# THE COURIER-JOURNAL
# KENTUCKY COOKBOOK

*Edited by John Finley*

# CREDITS

John Finley, Editor
Stephen Sebree, Designer
Bill Norton, Copy Editor
Alice Colombo, Proofreader
Jane Fleischaker, Proofreader
Nick Bachert, Typography
  Technician
Paul Wirth, Typography
  Technician
Terry O'Brien, Typist

Published by The Courier-
Journal and Louisville Times
Company
525 West Broadway
Louisville, Kentucky 40202

© 1985 The Courier-Journal and
Louisville Times Company

Library of Congress Catalog
Card Number: 85-071929

Printer: Gateway Press Inc.
Louisville, Kentucky

First printing: October, 1985

*Pictured on the cover is one of
Kentucky's most noted and popular
dishes, burgoo. Photograph by H.
Harold Davis.*

# DEDICATION

To Carol Sutton Whaley, who wanted this cookbook to reflect her love for the state of Kentucky, its people and its food.

# ABOUT THE EDITOR

John A. Finley is a Louisville writer. During nearly 15 years at The Courier-Journal, he held a variety of writing jobs, including that of restaurant reviewer. He is a graduate of the University of Illinois and has lived in Louisville for 20 years.

# INTRODUCTION

Among the thousands of recipes in the files of *The Courier-Journal* kitchen is one for "frittered bear paws." This is not a recipe that was culled from an obscure and aged publication and then filed for its historical interest. It was actually tested and published in *The Courier-Journal.* The *C-J* kitchen has, in fact, about a half dozen recipes explaining how to cook bear meat.

Lest this lead to conjecture that *C-J* food editors have been answering how-to questions since the days of Daniel Boone, it must be pointed out that newspaper food editors came about in the 20th century, as wood and coal cook stoves gave way to ranges and ice boxes yielded to refrigerators. The changeover to an electrified society was gathering momentum, and the food-processing industry, seemingly non-existent one moment, suddenly was a growing giant. Where housewives once got a jar of home-canned beans from a dark, cool corner of their own basement, they now picked canned beans from shelves at the grocery store.

Utility companies sought to stimulate the use of electricity and gas in the kitchen. Appliance makers and food packagers set out to encourage sales by helping consumers understand how to use their products. Home economists were hired to give demonstrations and write recipes that used a manufacturer's product. Food editors were needed to sort through the torrent of information newspapers were receiving about new food and kitchen products and to make sense out of it all for the readers.

Gladys Marie Wigginton, who wrote under the name of Marie Gibson, was *The Courier-Journal*'s first food editor. She had been trained as a dietitian and was working at the old Norton Infirmary when she was hired. Her byline began appearing in 1936.

"It was the greatest fun in the world because they'd let us do anything we wanted to," Mrs. Wigginton recalled in an interview this year.

Food *is* fun. Human beings have always used it to celebrate important occasions. But food also is essential to survival, and it remains a topic that demands serious and knowledgeable attention.

Mrs. Wigginton began writing about food during the Great Depression, when stretching the food budget was a very real concern for families. Many women were learning how to cook for the first time, Mrs. Wigginton says, because their families had always employed cooks before.

In the 50 years since Marie Gibson's first column, there has been a great world war, with food shortages and rationing. There has been a revolution in nutritional information related to health and longevity. New appliances have dramatically reduced food-preparation time. We have sampled heretofore exotic cuisines and embraced some of the dishes as our own, producing everyday menus that are a melange of foreign words. And today, while many still face the problem of getting enough to eat, a broad class of Americans has the luxury of treating food as an item of fashion. Their concerns are for the "in" foods and the "in" restaurants.

Marie Gibson, Cissy Gregg, Loyta Higgins, Lillian Marshall, Deni Hamilton and Elaine Corn are the food editors who have guided us through those years, and a lot of history is reflected in their recipes. There are recipes that tell us something about our state and our nation, and there are recipes that tell us something about our community and the people who were cooking up tasty dishes here before us.

Some punctuation was changed to clarify the instructions, but otherwise, the recipes are reprinted pretty much as they originally appeared in *The Courier-Journal.* You'll find "catsup," "catchsup" and "ketchup" all listed as ingredients. You'll see that in addition to being a creative cook, Cissy Gregg was probably the most imaginative user of the dash ( — ) journalism has ever known. Not only that, Cissy was permitted to get away with writing about "whisky" when she meant bourbon "whiskey," a lapse that today would drive many a newspaper copy editor to bite through his lower lip.

To capture the flavor of the time and the spirit of Cissy Gregg's cookery, a lot of the Cissy's recipes are reproduced exactly as she wrote them. That means there is no separate list of ingredients for a few of the older recipes. In those days, the format of recipes called for the ingredients to be encompassed among the instructions. The disadvantage of the format is that it is difficult to tell at a glance what goes into a dish. There is a positive side to the format, however: It forces a cook to read a recipe all the way through before starting to make it, and that's always a good idea. More than a few cooks, especially ones in a hurry, have been subjected to some nasty surprises because they started throwing ingredients together before they read a recipe to the end.

But for the most part, Cissy's recipes have been left as she wrote them, ambiguities and all, because the *way* she expressed herself was a big part of what made her so special to an entire generation — make that two generations — of *Courier-Journal* readers.

"I've pondered a lot on why Cissy was so popular," Deni Hamilton wrote in 1981 for the introduction to *Cissy Gregg's Cook Book (Volume 1 and 2).* "Some of it, sure, was because she wrote so much for so many years.

"But I think most of it was because of the way she wrote about cooking. Reading Cissy was like standing beside her at the stove. She conjured up a good picture of what the cook was getting into in the preparation of a dish, and exactly what to expect when it was prepared, even though she was a bit 'wordy' by today's journalistic standards."

There are no recipes from Marie Gibson in this book because she wrote about what others cooked. She oversaw a weekly contest in which readers were invited to send in favorite recipes for a certain type of dish. The prizes were $5, $3 and $1 for first, second and third — no small amount of money for that time — and the contests typically evoked 200 responses from all over Kentucky and its border states.

Ms. Gibson eliminated the duplicates and the obvious losers, then selected six or seven recipes as finalists. *The Courier-Journal* had no test kitchen during her tenure, so she tested the recipes at her home on Glenmary at Ray. She conducted tastings among neighbors and friends. Then she selected the winners.

Marie Gibson left the newspaper in 1941 when her husband, an officer in the Army reserve, was called to active duty and transferred to Pennsylvania.

*The Courier-Journal* got its test kitchen during Cissy Gregg's 21-year tenure, and it remains one the few newspapers in the nation to have one. But it is not a fancy kitchen; it is not the most modern kitchen. The visitor's head will not spin with visions of shiny copper utensils, sleek stainless cookware and electronic, digital appliances. Most visitors, in fact, would probably conclude that they'd just as soon work in their own kitchens, thank you.

But the *C-J* food editors always have recognized that having the very latest in kitchen gadgetry is not what matters. "The secret to this sort of thing is keeping in touch with the public," Marie Gibson said in an interview. Cissy Gregg did that. So did Loyta Higgins, Lillian Marshall and Deni Hamilton. So does Elaine Corn. It is reflected in their recipes. It is reflected in this cookbook.

**John A. Finley   1985**

# FOREWORD

In the four years I have been food editor of *The Courier-Journal,* I have come to a conclusion about Kentucky food now clearly evinced in the pages of this book — that it can be as predictable as meat and potatoes, yet as disparate as grits and guacamole.

We like honeyed chicken wings, pasta salad, Greek soups and Irish stew. We eat pole beans with ham one day and hearts of palm the next. We've become downright spoiled in the lap of greengrocer luxury. Raspberries and rhubarb grow in our back yards, and big-city chefs would like nothing better than to have our access to them.

It's a food region with boundaries we blur at whim. Sometimes we cling to the history of Hot Browns, burgoo, Kentucky trout and dove. Since refrigerated trains first passed through this region, there has been an almost insatiable appetite for oysters and crabmeat. We like the familiarity of corn pudding and fried tomatoes, but in recent years we have been persuaded to try fettucine Alfredo, yogurt, avocados, chili con queso and phyllo dough. Still, for every marinated salmon there is river channel catfish; for every chocolate truffle, a mayonnaise cake.

Perhaps this brand of gastronomic promiscuity is due, in part, to functions of tradition, geography and a hellbent curiosity. It may also stem from 50 years of influence from the food pages of *The Courier-Journal,* which by definition, were duty-bound to reflect the tastes, trends and economy of the times.

Every week they were crammed with recipes. Five decades of food editors wrote about people from here, other states and countries who have shared their experiences and, like many *C-J* readers, cooked with a vengeance.

Few newspapers in this country can claim such a culinary legacy. No one knew this better than Courier-Journal senior editor Carol Sutton, to whom this book is dedicated. She was both an accomplished journalist and cook. She also traveled extensively, particularly in Latin America, where she picked up many cooking influences. But the first time she made an Ecuadorian feast here, she didn't waste time researching books. Carol dialed the embassy in Washington, D.C.

In the early stages of this project, she discussed with me how one would go about sizing up Kentucky's cuisine in a couple of hundred pages. We had noticed the trend to books with chapters based by seasons. We hashed through a long lunch talking about Kentucky's big entertaining events and wondered if Derby and holidays would provide the backdrop for interesting recipes.

Finally, Carol set her own plan on paper. After her death on Feb. 19, 1985, the notes were found, and John Finley was asked to finish the project.

It is estimated that between 12,000 and 20,000 recipes are on file in the office of the C-J test kitchen, although no one has actually counted all the index cards. John spent nearly two months leafing through them for this book and culled his take to 600. From the looks of the file drawers, he says, he scarcely made a dent.

Through careful selection and elimination, John set up an engrossing compilation of Kentucky's food — what it was, is and will continue to be, according to the chronicles of *The Courier-Journal.* In maintaining the integrity of the older recipes, he kept them as close to their original form as possible.

You might want to take in the first reading of this book without cooking from it. Remember your parents' meals. Think back to all those cakes and pies.

"There must not have been a meal unless there was a cake or a pie," John said, after all the recipes were in hand. "Perhaps the real criterion of a cook then was the way you did cakes or pies, and everything else was meat and potatoes — ordinary fare that did not seem worthy of praise."

Keep looking and you'll see what John began to notice, that "we've gone toward cooking our vegetables a more reasonable amount of time and getting the most nutrition from our cooking. There are more foreign influences and a trend toward lighter entrées and desserts, to lighter meats like veal and chicken and away from nitrated and preserved meats."

As you flip from appetizer to breads, beverages to casseroles, you'll be able to taste Kentucky, savor its most memorable culinary moments, and perhaps pronounce this collection a pretty good chew.

**— Elaine Corn, Courier-Journal food editor   1985**

# CONTENTS

# APPETIZERS & PARTY FOODS

# STEAK TARTARE

*Don Grisanti created this recipe for a 1980 Sunday Magazine article by Deni Hamilton. Grisanti, along with brother Michael, was one of the forces behind the national recognition accorded Casa Grisanti today.*

1-2 anchovy fillets
2 pounds finely ground sirloin or
   top round
1 tablespoon finely chopped
   shallots
1 tablespoon finely chopped parsley
1 tablespoon chopped capers
4 drops Worcestershire sauce
3 drops Tabasco
1 teaspoon dry Dijon mustard
   powder
1 ounce (2 tablespoons) olive oil
2 raw egg yolks
Ground fresh pepper
Pinch salt

Make a paste with anchovy fillet. Combine it with shallots, parsley, capers, Worcestershire sauce, Tabasco, mustard and oil, and blend well. Add raw egg yolks to mixture. Combine mixture with ground meat. Finish with freshly ground pepper and salt to taste. Serve on a bed of romaine, or garnish with fresh watercress. Serves 8-10 persons.

# GRILLED PEPPER HORS D'OEUVRE

Split large green peppers in half lengthwise, and remove the stems, seeds and membranes. Soak the peppers in a little olive oil for 30 minutes. Drain and broil them under a low flame, turning occasionally. Broil until slightly blistered and browned. Cut the peppers into thin strips and sprinkle them with a little finely minced onion. Marinate them for an hour or more in a French dressing made of 1 part vinegar to 3 parts oil, and mustard, salt and pepper to taste. Serve chilled but not cold.
— Cissy Gregg, 1960

# PESTO DIP

3 cloves garlic
½ cup pine nuts
2 cups densely packed basil leaves
Salt and freshly ground pepper, to
   taste
1 cup olive oil
½ cup grated parmesan
¼ cup grated romano
2 cups sour cream

Pulverize the garlic and pine nuts in a food processor or blender. Add basil and keep grinding. With machine running, add oil in a steady stream until mixture is smooth. Stir in parmesan, romano and sour cream. Chill. Use before 3 days. Makes about 3 cups.
— Elaine Corn, 1982

# SUSAN WILLOUGHBY'S MEXICAN PEPPER DIP

*A class of sixth graders at Belknap School came up with this recipe, and they prepared it and other south-of-the-border dishes for a study project on Central America. Lillian Marshall wrote a feature article about the children in 1974.*

Mix ingredients in blender until well mixed. Then serve as a dip with corn chips. It's hot, but very good. Makes a cup.

An 8-ounce package cream cheese
A 4-ounce can of roasted, peeled, green chili peppers
3 strips crisp bacon
½ teaspoon salt
A tablespoon light cream
2 teaspoons onion juice
A tablespoon Worcestershire sauce

# HOT CLAM BITS

Mix together a cake (3 ounces) cream cheese, a can (about 7 ounces) drained, minced clams, a teaspoon lemon juice, a teaspoon hot mustard, generous dash crushed red peppers; salt and pepper to taste.
— Cissy Gregg, 1962

# CHUNKY GUACAMOLE

Peel and cube avocados and place in a mixing bowl. Quickly coat with lime juice so avocados won't blacken. Stir in remaining ingredients with a fork, breaking up avocado cubes slightly. Chill briefly. Serve within an hour or so of preparation. Makes 3 cups.

4 very ripe avocados
Juice of 2 large limes
1 large tomato, seeded and coarsely chopped
½ cup red picante sauce (recipe follows)
1 jalapeño, seeded and minced

## RED PICANTE SAUCE

Combine tomatoes, onion, garlic, jalapeños and juice in a blender or food processor. Mixture will be thick. Transfer to a small saucepan and simmer 15 minutes. Cool. Add herbs and seasoning. Chill a few hours. Makes 2 cups.
— Elaine Corn, 1982

4 tomatoes, seeded and chopped
1 tiny onion, diced
1 garlic clove, minced
4 pickled jalapeños, stemmed
¼ cup juice from can of pickled jalapeños
½ teaspoon marjoram
½ teaspoon chili powder
Salt and freshly ground pepper

# DIP OF TAPENADE

¾ cup capers
1½ 2-ounce cans flat anchovies
1 cup tuna
½ onion
18 black Mediterranean olives
½ cup chopped parsley
½ cup minced green onion tops
4 cloves garlic
1 teaspoon dry mustard
1 tablespoon cracked black pepper
Juice of 2 lemons
Dash of Worcestershire
2 tablespoons olive oil
¼ cup cognac
12 ounces cream cheese
8 ounces sour cream

Pulverize capers, anchovies, tuna, onion, olives, parsley, green onion tops, garlic, dry mustard, black pepper with lemon juice until an oily paste. Transfer to bowl. Cream remaining ingredients, then fold into paste. Chill. Makes about 3½ cups. Delicious with rice crackers, crusty bread, bread sticks and raw vegetable sticks.

— Elaine Corn, 1982

# TULIP APPETIZER

Pick out small green peppers. Flute them around the edge to make them look "tulip-pee". Have ready hard-cooked eggs, and the number depends on the size of the peppers and the number of people you are serving. For 1 to 1½ hard-cooked eggs, a pepper should be about right. Mix shelled and chopped eggs with a well-seasoned mayonnaise; then you come into your own as a seasoner. Use red caviar, or black if you don't mind the color, anchovy paste, Tabasco and anything else in the way of seasonings you have and think would make the mixture better and better. I season mine until I think they are just about right and then chill. Taste and season again if necessary.

Pile the mixture in the pepper-tulip cups and make them more realistic tulips by adding the stems and leaves of real tulips to the serving plate.

— Cissy Gregg, 1948

# CHILI DIP

4 cans chopped green chilies, drained
1 can jalapeños, drained
5 eggs
1 pound cheddar, shredded

Spread the chilies and the jalapeños on the bottom of a 9-by-13-by-2-inch baking dish. Lightly beat the eggs and pour over. Cover with cheese. Bake at 350 degrees for 30 minutes, or cook on covered grill until eggs are set and cheese melts. Makes a great snack when supper is still a few hours away.

— Elaine Corn, 1981

# DOUBLE-CHEESE BOURBON DIP

Mash cheeses with a fork until combined well. Add bourbon a tablespoon at a time. Taste. Mixture will take on potency during storage. Cover well and chill. Keeps in the refrigerator for two weeks. At serving, thinly slice apples to use as dippers and quickly toss with lemon juice to prevent darkening. Serve dip ringed with apples. Makes 4 cups dip.

— Elaine Corn, 1984

**⅔ pound Roquefort cheese**
**2 8-ounce blocks cream cheese**
**6 tablespoons bourbon**
**5 apples**
**Lemon juice**

# CHICKEN PUFFS

Beat egg white until stiff. Fold in the remaining ingredients. Spoon onto crackers or toast, and broil 2 minutes or until puffy and lightly brown. This should give you about 24 puffs — nice fat ones.

— Cissy Gregg, 1958

**1 egg white**
**5 ounces boned cooked chicken, minced**
**1 tablespoon grated onion**
**Salt and pepper to taste**

# COUNTRY HAM BALLS

*This recipe was supplied to the Cook's Corner column in 1983 by the Doe Run Inn, near Brandenburg, Ky.*

Mix ingredients thoroughly and chill. Roll into bite-size balls. Place in a shallow baking dish. Pour half the sauce over the balls and bake at 350 degrees for 30 to 45 minutes. Heat remaining sauce. Pour over cooked balls and serve warm. Makes about four dozen.

**4 pounds cooked, ground country ham**
**2 pounds pork sausage**
**4 cups bread crumbs**
**4 cups milk**
**4 eggs**
**Sauce (see recipe)**

## SAUCE

Mix thoroughly.

**4 cups light-brown sugar**
**4 cups vinegar**
**2 cups water**
**4 tablespoons mustard**

# STUFFED MUSHROOMS

12 large mushrooms
4 tablespoons butter or margarine
2 tablespoons minced onion
2 strips raw bacon, cut into snibbles
2 cups fine bread crumbs
1 teaspoon salt
⅛ teaspoon pepper
2 tablespoons chili sauce
2 tablespoons lemon juice
2 tablespoons parsley
Light cream

Wash and dry mushrooms. Remove the caps. Chop stems fine and saute in butter or margarine along with the onions and the bacon. Stir in the other seasoning ingredients and cook for a few minutes. Add bread crumbs last. Stuff the caps with this mixture and pour one-half cup cream over them to moisten. Bake in a moderate oven, 350 degrees, for 40 minutes. More cream may be added if necessary.

These have one handicap: they won't stand around waiting to be served. So it must be a last-minute doings, although the preparation of the stuffing can be done ahead of time, if that helps you plot and plan.

— Cissy Gregg, 1950

# CUCUMBER BALLS

Peel cucumbers and cut into small balls with a French ball cutter. It makes them look most attractive but is rather extravagant with the cucumbers. I see no reason why they couldn't be cubed just as well. Sprinkle small balls or small cubes with salt and let stand for a least 2 hours in the refrigerator. Drain thoroughly. Dress with a little French dressing — on the piquant side — to which has been added a little prepared mustard and a little squeezed, prepared horseradish. If possible, dust the bowlful with some chopped chives or parsley and stick each with a toothpick for handy hand eating.

— Cissy Gregg, 1951

# COUNTRY HAM BALLS

2 cups finely ground ham (cooked)
1 cup fine, fresh bread crumbs
1 egg, beaten
3 tablespoons milk
⅓ cup light corn syrup
2 tablespoons vinegar
1 teaspoon Worcestershire sauce
2 tablespoons prepared mustard
¼ teaspoon ground cloves

Combine ham, crumbs, egg and milk. Form mixture into one-inch balls. Place close together in small baking dish. Combine remaining ingredients, and pour over ham balls. Bake 20 minutes at 350 degrees. Makes about 1½ dozen or enough for about six party guests. Recipe is easily multiplied. May be refrigerated or frozen, then heated at serving time. Nice for chafing dish.

— Lillian Marshall, 1978

*Marinated chicken wings and chicken wings in honeyed barbecue sauce. Photograph by Robert Steinau.*

# BOURBON HOT DOGS

Cut hot dogs in ½-inch slices. Put these into a heavy fry pan, or electric skillet, with all other ingredients and simmer, covered, for 4 hours. Be certain it does not boil; simply simmer on very low heat. If the liquid evaporates too much, add more bourbon.

— Lillian Marshall, 1974

A pound hot dogs
¾ cup bourbon whisky
1½ cups catsup
½ cup brown sugar
1 tablespoon grated onion

# BRANDIED BLUE CHEESE CROCK

Combine blue and cream cheeses and blend until light and creamy. Stir in nutmeg and enough brandy for a good spreading consistency. Let it mellow in the refrigerator for a few days, then pack it into decorative jars or crocks for gifts. This recipe will make about 2 cups.

— Lillian Marshall, 1970

½ pound blue cheese, crumbled
1 (8-ounce) package cream cheese, softened
⅛ teaspoon nutmeg
⅓ to ½ cup brandy

# ALMOND-STUFFED MUSHROOMS

Wash mushrooms; remove and mince stems. Place caps, gill-side up on cookie sheet. Sprinkle with sherry. Mix bread crumbs, butter, chopped almonds and minced mushroom stems well. Add just enough sherry to moisten, so a pinch maintains its shape when made into a ball. Stuff mushroom caps with mixture, formed into balls. Bake in a preheated 425-degree oven about 8 minutes, and serve hot. Makes about 2 dozen.

— Deni Hamilton, 1979

½ pound small, fresh button mushrooms
Medium dry sherry
1 cup dry bread crumbs
4 tablespoons melted butter
1 cup finely chopped almonds

# SHERRIED, BROILED GRAPEFRUIT

Arrange grapefruit halves on baking pan and sprinkle each half with a tablespoon of sugar. Broil until sugar bubbles and fruit is hot. Place on serving dishes and put a tablespoon of sherry in center of each. Garnish with a maraschino cherry.

— Lillian Marshall, 1974

½ grapefruit (per person)
A tablespoon sugar
A tablespoon sherry
A maraschino cherry

# CHEESE WAFERS

1 cup butter
2 cups flour
½ pound sharp cheese, grated
1 beaten egg
Pecans

Mix butter, flour and cheese together with your hands; then roll out on floured board and cut with a very small biscuit cutter.

Place on cookie sheet and brush tops with beaten egg. Put pecan half on top of each and bake at 350 degrees for 10 minutes. As soon as you take them out of the oven, sprinkle them with salt and remove from cookie sheet. Makes about 75 wafers.

These are delicious as snacks and tidbits. You may leave the pecans off some of them for variety; they are just as good.

— Lillian Marshall, 1970

# CHEESE WAFERS

Cream ½ cup butter or margarine until it is quite soft. Gradually add to it 1 cup flour. Then, just as gradually, work in ½ pound of grated American or cheddar type cheese. Finally add a good dash of cayenne pepper. Next form the dough into long rolls as thick as you want the diameter of your wafers. There are no real rules about the size except someone has worked out that they should be "half a dollar size for tea, and a quarter size for cocktails". They will spread a little in baking. Wrap the roll in wax paper and keep in the refrigerator until ready to use. They should spend one night cooling their heels before you try to slice them. Slice paper-thin and bake in a moderate oven, 350 degrees, for 3 to 4 minutes. They should come out with their edges slightly tinged with brown. The rolls of dough will keep for several weeks.

— Cissy Gregg, 1948

# CHEESE PUFFS

½ pound butter or margarine
2 cups grated sharp cheese
1 egg white, slightly beaten
¼ teaspoon salt
1 tablespoon cream
1 loaf unsliced white bread

Have all ingredients at room temperature, with cheese very soft; combine all ingredients, except bread, in large bowl of mixer, then beat until smooth and creamy. Remove crust from bread and cut bread into 1½-inch cubes. Coat five sides of each cube with cheese mixture. Use a fork to hold each piece, if you wish, then spoon mixture over and around it. Place, uncoated side down, on greased cookie sheet and bake at 375 degrees for about 12 minutes. Makes about 50.

Or freeze on cookie sheets, then package well to store in freezer for later use. Bake frozen cubes at 375 degrees for about 15 minutes, or until lightly browned.

— Lillian Marshall, 1974

# CHICKEN LIVER PÂTÉ

Place chicken livers in a saucepan with water enough to cover them. Add parsley, onion and thyme. Simmer 20 minutes. Drain well and put through fine blade of food chopper.

Beat the melted butter into the liver and add remaining ingredients. Pack firmly, in an oiled one-quart mold. To serve, unmold and sprinkle with chopped parsley. Makes a quart.

— Lillian Marshall, 1969

**2 pounds chicken livers**
**3 or 4 sprigs parsley**
**A tablespoon chopped onion**
**¼ teaspoon thyme**
**A cup melted butter**
**1½ teaspoons salt**
**1½ teaspoons dry mustard**
**¼ teaspoon pepper**
**3 tablespoons cognac**

# CHICKEN LIVER AND MUSHROOM DIP

Sauté chicken livers in butter or margarine until done. Remove to a chopping board or bowl. Chop the livers and drained mushrooms, then add remaining ingredients and blend well. Add a bit more mayonnaise to make good dipping. Makes about 1½ cups.

— Cissy Gregg, 1953

**½ pound chicken livers**
**3-ounce can mushrooms, sliced or whole**
**2 tablespoons chopped chives**
**¼ cup chopped parsley**
**½ cup mayonnaise**
**Salt and pepper to taste**

# BENEDICTINE SPREAD

This recipe was originated in the 1920s by a Louisville caterer named Jennie Benedict. The spread became a regular feature at cocktail hours and weddings, and still is. Before blenders and food processors, the ingredients were grated and the cheese beaten by hand. It is said that Miss Jennie's mayonnaise was made of three ingredients; lemon juice, olive oil and egg yolk. The spread traditionally is tinted with a droplet of green food coloring, but that addition is up to the cook.

Blend all ingredients until a spreadable consistency. If making by hand, mash and beat the cheese with a fork, working in the cucumber and onion. Add onion juice to taste. Beat in remaining ingredients, adding only enough mayonnaise to thin. Place in crocks. Serve chilled on crackers or as a sandwich filling. Serves 10.

— Elaine Corn, 1983

**12 ounces cream cheese, at room temperature**
**1 medium cucumber, grated pulp only, drained**
**1 medium onion, grated, drained and some juice reserved**
**1 teaspoon salt**
**Pinch cayenne or Tabasco**
**Mayonnaise, to thin**
**Drop of green food coloring**

# CRAB NEWBURG APPETIZER

1 pound crab meat, fresh or canned
4 hard-cooked eggs
Salt to taste
½ pound cheddar cheese
Juice of 1 onion, or to taste
Cayenne pepper or Tabasco sauce
2 tablespoons butter
3 tablespoons flour
2 cups milk

We always suggest one hot something on the snack table. It breaks the monotony of the small cold items. Since we live in the era of the revival of the chafing dish in many forms having something hot has been greatly simplified.

Pick over the crab meat very well and remove all the whiffs of shells that lurk therein. We pick ours over twice to be sure as possible. To the crab meat add the grated hard-cooked eggs, onion juice, salt and cayenne.

Melt butter in the top of a double boiler. Add flour and blend until smooth. Then add milk and cook until the mixture has thickened. Add cheese, stir and cook over hot water until it has melted and become part of the sauce. Add crab-meat mixture and cook until hot. Pour into a chafing dish or a keep-hot server, and have close by a supply of Melba toast to act as the backbone for the crab Newburg.

— Cissy Gregg, 1955

# SQUASH CAVIAR

Two or three small summer squash
3 tablespoons olive oil
A small sliced onion
A small tomato, peeled and
  chopped
½ teaspoon salt, or to taste
¼ teaspoon marjoram or oregano
A pinch basil
A clove garlic, crushed

We have made caviar from eggplant, but we had never tried it with squash--the summer kind. It's an interesting dip and goes well with potato chips and corn chips.

Our squash was very tender. If yours are the same don't peel but cut into cubes. Cook in the olive oil with the onion, clove of crushed garlic and the tomato. Season with salt, marjoram or oregano and basil to taste. Cook tightly covered without water, until squash is tender, about 6 minutes.

Force through food mill or mash in electric blender until thickened and smooth. Add about a teaspoon vinegar. Serve chilled.

— Cissy Gregg, 1958

# BRAUNSCHWEIGER OLIVES

Braunschweiger olives are quite easy, and nice for serving on toothpicks. Mash braunschweiger sausage. Form a spoonful at a time into a small patty. Place a small stuffed cocktail olive in the center and roll in a ball to cover the olive. Then roll the ball in finely chopped parsley or finely chopped nuts. It is usually best to add a little butter to the sausage when mashing it if the nuts are to be used; the butter in the sausage makes the nuts stick a little easier.

— Cissy Gregg, 1955

# HONEYDEW FINGERS

Cut the melon into long pieces about the thickness of your middle finger. Cut off some of the fat of the ham, but I like to leave a little of it. Wrap the meat around the melon fingers. Place in the refrigerator until serving time.

Some people like to wrap the melon fingers so completely, they come as a surprise. But the color combination of the green melon and red of the ham is too pretty to hide, we thought.

A word about *prosciutto,* which is pronounced pro-SHOOT-toe. It is ham that is dried, salted, spiced and pressed, but it is not sugar-cured or smoked. It has a peppery-spicy covering that is very good, too, and that's another reason why we hated to cut it off. What you do cut off, save for seasoning something else.

The processing of the covering cooks the ham, so to speak, I was told, but if you have any left over — or get too much for the melon fingers — try cooking it as you do bacon — it makes enthusiastic breakfast partakers.

— Cissy Gregg, 1951

**1 ripe honeydew melon or cantaloupe**
**1 pound of thinly sliced Italian ham (prosciutto). (You also can use thinly sliced old ham, but that's hard to round up sometimes.)**

# CHILE CON QUESO

In a large skillet over medium heat, sauté the onions and garlic in the butter until limp. Add the chilies and jalapeños. (Three jalapeños, and you're smokin'.) Cook 5 minutes, stirring occasionally. Turn the heat to low. In batches, add the cheese, stirring constantly until all cheese has been added and is completely melted. Season with salt and pepper. Serve immediately with tortilla chips or other dippers.

— Elaine Corn, 1981

**2 onions, chopped**
**6 cloves garlic, minced**
**½ stick butter**
**10 Anaheim chilies, roasted, peeled and seeded, or 3 cans whole green chilies, coarsely diced**
**2 to 3 fresh jalapeños, seeded and minced**
**1½ pounds monterey jack cheese, cubed**
**Dash salt**
**Freshly ground black pepper, to taste**

# TOASTED PUMPKIN SEEDS

**2 cups pumpkin seeds, unshelled**
**1 tablespoon oil**
**Salt**

Toss the seeds in the oil, and salt to taste. Scatter on a baking sheet, and bake in a preheated 250-degree oven 30 to 40 minutes or until seeds have browned and crisped. Stir frequently. Cool, and store in tightly closed containers. Shell before eating. Makes about a cup of edible seeds.

— Deni Hamilton, 1980

# STUFFED VINE LEAVES WITH EGG-LEMON SAUCE

*For this recipe, Elaine Corn picked her own leaves from vines growing wild around Louisville — along River Road, in Cherokee Park, in alleys and elsewhere. She wrote about it in 1983.*

**40 fresh vine leaves, or grape leaves**
  **bottled in brine**
**1 teaspoon baking soda**
**¾ to 1 pound ground lamb**
**¼ pound extra-lean ground beef**
**1 large onion, minced**
**1 clove garlic, minced**
**½ cup pine nuts, optional**
**¼ cup fresh, minced mint**
**¼ cup fresh, chopped parsley**
**¼ cup fresh, chopped dill**
**2 teaspoons cinnamon**
**½ cup olive oil**
**2 teaspoons salt**
**½ cup raw rice**
**Juice of 1 lemon**

If using fresh vine leaves, rinse well. Drop into a 4-inch depth of boiling water to which baking soda has been added. Boil leaves 5 to 7 minutes, lid on. Drain liquid and rinse leaves again. (If using bottled grape leaves, rinse off brine and boil leaves 5 minutes without baking powder.)

Select 6 or 8 of the largest leaves to line the bottom of a Dutch kettle. Snip out thick bottom stem of each remaining leaf, making an incision like an inverted V into each base.

Combine remaining ingredients, except the lemon juice, until smooth. Place 1 teaspoon meat mixture on underside of leaf at base. Fold sides over, then roll toward the point to form a snug packet. Place seam-side-down into kettle as you go.

Pour enough water over packets to barely cover, about a 2-inch depth. Add lemon juice. Weight down with a heavy plate, or use a heat-proof plate held down with a heat-proof bowl filled with water. Cover and simmer 45 minutes to 1 hour. Remove *dolmathes* with tongs to a rack to drip dry. May be served hot or chilled.

Prepare egg-lemon sauce with liquid remaining in kettle. Makes about 3 dozen *dolmathes.*

## EGG-LEMON SAUCE

**Juice of 3 large or 4 medium lemons**
**3 egg yolks**
**1 tablespoon cornstarch**
**Cooking liquid from dolmathes,**
  **warm.**

Beat the lemon juice, yolks and cornstarch. Whisk into warm cooking liquid. Heat through, whisking out lumps. Serve with dolmathes. Makes about 2½ cups sauce.

# ROLLUPS

*Monica Kaufman, former reporter and weekend anchor for WHAS-TV, and her husband were among the couples featured by Lillian Marshall in the 1974 holiday entertainment issue. This is one of Monica's recipes.*

Combine soy sauce, sugar and onion in bowl. Set aside. Put a piece of liver and a chestnut on the bacon and roll it up. Secure with a toothpick and put in the marinade. Cover and refrigerate for at least four hours. This tastes better if marinated all night. Stir gently two or three times to marinate evenly. Drain well before cooking. Place the rollups on a cake rack that has been set on a foil-lined cookie sheet. Bake 20 to 30 minutes at 400 degrees. Turn once for even browning. Arrange on platter and serve. Makes 24 rollups.

½ cup soy sauce
½ cup light brown sugar
1 tablespoon minced dry onion
12 chicken livers, halved
12 water chestnuts, halved
12 bacon slices, halved

# MARINATED CHICKEN WINGS

To make preparation easier, place the chicken wings in freezer for about 30 minutes.

With a knife or cleaver, remove wing tips and save for stock. Then, cut through connecting joint between upper and lower part of each wing. Using a sharp, pointed knife, loosen skin, meat and cartilage from end of wing bone. Cut off excess fat and skin with scissors. Gently pull meat away over the other end of the wing, as if turning a glove inside out. You will have a smooth piece of bone with a ball of meat at the other end, skin inside, like a lollipop.

Combine marinade ingredients, pour over the wings and refrigerate for several hours. Combine coating ingredients, except for sesame seeds.

Preheat broiler. Line the broiler pan with foil. Place wings on foil and brush with half the coating.

Broil, not too close to the heat source, for about eight minutes. Sprinkle with 1 teaspoon sesame seeds and broil for another few minutes. Turn wings over with tongs, brush with remaining coating and sprinkle with remaining seeds. Broil for another 10 minutes, or until brown on outside and soft inside.

These easy-to-prepare chicken wings can be served hot or cold.

Elaine Corn, 1984

10 chicken wings

## MARINADE:
1 tablespoon thin Chinese soy sauce
1 tablespoon vegetable oil
½ teaspoon kosher salt
¼ teaspoon sugar

## COATING:
1 tablespoon thin Chinese soy sauce
1 tablespoon vegetable oil
1 tablespoon hoisin sauce
1 tablespoon ketchup
2 to 3 teaspoons sesame seeds

# CRABMEAT-STUFFED MUSHROOMS

3 dozen medium, or 2 dozen large, mushrooms, cleaned and stems removed
2 6-ounce cans lump crabmeat
2 tablespoons butter
1 shallot, minced
2 tablespoons sherry
⅓ cup ricotta cheese
1 egg, beaten
¼ cup packed, minced watercress leaves
1 tablespoon white horseradish
1 tablespoon Dijon mustard
⅔ cup bread crumbs
Few dashes Tabasco
Few dashes Worcestershire
White pepper, to taste

Blanch the mushrooms in rapidly boiling water for five minutes. (Mushrooms freeze nicely if first blanched.) Drain, rinse under cold water and place cavity-down on paper towels.

Drain crabmeat on paper towels. In a medium skillet over medium-high heat, sauté the shallot in butter for two minutes. Add sherry and cook down until mixture is thick, about 1½ minutes. Set aside. In a bowl combine all other ingredients, except the crabmeat. Stir in shallots. Fold in crabmeat. Mound stuffing high in mushroom caps.

To make ahead, freeze on a cookie sheet for 2 hours. Wrap in foil or place in freezer bags. To reheat, place frozen mushrooms, uncovered, on a cookie sheet in a preheated 400-degree oven for 15 to 18 minutes. Sprinkle with paprika, if desired.

Makes 2 or 3 dozen.

— Elaine Corn, 1984

# FOWLED OUT (CHICKEN WINGS IN HONEYED BARBECUE SAUCE)

3- to 4-dozen chicken wings
Honeyed barbecue sauce (see recipe)

Slice bony tips off wings and freeze for soup stock. Cut remaining wing sections at joints so you have one piece with one bone and a second piece with two smaller bones.

Melt a generous amount of butter in one large, or two medium, baking pans. Or, use shallow, oven-proof crocks you can bring to the table.

Arrange wings in butter. Pour sauce over wings. Bake at 350 degrees for an hour. Baste often! This is the secret to juicy chicken wings. It also prevents singeing.

Serve wings hot or cold with chutney and barbecue sauce drippings. Serves about 30.

## HONEYED BARBECUE SAUCE

Adjust sauce ingredients to suit your own tastes. Combine in a bowl with a spout. Sauce should have some body and be of a pourable consistency. It doesn't have to be thick.

Elaine Corn, 1985

¼ cup soy sauce
½ cup lemon juice or cider vinegar, or combination of both (or try lime juice)
½ cup honey
¼ cup vermouth, sherry or beer
3 tablespoons brown sugar
3 tablespoons chili powder or any Mexican seasoning
1½ cups ketchup, chili sauce or tomato sauce
2 tablespoons Worcestershire
Many dashes of Tabasco or cayenne pepper
Minced garlic
Salt and lots of freshly ground black pepper

# BAVARIAN SAUERKRAUT BALLS WITH CARAWAY-TOMATO SAUCE

Sauté onion in oil until tender. Add ham and corned beef. Heat thoroughly. Sprinkle on mixture of flour, parsley, salt and mustard. Mix well. Pour on tomato sauce. Simmer about 5 minutes. Stir in sauerkraut and cook stirring constantly until thick. Cool.

Form into bite-size balls. Roll in flour; dip in egg and roll in crumbs. Fry in oil heated to 375 degrees until golden brown, about 3 minutes (we used a deep fat fryer). Serve hot or cold with the tomato sauce.

½ cup finely chopped onion
2 tablespoons salad oil
½ pound lean boneless ham, ground
½ cup corned beef or pastrami, ground
½ cup flour
A tablespoon minced parsley
A teaspoon salt
A teaspoon dry mustard
An 8-ounce can tomato sauce
A pound, 11 ounce can sauerkraut, drained and chopped
An egg slightly beaten
Bread crumbs
Caraway tomato sauce (see recipe)

## CARAWAY TOMATO SAUCE

Pour an eight-ounce can of tomato sauce into a saucepan. Add 2 teaspoons dark brown sugar and ½ teaspoon caraway seed. Simmer slowly 10 to 15 minutes.

If you are a careful measure-outer this should give you about 60 sauerkraut balls and sauce for dunking.
— Cissy Gregg, 1962

# DONNA GILL'S SAUERKRAUT BALLS

*This dish was among those served by C.H. and Betty Lou Amster in 1974 at a cocktail buffet given for the Garvin Place-Ormsby Association, an event catered by Louisville restaurateur Tim Barnes. Lillian Marshall included the party menu in the holiday entertaining issue of the Magazine. Donna Gill is chef at the Science Hill Inn, Shelbyville.*

1 pound sauerkraut, rinsed and
    drained
1 15½-ounce can corned beef,
    chopped
3 eggs, slightly beaten
½ cup finely chopped onion
2 cups fine bread crumbs

Wrap the sauerkraut in a cloth and squeeze out excess water. Mix with the corned beef, two of the eggs and chopped onion. When mixed well, form into walnut-sized balls and freeze overnight. Remove from freezer and dip in beaten egg. Roll in bread crumbs and deep fry at 350 degrees until golden brown. Makes about 75 balls.

# BACKLAJANNAYA ICKRA

*"There is always a method of handling a delicate situation," Cissy Gregg wrote in introducing this recipe in 1955. "You wouldn't just blurt out that an eggplant mixture had a place among the appetizers, for noses might go up. But say it is Backlajannaya ickra, and people would be too curious to pass it up. Backlajannaya is eggplant cavier in Russia, I'm told."*

1 large eggplant or 2 smaller ones
4 large onions, chopped fine
Vegetable oil
1 chopped green pepper
1 tablespoon dried dill
2 tablespoons lemon juice
1 tablespoon sugar
1 small can tomato paste
2 tablespoons olive oil or salad oil

Prick the eggplant or eggplants in a few places with a fork. Place on a baking sheet and bake 1 to 2 hours in a 350-degree oven. (Ours were small this time, and we didn't need to bake them more than 45 minutes. They must be soft.) When ready, peel off the skin and chop the meat of the eggplants fine. You could put it through a food mill, but we chopped ours. Add the chopped-fine onions, which have been browned in a little oil. Then add the chopped green pepper and the dill, which has been soaking in the lemon juice long enough to give up its flavor. Strain the dill seeds out before adding. (I make dill vinegar from either fresh dill or dill seeds and use it instead of the lemon juice plus the dill. You can use dill juice from dill pickles.) Add sugar and tomato paste. Season with salt and pepper and blend in the 2 tablespoons of olive or salad oil. Mix it all well together and pour into a greased baking dish. Bake uncovered in a 350-degree oven for about 1 hour or until "sloppy-done." Serve cold as an appetizer with dark pumpernickel toast. We have made this a number of times, and we change the seasonings each time. We just work on it until it is good and tasty. It can be used as a filling for sandwiches or as a relish in a meal.

# VEAL-BLUE CHEESE PHYLLO TRIANGLES

Heat oven to 350 degrees. Have roll of phyllo dough at room temperature. Slice through roll at 3-inch intervals. Unfurl one 3-inch section. Carefully peel off first strip. Lay flat and brush with butter. Cover with a second strip. Brush with butter. Cover with a third strip. Brush with butter.

At one end of the layered strips place a well-heaped teaspoon of veal forcemeat. Top with ½ teaspoon blue cheese. Fold up in triangle shape, like a flag, tucking ends underneath or twisting into a topknot on top of triangle. Place triangles on an ungreased cookie sheet as you go. Brush tops with butter. Bake 18 to 20 minutes. Cool thoroughly.

If making ahead, freeze triangles on a cookie sheet for two hours. Transfer to freezer bags or wrap in foil. To reheat, place frozen triangles uncovered on a cookie sheet in a preheated 350-degree oven for 15 to 18 minutes.

Note: This recipe may be made from one roll of phyllo dough, but have another on hand in case of breakage or splitting.

Makes 3 dozen triangles.

**2 boxes phyllo dough (see note)**
**1 to 2 sticks butter or margarine, melted (for brushing)**
**Veal forcemeat (see recipe)**
**¼ pound crumbled blue cheese**

## VEAL FORCEMEAT

If you don't have a food processor or blender, have butcher grind the veal on smallest grind.

Trim veal of all fat. Cut into small bits. Place ½ cup veal pieces in a food processor or blender with celery leaves. Process until smooth. With machine running, drop in remaining veal a handful at a time. Add remaining ingredients in order and keep machine going until mixture resembles the "stiff peak" stage of beaten egg whites. Taste for flavor. Forcements traditionally are heavily seasoned. Best if made a day or two ahead.

Makes about 3 cups forcemeat.

— Elaine Corn, 1984

**1 pound veal sirloin tip, cubed**
**¼ cup packed celery leaves**
**2 tablespoons dried thyme**
**1 tablespoon fresh minced basil, or 2 teaspoons dried**
**1 teaspoon freshly grated or ground nutmeg**
**2 teaspoons salt**
**1½ teaspoons freshly ground black pepper**
**2 tablespoons sherry**
**¼ cup cream**
**3 eggs**

# CRAB PUFFS

1 6½-ounce can crab meat
2 tablespoons butter
¼ cup sliced green onions
1 cup chopped mushrooms
1 8-ounce package cream cheese,
    room temperature
½ teaspoon Worcestershire sauce
⅓ cup mayonnaise
2 tablespoons minced fresh parsley
½ cup melted butter
¼ pound phyllo pastry sheets

Shred crab; remove any bits of shell. Melt 2 tablespoons butter and add onions. Sauté 1 minute to bring up bright green color. Add mushrooms and combine with crab, cream cheese, Worcestershire sauce, mayonnaise and parsley. Spread phyllo sheets in layers of two. Cut into strips about 2 inches by 10 inches. Brush each strip with melted butter. (Keep strips you're not working with between moist towels so they won't dry out.) Spoon a tablespoon filling onto end of each strip. Fold pastry over filling to form a triangle. Continue folding in triangles, as you would a flag, the length of the strip. Brush completed triangle liberally with melted butter. Place, seam side down, on greased baking sheet. Bake in preheated 350-degree oven 30 minutes or until crisp and golden. Serve hot. Makes about 3 dozen.

— Deni Hamilton, 1979

# FAYE'S CRABMEAT DIP

1 cup drained crabmeat, chopped
½ cup sour cream or yogurt
½ cup mayonnaise
1 tablespoon fresh parsley, chopped
1 tablespoon sherry
1 teaspoon lemon juice
Salt and pepper to taste

Combine all ingredients, saving some parsley. Mix well. Pour into bowl, allowing to set. Garnish with parsley.

— Lillian Marshall, 1967

# SALADS, SALAD DRESSINGS & RELISHES

# TOFU-CUCUMBER DRESSING

½ medium cucumber, peeled,
   seeded and coarsely chopped
Juice of 1 lemon, or 2 tablespoons
   white wine vinegar
1 clove garlic
1 teaspoon dry mustard
1¼ cups cubed tofu
¼ cup commercial mayonnaise (not
   salad dressing)
¼ cup plain yogurt
3 tablespoons olive oil

Place all ingredients in a blender and blend until very smooth and of a medium thickness. Makes 2 cups.

— Elaine Corn, 1985

# BIBB SALAD WITH MUSHROOM MARINADE

3 tablespoons olive oil
Juice of 1 lemon
½ teaspoon ground coriander
1 clove garlic, crushed
1 tablespoon fresh chopped parsley
1 tablespoon minced green onion
   tops (green parts)
1 tablespoon chopped black olives
8 medium white mushrooms, thinly
   sliced
1 head bibb or Boston lettuce

Combine all ingredients except the bibb. Let soak 1 hour. Arrange lettuce in petal fashion on 4 salad plates. Remove garlic and spoon mushroom mixture into center of leaf arrangements. Serves 4.

— Elaine Corn, 1985

# MAMMA GRISANTI'S HOUSE SALAD

*The Mamma Grisanti house salad is a favorite of many who visit the Louisville restaurant. This recipe was printed in the Cook's Corner column in 1983 at the request of a reader.*

¼ head iceberg lettuce
6 to 8 leaves fresh spinach
1 tomato, cut into quarters
2 ounces red onion, thinly sliced
2 ounces mushrooms, thinly sliced
4 black pitted olives
2 artichoke hearts
½ ounce romano cheese, freshly
   grated
1 ounce Italian dressing (see recipe)

Mix together ingredients, then add dressing. Mix again.

## MAMMA'S ITALIAN DRESSING

In bowl combine salt and seasonings. Add oil and mix. Add vinegar slowly, continuing to mix. Taste to adjust for personal preference.

**Pinch salt**
**Pinch thyme**
**Pinch basil**
**1 teaspoon dry mustard**
**Pinch oregano**
**Pinch pepper**
**1 pint salad oil (olive oil is suggested)**
**½ pint wine vinegar**

# NEW ORLEANS HOUSE BLEU CHEESE DRESSING

*This recipe from the Louisville seafood restaurant was requested in 1979 in a letter to the Cook's Corner column.*

Mix together well. Makes approximately 2 quarts.

**1 quart salad dressing**
**2¼ cups sour cream**
**1¾ pound bleu-cheese crumbles**
**¼ cup lemon juice**
**⅛ cup salad oil**
**1½ teaspoons salt**

# CUCUMBER-YOGURT DRESSING (LOW CALORIE)

Blend all ingredients in a jar or blender, adding oil last, if using. Use with mixed lettuces. About 25 calories per tablespoon. Makes 1½ cups.
— Elaine Corn, 1985

**1 cup plain yogurt**
**1 cucumber, peeled, seeded and shredded or chopped**
**1 clove garlic**
**Juice of 1 lemon**
**⅛ teaspoon cayenne or paprika**
**Salt, to taste**
**2 tablespoons olive oil, optional**

# BUTTERMILK-HERB DRESSING (LOW CALORIE)

1 cup buttermilk
Few sprigs watercress, optional
2 green onion tops (green part),
   coarsely chopped
¼ teaspoon dried oregano or
   marjoram
¼ teaspoon dried tarragon
¼ teaspoon dry mustard
6 to 8 sprigs parsley
¼ teaspoon sugar
Salt and white pepper, to taste

Place all ingredients in a blender or food processor and blend until smooth. Approximately 14 calories per tablespoon. Makes 1½ cups.
— Elaine Corn, 1985

# CUCUMBER-DILL DRESSING

½ cup oil
¼ cup lemon juice
Pinch sugar (optional)
½ teaspoon dried dill weed
½ teaspoon dry mustard
¼ teaspoon garlic salt
Pinch pepper
½ cup peeled, seeded and finely
   chopped cucumber
1 green onion, minced

Blend all ingredients very well, and chill overnight. Shake well before serving over mixed green salad. Makes about 1¼ cups.
— Deni Hamilton, 1980

# WILTED LETTUCE

6 slices breakfast bacon
¼ cup vinegar
¼ teaspoon salt
1 teaspoon sugar
⅛ teaspoon pepper
Lettuce

Have a large bowl warmed by pouring boiling water into it. Let it stand a-heating while you make the dressing.

Cut the bacon in pieces and fry crisp. Remove from pan and keep hot.

Mix the other ingredients together and pour into the hot grease. Watch out — it spatters! Quickly pour the water out of the bowl. Dry. Dump lettuce into warmed bowl, pour the hot contents of the skillet over the lettuce. Cover bowl closely and let lettuce wilt for 5 minutes. Uncover, sprinkle the bacon pieces over the top and hurry it to the table.
— Cissy Gregg, 1954

# KILLED LETTUCE

*Cissy Gregg wrote in 1962 that "killed lettuce," a variation on wilted lettuce, is "another greenery we all love in this part of the country." She found in Myrtle Ellison Smith's "A Civil War Cook Book" that the recipe is from Tennessee, "but somehow or other, it must have crept over the southern boundary of Kentucky," Cissy added.*

Tear the washed tender leaves of lettuce and drain well. Add about 6 to 8 young tender green onions that have been cut into small pieces. Sprinkle with salt and pepper and stir gently so that all the lettuce is well-seasoned.

Cut 4 slices of bacon in small pieces. Fry and drain. Add ½ cup vinegar to the fat and let come to boil. Add the hot vinegar dressing to the lettuce and toss gently. Take the crisp bacon and sprinkle over the top of the "killed lettuce."

# GERMAN POTATO SALAD (HOT)

Boil the potatoes for 20 to 30 minutes, until tender. Drain, cool and slice. Fry the bacon in a heavy skillet until crispy. Remove to paper towels to drain. In the same skillet, but with most of the fat removed, sauté the onion. Add flour, sugar, seasonings, celery seed, wine vinegar and water, stirring well until mixture begins to thicken slightly. Add reserved bacon, potatoes and crumble in the eggs. Garnish with parsley and serve hot. Serves eight.

— Elaine Corn, 1982

**7 medium potatoes**
**8 slices bacon**
**1 onion, chopped**
**2 tablespoons flour**
**2 tablespoons sugar**
**Salt and freshly ground pepper, to taste**
**1 teaspoon celery seed**
**½ cup white wine vinegar**
**½ cup water**
**2 hard-cooked eggs**
**2 tablespoons chopped parsley**

# CHICKEN SALAD

Sprinkle lemon juice over chicken and apple. Toss lightly. Add chopped egg, celery and almonds. Blend mayonnaise with seasonings. Fold into chicken mixture. Serves 8.

— Cissy Gregg, 1952

**2 cups diced cooked chicken**
**1 cup diced celery**
**2 hard-cooked eggs**
**½ cup diced apple (red-skinned preferred and leave the skin on)**
**¼ cup chopped toasted almonds**
**Juice of 1 lemon**
**⅓ cup mayonnaise**
**½ teaspoon salt**
**Dash pepper**
**½ teaspoon sweet basil**

# CHICKEN NECTARINE SALAD

3 cups diced, cooked chicken
3 or 4 fresh nectarines, diced
½ to ¾ cup thinly sliced water
   chestnuts
¼ cup diced celery
¼ cup diced green pepper
¾ cup mayonnaise
1 tablespoon vinegar
1½ teaspoons sugar
¾ teaspoon salt
½ teaspoon dried rosemary leaves,
   crushed
1 head iceberg lettuce, cut crosswise
   into 6 slices

Combine chicken, nectarines, water chestnuts, celery and green pepper in salad bowl. Mix the mayonnaise with vinegar, sugar, salt and rosemary. Pour dressing over salad and toss lightly. Serve heaped on lettuce slices. Six servings.

— Lillian Marshall, 1977

# FIESTA CHICKEN SALAD IN SNOW PEA BASKET

4 cups diced, cooked chicken
1 large onion, chopped
2 cloves garlic, minced
1 bunch fresh cilantro
2 to 3 fresh jalapeños, seeded,
   minced
1 teaspoon marjoram
1 tablespoon thyme
Salt, to taste
Freshly ground pepper, to taste
Favorite mayonnaise, to taste (at
   least ½ cup)
1 8-ounce package cream cheese,
   cubed
Green beans, washed, lightly
   steamed
Snow peas, washed, lightly steamed
Easy vinaigrette (recipe follows)

In a large mixing bowl, combine the chicken, onion, garlic, cilantro, jalapeños, marjoram, thyme, salt and pepper until thoroughly incorporated. Mix in mayonnaise. Fold cream cheese into mixture, being careful not to mash the cubes. Chill until ready to use.

To build the salad, first line a pretty single-serving bowl with steamed green beans in a pinwheel design. Brace and stack about 4 circles of snow peas against the beans. Place scoop of chicken salad in center of snow peas. Garnish with sprig of cilantro. Spoon over with easy vinaigrette. Serves one for a light lunch. About 4 or 5 salads in all.

— Elaine Corn, 1981

## EASY VINAIGRETTE

In a bowl, stir with a fork ¼ cup red wine vinegar, ¼ teaspoon of any prepared mustard, salt and pepper. Add optional herbs: marjoram, tarragon. Beating vigorously, add 1 cup oil (safflower, olive or peanut). Drizzle over salad, or refrigerate in tightly covered jar. Keeps 1 month. Makes 1 cup.

# CHICKEN SALAD

*This recipe, from Teresa Clare, was among those in a 1984 Magazine feature by Elaine Corn about the backstage buffets at the Louisville Ballet.*

Boil chicken with lemon-pepper seasoning 40 minutes. Cool, remove meat from bones and chop. Combine with remaining ingredients. Chill overnight. Add a splash of lemon or lime, to taste. Serves 6.

**4 chicken breasts**
**2 tablespoons lemon-pepper seasoning**
**1 teaspoon dill weed**
**4 tablespoons yogurt**
**2 tablespoons mayonnaise**
**1 rib celery, chopped**
**½ cup raisins**
**Small pieces of carrot, for color**

# RAINBOW CHICKEN SALAD

In a deep saucepan, simmer chicken in water, salt and pepper, covered, for 45 minutes. Cool. Separate meat from bones. Discard bones and skin. Reserve broth for later use, if desired. Cut chicken into thin strips and set aside. On a large platter, arrange leaves of romaine with stalks toward center of platter and tips outward. Alternate slices of avocado and grapefruit in outer ring. Sprinkle with lemon juice. Alternate orange and onion slices for an inner ring. In the center, arrange chicken. Pour orange-mustard mayonnaise over chicken and serve remainder in a separate bowl. Serves 4.

**2 whole broiler-fryer chicken breasts**
**2 cups water**
**1 teaspoon salt**
**¼ teaspoon pepper**
**1 head romaine lettuce**
**2 avocados, peeled and sliced lengthwise**
**2 grapefruits, peeled, seeded and sliced into sections**
**1 lemon, juiced**
**4 navel oranges, peeled, seeded and sliced into sections**
**1 small sweet red onion, sliced**
**Orange-mustard mayonnaise (see recipe)**

## ORANGE-MUSTARD MAYONNAISE

In a medium bowl, beat egg yolks with Dijon mustard and lemon juice. Whisk in olive oil, adding very slowly in a thin stream, until mixture thickens. Add grated peel from orange and the juice from ½ orange. Add salt and pepper, to taste.
— Elaine Corn, 1983

**2 egg yolks**
**2 teaspoons Dijon mustard**
**1 teaspoon lemon juice**
**1 cup olive oil**
**1 orange**
**Salt and pepper, to taste**

# CHICKEN SALAD

It isn't always that a new recipe makes for excitement in eating. In fact, most often, something exciting comes from shaking one's imagination until it becomes active again.

There is no doubt that chicken salad is one of our favorite recipes. You know you can't miss on it. This one was borrowed from the French. Of course, it's made of the same ingredients that go into our chicken salad, but they have a little different way of putting it together. This is it:

Shred finely the lettuce you'd use as the base for the salad and toss with it an equal amount of diced celery — the amount you would be using ordinarily. Along with these two toss in a few tablespoons of mayonnaise, and mix lightly but well.

Then to the chicken add chopped green olives or capers and a generous amount of mayonnaise.

Put the lettuce mixture over the bottom of a pretty salad bowl or plate and carefully spoon the chicken mixture on top. So simple — but you'll be surprised the difference this simple change in mixing chicken salad can make.

— Cissy Gregg, 1956

# CHICKEN SALAD

*This 1961 recipe is vintage Cissy Gregg, incorporating her belief that some cooking instructions should be left deliberately vague. She has some definite rules that shouldn't be violated, but within certain guidelines Cissy urges that you do a recipe your own way. Taste and adjust, she says.*

Cook your chicken, capon or whatever you are using, as follows. After the chicken or chickens are picked over, put them over the tender confines of a pot of water in which has been added a carrot, a few sprigs of parsley, and some of the outer ribs of celery, plus leaves. When the chicken pieces come back to a boil, turn the heat down to simmering and allow them to slowly cook until tender. Add salt when they are about half done. Let them stand in the cooking water until they are cool enough to handle. Remove all of the skin and take the meat off the bones.

We used both dark and white meat in this salad. To some that would be heresy, but I have never been able to understand why — both are off of the same chicken. As the skin is taken off and the bones are picked of their meat, the bones and the skin go back into the pot to be cooked down into a rich broth for soup. From about 5 pounds of chicken, we come up with a quart of diced, cooked chicken.

Diced celery is a wonderful helper to chicken salad, but in our opinion, don't get carried away with yourself. We use about ⅓ cup celery to one cup of the diced chicken.

Toss the celery and chicken together. Cut the salad dressing with about ⅓ mayonnaise. Mix it up gently and add it to the chicken-celery mixture. Take a taste. We added lemon juice and salt, but this is all according to taste.

Then add as many almonds as the budget will afford. We started out with a cup of the blanched almonds, using some whole and the others slivered. Then, horrors on us, we started tasting, picking out the almonds and a piece of chicken to boot, which we call tasting.

Don't make your chicken sloppy with salad dressing, just enough to give all of the ingredients a thin coating of the dressing.

Then we shoved it all into the refrigerator and let it stand to wait until morning. It always tastes better if it has had a little resting time anyway. For the final push, the mixed-up salad goes to a pan that suits the type of platter you are using. It just stands there until it is well chilled, and the final touch is to turn the whole beauty out on the platter and garnish as you please.

# HOT SLAW

Snip up the bacon into snibbles and fry until crisp. Take out and drain on a paper towel. Sauté the onion in the bacon drippings until it is a golden brown. Combine the sugar, flour, salt and pepper and stir into the drippings. Gradually add vinegar, and cook slowly until thickened, stirring constantly. Add the bacon to the sauce, and heat hot. Pour over the shredded cabbage and toss to mix well.

You'll find this same dressing good with lettuce, or even on potato salad.
— Cissy Gregg, 1953

**3 slices bacon**
**1 medium onion, chopped**
**½ teaspoon salt**
**¼ teaspooon pepper**
**1 tablespoon sugar**
**1½ teaspoons flour**
**1 cup vinegar**
**1 medium-sized cabbage, shredded**

# "C" AND "C" AND "A" SALAD

One C is for cabbage, the other is for celery and the A is for apple.

Mix together 1 cup of finely minced cabbage, 1½ cups of diced celery, 1 tart red apple, diced with the skin left on but cored, and ¾ cup broken nut meats. Mix lightly with a tart mayonnaise and place on a bed of greens — we used pieces of chicory and Bibb. Sprinkle the top of the salad with poppy seeds. Quite simple, yet good and perky.
— Cissy Gregg, 1953

# SLAW

Heat vinegar with seasonings. Cool. Pour over cabbage and pepper. Toss to blend. Garnish with wedges of tomato, carrot strips or as you wish.
— Cissy Gregg, 1957

**2 cups finely chopped cabbage**
**1 green pepper, chopped fine**
**⅓ cup vinegar**
**½ teaspoon salt**
**3 tablespoons sugar**
**⅛ teaspoon red pepper**
**1 teaspoon celery seed**

# ROQUEFORT SLAW

A medium head of cabbage
2 ounces Roquefort cheese
½ clove garlic
Vinegar
1 cup mayonnaise (homemade
    makes it mighty good)

Shred your cabbage. Cream Roquefort cheese. Add garlic, sliced very thin, and then add enough vinegar to make a smooth paste. Mix in mayonnaise and let stand for at least 30 minutes. Add dressing to cabbage just before serving. A medium head of cabbage should serve from 6 to 8.

As a garnish we used pickled immature ears of corn. Unless you have a corn patch of your own you must buy them, but they are so good. And then we added a few radishes, crisp and tender, to give color to the individual servings. This time we didn't even make them into radish roses but left them as little red balls into which you can sink you teeth.

— Cissy Gregg, 1956

# TABOULEH

1 cup bulghur wheat
3 medium tomatoes, seeded and
    chopped
1 medium cucumber, chopped
1 cup chopped parsley
1 bunch green onions, chopped
¼ cup fresh lemon juice
3 tablespoons olive oil
Salt and pepper, to taste
About 2 heads Romaine lettuce

Soak bulghur in water for 10 minutes. Drain and combine with next 7 ingredients. Chill well. Arrange lettuce on a large platter and spoon tabouleh into center. Makes about 10 cups.

— Elaine Corn, 1983

# TURKEY SALAD

6 cups chopped turkey, light and
    dark meat
½ cup chopped celery
½ cup chopped olives
5 hard-cooked eggs, chopped
¼ cup chopped sweet pickles
½ cup cashews, optional
1½ cups mayonnaise
Salt and pepper, to taste

Combine all ingredients and chill until serving. Serves 12.

— Elaine Corn, 1981

# TACO SALAD

Mix avocados or prepared guacamole with chili powder and onion. Combine the canned and fresh tomatoes. In a large bowl, place in this order: lettuce, tomatoes, crumbled corn chips, guacamole, cottage cheese, hot sauce, cheddar. Chill well. Serves six.

— Elaine Corn, 1983

2 avocados, chopped and mashed
    with 1 tablespoon lemon juice, or
    2 6-ounce cans frozen
    guacamole, defrosted
1 tablespoon chili powder
½ cup minced onion
½ 10-ounce can tomatoes with
    green chilies
2 medium tomatoes
1 head lettuce, torn into bite-sized
    pieces
1 6-ounce bag corn chips
8 ounces cottage cheese
½ cup hot sauce
½ pound grated cheddar cheese

# ZESTY TUNA SALAD

*"Sometimes we feel that there are recipes so simple we don't need to give them," Cissy Gregg wrote. "Yet, we get many requests for such. One of these is tuna salad. We use this one ourselves."*

Cut olives into large pieces. Dice eggs. Flake tuna coarsely over olives and eggs. Add celery and green pepper. Blend mayonnaise with vinegar, salt, pepper and onion. Pour over salad mixture and blend lightly. Serve on crisp salad greens. Makes three to four servings.

½ cup ripe olives
2 hard-cooked eggs
1 (6½ or 7-ounce) can tuna
1 cup chopped celery
2 tablespoons chopped, green sweet
    pepper
½ cup mayonnaise
2 teaspoons vinegar
¼ teaspoon salt
Black pepper to taste
1 teaspoon grated onion
Salad greens

# WALDORF SALAD

Combine all ingredients except the nuts, mixing well in a large bowl. Line a platter or individual salad plates with lettuce. Spoon salad over lettuce. At serving, sprinkle with nuts. Serve well chilled. Makes six to eight servings.

— Elaine Corn, 1984

3 cups cubed apples, peeled or not
1 cup finely chopped celery
1 cup mayonnaise
Pinch nutmeg
2 tablespoons lemon juice
Lettuce leaves
½ cup chopped pecans

# CRANBERRY-PECAN SALAD RING

*This was one of the recipes given to Elaine Corn by the family of Gov. Martha Layne Collins and Chef Vincent Ashby of the governor's mansion for the 1984 holiday-entertaining issue of the Magazine.*

**4 cups fresh cranberries**
**1½ cups sugar**
**1 cup water**
**2 tablespoons plain gelatin**
**¼ cup cold water**
**1 tablespoon fresh lemon juice**
**⅔ cup chopped pecans**
**1 cup diced celery**

Wash cranberries. Boil sugar and water for 5 minutes. Add berries and cook until they burst, about 5 minutes more. Soften gelatin in cold water, then add to hot cranberry mixture, stirring until dissolved. Add lemon juice. Cool slightly. When mixture begins to thicken, fold in pecans and celery. Place in an oiled mold. Chill at least 6 hours. Garnish with endive, grapes and orange sections. Serves 8 to 10.

# LEND-ME-YOUR-FEARS CAESAR

*Elaine Corn wrote that this recipe, published in 1983, "avoids the theatrics" of the usual Caesar "but leaves the taste. There is no particular order of appearance, except to add oils and cheese last. Make it ahead. Have more dressing on hand if anyone asks for Caesar on the side. The dressing also makes a great steak baste."*

## DRESSING:

**5 cloves garlic**
**Juice of 2 lemons**
**2 eggs**
**½ cup red wine vinegar**
**4 whole anchovy fillets**
**Dash Tabasco**
**1 tablespoon Worcestershire**
**Freshly ground black pepper**
**1 cup olive oil**
**½ to ¾ cup salad oil**
**1½ cups freshly grated parmesan cheese**

Whirl first eight ingredients in a blender or food processor, adding extra Tabasco, Worcestershire or pepper to taste. With machine running, add oils. Dressing will thicken. Stir in parmesan cheese. Chill until ready for use. Wash the inner leaves of the romaine. Pat dry thoroughly. If large, tear leaves gently into bite-sized peices. Place romaine in a large bowl. Toss with croutons. Spoon into the bowl just enough dressing to coat the leaves, or pass around a cruet of Caesar dressing at the table. Garnish salad with red onion rings. Serves 10 to 12.

## SALAD:

**2 heads romaine, limp outer leaves removed**
**1 box plain croutons**
**Thinly sliced red onion rings**

# MRS. HALL'S LIME-PEAR SALAD

*This is a favorite recipe of Mary Hall of Shelbyville, mother of Gov. Martha Layne Collins. It was given to Elaine Corn by the governor's family for the 1984 holiday-entertaining issue of the Magazine.*

Drain and dice pears, reserving juice. Heat juice and combine with gelatin. Allow to set slightly. Beat in cream cheese. Add pears. Whip the cream to medium peaks and fold in. Place in oiled mold and chill. Serves 8 to 10.

**1 large can pears**
**1 small package lime-flavored gelatin**
**2 8-ounce packages cream cheese, softened**
**1 cup whipping cream**

# DEVILED POTATO SALAD

Cut eggs open and remove yolks. Mash yolks. Blend egg yolks with vinegar, horseradish and mustard. Mix in mayonniase, sour cream and the salts. Chop egg whites, and mix with potatoes, celery, onion and green pepper. Stir in egg-yolk mixture and chill. Serves 15 to 20.
— Deni Hamilton, 1979

**16 hard-boiled eggs**
**¼ cup vinegar**
**2 tablespoons horseradish**
**5 tablespoons Dijon mustard**
**2 cups mayonnaise**
**2 cups sour cream**
**1 teaspoon celery salt**
**2 teaspoons salt**
**12 large potatoes, peeled, cubed and cooked until tender (about 13 cups)**
**2 cups chopped celery and tops**
**½ cup chopped onion**
**¼ cup chopped green pepper**

# BIBB, HEARTS OF PALM AND ARTICHOKE SALAD

Separate the leaves of the Bibb lettuce, wash, dry and keep cool. Slice the hearts of palm. Drain the artichokes well, reserving the marinade. Place several leaves of lettuce on eight salad plates. Divide the hearts of palm slices and artichokes among the plates. Sprinkle each with sprouts. Drizzle the reserved marinade over all. Makes eight salads.
— Deni Hamilton, 1980

**4 medium heads of Bibb lettuce**
**1 14-ounce can hearts of palm, chilled and drained**
**2 6-ounce jars marinated artichokes**
**½ cup alfalfa sprouts**

# SALADE NICOISE

2 pounds potatoes
¾ pound green beans
2 heads Boston or 3 heads bibb
    lettuce, rinsed
3 tomatoes, cut in eighths
3 hard-boiled eggs, halved
6 to 8 anchovy fillets
¼ cup niçoise olives, or good black
    Greek olives
1 to 1¼ cups drained tuna
1 tablespoon capers
Vinaigrette (see recipe)

Peel the potatoes and boil 15 to 20 minutes. Slice and toss with ¼ of the vinaigrette.

Wash and cook the beans in boiling water for 5 minutes. Drain and toss with 3 tablespoons of the vinaigrette.

Place the potatoes in the center of a platter, or place equal portions on six salad plates.

Toss the lettuce with remaining vinaigrette and surround potatoes. Arrange in clumps or symmetrical decoration the tomatoes, eggs, anchovies, olives and tuna. Sprinkle with capers. Chill. Present at the table without stirring. Serves 6.

Serve as a cooling lunch entree or to begin an evening meal. Its flavors are robust yet gleaned from simple, native ingredients.

For best flavor, use high-quality tuna (or fresh tuna poached 8 minutes in wine, if available), virgin or extra-virgin olive oil and a well-aged red or white wine vinegar to top off the vinaigrette. As always, fresh herbs will help the illusion that the Mediterranean is closer than we think.

— Elaine Corn, 1984

# VINAIGRETTE

4 tablespoons red or white wine
    vinegar, or half vinegar and half
    fresh lemon juice
2 teaspoons prepard Dijon-style
    mustard
¼ teaspoon dried tarragon, or 1
    teaspoon minced fresh
½ teaspoon dried thyme, or 1
    teaspoon minced fresh
Salt and white pepper, to taste
½ to ¾ cup fruity olive oil
1 clove garlic, finely minced

In a small bowl, combine the vinegar or lemon juice with the mustard, herbs and seasonings. Beating constantly with a small wire whip, add the oil by dribbles until mixture thickens. Stir in garlic. Dressing also may be made by shaking all ingredients vigorously in a jar with a tight-fitting lid.

# SPICY FRENCH DRESSING

Mix all ingredients and shake well before using.
Makes ½ cup.

— Deni Hamilton, 1979

3 tablespoons tarragon vinegar
⅓ cup oil
¼ teaspoon (or more to taste) hot
    red-pepper sauce
½ teaspoon salt
½ teaspoon dry mustard

# GREEN GODDESS DRESSING

Mix all ingredients together until smooth. May
be whirled in blender or food processor. Refrigerate,
covered, at least 2 hours or overnight. Whisk to
serve. Makes about 1¾ cups.

— Deni Hamilton, 1980

1 clove garlic, minced
¾ cup finely chopped, packed
    parsley springs
1 cup mayonnaise
½ cup sour cream
3 tablespoons tarragon wine
    vinegar
2 tablespoons anchovy paste or
    minced anchovies
2 tablespoons minced chives
1 teaspoon lemon juice
½ teaspoon Worcestershire sauce
Salt and pepper to taste

# CAULIFLOWER WITH AVOCADO DRESSING

For this salad the cauliflower may be left as a
whole head or divided into florets, as you wish. We
like to cook salad vegetables until just tender and
then drop them into ice water to chill quickly. This
stops the cooking at once, and they don't seem to
shrivel in the chilling so much. To serve whole,
place cooked cauliflower on platter, garnish the base
with the greens, and pour the dressing made of the
other ingredients over the top. We used the
cauliflower as florets and masked the serving with
the dressing. The amount of lemon juice depends on
the tartness of your mayonnaise, and so will the
other seasonings, for that matter.

— Cissy Gregg, 1956

1 head of cauliflower, cooked and
    chilled
Watercress, chicory or Bibb lettuce
½ cup mayonnaise
1 small ripe avocado, sieved
¼ cup sour cream
2 tablespoons fresh onion juice
3 drops Worcestershire sauce
Lemon juice to taste
¼ teaspoon curry powder, or more
    to taste

# CUCUMBERS IN SOUR-CREAM SALAD

2 teaspoons salt
1 tablespoon lemon juice
1 teaspoon dill weed
1 medium onion, sliced and
    separated into rings
1 cup sour cream
3 medium cucumbers, sliced thin

Combine all ingredients, cover and chill in refrigerator. Stir once or twice while they chill to blend the flavors. Serves six.

— Lillian Marshall, 1977

# SALPICON (COLD MEAT SALAD)

## FOR THE MEAT:

3 pounds brisket or flank steak
1 pat butter
1 garlic clove, minced
1 small onion, quartered
1 whole garlic clove
2 carrots
1 teaspoon oregano
1 tablespoon fresh mint
5 cloves
¼ cup cilantro leaves
8 peppercorns
Salt

## DRESSING:

⅓ cup olive oil
⅓ cup red wine vinegar
1 garlic clove
Juice of 2 limes
1 teaspoon marjoram
½ bundle cilantro

## MIXTURE:

½ red onion, chopped
1 jalapeño, seeded and minced
1 avocado, cubed
1 cup queso blanco or cream cheese,
    cubed
Juice of one more lime
Romaine leaves

Heat butter in deep pot. Stir in minced garlic. Sear meat. Add water to cover, and add remaining ingredients for meat. Bring to a boil, lower heat and simmer covered for 1¾ hours. Remove meat and cool. Pour broth through a strainer, discarding solids and saving broth for another use. When meat is cool, slice in the direction of the grain, then shred each slice with two forks until fine.

Combine all dressing ingredients in a blender or food processor. Stir into meat. Cover and marinate overnight.

At serving, add mixture of red onion, jalapeño, avocado, cheese and lime juice. Spoon meat onto tostadas or place all on a bed of romaine leaves. Serves 10 to 12.

— Elaine Corn, 1982

# AVOCADO-ORANGE SALAD

Line 6 individual salad plates with lettuce. Arrange avocado slices, orange segments, pepper strips and onion rings on lettuce. Garnish with watercress sprigs and lime wedges. Pour dressing over. Serves 6.

— Deni Hamilton, 1981

**6 lettuce cups**
**2 avocados, halved, pitted and sliced into wedges**
**1½ cups fresh orange segments (about 3 oranges)**
**12 fresh sweet red pepper strips or 12 strips pimento**
**12 red onion rings**
**Watercress sprigs**
**Lime wedges**
**Lime mustard dressing (see recipe)**

## LIME MUSTARD DRESSING

Into a blender, put the lime juice, marmalade, vinegar, mustard, salt and oil. Whirl just long enough to chop the marmalade fine. Pour into container and add garlic. Cover and chill 2 hours. Stir well and remove garlic before serving. Makes about ¾ cup, or 2 tablespoons for each of 6 servings.

**2 tablespoons each lime juice and orange marmalade**
**1 tablespoon white wine vinegar**
**2 teaspoons Dijon mustard**
**½ teaspoon salt**
**¼ cup oil**
**1 clove garlic, peeled and halved**

# VINAIGRETTE SAUCE

Mix well and chill.

— Cissy Gregg, 1955

**⅓ cup red wine**
**¼ cup red wine vinegar**
**¾ cup olive oil — or you can use salad oil**
**1 teaspoon salt**
**½ teaspoon freshly ground black pepper, or the coarse ground pepper from the jar**
**2 scrapings across an onion, or to taste**
**1 tablespoon capers, and the juice that comes with them**
**1 tablespoon chopped olives, ripe or green**
**A pinch of thyme**

# VINAIGRETTE DRESSING (USE FOR A MARINADE)

¼ **cup vinegar**
¾ **cup oil**
¼ **teaspoon basil**
¼ **teaspoon rosemary**

Mix all ingredients, and pour over lightly cooked vegetables such as celery, well-drained canned vegetables or just-tender frozen vegtables.
— Deni Hamilton, 1978

# CARAWAY SALAD DRESSING

1 **tablespoon caraway seeds, crushed**
2 **tablespoons water**
¾ **cup salad oil**
⅓ **cup red-wine vinegar**
1 **teaspoon salt**
½ **teaspoon black pepper**
2 **teaspoons grated onion**
¼ **teaspoon garlic juice**

Cook seeds in water over very low heat until water is absorbed. Combine all other ingredients in a jar. Add seeds, shake and chill overnight. Remove from fridge about 10 minutes before serving. Makes about 1¼ cups.
— Deni Hamilton, 1979

# PICKLED EGGS

4 **cups vinegar**
1 **cup juice drained from canned beets**
6 **peppercorns**
1 **large onion, sliced and separated into rings**
1 **clove garlic, crushed**
½ **teaspoon salt**
1 **small whole red pepper**
1 **dozen hard cooked eggs**

Place vinegar and beet juice in a saucepan and add the peppercorns, onion, garlic, salt and red pepper. Boil 10 minutes. Place shelled eggs in bowl or crock and pour the vinegar solution over them. Let stand several days before using.

As a practical matter, you may add the beets themselves to the marinade along with the eggs. The combination is sharp and tasty as a salad, appetizer or colorful addition to an antipasto arrangement.
Lillian Marshall, 1967

# MARINATED RADISHES

**About 20 radishes**
1 **green pepper (optional)**
1½ **tablespoons soy sauce**
2 **tablespoons vinegar**
1½ **tablespoons sugar**

Cut off tops and tails of the radishes, and either slice them thinly or crush them. Cut the pepper into slivers. Marinate in a mixture of the soy sauce, vinegar and sugar. Adjust the seasonings as you wish. Count on about 20 radishes for 2 servings.
Cissy Gregg, 1956

# ANTIPASTO A LA WEBBER

*Bill Webber was chef at the resort hotel in French Lick, Ind., when he gave this recipe to Cissy Gregg in 1957. At the time, he was trying to feed everyone at a big music festival. For all of the ingredients, the recipe is simple — even fun.*

*The folks at Joseph A. Dattilo & Sons tell us that a half crate of celery is 15 bunches and that a crate of cauliflower is 12 heads.*

You chop and chop and chop the vegetables. Then you mix and mix the unchoppable ingredients — on the first day. The second day this mixture rests and components become companionable. The third day it is all eaten up, and the whole business starts again. Makes 17 gallons.

½ **crate celery**
6 **cans pimentos**
A **crate cauliflower**
2 **gallons ripe olives**
10 **pounds of mushrooms**
6 **cans tuna**
6 **eggplants**
2 **dozen green peppers**
2 **gallons pearl onions**
6 **cans of artichoke bottoms**
3 **gallons dill pickles**
15 **pints tomato purée**
½ **pound raw garlic**
2 **pounds salt**
2 **bottles of Worcestershire sauce**
A **bottle A-1 sauce**
2 **gallons of vinegar**
5 **gallons olive oil**
½ **pound English mustard**
6 **bay leaves**

# ELIZABETH SHELTON'S CRANBERRY RELISH HORS D'OEUVRES

*This recipe was served at an Actors Theatre Patrons Party in 1976. Deni Hamilton wrote about the food preparations for the party.*

Wash and sort cranberries. Put in heavy saucepan and cover with the water. Cook over medium heat until tender. Add the raisins, chopped orange pulp and rind. Cook slowly ten minutes. Add sugar and cook until thick. Remove from heat and add nuts. Cool and freeze. To serve, defrost and spoon into celery ribs cut into bit-sized pieces.

1 **quart fresh cranberries**
1 **pint water**
1 **cup chopped raisins**
**Pulp of two oranges, chopped**
**Rind of two oranges, grated**
3 **cups sugar**
½ **cup chopped pecans**
**Celery ribs**

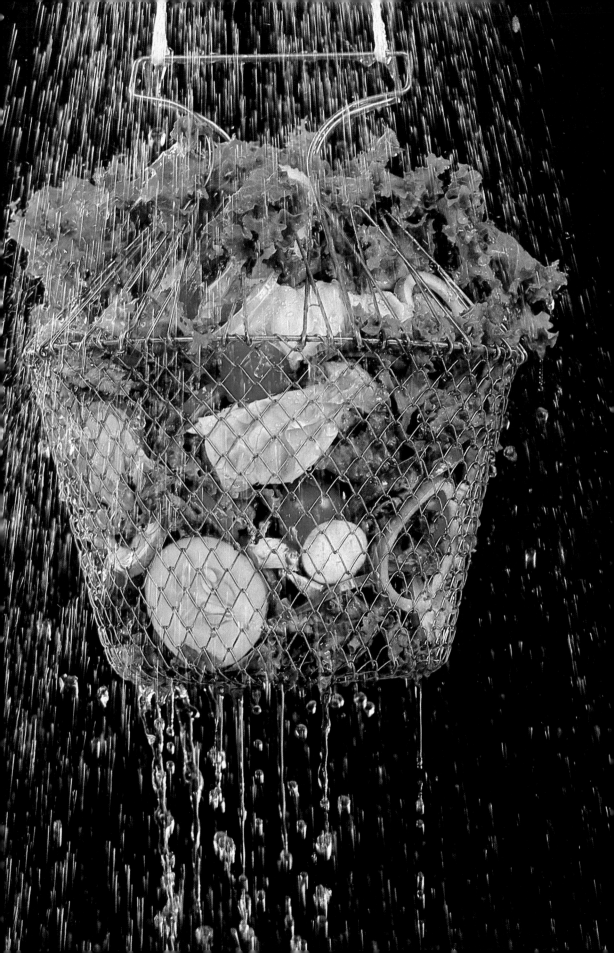

# SOUPS, CHILI & BURGOO

# KENTUCKY BURGOO

*Every cook is tempted to put his or her own stamp on this Kentucky classic, and the Courier-Journal food editors have steered pretty carefully around the many and varied claims of authenticity and originality. The following is known as the Hart County burgoo, and it has been a popular version. The recipe, which was published in the Sunday Magazine in 1979, appears in "Recipes From Around an Old Inn," compiled by the Munfordville Woman's Club.*

*Lillian Marshall did as much experimenting with burgoo as anyone, maybe more, and she came up with versions that could cook — with little attention — in the oven. "This is a loose-knit recipe," she wrote of one particular version. But "burgoo is that kind of thing," she continued. "You can juggle the vegetables to your heart's content."*

2 pounds pork shank
2 pounds veal shank
2 pounds beef shank
2 pounds breast of lamb
1 4-pound hen
8 quarts water
1½ pounds potatoes
1½ pounds onion
1 bunch carrots
2 green peppers
2 cups chopped cabbage
1 quart tomato purée
2 cups whole corn, fresh or canned
2 pods red pepper
2 cups diced okra
2 cups lima beans
1 cup diced celery
Salt and cayenne to taste
Tabasco to taste
A-1 Sauce to taste
Worcestershire sauce to taste
Chopped parsley

Put all the meat into cold water and bring slowly to a boil. Simmer until it is tender enough to fall from bones. Lift the meat out of the stock. Cool and chop up the meat, removing the bones.

Pare potatoes and onions. Dice. Return meat to stock, and add potatoes and onions. Dice and add remaining ingredients except the last five. Allow to simmer until thick. Burgoo should be very thick, but still "soupy." Add seasonings to taste, a bit at a time, continuing until the burgoo is almost done. Add chopped parsley just before serving.

Stir frequently with a long-handled spoon or paddle during the first part of the cooking and almost constantly after it gets thick. Use at least a 4-gallon kettle and cook approximately 10 hours. Makes about 12 quarts.

# ELAINE'S CHICKEN SOUP

1 stewing hen or large fryer
   chicken, about 3 pounds
Water, to cover
1 whole, peeled onion
6 carrots
6 ribs celery
½ bunch fresh parsley
2 to 3 garlic cloves, optional
2 to 3 tablespoons dill weed, or a
   stalk if fresh
Salt and pepper to taste

Wash bird, place in large pot with water. Cover and bring to a boil. Skim. Add remaining ingredients except salt. Tie carrots, celery and parsley with string, if desired. Cover and return to a boil. Lower heat and simmer for 1½ to 3 hours, keeping cover slightly askew. Remove bird. Strain soup and return to pot. Add salt and adjust pepper, if necessary. Heat through.

The meat from the bird can be used in another recipe or chopped and added to the soup.

— Elaine Corn, 1985

# OKRA-CHICKEN GUMBO

Clean and cut up the chicken as for fricasseeing; cut the ham into small squares or pieces and chop the onions and parsley. Skin the tomatoes and chop fine, saving the juice, or dump the canned tomatoes in as they come, drained but without chopping. Wash and stem the okra and slice into half-inch slices.

Put the shortening (or use butter) into the bottom of a deep, heavy kettle. When the fat is hot, add the chicken and the ham. Cover closely and simmer for about 10 minutes. Then add the chopped onions, parsley and tomatoes, drained of their juice, stirring frequently to keep the mixture from scorching. Next add the okra and brown, but stir frequently — if not constantly — to keep from scorching.

When the okra is browned, add the juice from the tomatoes. The browning of the okra is what imparts a wonderful flavor, but it must not scorch, one iota, since the least scorch taste harms the delicious flavor, and for this reason many Creole cooks brown the okra in a frying pan separately — and I prefer to follow such an idea rather than take a chance.

Salt and pepper goes in now, and finally enough boiling water to cover. We figured about 3 quarts.

Bring to a boil, turn down the heat and allow to simmer for at least an hour longer, according to the thickness desired. We simmered ours until the chicken disintegrated off the bones practically. Remove from the stove and while boiling hot gradually drop in 2 tablespoons of filé and mix thoroughly. Pour into a hot tureen and serve in bowls with about 2 tablespoons of cooked rice in the center. Never boil the rice with the gumbo — it isn't done — but cook the rice separately so each grain takes that lone stand, and serve in the bowl with the gumbo.

It is a whole meal, with additions only of perhaps crackers or the typical hard French bread and salad and then perhaps dessert.

— Cissy Gregg, 1950

1 chicken (we used a between 4- and 5-pound young hen)
1 onion
6 large fresh tomatoes or a No. 2½ can of tomatoes, reserve juice
2 pints of okra or 50 counted by their noses
½ pod of red pepper, without the seeds
1 slice of ham
1 bay leaf
A couple sprigs of parsley
1 tablespoon shortening
Salt, pepper and cayenne, if you please, to taste
2 tablespoons filé

# MAISONETTE'S CREAM OF SPINACH SOUP

*Vallie Comisar Geier, owner of Cincinnati's renowned French restaurant, supplied a family-size recipe for this soup in 1984 at the request of our Cook's Corner column.*

2 ounces butter
½ cup chopped leeks
½ cup chopped celery
1 cup chopped onions
3 pounds fresh spinach
1 gallon chicken stock
Salt and pepper, to taste
1 cup cream

Melt butter in large pan. When it foams, add leeks, celery and onions. Cook without browning. Add the spinach; mix well. Add the chicken stock and bring to a boil. Simmer for 30 minutes. Remove from stove, purée in blender and cook again until reduced to a half gallon. Check seasoning. Add the cream and bring to boil again. Serve immediately.

Makes approximately ½ gallon.

# JULIAN'S CHILI

*Gov. and Mrs. Julian Carroll supplied this recipe to the Cook's Corner column in 1979 in response to a reader's request.*

2 pounds ground beef
1 medium onion, chopped
1 8-ounce package spaghetti
2 16-ounce cans chili beans
¾ cup sugar (optional)
2 3-ounce cans tomato paste
1 quart home-canned tomato juice
4 to 6 tablespoons chili powder
Salt and garlic to taste
½ cup red wine

Brown ground beef and onions together. Cook spaghetti in three quarts salted water. Retain water for part of liquid. Add chili beans, sugar, tomato paste, tomato juice, chili powder, salt and garlic. Simmer for 1½ hours. Add red wine last 30 minutes of cooking time.

# COLD HERBED TOMATO SOUP

4 cups tomato juice
¼ cup olive oil
¼ cup tarragon vinegar, optional
2 tablespoons lemon juice
1 clove garlic, minced
1 teaspoon dry mustard
½ teaspoon dry rosemary leaves,
    crushed
1½ teaspoons basil, crushed
½ teaspoon thyme
Salt and pepper to taste

Mix all ingredients in blender, and whirl until smooth. Chill, covered, overnight. Makes 4½ cups.
— Deni Hamilton, 1978

# BOWL OF RED

*This recipe calls for "pure" chili powder, and when she wrote about several variations on chili in 1983, Elaine Corn noted that some commercial brands of chili powder contain not just the powder of chili pepper pods but also cumin, oregano and cayenne.*

In a large kettle, sauté the suet until browned and curled. Add steak and garlic and stir until meat is browned on all sides. Add remaining ingredients. Bring to a boil. Place cover askew and simmer 1 hour. Remove cover and simmer 30 minutes more, or until chili thickens. Serve with cornbread. Serves 16.

— Elaine Corn, 1983

¼ **pound suet**
4 **cloves garlic, minced**
6 **pounds round steak or sirloin, trimmed and cut into 1-inch cubes**
9 **dried red chili pods**
¼ **cup pure chili powder**
¼ **cup oregano**
¼ **cup ground cumin**
¼ **cup paprika**
2 **tablespoons salt**
⅛ **cup cayenne**
3 **quarts water**

# BRAZILIAN CHICKEN SOUP

Bring the broth and chicken to a simmer and add remaining ingredients. Simmer just until vegetables and rice are tender, about 20 minutes. Makes about 10 cups.

— Deni Hamilton, 1980

1¾ **quarts chicken broth**
2 **to 3 cups cooked chicken in big chunks**
¼ **teaspoon black pepper**
¼ **teaspoon thyme**
½ **teaspoon ground cumin**
2 **bay leaves (if none were used to flavor broth)**
1 **pound zucchini, cut in 1-inch-thick slices**
⅓ **cup raw rice**
2 **medium onions, quartered**
1 **cup cubed, cooked, smoked ham (about 5 ounces)**
2 **cups frozen, fresh or canned whole corn kernels**
1 **7-ounce jar whole pimetos, drained and coarsely chopped**

# MAUDE'S BEAN SUPREME

*Deni Hamilton prepared this soup for the old Red Dog Saloon on East Washington Street during the late 1960s, long before she became food editor. It is her mother's recipe.*

1 cup dried garbanzos
1 cup dried black beans
1 cup dried baby limas
1 cup dried great northern beans
1 cup dried pink or pinto beans
1 cup dried lentils
1 cup dried black-eyed peas
2 tablespoons salt
4 huge, meaty ham hocks

Wash and pick over all beans, keeping garbanzos separate. Put garbanzos in 6 quarts of water, and boil for 5 minutes. Put in rest of beans and salt, and return to boil for 2 minutes. Cover, turn off heat and allow to stand for an hour. Add ham hocks, and return to boil. Cover and simmer about 5 hours or until beans are tender and lentils have broken up and are hard to find. If not thick enough to suit you, use a potato masher and mash the contents of the soup pot about 3 times, and simmer another half hour with the lid off. Garbanzos never get as tender as other beans, so don't worry. That's the way they're supposed to be. Makes about 5 quarts of soup.

# POTATO SOUP

¼ stick butter or margarine
A 2-ounce chunk salt pork
3 large potatoes, peeled and cut in ½-inch cubes
2 small onions, or 1 medium one, sliced thin
1 whole clove garlic, on a wooden pick
1 small bay leaf
1 or 2 sprigs fresh parsley
½ cup water
4 cups milk
Salt and pepper to taste
For garnish: chopped chives or parsley

Cut the salt pork into tiny cubes. Melt butter in heavy saucepan, add pork and fry slowly until done and crisp. Add potatoes, onions, garlic, bay leaf and parsley. Add water and one cup of the milk. Cover and steam over low heat until vegetables are soft. Discard garlic, bay leaf and parsley. Reserve a few pieces of potato to add to soup at serving time. Puree, mash or rice remaining potatoes and onions with the liquid left from cooking. Return to saucepan, and gradually stir in the remaining milk. Heat to serving temperature. Garnish each bowl with potato cubes and a sprinkle of chives or parsley. About six servings.

— Deni Hamilton, 1978

# SAUSAGE CORN CHOWDER

Brown link sausages very slowly all over until done through, about 20 minutes. Cut into small pieces and reserve. Drain all the grease but a tablespoon or so and sauté the onion and green pepper in it. Toss in diced potatoes, bay leaf, parsley and sage. Barely cover with corn juice and extra water, if needed. Cover and cook until potatoes are very tender. Remove bay leaf and thoroughly mash the potatoes. Put in corn. Mix flour and three-quarters cup milk or half-and-half well and add to pan, stirring. Bring to simmer, stirring constantly, and cook gently 10 minutes. If too thick, add more milk. Pour a little of the hot liquid into the egg yolks and beat. Pour in a little more, beating, until the yolks are hot. Then stir in that mixture to the pot. Add reserved sausage pieces. Salt and pepper to taste. Serves four.

— Deni Hamilton, 1976

8 sausage links (an 8-ounce package), uncooked
1 small onion, chopped
2 tablespoons chopped green pepper
1 cup peeled and diced potatoes
1 1-pound, 1-ounce can whole-kernel corn, drained and juice reserved
1 small bay leaf
1 teaspoon chopped parsley
1 pinch sage
2 tablespoons flour
1 cup or so milk or half and half
2 egg yolks, beaten together
Salt and pepper to taste

# OXTAIL SOUP FOR EIGHT

Dredge pieces of oxtail in flour and brown them in the shortening, heated in a large kettle or Dutch oven. Add water, salt, pepper, parsley and bay leaves. Cover and simmer for 2 hours. Add remaining ingredients and simmer 1 to 1½ hours longer. Taste and correct seasonings. Serve hot in heated pottery bowls.

— Lillian Marshall, 1969

3½ to 4 pounds oxtail, sliced 1½ inches thick
¾ cup flour
3 tablespoons shortening
2½ quarts water
4 teaspoons salt
¾ teaspoon pepper
2 tablespoons dried parsley flakes
2 or 3 bay leaves
2 medium onions, sliced
1 quart canned tomatoes
3 tablespoons Worcestershire sauce
4 teaspoons sugar
1 tablespoon celery salt
¼ teaspoon powdered cloves
1 pound carrots, sliced thin
1 1-pound can green beans, drained
4 large potatoes, peeled and diced small
½ cup pearl barley

# LEO'S SEAFOOD HIDEAWAY RED-SNAPPER GUMBO

*In 1975, Lillian Marshall indulged in a little nostalgia about Leo's Seafood Hideaway, the Louisville area's first all-seafood restaurant. It was on Jefferson Street and went out of business in 1966. The owner was Leo Weil, who established the Fulton Fish Market and was first president of the American Seafood Distributors Association.*

½ pound margarine
1 pound potatoes, diced
1¼ pounds onions, diced
½ a medium bunch celery, chopped
   (that's a bunch, not just a stalk)
3 tablespoons salt
2 teaspoons white pepper
6 cups canned tomatoes
6 cups sliced okra
1 gallon fish stock (see recipe)
3 quarts water
½ pound rice
3 cups tomato juice
3½ pounds red-snapper fillets, cut
   crosswise in 1-inch pieces

Heat the margarine in a large, heavy pot which will accommodate the two gallons of gumbo you will have when finished. Add the cut-up vegetables and sauté them until wilted and tinged with color. Add salt, pepper, tomatoes, okra, fish stock, water, rice and tomato juice. Simmer, covered, until everything is tender, an hour or more. Add the fillets and simmer 20 to 30 minutes. Estimating a pint per person, it will make double helpings for 16 — more, if you serve it with a scoop of cooked rice under it.

## FISH STOCK

3 or 4 pounds fish bones (get them
   when you buy the fish)
5 quarts water
1 small onion, quartered
¼ cup parsley
2½ teaspoons salt
12 peppercorns
1 bay leaf
½ lemon, squeezed over the pot and
   the rind dropped in too
½ teaspoon thyme
¼ cup dry white wine

Combine ingredients and simmer for 30 minutes. Strain and discard solids. You should have roughly a gallon of stock for the gumbo recipe.

# PUMPKIN SOUP

Add 1 cup mashed pumpkin to 4 cups of scalded milk and season with salt, pepper, a couple of tablespoons of butter and ½ teaspoon sugar. Heat, stirring constantly. Pour over fried croutons — small squares of bread, fried in butter or margarine, you know, and serve immediately. Should serve four.

— Cissy Gregg, 1951

*From foreground: Cream of mushroom soup; quick, fresh tomato soup; potato chowder; chunky cream of asparagus soup. Photograph by Durell Hall Jr.*

# PUMPKIN SOUP

Sauté onion in butter or margarine for 2 minutes. Add tomatoes and pumpkin and heat thoroughly over low heat. Add remaining ingredients and reheat to simmering. Remove from fire; serve immediately. Makes 2 or 3 servings.

Of course, it's true sometimes we cook foods merely because we like them. But there are many times when we cook just to get rid of something we happened to buy or have.

Pumpkin luck to you!

— Cissy Gregg, 1947

1 tablespoon finely chopped onion
1 tablespoon butter or margarine
1½ cups cooked tomatoes
1 cup cooked pumpkin
1 cup thin cream
½ cup milk
¾ to one teaspoon salt
Pepper to taste

# PEANUT BUTTER SOUP

Melt butter or margarine in a large saucepan, add onion and cook until tender. Stir in flour and seasonings. Gradually add milk and chicken broth, and cook until smooth and thickened, stirring constantly. Blend in peanut butter. Serve hot with slivered peanuts afloat, or if you don't have the peanuts, use a little minced chives. These should be growing in your garden or in a pot in the window.

— Cissy Gregg, 1949

2 tablespoons butter or margarine
2 tablespoons finely minced onion
3 tablespoons flour
1 teaspoon salt
¼ teaspoon celery salt
⅛ teaspoon pepper
3 cups milk
1 cup chicken stock or, you know, the stock that's made from a bouillon cube
½ cup peanut butter
A few slivered salted peanuts, if handy

# GERMAN GREEN BEAN SOUP

Place ham and bone with beans, potatoes, water, salt, pepper and garlic powder in Dutch oven. Boil, covered, for 30 minutes or until potatoes are tender. Meanwhile, sauté onion with bacon. Add to soup. Mix flour with milk and stir in, too. Simmer, covered, for 15 minutes. Garnish with parsley. Makes six to eight servings.

— Lillian Marshall, 1976

2 cups leftover ham and ham bone
1 pound fresh green beans
2 large potatoes, peeled and cubed
3 quarts water
2 teaspoons salt
1 teaspoon pepper
½ teaspoon garlic powder
1 medium onion, minced
4 slices bacon, cubed
3 tablespoons flour
1½ cups milk

# GAZPACHO SOUP

3 cups cored, chopped fresh
   tomatoes
1½ cups peeled, chopped cucumber
1 green pepper, cored, seeded and
   coarsely chopped
1 clove garlic
½ cup water
5 tablespoons olive oil or corn oil
¼ cup wine vinegar
Salt to taste
2 slices untrimmed fresh bread,
   cubed

Combine all ingredients in an electric blender (or processor) and blend at high speed, stirring down with a rubber spatula as necessary. Place in large, ordinary kitchen sieve inside a mixing bowl. Pour mixture into sieve. Press and stir with a spoon to extract as much liquid as possible. Discard solids in the sieve. Taste for seasoning and add more salt and vinegar if desired. Chill thoroughly before serving. Makes 6 servings.

— Lillian Marshall, 1969

# GAZPACHO, ANOTHER VERSION

*Technically, gazpacho is a salad, albeit a liquid one, but we're including this recipe here to keep three soupy versions together.*

2 cucumbers, peeled and finely
   diced
4 tomatoes, seeded and finely diced
2 green peppers, seeded and
   slivered
1 onion, finely chopped
Salt and pepper
Rolled anchovies
Black olives
2 garlic cloves
Pinch of ground cumin seed
¼ cup vinegar
½ cup olive oil
2 tablespoons finely chopped
   shallots
1 tablespoon chopped parsley
Juice of 1 lemon

In a deep bowl or glass jar arrange alternate layers of cucumbers, tomatoes, green peppers and onion. Sprinkle layers lightly with salt and pepper, and intersperse the vegetables with rolled anchovies and black olives. In a wooden bowl, mash to a paste 2 garlic cloves with a little salt and a pinch of cumin seed. Beat in the vinegar and olive oil, and stir in parsley and shallots. Pour this dressing over the salad and chill for 2 or 3 hours. Sprinkle with the juice of 1 lemon and serve in chilled bowls as an hors d'oeuvre or salad. About 4 servings.

— Lillian Marshall, 1971

# NEARLY CLEAR GAZPACHO

Place the garlic and the cucumbers cut in chunks into a blender and liquefy. Transfer to a large bowl and stir in the chicken broth. Add the vinegar, lemon juice and salt. Stir in the olive oil. Cover and chill at least 6 hours. At serving time, divide the remaining cucumbers and tomatoes among 6 chilled bowls and ladle over with the chilled soup.

Garnish: Freshly snipped chives, diced bell pepper and whole toasted almonds.

— Elaine Corn, 1981

3 medium cucumbers, peeled, seeded, cut in chunks
2 or 3 cloves garlic
3 cups freshly made or canned chicken broth
¼ cup white vinegar
Juice of ½ lemon
1½ teaspoons salt
½ cup olive oil, optional
3 medium cucumbers, peeled, seeded, quartered and thickly sliced
4 tomatoes, peeled, seeded and coarsely chopped

# BLACK OLIVE SOUP

Place broth in saucepan and bring to boil. Add onion juice and garlic, reduce heat and simmer for 10 minutes. Beat eggs in a large bowl and slowly add the hot broth, being careful not to curdle the eggs. Add remaining ingredients and cool. Refrigerate overnight. Makes about two quarts. Serve chilled in chilled soup bowls. Serves 12.

— Lillian Marshall, 1974

1 quart rich chicken broth, defatted
2 cups (drained and measured) pitted ripe olives, sliced thin
2 teaspoons onion juice
1 small clove garlic, minced
2 eggs
2 cups half-and-half
2 teaspoons thick, bottled steak sauce
¼ cup dry sherry

# POTATO CHOWDER

Stir bacon and onion in a saucepan over a low fire until the bacon is crisp and the onion is cooked clear, which means it is yellowish looking but not brown. Add the water, salt, pepper and the diced potatoes. Cover and simmer slowly until the potatoes are tender. Mash the potatoes or leave them in cubes as they are, just as you feel about it. Add the milk, shredded carrots and chopped spinach. Heat to the simmering point, but do not boil. This will serve six or eight a grand nourishing repast without much trouble to the preparer.

— Cissy Gregg, 1943

6 slices diced bacon
3 tablespoons diced onion
2 cups water
1 teaspoon salt
⅛ teaspoon pepper
5 potatoes, peeled and diced
1 cup finely chopped carrots
1 cup finely chopped raw spinach
4 cups milk

# CHERRY SOUP RUSSE

1 can (1 pound, 4 ounces) frozen
   cherries
1 quart water
2 teaspoons cornstarch mixed with
   2 tablespoons cold water
2 cardamom seeds crushed, or ⅛
   teaspoon powdered cardamom
1 lemon
2 tablespoons sugar (or more, if
   desired)

Pare rind from lemon, as thin as possible, then squeeze and strain juice. Place the cherries, water, cardamom and the rind of the lemon into a saucepan and simmer 15 minutes, or until cherries are very tender. Rub mixture through a sieve or puree in an electric blender (or processor). Return to saucepan and add the cornstarch mixed with water. Stir and cook for about 5 minutes, or until slightly thickened. Stir in lemon juice. Chill and serve sprinkled with parsley or garnished with a thin lemon slice. Serves 8.

— Lillian Marshall, 1968

# RED CHERRY SOUP

*Lillian Marshall recommended this soup for the start of a Christmas dinner spread in 1971.*

1 can (1 pound) red, sour pitted
   cherries in water pack
¼ cup sugar
2 teaspoons cornstarch
¼ teaspoon salt
¼ teaspoon cinnamon
½ cup orange juice
½ cup claret (bordeaux) wine, or
   any dinner wine that is being
   served with the meal
Sour cream for garnish

Drain cherries; reserve liquid and a few whole cherries for garnish. Chop remaining cherries very fine, or purée in an electric blender (or processor). Combine sugar, cornstarch, salt and cinnamon in saucepan; stir in cherry liquid, chopped cherries and orange juice. Cook over medium heat, stirring constantly, until mixture comes to a boil; boil ½ minute. Remove from heat; stir in wine. Serve hot or chilled, garnished with a spoonful of sour cream and whole cherries. Makes 4 to 6 servings.

# MADEIRA CONSOMMÉ

3 or more pounds beef soup bones,
   or roast and steak bones
2 quarts water
Celery leaves
⅓ cup Madeira wine
Salt and pepper to taste
Thin lemon slices and mint leaves
   for garnish

Boil the bones and celery in the water for 1 to 1½ hours. Strain soup, and add salt and pepper to taste. Bring to boil again and add wine. Garnish each serving with a thin slice of lemon and a mint leaf. Makes 8 servings.

— Lillian Marshall, 1974

# TURKEY BONE SOUP

Cover the bones, any pieces of leftover skin and a little stuffing, if available, with cold water. Add the celery and a few leaves, too, if you have them, the carrot, onion and barley. Cover and simmer gently for two to three hours. Strain, add bouillon cubes and bring to the boiling point. Season to taste and serve hot. It you didn't have the stuffing to add, drop in a pinch of mixed herbs.

— Cissy Gregg, 1950

**Turkey carcass and water to cover**
**1 stalk celery, diced**
**1 carrot, sliced**
**1 onion, sliced**
**2 bouillon cubes**
**¼ cup barley, presoaked an hour in cold water**
**Salt and pepper to taste**

# SPANISH BEAN SOUP

Drain salt water from soaked beans and pour beans into 6 cups of boiling water. Add remaining ingredients, seasoning to taste as soup simmers. Add boiling water as needed and stir to keep from scorching. Simmer several hours, until beans are nicely tender. About 6 or 7 servings.

— Lillian Marshall, 1969

**1 8-ounce package garbanzo beans, soaked overnight in salted water**
**⅛ teaspoon saffron**
**½ pound or more smoked ham, or a meaty smoked ham bone**
**3 medium potatoes, diced**
**1 small onion, diced**
**Salt and garlic to taste**

# DOLLY GOFF'S APPLE-ONION SOUP

In soup kettle, boil the beef bone in the water for ½ hour. Strain broth, wash kettle, then return bone and stock back into kettle. Again, there should be 2 quarts liquid. If not, add water to make it up. Add tomatoes, apples, onion with cloves stuck in, and the cinnamon. Boil 3 hours gently, take out bone and season broth with salt and pepper. Put mixture through sieve, or use an electric blender, pureeing 2 cups at a time, until mixture is perfectly smooth. Add water again if necessary to make 2 quarts. Now add the thickening made by blending the butter with the flour. Stir over low heat until thickened and very hot. If desired, garnish each bowlful with 1 teaspoon of whipped cream. Serves 10-12 as first course.

— Lillian Marshall, 1971

**1 medium-size beef bone, all fat removed**
**2 quarts water**
**1 can (2 cups) tomatoes, sieved**
**3 apples, quartered and cored but not peeled**
**1 large onion quartered, with 2 cloves stuck in each quarter**
**3 sticks cinnamon, broken small**
**Salt and pepper to taste**
**2 tablespoons butter**
**2 tablespoons flour**
**For garnish: whipped cream, if desired**

# CARROT SOUP WITH CHIVES

**4 large carrots**
**4 cups water**
**Salt**
**4 tablespoons rice**
**2 tablespoons butter or margarine**
**1 egg yolk**
**Pepper**
**Chopped chives**

Scrape carrots and cook in salted water until tender. If you like, cut up the carrots for quicker cooking — they're going to be run through a sieve anyway. Save the water in which the carrots are cooked, and put the carrots through a sieve or food mill. (Or purée in blender or food processor.) Bring the water in which the carrots were cooked to a boil and add rice. Simmer until the rice is tender. Add the carrot pulp and butter or margarine to the rice mixture. Stir egg yolk into a little of the hot liquid then add to the soup. Whip with an electric beater or a rotary hand beater. Serve with a garnish of chives.

The size of carrots used will make a difference in the thickness of the soup. In case it gets a little too thick for your liking, add a little boiling water before adding the egg yolk. The yolk will thicken the soup slightly, but it also adds richness, and we liked the addition of the egg yolk rather than letting the rice complete the job of thickening.

— Cissy Gregg, 1951

# WATERCRESS SOUP

**2 potatoes**
**1 onion**
**1 quart boiling water or chicken**
**  stock**
**1 large bunch of watercress or 2**
**  small ones**
**2 beaten egg yolks**
**4 tablespoons cream**
**Salt and freshly ground black**
**  pepper**
**Paprika**

Peel and slice the potatoes and onion. Set them to boil in the quart of water. It is much better, we think, to use stock instead of water. It can be chicken stock, or chicken stock made from bouillon cubes, or the canned. While the potatoes and onion are cooking, wash well and pick over the watercress. We used two bunches but have no idea whether they would be called large or small. We just like plenty of watercress. Chop up the watercress or, better still, cut fine with the kitchen scissors.

When the potatoes and onion are mushy done, put through a food mill or whatever device you use for puréeing. Mix puréed vegetables and liquid in which they are cooked together and heat hot. When it is boiling again, add the snipped watercress. Let it return to a boil and after a minute, remove from the fire. Add salt as is needed, and freshly ground black pepper. Then add the beaten egg yolks mixed with the cream and heat for a minute but do not boil. Serve with a sprig of cress in each bowl.

— Cissy Gregg, 1955

# CORN CHOWDER

Fry the pork until the fat comes out freely, then remove and save the crisp scraps. Cook the onion in the fat until a light brown. Add corn, potatoes and water, and simmer until the vegetables are tender. Add scalded milk and thicken with flour and butter or margarine creamed or rubbed together. Simmer 5 minutes, season and, just before serving, stir in the cracker crumbs and the reserved pork scraps.

If you have the whole-kernel corn, vacuum pack, add about ½ cup more milk. Also, I shall remind you that this is a good place to make use of the dry-milk solids.

If you are oyster-minded, use 1½ cups of oysters, carefully picked over and scalded in their own juice, instead of 1½ cups of milk. Chop or leave the oysters whole, according to your own wishes.

— Cissy Gregg, 1950

⅛ pound of salt pork, diced
1 onion, minced
2 cups canned creamed corn
2 cups diced potatoes
2 cups boiling water
1 quart milk, scalded
2 tablespoons flour
1 tablespoon butter or margarine
1 teaspoon celery salt
A pinch of pepper
⅓ cup cracker crumbs

# COOL CUCUMBER SOUP

Cook together until very tender the unpeeled cucumber, onion, salt, pepper and chicken broth. Blend cornstarch and a little cold water until smooth. Add cornstarch to cucumber-chicken broth mixture, cook, stirring constantly for 2 minutes. Put all through a food mill or a sieve — mashing it through. (Or use blender or processor.) Chill. When ready to serve, add cream and chilled peeled and chopped raw cucumber. Serve cold with mint or chives and, if you like, a little whipped cream on top.

— Cissy Gregg, 1949

2 cups unpeeled, chopped cucumber
1 medium sized onion, chopped
1 teaspoon salt
⅛ teaspoon cayenne pepper
2 cups chicken broth, or 2 cups water and 2 chicken bouillon cubes
2 tablespoons cornstarch
1 cup light cream or 1 cup sour cream
1 cup peeled, finely chopped cucumber
Chopped fresh mint or chives

# CHILI-BEAN CHOWDER

*Cissy Gregg gave a little lesson in seasonings along with this 1947 recipe. She also took the position that garlic "does the best job when it's hard to tell it's there even."*

1 No. 2½ can of kidney beans,
   about 30 ounces or 3½ cups
2 cups water
1½ teaspoons salt
1 medium onion, chopped
2 cloves garlic
1½ teaspoons chili powder
1 tablespoon oregano, powdered
1⅔ cups evaporated milk, which is
   one tall can

Add water, salt, onion and garlic, chili powder and oregano to kidney beans and simmer slowly until onion is tender and spices are fully blended. Take out the garlic because all you want is the flavor. A good retrieving way is to stick each clove with a toothpick. Then the toothpick leads the way to keep one single piece of the garlic from landing in somebody's bowl.

Just when you are ready to serve, add the milk and heat to serving temperature. Don't boil, or the mixture may curdle.

This will make the first course of a meal for about six, but if you want to make a meal off of it, I don't believe it would do for more than three.

The seasonings we liked as given. Oregano has a sagey flavor that's interesting for those who like the unusual. For the young, always take the high and unusual seasonings in small steps. The youngsters don't have jaded taste buds, and seasonings are very pronounced to them.

Another good point about this soup is that the basic part up to adding the milk can be done way beforehand and the milk added a few minutes before supper or lunch time.

# COLD AVOCADO SOUP

5 medium sized avocados
6 cups chicken stock or broth
¼ cup lemon juice
¼ cup sherry (optional)
Salt and pepper to taste
3 tablespoons chopped olives or
   parsley
1 cup sour cream

Remove skin and seeds from avocados. Purée in blender (or sieve) and combine with clear chicken stock. Add sherry, lemon juice and salt and pepper to taste. Chill thoroughly until serving time. (If you wish to make it a day in advance, you may like to put the avocado seeds in the soup until serving time; they help keep the color bright.) At serving time, spoon sour cream on each serving and sprinkle with chopped chives or parsley. Makes 12 servings.
— Lillian Marshall, 1968

# RICH SHERRIED CONSOMMÉ

Brown bones at 350 degrees for 40 minutes, turning once. Halve peeled onion and place in a cast-iron skillet, flat sides down, over medium-high heat until blackened.

Place bones, blackened onion and all except last 3 ingredients in a large pot or Dutch kettle. Bring to a boil, skim, reduce heat to no hotter than a gentle simmer for 5 hours, uncovered. Skim again, if necessary. Strain through metal strainer, returning soup to the pot over medium-high heat and discarding solids.

Beat the whites to firm peaks. Add with shells to soup. Simmer gently 20 minutes. (Soup will look like a mess. The egg whites and shells clarify the liquid.) Strain twice through strainer lined with two thicknesses of cheesecloth, discarding solids. Add sherry and salt. Serves 8 to 10.

— Elaine Corn, 1984

**3 pounds meaty short-rib bones, or other kind of meaty marrow bones, plus 1 pound bony chicken parts, such as necks or wing tips**
**1 large onion, peeled and halved**
**3 quarts water**
**1 large onion, unpeeled**
**2 ribs celery**
**2 garlic cloves**
**2 carrots, scrubbed**
**1 turnip, peeled**
**4 generous sprigs fresh parsley**
**8 whole black peppercorns**
**4 whole cloves**
**1 leek, white part only, washed well**
**1 bay leaf**
**½ teaspoon thyme**
**2 egg whites, plus egg shells**
**2 tablespoons dry sherry**
**Salt, to taste**

# ICED CUCUMBER SOUP WITH SOUR CREAM

For 1 quart homemade chicken stock, from which the fat has been skimmed, or 1 quart chicken bouillon from cubes, use 2 medium unpeeled cucumbers. Dice them and simmer them in butter, along with a small sliced onion, until they are tender. Add 1 cup light cream and a pinch of thyme, salt and white pepper, as needed, and simmer another 5 minutes.

Rub the cucumber-onion mixture through a sieve into the chicken broth, add some chopped fresh tarragon, heat again, and thicken slightly with the yolks of 2 eggs beaten with a little of the stock.

Chill thoroughly, and garnish with a slice of lemon in each bowl and 1 teaspoon sour cream. Top with almonds that have been blanched, sliced very thin, roasted brown on top of the stove in a skillet with butter, then drained and salted. Serve while the almonds are still warm. It's a pleasing contrast.

— Lillian Marshall, 1968

# BLACK BEAN SOUP

*Cissy Gregg made one further note among her list of ingredients for this 1943 recipe: "If you are an addict to spices in soup, a bay leaf and a couple of cloves will go good along with the rest of the ingredients." Obviously, Cissy would have used a blender or a food processor instead of sieving the beans.*

**1 pint of black beans**
**2 quarts of water**
**½ onion, chopped, grated or minced**
**½ cup celery, chopped, too**
**2 teaspoons salt**
**1 teaspoon pepper**
**3 tablespoons butter**
**2 tablespoons flour**
**1 lemon**
**2 hard-cooked eggs**

Soak the beans overnight, pour off the soaking water. Fry the onion in two tablespoons of the butter, add to the beans along with the celery and the water. Cook at the slow pace until the beans are tender, which will be at least three hours. Add more water as it boils away. Then when the beans are soft and squashy rub through a strainer or sieve. This is the worst part for me, but keep at it and soon the job will be finished.

Add the other seasonings. The butter left and the flour are for thickening, and, to get it in properly, it is practically necessary to melt the butter, add the flour, then a cup of the soup and pour one way or the other until all are together. The lemon gets sliced and goes for a swim on top of the soup in the company of the thinly sliced egg. A dash of sherry is an asset, too, if you have it about the house.

# MINESTRONE

**1½ pounds meaty soup bones**
**4 quarts water**
**3 teaspoons salt**
**¼ teaspoon pepper**
**1 1-pound 3-ounce can tomato purée**
**2 6-ounce cans tomato paste**
**1 1-pound can tomatoes**
**2 or 3 tablespoons olive oil**
**3 medium onions, chopped**
**1 clove garlic, minced**
**1 cup chopped celery stalk and top**
**1 cup fresh chopped parsley**
**3 large carrots, thinly sliced**
**½ teaspoon oregano**
**½ teaspoon basil**
**1 cup finely chopped cabbage**
**1 cup finely chopped escarole**
**2 small zucchini, thinly sliced**
**1 15-ounce can navy beans, drained**
**2 15-ounce cans garbanzo beans,**
**   drained**
**2 ounces pasta of your choice**

Simmer meaty bones in water and salt and pepper one hour, uncovered. Add tomato purée, paste and tomatoes. Meanwhile, sauté in olive oil the onions, garlic, celery and parsley until the leaves are wilted. Add to soup. Put in carrots and herbs and simmer another hour or until meat is tender and can be pulled off bones. Chop meat coarsely. Discard bones, making sure to leave the marrow in the soup. Add cabbage, escarole, zucchini and beans and simmer until cabbage is just tender. Add pasta and cook until just tender. Pass fresh grated parmesan cheese along with soup for topping. Makes about 6½ quarts.

— Deni Hamilton, 1976

# GULF HILLS LEMON SOUP

*Over the years, Cissy Gregg used several recipes from Gladys Hill of Ocean Springs, Miss., including this one in 1951. We haven't found Cissy's first reference to Mrs. Hill, so it's not clear whether she was associated with a restaurant or inn with the "Gulf Hills" name.*

Simmer onions and garlic in the beef stock until both are tender. You can use canned beef stock, but if you'll take the time to make a good beef stock on your own, the soup will be more individually flavored.

Stir in the cooked rice and let come to a boil. Pour the boiling hot stock over the beaten eggs — a little at first and then more, stirring vigorously, of course, until all the stock has been added.

After the eggs are in, don't allow the soup to come to a boil again. You have to watch this to keep the soup from curdling. We don't find it unruly at all — but it can be temperamental, they say.

Serve hot with a thin slice of lemon, sprinkled with minced parsley on top of each serving. This amount will serve four to six, depending on the size of your soup bowls.

**3 cups beef stock**
**1 small onion, minced**
**1 clove of garlic, minced**
**2 eggs, well beaten**
**Juice of 1 lemon**
**½ cup cooked rice**
**Salt and pepper to taste**

# MISS NELL'S LIMA BEAN SOUP

*Miss Nell Westmeier was a "queen soup maker for a well-known restaurant" in Louisville, Cissy Gregg wrote in 1955. Cissy said she decided to write about Miss Nell and her recipe after her husband came home raving about the soup.*

Soak lima beans overnight. Cook ham hock and bone with celery, onion, red pepper pod and green pepper until thoroughly done. The ham should be cooked until the meat is willing to fall off the bone If any clings, strip it off down to the last fragment. Drain soaked lima beans and add to mixture. Cook the beans quickly in the broth until tender. Here you have to be on your own as to the amount of liquid and lima beans. Don't hesitate to add boiling water if necessary. Season with salt to taste. The amount will depend on the saltiness of the ham broth.

The amounts of these ingredients, Miss Nell said, may be varied to suit what you have on hand. More celery, and she uses quite a bit in hers, and the green pepper or the onions, is a matter of taste.

Her beans are tender as can be, but "don't let them cook until they mash up," she advised.

**1 pound dried lima beans**
**1 good-sized ham hock and bone**
**½ medium-sized stalk celery, cut fine**
**3 good-sized onions, cut fine**
**½ green pepper, cut fine**
**1 red pepper pod or the equivalent**

# CHILLED CUCUMBER-YOGURT SOUP WITH WALNUTS

½ cup chopped walnuts
2 to 3 cloves garlic
¼ cup olive oil
Juice of 1 lemon
3 cups yogurt
1 cup chicken broth, or 2 chicken bouillon cubes dissolved in 1 cup hot water, cooled
1 cucumber, peeled, seeded and chopped
Dash paprika
Salt and white pepper
Fresh chopped mint, for garnish

In blender, food processor or with a mortar and pestle, mash the walnuts and garlic with the oil and lemon juice. Place in a bowl with yogurt and stir to combine. Stir in broth and remaining ingredients. Adjust seasonings. Chill several hours before serving ice cold. Garnish. Serves 4 to 6.

— Elaine Corn, 1983

# CREAM-OF-MUSHROOM SOUP

2 pounds mushrooms
6 cups chicken stock, preferably homemade
3 tablespoons unsalted butter
3 tablespoons flour
1 cup heavy cream
¼ cup sherry
Few dashes Tabasco or pinch cayenne
Freshly ground pepper to taste
Dash salt

Wipe the mushrooms with a damp cloth. Untwist stems and coarsely chop. Thinly slice the caps and set aside. In a large saucepan, simmer 4 cups of chicken stock with the chopped stems 20 minutes, or until the stock is deep brown and mushrooms give off no flavor. Strain. (Reserve pieces to use in stuffing or to purée in other soups, or discard.) Return mushroom broth to heat. Add 1½ cups more stock. Bring to boil. Add butter. In a small cup, dissolve the flour in the remaining ½ cup stock. Pour slowly into soup and stir, or whisk, until smooth. Add sliced mushroom caps. Simmer 5 minutes. Remove from heat. Stir in the cream. Add sherry and Tabasco. Season after tasting. Serve immediately. Serves 6 to 8.

— Elaine Corn, 1981

# CREAM OF BUTTERNUT SQUASH AND SHRIMP SOUP

*In October 1983, Elaine Corn wrote about a variety of winter squashes and told how to use them. The butternut is one of the most popular, she wrote, and "one of its finest moments is as soup."*

Halve squash. Scoop out seeds. Lay cut side down on baking sheet. Bake at 350 degrees for 30 to 40 minutes. Cool. Remove pulp and purée, beating in stock until velvety smooth. In a large saucepan, melt butter. Add shrimp and sauté until translucent, about four minutes over medium-high heat. Add squash-stock purée, half-and-half, curry, cinnamon, salt and pepper. Stir well and heat through. Serve hot. Makes six servings.

**1 medium butternut squash, or 2 cups purée (or equivalent of acorn, buttercup, pumpkin or Hubbard purée)**
**2 cups chicken stock**
**2 tablespoons butter**
**¾ pound small to medium shrimp, shelled**
**1½ cups half-and-half**
**½ teaspoon curry**
**Pinch cinnamon**
**Salt and white pepper, to taste**

# TOMATO AND SEAFOOD SOUP

(Clams may be used in this dish, or even two cans of clam broth. We used shrimp and some frozen crab meat, fresh-frozen, because we had it lurking in the freezer).

Leave the shrimp unpeeled but well washed, and cook for 5 minutes in salted water to which have been added a slice of onion, half a lemon squeezed of the juice but the peel added, a small pod of red pepper and a little celery — especially the tops, since they are so flavorful.

When the shrimp are withdrawn from the cooking, let them cool in the broth. Peel and devein them. Strain the broth and use it in the soup.

Cook the onions, garlic and tomatoes in the olive oil (we used the canned tomatoes — one large can, a small can of tomato purée and two tablespoons of paste). Simmer a little until somewhat tender. Add the strained shrimp broth to make 6 cups; if you don't have enough, add tomato juice or water. Add the bay leaf and thyme and simmer 15 minutes. If you are a perfectionist, strain again, through a course sieve. We simply fished out the bay leaf and left the rest in the soup. Add the cooked shrimp and about ½ pound of picked over crab meat, chopped parsley, salt and pepper. Taste for the true flavor, and it should be so good you puff up like a pigeon with pride.                     — Cissy Gregg, 1961

**2 pounds shrimp**
**2 cups diced onions**
**2 cloves garlic, crushed**
**4 large tomatoes, skinned and sliced, or canned tomatoes**
**⅔ cup olive oil**
**1 bay leaf**
**1 teaspoon thyme**
**Chopped parsley**
**Salt and pepper**

# TURTLE SOUP

*Cissy Gregg went to Charles L. Bronger, "a recognized turtle-soup authority," for this 1948 recipe. Bronger was superintendent of the newspapers' engraving department at the time. A blender or a food processor would be a labor-saver in this recipe, although it is clear that the food should be chopped fine but not liquified.*

**7 pounds of turtle (If you don't have that much, fill out the amount with fresh beef tongue.)**
**¼ medium-sized head of cabbage**
**6 medium-sized carrots**
**1 pound fresh green beans**
**1 whole bunch of celery**
**8 onions about 2½ inches in diameter**
**8 potatoes about 3 inches in diameter**
**1 10-ounce can tomato purée**
**3 lemons**
**6 eggs, hard cooked**
**2 No. 2½ cans tomatoes or 6 cups of canned tomatoes**
**½ cup whole allspice**
**1 can peas**
**Kernels from 2 ears of corn, if you like**
**1 bottle catsup**
**1 red pepper**
**Salt to taste**
**About 1 cup of browned flour**
**1 bottle of claret, or any dry red wine**
**About 3½ gallons of water**

Put turtle meat or turtle and fresh beef tongue on in cold water and allow it to come slowly to a boil. Turn down the heat and simmer gently until the meat is falling-apart tender. The turtle meat will cook more quickly than the tongue, but as a guess of time so you'll have some idea of what you are getting yourself into, we would say allow at least 2½ to 3½ hours to cook the meat.

While the meat is cooking, get the vegetables ready and have the seasonings in hand. When the meat has cooked, lift out of the broth, take out bones and trim the tongue if it is used. Next everything must go through the meat chopper; yes, corn, peas, 5 of the 6 eggs and 2 of the 3 lemons. The extra hard-cooked egg and the lemon can be sliced and added as a garnish. We didn't put the tomatoes through the chopper, and that was a mistake, so remember to grind all ingredients. This means to put the canned tomato pulp through the chopper with everything else except the red pepper.

We found by waiting until the meat was cooked that we could use some of the easy-to-grind vegetables to help the meat and the softer vegetables through the chopper. The celery and carrots are excellent grinding helpers. Use either the medium or the fine knife. Mr. Bronger specifies that the grinding gauge should not have a larger opening than ¼ inch. Save all juice that drips from the grinder and put it with the other ground ingredients back into the stock. Add catsup and red pepper. Add some salt but wait until the last to finish off, so don't add too much at first. Tie the allspice in a cloth or small bag and toss it into the pot. Simmer all together for approximately 4 more hours. The sliced lemon can go in then too if you like, but we saved the final egg to put on the top.

The cooking is very simple — in fact the fire does the work, or most of it. There must be stirring, especially toward the last. When the soup thickens up with all the vegetables added, plus the natural evaporation in cooking, turtle soup will scorch as easily as jam. It's best to cook it with an asbestos mat between the fire and pot. If that isn't possible, stir oftener than occasionally. We won't say all of the time, but often enough to keep the mass from becoming too attached to the bottom and the heat. Also keep the fire turned low.

To brown the flour, put perhaps a little more than the amount called for in a shallow pan under the broiler. Stir frequently to keep the flour from lumping and scorching. Aim for a good brown tinge, but don't let the flour burn — and when flour gets to a certain spot, it seems to take delight in burning.

If the broiler way doesn't suit you, put the flour in a skillet and burn it by swishing it to and fro until the desired color is reached.

If any water needs to be added after the initial quantity, add only boiling water. Turtle soup blanches in horror at having cold or even tepid water dashed into it.

This sounds like a lot of soup, and believe me it is, but, my, how it can disappear! Don't try to figure the number of servings by any rule given for other soups. The smallest appetite can take on a quart, and some capacities are seemingly without limit.

Of course, when you have cooked turtle soup, you have cooked the meal.

The only thing that goes with it would be a few knickknacks and an assortment of bread and crackers. We offered thin slices of rye bread, melba toast and crisp bread sticks besides crackers. There are also carrot curls and celery sticks.

# SUMMER SOUP

Cut cabbage, carrots and beets into short narrow strips. Sauté onions, carrots and cabbage in butter or margarine in large heavy pot. Add a quart of water, salt and pepper and cook until vegetables are tender crisp. Add beets. Heat the second part of water and dissolve beef bouillon cubes in it. Combine with vegetable mixture; thicken with paste of flour and a little cold water. Bring to a simmer and add lemon juice or vinegar. Serve garnished with dollop of sour cream. Sprinkle with chopped parsley, if desired. Serves 8 to 10.

— Lillian Marshall, 1972

½ head green cabbage
2 carrots
3 cooked beets or a can sliced beets
2 medium onions, chopped
4 tablespoons butter or margarine
4 tablespoons flour
5 beef bouillon cubes
2 quarts water
1 teaspoon salt
⅛ teaspoon pepper
1⅓ tablespoons vinegar or lemon
   juice
Sour cream

# CHUNKY CREAM OF ASPARAGUS SOUP (WITH EXTRA-CREAMY VARIATION)

2 tablespoons butter
1 cup chopped onions
¾ pound thin fresh asparagus,
    sliced diagonally in 1-inch pieces
    (reserve the best-looking tips)
2 tablespoons all-purpose flour
1¾ cups chicken broth, or 1 (13¾
    ounce) can
1 cup cream, half-and-half or milk
Dash salt
Pinch thyme
¼ teaspoon white pepper

In a medium pot over medium-high heat, melt the butter. Add onions and asparagus and sauté, stirring now and then, for 6 minutes. Add flour, stirring mixture constantly for a minute. Asparagus may make mixture sticky. Stir while slowly adding broth until soup is smooth. Bring to a boil. Reduce heat slightly, add cream, salt, thyme and pepper. Serves 4.

## EXTRA-CREAMY VERSION

Cool above soup slightly. Purée half the recipe in a blender or food processor until smooth. Add back to soup, stirring to combine well. Reheat and serve.

— Elaine Corn, 1984

# QUICK FRESH TOMATO SOUP

2 tablespoon olive oil
1 cup chopped onions
1 cup chopped celery
4 cloves garlic, minced
2 tablespoons all-purpose flour
2 cups canned whole plum Italian
    tomatoes, including juice, or use
    fresh, skinned and seeded
Pinch sugar
1¾ cups beef broth, or 1 (13¾-
    ounce) can
Dash salt
¼ teaspoon freshly ground black
    pepper
½ teaspoon crumbled, dried
    oregano

Heat the olive oil in a medium pot over medium-high heat. Add onions, celery and garlic and sauté 3 minutes, stirring now and then. Add flour, stirring the pasty mixture around the pot for 2 minutes. Slowly add the tomatoes and their liquid, breaking up tomatoes slightly as you stir. Add sugar. Bring to a boil. Slowly add broth. Bring to a second boil. Add salt, pepper and oregano. Serves 6.

— Elaine Corn, 1984

*Minestrone. Photograph by Carl Rainbolt.*

# CORN AND OYSTER BISQUE

In a large saucepan or Dutch kettle, heat the butter. Add the onion, carrot and celery and sauté 15 minutes. Stir in 4 cups of the corn, the stock and reserved oyster liquor and bring to a boil. Cool slightly, then purée mixture in a food processor or blender until very smooth. Press purée through a sieve, discarding solids. Return soup to kettle with cream, remaining corn and pepper.

Heat through and keep warm. At serving, add oysters and heat for about 3 minutes (until edges curl and turn white). Serve immediately. Serves 6.

— Elaine Corn, 1984

**3 tablespoons butter**
**1 onion, diced**
**1 carrot, diced**
**1 rib celery, diced**
**6 cups fresh or frozen corn kernels**
    **(if frozen do not thaw)**
**2 cups chicken stock**
**1½ cups cream, half-and-half,**
    **whole or skim milk**
**White pepper, to taste**
**1 pint fresh shucked oysters,**
    **drained, and liquor reserved**

# SOUTHERN FISH CHOWDER

*The fish in this 1951 recipe tested by Cissy Gregg is cooked tender, then simmered about 40 minutes more. By today's standards, that's decidedly overcooked. If you want the fish in bite-size chunks, you may want to cook it first, as the recipe suggests, but then cut it to size and add it to the broth near the end of the cooking, along with the pork scraps, egg and lemon slices.*

Clean the fish thoroughly, but I hope you only have to do the finishing touches of same. Then simmer in the water until tender. Drain and save the liquor. Discard the skin of the "red" and take out the bone. Fry pork until the fat flows freely. Remove the crisp scraps and cook the onion and garlic in the remaining fat until light brown. Add the green pepper and cook 3 minutes longer. Add fish — on the return trip, fish stock, celery, potatoes, tomatoes, bay leaf and seasonings all go in — and simmer until the potatoes are tender, which sums up to about 40 minutes. Finally add the pork scraps, egg and lemon slices, then the wine, if you are using it, and heat until very hot. Then serve. We thought what we came up with was quite delish, and you can do the same. It was our first time, too. Like many teachers, we were just one step ahead.

— Cissy Gregg, 1951

**1½ pounds red snapper**
**1½ quarts water**
**½ pound salt pork, diced**
**2 onions, minced**
**1 clove garlic, finely minced**
**1 small green pepper, but if Nature**
    **doesn't cooperate — a green**
    **pepper any size**
**⅓ cup minced celery**
**2 large potatoes, diced**
**1 cup canned tomatoes — but we**
    **like the color red and probably**
    **used more**
**1 small bay leaf, and I do watch the**
    **flavor of even a small bay leaf**
    **carefully**
**1 teaspoon salt**
**¼ teaspoon pepper**
**1 hard-cooked egg, sliced**
**½ lemon, thinly sliced**
**⅓ cup sherry (optional)**

# CHILLED LEMON SOUP WITH MINT

*This recipe is from Molly Clowes, editor of The Courier-Journal editorial page when she retired in 1971. The soup was part of a cold buffet menu in a 1966 issue of the Magazine.*

**4 cups chicken stock, fresh or canned**

**2 tablespoons tapioca**

**3 egg yolks**

**2 tablespoons lemon juice**

**1 tablespoon grated lemon rind**

**½ teaspoon salt**

**⅛ teaspoon cayenne**

**1 cup heavy cream**

**2 tablespoons fresh mint, finely cut with scissors**

**½ to 1 cup light cream, if necessary**

This is a chilled version of the famous Greek lemon soup known as avgolemono. Tapioca, instead of the traditional rice, lightly thickens the chicken broth, which is then flavored with lemon and given a velvet-like consistency with egg yolks and heavy cream. This recipe serves six.

In a heavy 2-quart saucepan, bring the 4 cups of stock to a boil and sprinkle in slowly 2 level tablespoons of tapioca. Cook rapidly for 2 or 3 minutes, then lower the heat and simmer, partially covered, for about 5 minutes.

Meanwhile, with a wire whisk or fork, beat together in a small bowl the 3 egg yolks and the lemon juice, grated rind, salt and cayenne. When they are about combined, mix in cup of heavy cream. Now, tablespoonful by tablespoonful, add the simmering stock to the cream mixture, stirring well after each addition. At about the 10th spoonful, reverse the process and pour now-heated cream back into saucepan all at once, stirring constantly.

The next step, always fraught with potential disaster, is to cook the soup until it thickens to a smooth, light custard. But don't bother doing this in a double boiler, a wearisome, unnecessary process. Cook it over direct heat. If you are really careful not to let the soup get too hot (to say nothing of letting it boil), it won't curdle.

Place the saucepan over moderate heat and, stirring deeply and around the sides of the pan with a wooden spoon, cook the soup until it begins to thicken and you feel a barely perceptible resistance to the spoon. Still stirring, lift the pan above the heat to cool it a bit, then return it to the heat once more. Continue to cook, lifting the pan from time to time, until the soup has thickened enough to coat the back of the spoon lightly. Don't worry if the soup seems thin; it will thicken more as it cools. Pour it at once into a cold bowl, preferably stainless steel, and allow the soup to come to room temperature before covering it tightly with adhesive plastic wrap or waxed paper. Place in the refrigerator and chill until icy cold. If the soup thickens too much, it can be thinned with light cream. Garnish each cup with some finely cut mint and sprinkle a little grated lemon rind on top if you wish. Serve at once.

# PUMPKIN-APPLE CREAM SOUP

Wash pumpkin with a scrub brush. Quarter pumpkin. Remove seeds and reserve, then scrape off sinews. Chop quarters into coarse chunks, but do not peel.

In a large pot or Dutch kettle, cook pumpkin pieces and apples in simmering stock for 1 hour, covered. Strain contents of pot, returning cooking liquid to pot. Allow pumpkin to cool. Slip off skin and purée pulp with apples in a food processor or blender, or run through a food mill, until very smooth. You should have between 3 and 4 cups.

Add purée to stock, stirring in cream. Heat through. Season with nutmeg and salt. Garnish with toasted pumpkin seeds. Serves 10 to 12.

Note: Wash reserved seeds in a colander under running water. Remove any pumpkin fibers with your fingers. Spread seeds on a foil-covered baking sheet. Sprinkle with coarse salt. Broil 3 to 5 minutes, then stir with fork. Return to broiler another 3 to 5 minutes, stirring now and then to toast evenly. May need more or less heat, depending on your broiler. You may also sauté the seeds in a non-stick fry pan until browned. Seeds are ready for snacking or garnish.

— Elaine Corn, 1984

1 small pumpkin, or "pie"
  pumpkin, about 5 to 7 pounds
2 medium tart green apples, peeled
  and cored
6 cups chicken stock
2 cups cream
Freshly ground nutmeg
Dash salt
Toasted pumpkin seeds, for garnish
  (see note)

# BORSCH (BEET SOUP)

Scrub, then thinly peel and shred the beets fine. Melt butter or margarine and when hot add beets and cook 15 minutes, stirring occasionally. Add ⅓ of the stock, sugar, salt and pepper — these exact amounts will depend on the original seasoning of the stock. Then add the rest of the stock. Cover and simmer 20 minutes longer. Add vinegar or lemon juice, taste and reseason as you wish. Instead of the sour cream we used slices of avocado for the "buttery touch" to the soup.

— Cissy Gregg, 1962

6 large beets
3 tablespoons butter or margarine
2 quarts stock
1 teaspoon sugar
Salt and pepper
1 tablespoon vinegar or lemon juice
Sour cream, if you wish

# FRUIT SOUP

1 quart berries
1 cup boiling water
¼ teaspoon salt
3 tablespoons quick-cooking
  tapioca
1 quart cold water
1 to 3 cups sugar
¼ lemon cut in slivers
1 three-inch stick cinnamon
½ cup sweet wine — port or sherry
  — if desired

Use only ripe, solid fruit. Pit, cap or prepare in the manner called for by the fruit used.

Put the cup of boiling water in the top of a double boiler over direct heat. When it comes to a boil, add salt and tapioca, sprinkling it slowly into the water, stirring continuously for five minutes.

Then add the quart of water and stir until it comes to a boil. Add sugar, fruit, cut lemon and cinnamon. Stand over lower part of the double boiler containing boiling water and cover. Cook in this way for 20 to 25 minutes or until the fruit is tender. Stir frequently from the bottom. Remove the stick of cinnamon, and add wine if it is used. Chill and serve cold.

Fruit soup can be served hot, but my preference is for the chilled way.

— Cissy Gregg, 1950

# MEATS

# TENDERLOIN OF BEEF WITH BURGUNDY SAUCE

*Vincent Ashby, chef of the governor's mansion for Gov. Martha Layne Collins supplied this recipe to Elaine Corn for the 1984 holiday entertaining issue of the Magazine.*

**5 pounds beef tenderloin**
**3 teaspoons salt**
**2 teaspoons pepper**
**2 tablespoons butter, softened**
**2 tablespoons minced shallots**
**4 tablespoons butter, chilled**
**¼ cup burgundy wine**
**1 tablespooon tomato paste**
**1 cup brown sauce (see recipe)**

Heat the oven to 425 degrees. Sprinkle the meat with salt and pepper. Rub soft butter all over meat. Place in a shallow pan in the middle of the oven for 30 minutes, or until a meat thermometer reaches 120 to 125 degrees. Let meat rest on a heated platter for 10 minutes. Make the sauce.

Sauté the shallots in 2 tablespoons of remaining butter. Add wine and cook 2 to 3 minutes. Add tomato paste, stirring constantly. Add brown sauce, reduce heat and simmer 8 minutes. Add final 2 tablespoons butter and pass sauce in a sauce boat.

## BROWN SAUCE

**½ cup beef drippings**
**2 tablespoons each chopped celery, onions and carrots**
**½ cup flour**
**2 cups peeled and drained tomatoes (about 3 if fresh)**
**1 cup tomato purée**
**½ cup coarsely chopped parsley**
**8 cups rich beef stock**

In a large, heavy kettle, sauté the celery, onions and carrots in the drippings over medium heat until onions are transparent. Stir in the flour and cook until the mixture becomes medium brown. Add tomatoes, purée, parsley and stock. Simmer 2 hours, uncovered, until reduced by half. Skim now and then. Strain and return to pot without heating and stir to prevent skim from forming. Sauce should be the consistency of cream. Serves 6.

# STANDING RIB ROAST OF BEEF WITH HORSERADISH SAUCE

A whole prime-rib standing roast usually weighs 20 to 22 pounds. Your butcher will cut one to fit the size of your dinner needs. The first three ribs are the choicest.

For a 6- to 8-pound roast, place beef, fat side up, in a roasting pan. Roast at 500 degrees for 20 minutes. Reduce heat to 350 degrees. Roast for one hour for medium-rare. Or roast 20 minutes per pound for rare, 25 minutes per pound for medium and 30 minutes per pound for well-done. Internal temperatures are rare, 130 degrees; medium, 150 degrees; well-done, 160 degrees. Reserve pan drippngs for Yorkshire pudding.

Place on serving platter. Carve from the top. Serves six to eight.

— Elaine Corn, 1982

## HORSERADISH SAUCE

Combine all ingredients except the cream. Whip the cream. Fold into horseradish mixture. Keep chilled. Makes about 2 cups.

**½ cup prepared white horseradish, drained**
**½ cup mayonnaise**
**1 tablespoon white wine vinegar**
**Pinch sugar**
**Salt and white pepper**
**1 cup heavy cream**

# REUBEN SANDWICH GUIDELINES

This operation calls for guidelines, not a recipe. To make the Reuben, you'll need cooked corned beef, sliced paper-thin; Swiss cheese; dark rye or pumpernickel bread; sauerkraut; Thousand Island dressing; and butter to spread on the bread for grilling.

Line up pairs of bread slices and spread them with a light coat of dressing. On one slice, arrange several slivers of corned beef. On the other slice of bread place a generous slice of Swiss cheese. Drain the sauerkraut well. Then, with a fork, cover either the beef or the cheese with the kraut. When all sandwiches are filled, butter both outside pieces and grill slowly until browned. The sandwiches should be weighted a bit; best of all is a grill with its own fitted cover. Serve immediately, hot.

— Cook's Corner column, 1979

# BRAISED FLANK STEAK

Score both sides of each flank about ⅛-inch deep, as you would for decorating ham. Dust with flour. Sauté in a combination of the butter and oil. Put in a heavy Dutch oven, and add salt and pepper and vegetables. Mix the lemon juice and catsup, and pour it over the meat and vegetables. Cover tightly. Bake in a preheated 325-degree oven for about 2 hours, or until meat is very tender. You may want to rearrange the meat in the pot after it has cooked an hour or so. Remove steaks, keeping pot juices warm, and slice very thin, on the diagonal. Serve at once with the pan juices as gravy. Serves 6 to 8.

— Deni Hamilton, 1979

**3 flank steaks (about 4 pounds altogether)**
**2 tablespoons flour**
**2 tablespoons butter**
**2 tablespoons oil**
**1 teaspoon salt**
**¼ teaspoon pepper**
**¾ cup finely chopped celery**
**¾ cup finely chopped carrots**
**¾ cup finely chopped onions**
**¼ cup lemon juice**
**½ cup catsup**

# SPICY BEEF STEW

**Two pounds beef stew meat, cut in
   2-inch cubes**
**⅓ cup flour**
**2 tablespoons fat**
**½ teaspoon celery salt**
**¼ teaspoon garlic powder (or a
   clove of garlic, chopped)**
**¼ teaspoon dry thyme**
**1½ cups water**
**1 teaspoon whole cloves**
**6 medium-sized onions**
**6 carrots**
**6 medium-sized potatoes**
**¼ cup sliced green pepper**

The meat for this stew comes from several cuts of beef. They are the less tender cuts, but possess the good beef flavor. The cuts are the same as used for pot roasting; for stew, however, the meat is cut into large cubes, meaty enough for a good serving. Sometimes you'll find stew meat cheaper if bought by its name and already cut up than when you ask for a certain cut of beef and then ask to have it cut for stewing.

As a guide rule, buy from ¼ to ⅓ pound of meat per serving. Careful browning is the secret of a good stew, no matter what other flavoring you happen to want to incorporate.

One important part about a stew is that the same kind of meat can make entrance after entrance to your table and never be the same. It's like a fashionable woman with a large and attractive wardrobe.

If you have got into the habit of always putting the same outfit on the stew, we have a suggestion for really spicing up its appearance, as well as flavor.

Spread meat out on a piece of waxed paper. Sprinkle flour over meat. Turn meat to coat on all sides. (Save extra flour.) Brown floured meat on all sides in fat in a kettle. Remove browned meat from kettle. Sprinkle extra flour, celery salt, powdered garlic and thyme into kettle with fat. Gradually add water.

Stir and cook until the gravy is smooth and thickened. Return browned meat to the kettle with gravy. Cover and cook for an hour. Stick whole cloves into onions. Add onions, carrots, potatoes and green pepper to kettle. Cover and continue cooking over low heat on top of range or in moderate oven, 350 degrees, for an hour or until meat and vegetables are tender.

If any water is needed, be sure to add boiling water, and only a little of it at a time.

— Cissy Gregg, 1953

*Kentucky country ham with grits casserole. Photograph by Robert Steinau.*

# BEEF BOURGUIGNONNE

*Mrs. Liz Wise, an accomplished Whitesburg cook, gave these recipes to Elaine Corn for a 1985 Magazine feature.*

Cut meat into quarter-sized squares. Have skillet hot with shortening or kidney fat. Sear meat until brown. Don't crowd the skillet. Brown on each side. As the meat browns, transfer it to a large pot (an enamel-coated cast iron pan is good) that has a fitted lid, and place over high heat. After all meat is browned and transferred, to the first pan add the onions and carrots. Stir thoroughly until onions begin to look glassy. Add mushrooms and turn down heat. Cover to let the vegetables exude juice.

In the meantime, heat the oven to 375 degrees. Continue to stir the meat with a large wooden spoon until nicely caramelized. This gives the finished dish a burgundy sheen. Sift part of the flour over the meat. Continue browning until a roux forms, but do not let meat burn. Add remaining flour over vegetables. Add wine to vegetables and bring to a boil. Add garlic and transfer mixture to the meat. Add bouquet garni and tie with string to handle of pan. Shake pan and then stir gently. You may need to add some stock. Heat the lid to the pan before covering and place pan in the oven for 20 minutes. Reduce heat to 275 degrees and bake 1¾ hours more, or until meat is tender. Add seasonings. Serve with flat noodles tossed in hot cream and butter. Serves 6.

Note 1: Mrs. Wise says beef kidney fat has the highest smoking point of any animal fat.

Note 2: Bouquet garni is made by wrapping parsley, thyme, 12 peppercorns and a bay leaf in damp cheesecloth. Pound with a cleaver before tying.

**5 pounds English roast, round or sirloin, or 4 pounds totally trimmed**
**Shortening, or beef kidney fat (see Note 1)**
**¾ pound onions, chopped**
**½ pound carrots, chopped**
**1 pound fresh mushrooms, chopped**
**¾ cup flour**
**1 bottle (750 ml) cabernet sauvignon, or other good red wine**
**¾ tablespoon chopped garlic**
**Bouquet garni (see Note 2)**
**Salt and pepper, to taste**
**Warmed beef stock**

# BARBECUED BRISKET OF BEEF

5- to 6-pound beef brisket

## SAUCE:

½ cup ketchup
1 cup tomato sauce
½ cup brown sugar
½ teaspoon cayenne pepper
1 onion, grated
1 clove garlic, mashed
¼ teaspoon dry mustard
½ stick butter or margarine
¼ cup vinegar
¼ cup Worcestershire sauce
1 bottle commercial barbecue sauce

Combine sauce ingredients in a saucepan and bring to a boil. Simmer 10 minutes. Place brisket on a hot charcoal grill and sear both sides well on high heat, about 10 minutes on each side.

Remove from grill and place in a roasting pan covered with foil. Roast at 325 degrees for two to 2½ hours. Remove foil and cover with sauce. Bake one hour more, basting frequently with sauce until meat is tender. Meat will shrink. Makes eight servings.

— Elaine Corn, 1984

# MRS. BISCHOFF'S BARBECUE

*This is Anna Bischoff's dish, and our readers liked it, judging by the requests for the recipe. Deni Hamilton printed it in 1978 for a story on quick recipes using hamburger.*

1 tablespoon oil
½ large green pepper, chopped
1 large onion, chopped
4 ribs celery, chopped
1 10-ounce can tomato purée
½ the same size can of water
2 tablespoons brown sugar
2 tablespoons vinegar
A 1-ounce package chili powder
1 tablespoon salt
2 pounds hamburger

In the oil, sauté the vegetables until soft. Add the purée, water, sugar, vinegar, chili powder and salt and mix well. Add the raw hamburger, breaking it in pieces, and mix well. Simmer on low heat about 45 minutes or until hamburger is cooked. Serve on buns.

Mrs. Bischoff recommends topping the sandwich with sweet pickle relish. Makes six to eight sandwiches.

# VEAL PICCATA

8 veal scaloppine, pounded thin
Flour for dredging seasoned with
    salt and pepper
3 tablespoons butter
3 tablespoons olive oil
½ cup dry white wine
2 lemons, juiced

Take veal pounded as thinly as possible and dip it into flour. Shake off excess. Heat butter and oil in a wide, heavy skillet over medium-high heat. When bubbling, lay in veal. Brown on first side, about 2 minutes. Turn, brown other side 1 minute. Do not crowd skillet; work in batches if skillet will not accommodate all scaloppine. Tip skillet and drain most of fat. Add wine. Let sizzle and cook down about 3 minutes while scraping up any bits of meat that may cling to the skillet. Add lemon juice. Place meat in overlapping fashion on warm platter. Pour thin sauce over. Serve garnished with buttered carrots, oregano zucchini and fried eggplant sticks.

— Elaine Corn, 1983

# WESTERN-STYLE JERKY

*When dried-beef products made their way onto snack counters in the late 1970s, cooks started digging through their cookbooks for recipes to prepare jerky. The Cook's Corner column printed this one in response to a reader's request in 1984.*

This recipe is for 7 pounds of meat. For best results, buy good-quality lean meat, such as round of beef. Have the butcher slice it about ¾- to 1-inch thick. Other flavorings may be adjusted, but be sure to use the full amount of salt. This recipe is fairly peppery.

Trim meat of all fat. Slice it across the grain no thicker than ¼-inch. Mix all the ingredients in a stoneware crock or deep enamel container.

Stir for five minutes. Let stand for five minutes. Add strips of meat, one at a time, placing each layer across the previous layer in a criss-cross pattern. Soak 24 hours. At intervals of three hours, lift from bottom and mix well to soak all meat equally. Drain well.

It is best to dry during the summer in very dry, hot, sunny weather. However, a clean, dry basement, attic or garage is fine. Use a large needle to pass a heavy string or thread through one end of the strips and stretch the string between two points. Meat strips should not touch so air can circulate evenly around them. Protect floors by covering with plastic. The meat should be cured and ready to eat in about three weeks if the humidity is low, longer if not.

**2½ gallons cold water**
**1 large onion, chopped**
**6 hot red peppers, chopped**
**1⅓ cups salt**
**⅓ teaspoon cayenne pepper**
**¼ teaspoon garlic salt**
**1 teaspoon black pepper**
**1½ tablespoons liquid-smoke flavoring**
**1 teaspoon vinegar**

# OSSO BUCO

**6 to 8 meaty veal shank (shin) bones, sliced at 1½- or 2-inch intervals**
**About ½ cup flour, for dredging**
**3 tablespoons butter**
**3 tablespoons olive oil**
**1 cup chopped carrots**
**1 cup chopped celery**
**1 cup chopped onion**
**2 cloves garlic, minced**
**Salt and pepper, to taste**
**1 cup white wine**
**1½ cups chopped (canned) Italian plum tomatoes, including some juice**
**1 cup chicken or beef stock**
**1 bay leaf**
**¼ teaspoon rosemary or sage**
**Gremolata (garnish), (see recipe)**

Tie kitchen string around each shank so meat around bones keeps its shape during cooking. Dredge bones well in flour, shaking off excess and being sure to coat edges. In a large, wide skillet, or two medium skillets, heat the butter and oil over medium-high heat. Add bones. Brown very well until dark on both sides and edges, about 20 minutes.

Remove meat to an oven-proof casserole. To skillet still on medium-high heat, add carrots, celery, onion and garlic. Brown well. Add salt and pepper. Add wine and simmer until wine evaporates, about 5 minutes. Stir in tomatoes, stock, bay leaf and rosemary. Bring to a boil, then pour sauce into the casserole, over and around the bones. Cover. Place in a 350-degree oven for 1½ hours. Baste bones with sauce now and then. Add more broth if sauce dries out. Meat should separate slightly from bones, and bone marrow should be very soft. Five minutes before serving, sprinkle osso buco with *gremolata.*

To serve, place bones on a platter and remove the string. Pour the sauce over the bones. Serve one shank per person. Provide a utensil, such as a small fork or spoon, to eat the marrow. Serves 6 to 8.
— Elaine Corn, 1984

## GREMOLATA

**1 tablespoon minced lemon zest**
**1 tablespoon minced orange zest**
**1 tablespoon minced garlic**
**1 tablespoon minced parsley**

Toss together lightly.

# BARBECUED PORK

**A 9- or 10-pound fresh pork shoulder**
**Salt and pepper**
**Sauce (see recipe)**

Rub the pork shoulder all over with salt and pepper; place on rack in roasting pan. Mop it generously with barbecue sauce and place in 210-degree oven. It should be falling-apart tender in about 16 hours. Brush meat with sauce once or twice while roasting. Cool enough to handle and pull meat apart in shreds, discarding bone and fat.

Serve on warm buns. About 4½ to 5 pounds, or about 32 bunsful at two ounces per bun.

## BARBECUE SAUCE, WESTERN KENTUCKY STYLE

Combine all ingredients in saucepan and boil for five minutes. Makes about two quarts of sauce. This is enough to do two pork shoulders. You may wish to divide it in half, as one quart is sufficient for one shoulder. After brushing the roasting pork with some of the quart of sauce, boil remainder up again and combine with the fine, shredded pork. You can keep the remaining quart indefinitely in a covered jar in refrigerator for the next occasion. Good for chicken or beef or spareribs.

— Lillian Marshall, 1975

3½ cups water
2¼ cups catsup
¾ cup Worcestershire sauce
2 teaspoons paprika
1½ teaspoons black pepper
1½ teaspoons garlic salt
1½ to 3 teaspoons cayenne pepper, according to how hot you like it
2 teaspoons mild dry mustard
5 teaspoons onion powder
3 tablespoons salt

# STUFFED BREAST OF VEAL

Preheat oven to 400 degrees. Stuff veal pocket, and skewer ends closed. Place, bone side down, in shallow roaster. Brush with oil and sprinkle with rosemary and garlic. Put in oven and bake until brown, about 1 hour. Reduce heat to 350 degrees. Pour off grease in pan. Pour sherry and broth in pan. Salt and pepper roast and continue baking, about another hour, until tender. Serves 8 to 10.

— Deni Hamilton, 1979

1 7- to 8-pound breast of veal with pocket cut in
½ teaspoon rosemary
⅛ teaspoon garlic powder
Oil
½ cup cream sherry
½ cup chicken broth or water
Salt and pepper
Pecan-mushroom stuffing (see recipe)

## PECAN-MUSHROOM STUFFING

Mix all ingredients and toss well. Stuffs a 7- to 8-pound veal breast.

2 quarts dry bread crumbs
2 cups coarse-ground pecans (about ½ pound)
2 to 3 cups chopped mushrooms, fresh or canned
4 tablespoons butter or margarine
½ teaspoon rosemary
1 teaspoon marjoram
⅛ teaspoon garlic powder
¼ cup cream sherry
1 large egg, well beaten
1 cup chicken broth or liquid from canned mushrooms
1 teaspoon salt
½ teaspoon pepper

# ROAST LITTLE PIG

*These instructions were printed in 1962, but Cissy Gregg wrote of "Master Pig" in a number of her other pork recipes. Most readers probably will not want to become that intimately acquainted with something they're about to pop into an oven.*

*Master Pig's "12" pounds apparently is a typographical error. The Wolfe Meat Market in New Albany, Ind., puts the minimum weight of pigs for roasting at 50 pounds.*

This one weighed 12 pounds. We thought we could get him in our oven, but . . . we don't know measurement. We could have cut off Master Pig's head, his tail or something, but that didn't seem fair. So I called my good friend Achille Mozzali, chef of the Pendennis, and told him my troubles. Well, the sky opened up and the sun came through. "Bring it over and we'll find an oven big enough for a wee pig!" Over Master Pig went.

Master Pig had to have a stuffing to make his little sides look filled out. (Of course, he had been tenderly cleaned inside and out.)

### Chef Mozzali's way with Master Pig

Sponge it off with a damp cloth inside and out. Salt the inside. Fill the cavity with stuffing of your choice. It will take 8 to 10 cups of stuffing. It can be made according to any stuffing recipe, except it should be kept dry with very little fat. The addition of chopped apples, a little onion, celery chopped fine and sage or poultry seasonings to the toasted bread crumbs will help. Anchor the stuffing in place by skewers and a lacing as one would for a turkey, but this opening is longer and we think the skewers — or clean nails will do and clean thread zig-zagging — to close the opening will do a good job. And close it firmly but not tightly.

Put the stuffed pig right side up on a rack in an open baking pan. Push the front legs forward and the back legs back so the pig rests firmly on the rack. Open the jaws and put a potato or a small block of wood between the teeth to keep the jaws open. Wrap the ears with oiled cheesecloth or use little teepees of foil to keep them from browning too quickly. Now into the oven it goes. But it's best to rub the body with a mixture of equal parts of flour and butter or fat — we would certainly want Master Pig to have an all over brown look.

Bake in a moderate oven, 350 degrees, for 3½ to 4 hours. If the skin begins to crack or get too brown, cover with a thin cloth or foil.

Put Master Finished Pig on a wooden board first — or on napkins or something like that so the stuffed body will drain. Replace the wooden block in the mouth with an apple, or we used these small tomatoes.

There are red roses around his head, an orchid to decorate his cute little curl of a tail, and since he was the star of the performance foodwise we put a rhinestone in his forehead.

Now to carve Master Pig: Take off the fore legs and hind legs. Take the meat off the bones and cut into servings. Also take off the jeweled and bedecked head — there's nothing you can gain meatwise from that part. Cut along the back bone to remove the chops — first on one side and then the other. Serve with the dressing and the piggie-pieces on top.

# ROAST LOIN OF PORK

Season with salt and pepper, and place in an open roasting pan with fat side up and ribs ends down to form a rack. Make an incision for the meat thermometer, if you have one, so the bulb reaches the center of the largest part. Don't cover or add water. Roast in a moderate oven, 350 degrees, until the meat thermometer registers 185 degrees. If you don't have one of the handy thermometers, don't worry yourself about it, but allow 30 minutes per pound for the roasting. It should come to the table crispy brown and glamorously oozing with its own juices.

When the roast gives a sidelong glance and sees that the thoughtful cook has nestled broiled peach halves along the platter with it, I have a feeling the roast realizes the beautiful end it is approaching.

— Cissy Gregg, 1947

# CROWN ROAST OF PORK

Have the butcher prepare the crown roast of pork chops for you from the center of the loin. There must be enough "chops" or "bones" to make a good circle or the roast will look as cramped as the old-fashioned feminine figure corseted into the hour-glass shape.

When the roast is to be used, take the frills off temporarily, and salt and pepper well. Then we put small chunks of salt pork on the bones — you know, cut a small square and jab a hole in the center, then stick it on the bone, to keep the bones from burning during the cooking.

Place the thus prepared crown in a hot oven, 550 degrees, for 15 minutes, then reduce the heat to 375 degrees and continue to cook for about 1¾ hours, basting frequently. When the roast is tender, remove it to a hot platter and pour off all the fat in the bottom of the pan. Add 1 cup water to all the brown residue that's been left behind. Stir until every bit of it is loosened and in solution form. Cook over a hot flame, and stir the juice until it has reduced itself to a thick glaze. Pour this over the meat. Replace the frills on the bones, and garnish as you wish.

How can one manage this and go to church? Well, I've lived long enough to have learned it is well to follow directions — but the good manager makes them fit into her own way of doing. One way would be to cook the roast underdone, and finish off after church. Or if dinner is to come in the middle of the afternoon, the cooking can be completed in approximately 2 hours, from scratch.

If there are young in the family, such a waiting period might be too much of an obstacle to live through, but sermons don't last two hours anyway, and if you know your oven, and if it's a new type, the basting might not be missed. Perhaps I'm not a trusting soul because when I have something in the stove, I get fidgety if I'm not there to peep in on it. So the half-and-half way would be my personal way if I couldn't do it all at one time.

— Cissy Gregg, 1950

# PHILOMINA POLIO'S ORIGINAL SAUSAGE

*Julio and Philomina Polio ran a fruit and vegetable store on South Brook Street in the late 1800s, and Philomina sold this sausage there. Elaine Corn gave this recipe and others in writing about the Polios' daughter, Juliet Drane, in 1981.*

Combine all ingredients in a large mixing bowl. Work well with the hands until mixture is completely smooth. Shape and fry.

**2 pounds coarsely ground pork**
**6 ounces ground veal**
**1 tablespoon whole fennel seed**
**1 teaspoon salt**
**1 teaspoon black pepper**
**1½ teaspoons crushed red pepper**
**1 teaspoon paprika**

# ROLLED PORK LOIN WITH PARSLEY-HERB STUFFING

**1 4- to 5-pound boneless pork loin**
**1 egg white**

## FILLING:

**½ cup raw rice**
**2 tablespoons butter**
**2 tablespoons minced shallots**
**3 cloves garlic, minced**
**⅓ pound fresh mushrooms,**
**    coarsely chopped**
**4 cups packed parsley (curly or flat**
**    Italian), leaves only**
**1 teaspoon summer savory**
**½ teaspoon thyme**
**1 egg yolk**
**Sesame seeds**
**1 egg, lightly beaten**
**Salt and pepper, to taste**

Have your butcher cut half a pork loin from the rib end, leaving the "lip" intact and defatting the top. It should weigh about 4 to 5 pounds. Then have the butcher split the loin open from the lip end, in butterfly fashion, and continue splitting until the loin lies flat.

Paint unfurled loin with egg white. Set aside while you prepare the filling.

Bring 2 cups water to a rolling boil. Add rice. Boil 5 minutes, lid off. Strain rice and reserve.

Heat the butter in a wide skillet. Sauté shallot and garlic a minute or two over medium heat, stirring a little. Add mushrooms. Place parsley leaves into skillet. Turn the leaves over and over with a spatula, rather than stir, until the mixture moistens enough to manage it. Sauté a total of 8 minutes. Mixture will decrease in volume by more than three-fourths. Purée just until small lumps remain. Transfer mixture to a mixing bowl. Mix in herbs and egg yolk. Stir in cooked rice. Add salt and pepper, to taste.

Spread filling evenly over surface of prepared pork loin, leaving a ½-inch border. Roll up. Tuck seam underneath, or slightly at the side, depending on how your piece of meat looks best. Secure with fishing line. (It doesn't show at the table, but be sure guests don't eat it.) Roll may be refrigerated overnight at this point.

Place roll on rack set in a roasting pan. Roast at 400 degrees for 30 minutes. Reduce heat to 325 degrees and roast 50 minutes to 1 hour more. Internal temperature of pork should reach between 140 and 160 for a barely pink center. Remove from oven. Let cool slightly. Increase oven temperature to 500 degrees.

Near serving time, paint top of roll with beaten egg. Press sesame seeds into place. Bake at 500 degrees for 10 to 12 minutes. Seeds should turn golden brown. Remove. Reserve 2 tablespoons drippings for sauce. Slice roll on the diagonal.

Place a little lagoon of about ¼-cup tinted wine-thyme sauce per plate, then center meat on top of sauce. Serve with steamed asparagus.

— Elaine Corn, 1983

## TINTED WINE-THYME SAUCE

Heat pan drippings and butter. Add garlic and shallots and sauté 1 minute. Stir in flour. Cook 1 minute, stirring and keeping mixture bubbling. Add wine gradually. Add thyme. Bring to boil. Boil 5 minutes. Strain. Return sauce to pan. Blend in tomato paste. Add stock or water, salt and pepper. Bring to a boil again. With pan off the heat, finish with butter, swirling until melted and sauce thickens slightly. Makes about 2¼ cups.

**2 tablespoons pan drippings**
**2 tablespoons butter**
**2 cloves garlic, minced**
**1 tablespoon minced shallot**
**1 tablespoon flour**
**¾ cup dry white wine**
**¼ teaspoon thyme**
**2 teaspoons tomato paste**
**½ cup stock or water**
**Salt and white pepper, to taste**
**Additional 2 tablespoons butter**

# BOHEMIAN SPARERIBS

Cut spareribs into individual servings. Season with salt and pepper. Mix caraway seeds with sauerkraut and place in an 8-by-12-inch baking dish.

Arrange all but two onion slices on sauerkraut and pour tomatoes over the mixture. Place spareribs on top and cover with remaining onion rings, and bake in a moderate oven, 350 degrees, for 2 hours.

This dish deserves the accolade, "das ist gut." We had never tried the combination of tomatoes with the sauerkraut, but we liked it very much.

No recipe ever seems to state whether you should cover a dish such as this one or cook it uncovered. When in doubt, we usually use a piece of cooking foil over the top of the mixture until it gets started and then set it aside. If it seems to be browning too fast or drying out, we put the foil back on top.

For all our modern adjustment of recipes, there has never seemed to be a way to take the personal touch out of making a good dish, no matter what it might be.

We liked Waldorf salad with this, boiled potatoes, and corn bread sticks. You might try muffins or whatever other way you like your corn bread.
— Cissy Gregg, 1959

**2 to 3 pounds spareribs**
**1 teaspoon salt**
**¼ teaspoon pepper**
**1 tablespoon caraway seeds**
**1 can (16 ounces) sauerkraut**
**1 medium onion, sliced**
**1 can (16 ounces) tomatoes**

# CROWN ROAST OF PORK WITH CHESTNUT DRESSING AND ROASTED POTATOES

1 crown roast of pork
Salt and pepper, to taste
1 tablespoon minced garlic
6 potatoes, quartered
Chestnut dressing (see recipe)

Have butcher tie a 10-pound center-cut pork loin from the rib end into a circle with chine bones cut off.

Heat oven to 350 degrees. Rub meat all over with salt, pepper and minced garlic. Place roast, rib-ends down, on a rack in a roasting pan. Roast 2 hours. Turn roast ribs up and return to pan without rack.

Fill center with as much chestnut dressing as will fit. Place quartered potatoes in pan around roast. Roast for 1½ to 2 hours more.

When done, let stand out 15 minutes. Decorate with frills. Transfer to a serving platter surrounded with Brussels sprouts, carrots and potatoes.

— Elaine Corn, 1982

## CHESTNUT-GINGER DRESSING

1½ pounds chestnuts, slit, parboiled and shelled
1 stick butter
1 large onion, chopped
2 cups chopped celery
4 cups plain bread crumbs
½ cup fresh chopped parsley
1 teaspoon ground ginger
Salt and pepper

Mince or purée the chestnuts and place in a large bowl. Sauté the onion and celery in butter until soft. Add to chestnuts with remaining ingredients. If too dry, add butter. Spoon into center of crown roast. Additional filling may be baked separately.

# BOAT-DECK GRILLED MARINATED PORK CHOPS

8 pork chops or steaks, about ½-inch thick each
½ cup grapefruit juice
½ cup soy sauce
½ cup dry white wine
1 teaspoon poultry seasoning
2 tablespoons oil

Mix the juice, sauce, wine, poultry seasoning and oil. Pour over the pork in a shallow roasting dish, or place the chops in a heavy plastic bag and pour in the marinade. Seal the bag. Turn chops in dish or in bag several times over the course of about four hours. Place on grill four inches above glowing charcoal coals, and slowly allow to brown, about 20 minutes. Turn and brown other side. Serves eight.

— Deni Hamilton, 1980

# SPIT-ROASTED LAMB

Select a leg or boned shoulder of lamb and marinate it for 24 hours in the marinade. Turn a few times during the marinating.

Place on a spit over the coals or on the rotisserie of your oven. A leg of lamb will take from 1 to 3 hours, depending on the size and the temperature, but the safest way is to use a meat thermometer, and get it up to 180-degrees to have it cooked, but if you like it juicy and rare, this temperature is much too high.

There is some place from which the idea has come that lamb should be well cooked. Take your choice. We aren't on that crusade at the moment, but if you have ever tasted juicy pink lamb — it is just as it is with tender beef. The life shouldn't be taken out of good lamb or beef.

I've told this story before, but perhaps you didn't read it, or have forgotten. In San Francisco we would go to a small restaurant. There was no decor, but perfect food, and one man. I could spot him. He ate a saddle of lamb, crusted and brown on the outside and pink on the inside, and out of a two-chop rack (on the double) he wouldn't leave enough for me to bring home to the doggie. He was French and he hand ate it. I've worked on this crusty brown touch, but I have never been able to turn up with something which they did on charcoal. On the rotisserie, and with this marinade, we have come the closest for home use.

Just try lamb juicy and pink once, and you'll get a new impression of two ways with lamb-bee pie — or take it fully cooked and flavorful. Either way you can't go wrong.

Your range will give you the directions on how to use an oven rotisserie for your own range oven. We are delighted with what we have done with ours.

We took the marinade and drippings and made a gravy, only thickening it slightly with corn starch and water. Then reseason as you wish.

— Cissy Gregg, 1960

## MARINADE:

**1 cup of olive or vegetable oil**
**2 cups of white vinegar**
**2 tablespoons each of chopped shallots, parsley, chopped carrots and celery**
**1 bay leaf**
**1 crushed clove of garlic**
**1 large onion chopped**

# LAMB FRIES — FRIED A LA ROBINSON

*Mrs. Ray Robinson, a Lexington native living in Louisville, gave this recipe to Cissy Gregg in 1957. She suggested lamb fries as a "Kentucky First" dish. Cissy, like most recipe writers, just couldn't come right out and say that lamb fries are lamb testicles.*

Now we come to the lamb fries. These are so easy to prepare, there is really not a recipe. Lamb fries must be skinned before they are cooked. I have skinned them, but unless you have had a little experience, it would be better to have your meat man do the work for you. It is much like learning to swim, I'll admit — you can't learn if you don't try — but for the first go-around, let this expert show you the technique.

Mrs. Robinson, a country girl, she says, does the skinning of the lamb fries herself. And once skinned, she places them in ice water for about 30 minutes. This, she says, "firms them up." Then they are sliced. We didn't soak ours, since they were skinned and cooled off at the market. We simply washed them in cold water and then sliced them.

Cut the lamb fries into about ¼-inch slices. Dip the slices in flour, then in beaten egg diluted with a tablespoon of water or milk to the egg, and then in seasoned flour again. Fry in deep fat or in a skillet with enough fat to let the slices swim. Drain and serve hot with a cream gravy, well seasoned, and asparagus.

The only change we made from this simple recipe was to mix a few dry fine bread crumbs in with the flour that made the final covering.

They are delicious! Of course, the cream gravy is a pleasant addition, and so is the asparagus, but the vegetable doesn't have to be asparagus — any green vegetable would be good. Sometimes lamb fries are served on toast. They should always be well peppered — or at least, I think so. The pepper has a way of giving lamb fries "life." And we like lemon wedges or slices served with ours, but we are prejudiced — we like lemon with everything.

# CASSEROLE OF LAMB, ARMENIAN STYLE

*If you can't find an envelope of tomato soup mix, try substituting 1 or 2 tablespoons of tomato paste.*

**1 green pepper cut in strips**
**1 medium onion, sliced thin**
**1 4-ounce can sliced mushrooms**
**3 tablespoons butter or margarine**
**Flour for dredging**
**1 medium eggplant**
**2 pounds lean lamb (from shoulder or leg)**
**An envelope tomato soup mix**
**½ teaspoon salt**
**⅛ teaspoon pepper**
**¼ teaspoon oregano**
**¼ teaspoon basil**
**1⅔ cup water**

Sauté green pepper, onion and mushrooms in butter or margarine. Dredge the lamb in flour and brown with vegetables, except eggplant. In a saucepan stir the soup mix and seasonings into the water. Bring to a boil to thicken the sauce. Meanwhile, peel and cut the eggplant in ¾-inch thick slices.

Arrange eggplant in casserole; cover with the sautéed meat and vegetables and pour on the tomato sauce. Cover and bake at 375 degrees for an hour. Makes four to five servings.

We were spurred on to making this casserole from a call that came asking us how eggplant could be prepared other than frying. When we found this one and it was easy to make for even a family dinner, we thought about this call we had had and that maybe others would like to prepare eggplant other than frying it.        — Cissy Gregg, 1962

# SPRIGGED LAMB

Wipe the meat with a cloth wrung out in hot water that has had a little vinegar added. Then with a sharp, pointed knife, make 25 to 30 incisions in the top and sides of the meaty part. Insert two or three leafy tops of the parsley in each incision. And if you like the lovely flavor of garlic — every so often stuff a snip of garlic in with the parsley.

Never use too much garlic, but a little is wonderful. Rub the roast with the seasonings. Place on a rack, rounded side up, in a regular roasting pan and roast uncovered in a moderately slow oven, 325 degrees, allowing 25 or 30 minutes per pound. Baste every 15 minutes after the first hour. If the top isn't crusty brown when the roasting time is up, turn the heat up to very hot, 500 degrees, and continue roasting for 5 minutes or so.

Remove to a hot platter and add a little boiling water to the drippings in the roasting pan. Bring to a boil and stir to mix in all the brown spatters. I prefer my gravy as a juice. However, if you would rather add flour and make it into a regulation gravy there's no law against it.

Scatter a few chopped almonds on top, and they'll make a glorious dish out of most anything. Or so it is in my family.

To accomplish this addition with speed, I've been buying small cans of chopped and slivered almonds. They come in handy. Almonds give squash great statue.

— Cissy Gregg, 1952

**1 5½- to 6-pound leg (boned and rolled if you prefer)**
**A bunch of parsley with all stems removed**
**1 teaspoon salt**
**⅛ teaspoon pepper**

# IRISH STEW

Cut 2 pounds of lamb breast in generous 2-inch pieces, then dredge with seasoned flour, using 1 teaspoon salt, 3 tablespoons flour and ⅛ teaspoon pepper. Heat 3 or 4 tablespoons of fat — any kind, in a stew pot, add the meat and sear lightly.

Then add ⅓ cup of chopped onions and continue searing 3 or 4 minutes longer. Add 10 whole peppercorns, one cup diced turnips, one large stalk of celery cut small, ½ cup of carrots cut into ½-inch pieces, 3 medium-sized potatoes quartered, 1 cup shredded cabbage and 5 cups cold water. Cover and bring to a boil. Reduce heat and simmer gently for one hour and a half. Taste for seasonings, and serve in a deep hot dish. Dust with finely chopped parsley.

— Cissy Gregg, 1951

# LAMB AND VEGETABLE STEW

4 shoulder lamb chops (about 1½ pounds)
2 tablespoons shortening (or cooking oil)
1 can (10½ ounces) condensed consommé
¼ teaspoon rosemary leaves, crushed
¼ cup water
A clove garlic, minced
8 small whole onions or the equivalent thereof
A package (9 ounces) frozen cut green beans
2 to 3 tablespoons flour

In skillet, brown the chops in shortening. Pour off the excess drippings. Add consommé, rosemary and garlic. Cover and cook over low heat 30 minutes. Add onions and green beans, cook covered an additional 40 minutes or until the vegetables are tender. Remove meat and vegetables. Blend flour and water until mixture is smooth. Gradually add to gravy, stirring constantly. Cook until thickened. Makes four servings.

— Cissy Gregg, 1963

# COOKING A LEG OF LAMB

| WEIGHT | APPROX. ROASTING TIMF | INTERNAL TEMPERATURE |
|---|---|---|
| 6 pounds | 3 hours | 175 degrees (medium) |
| | | 180 degrees (well done) |
| 8 pounds | 3½ hours | 175 degrees (medium) |
| | 4 hours | 180 degrees (well done) |

To roast a leg of lamb place it fat side up on a rack in an open pan in a slow oven, 325 degrees. Above is a schedule for roasting time. If you have a meat thermometer, it should give correct timing, but to have a knowledge of when the roast goes in the oven or to get it out at a certain time, we offer you this gauge.

About as large a leg of lamb as we have ever cooked is in the 6-pound range, but some, I'm told, can go as high as 8 pounds.

There is always the question of how one likes lamb roasted, just as with beef. It can be medium or well-done, so we give you both timings, roasting at 325 degrees.

Just be sure the lamb reaches the doneness your family likes it.

For us, we take a few liberties. We rub the leg over with salt and pepper. We make small incisions here and there and stick in small pieces of peeled garlic. We add a little paprika to the top after we have given it a sponge bath of lemon juice or tarragon vinegar — not too much but a little.

— Cissy Gregg, 1960

# GRILLED LAMB MARINATED IN OLIVE OIL AND HERBS

*Elaine Klein furnished this recipe to Elaine Corn for a 1983 feature on dishes for the Passover Seder.*

Place the lamb in a large bowl. Combine remaining ingredients for marinade and pour over the lamb. Cover very tightly with foil or plastic wrap and put the lamb in the refrigerator overnight, turning it occasionally. Before grilling, bring lamb to room temperature while you continue to turn the meat in its marinade.

Place the lamb, fat side up, on a hot grill (or run under your broiler), basting with marinade and turning over and over until nicely browned. This takes about 10 minutes. Transfer grilled lamb to a roasting pan. Cover with remaining marinade. Roast, uncovered, at 350 degrees for at least an hour or until internal temperature is 175 degrees for well-done, or 160 degrees for medium-rare. Serves six.

**5 pound leg of spring lamb, bone in**
**1 medium onion, finely chopped**
**3 large cloves garlic, minced**
**¾ cup olive oil (or vegetable oil)**
**½ cup dry white wine**
**¼ cup fresh chopped parsley**
**Juice of 1 lemon**
**2 to 3 tablespoons Dijon mustard**
**1 teaspoon salt**
**1 teaspoon basil**
**1 teaspoon oregano**
**½ teaspoon each: pepper, rosemary, thyme, marjoram**
**1 bay leaf, crushed**

# LUAU LAMB STEAKS OR CHOPS

Combine all ingredients except lamb, then pour over lamb in a shallow dish. Turn lamb over to coat both sides, and let stand half an hour. Turn again, and let stand another half hour. Broil lamb about 4 inches from heat source about 5 minutes on each side, or to desired doneness. Serves 4.

— Deni Hamilton, 1979

**8 lamb steaks or chops**
**1½ cups beef broth**
**¼ cup soy sauce**
**¼ cup honey**
**¼ cup vinegar**
**2 tablespoons dry sherry**
**1 garlic clove, crushed**
**¼ teaspoon powdered ginger**

# ROAST RABBIT WITH PORK STUFFING

**½ pound mild bulk pork sausage**
**4 tablespoons butter or margarine**
**1 large onion, chopped**
**⅓ cup diced celery**
**1½ cups dried bread cubes**
**1 domestic rabbit, about 3 pounds, cut into serving pieces**
**Butter or margarine**
**Salt and pepper**

Brown sausage, breaking into small pieces as it cooks. Remove from skillet; reserve. Add butter to drippings, and sauté onion and celery until soft. Add bread cubes and stir so they absorb drippings remaining. Stir in sausage. Put in bottom of 2-quart baking dish. Pat rabbit pieces dry with paper towels, and salt and pepper them. Arrange in one layer atop the stuffing. Dot with butter. Bake in preheated 350-degree oven, uncovered, until rabbit is tender, about 40 minutes.

— Deni Hamilton, 1980

# HASENPFEFFER

2 small rabbits, dressed and cut up
2 cups dry red wine
½ cup vinegar
1 onion, sliced and separated into
   rings
2 bay leaves
6 peppercorns
6 whole cloves
2 teaspoons salt
2 tablespoons brown sugar
6 juniper berries (optional, but
   good)
Small handful fresh parsley
¼ cup bacon drippings
½ cup red currant jelly
1½ tablespoons flour per cup liquid
   for making gravy later

Combine wine, vinegar, onion, bay leaves, peppercorns, cloves, salt, sugar, juniper berries and parsley to make marinade. Pour over rabbit in enamel pan (or in heavy plastic bag set in a bowl). Refrigerate 24 hours. Remove pieces of rabbit, saving marinade. Dry rabbit and brown in drippings. Place in casserole. Remove onion rings from marinade and sauté them in bacon drippings. Add to casserole. Strain marinade, discarding solids. Measure liquid and make paste of flour and some of the liquid. Add jelly and cook until thickened somewhat. Add to casserole, cover and bake an hour or more (until tender) at 350 degrees. Serve from casserole or platter with noodles. Serves eight.
— Lillian Marshall, 1975

# JINNY'S GAME STEW

*The Jinny of this recipe, printed by Lillian Marshall in 1968, is Jinny Schmeer Rose, a Louisville native living in North Carolina at the time. Game cookery was a specialty of hers.*

Game, soaked overnight in salt
   water
Seasoned flour
Fat to brown game (or cooking oil)
Water
6 peppercorns
2 or 3 teaspoons wine vinegar
1 small onion, sliced
1 bay leaf
1 can cream of chicken soup

You may use wild rabbit or squirrel, cut in serving pieces, or dove.

Dry the game and dredge in the seasoned flour. Brown all sides in hot fat or oil. Add water to barely cover. Then add peppercorns, vinegar, onion and bay leaf. Simmer, covered, until tender.

Remove game and reserve, keeping it warm. Strain the broth and discard seasonings. Combine strained broth with the soup. Put game back in the gravy.

Serve over rice, or do as Jinny does: Make pastry-style dumplings, rolled thin, cut and dropped into the simmering mixture. Cover closely and simmer 15 minutes without lifting the lid.

# FRIED SQUIRREL

Cut the dressed squirrel into serving pieces. Soak overnight in salt water. Dry and coat with seasoned flour. (Flour to which you have added salt and pepper). Fry in hot bacon fat until brown on all sides and fork-tender.
— Lillian Marshall, 1968

# SQUIRREL HUNTER'S STEW

*This 1971 recipe was from Mrs. C.J. Bolton of Ashland, Ky. In writing about the recipe, Lillian Marshall noted that Mrs. Bolton serves the squirrel from a chafing dish for a buffet. She suggested serving it with rice — especially wild rice — a green vegetable, slaw and hot rolls.*

Soak squirrels in salt water overnight. Drain and dry well. Dredge in seasoned flour. Heat shortening in skillets or large electric frying pan and brown squirrel on all sides. Remove from frying pan. Pour off excess fat.

Add 3 cups tomato juice, oregano, salt and pepper. Stir to loosen the browned crumbs. Replace squirrel in pan and, if necessary, add more tomato juice to cover. Cover completely with thinly sliced onions. Add wine, cover closely and cook very slowly until tender. Makes 6 to 8 servings.

**3 squirrels, cut up**
**Salt water to cover**
**Seasoned flour for dredging**
**Shortening for browning**
**3 to 4 cups tomato juice**
**¼ teaspoon oregano**
**Salt and pepper to taste**
**3 or 4 onions, sliced very thin**
**½ cup chianti or other dry red wine.**

# PINEAPPLE-GLAZED COUNTRY HAM

*This recipe is from Thelma Linton, who was cook for Jim Thomas, president of Shakertown at Pleasant Hill, Inc., when Elaine Corn featured Thomas and Mrs. Linton for the 1984 holiday entertaining issue of the Magazine.*

Soak ham overnight in water, to cover, with vinegar. Then place in a large roaster with clean water just to cover ham. Add brown sugar and pickling spice to the water. Cover and bake 4 hours at 300 degrees.

Remove from oven and let cool. Bone and skin, leaving a thin layer of fat. Mix brown sugar, bread crumbs and ground cloves. Press over fatted side of ham. Press pineapple chunks over sugar, then stick each piece of pineapple with a single clove. Return to oven and glaze at 350 degrees for 20 minutes. Cool ham thoroughly before slicing. Serves 30.

**1 15- to 20-pound Kentucky country ham**
**1 cup vinegar**
**1 cup brown sugar**
**4 tablespoons pickling spice**

## GLAZE:

**½ cup brown sugar**
**2 to 3 tablespoons bread crumbs**
**1 teaspoon ground cloves**
**1 can chunky pineapple, drained**
**Whole cloves**

# GERTIE GEURIN'S COUNTRY HAM AND RED-EYE GRAVY

*Gertie Geurin is a long-time Louisville cook whose mother baked pies at the Colonnade Cafeteria in the 1930s. At Elaine Corn's invitation, she gave a cooking demonstration to the National Food Editors and Writers Association's conference in Louisville in 1983.*

**8 slices raw country ham**
**¾ cup black coffee**
**1 teaspoon sugar**

Have skillet very hot with a drop of vegetable oil. Lay ham in skillet. Leave on one side eight minutes. Turn slices and fry eight minutes more. Pour coffee into skillet. Sprinkle in sugar. Cover. Let simmer over low heat for about five to 10 minutes. Serve ham and red-eye gravy together. Serves eight to 10.

# MRS. BOHON'S BONED AND BAKED OLD HAM

*Cissy Gregg ran this recipe in 1957. It came from Mrs. Henry Clay Bohon of Harrodsburg, Ky., and though it is for a baked, glazed country ham, just like the preceding recipe, it differs dramatically in style.*

Use a ham of 12 to 20 pounds. And, naturally, Mrs. Bohon recognizes none other than a sugar-cured, hickory-smoked rear leg of a Kentucky-born-and-bred hog.

Place the ham under running water and scrub well with a brush. Remove the hock. Place in an enamel or stoneware container. Cover with cold water, and add 1 pint of apple vinegar. Let stand 12 to 18 hours.

After the soaking, take the ham from its rejuvenating bath and scrub again. This second scrubbing depends on the state of the ham; sometimes it isn't needed; again, it's a good idea.

Take 2 pieces of heavy aluminum foil, fold together in a French roll so it will hold water. (Our first attempt wasn't so successful. We made the fold right down the middle and placed the ham on top of the fold. Then we had another bright idea — we would place the ham on the solid piece of foil and make the French seam to the side. The top piece was used as you would a lid.)

Before closing the ham up into a neat package, add 1 quart of sherry wine or water, and cover the ham with 1 pound of brown sugar. Close the foil to make it watertight. Place in oven on broiler with rack or in a shallow pan with the skin side down. (We learned the easy way to do this was to place the ham on the foil with the skin side down, pour the sugar over the cut side, and close up with the liquid added, doing all the work on the pan you had chosen for baking it. Then, when the folding-up was done, all the handling needed was to shove it into the oven.)

Heat oven to 300 degrees, and time the ham at 15 minutes a pound. When ready, turn off the heat and let ham cool to room temperature in the foil package. Open foil, place ham on board or marble, and skin. Then place on the board with the cut, or back side, up, and bone the ham. Truss if necessary.

Cut the surface of the boned ham about ⅛ inch deep in squares. Pat on heavy layer of brown sugar and stick a whole clove in each square. Place in oven (we use a 400-degree oven for glazing) and allow the sugar to carmelize. Let cool to room temperature. Place in refrigerator, and slice thin for serving. Wonderful with beaten biscuits.

There you have the details of a super-duper method of cooking a country ham. Actually, it took longer to write down the details than it did for our part in the preparation.

Of course, hams differ in loss. Ours weighed 17 pounds, 2 ounces. Cooked by Mrs. Bohon's method, the finished product, minus bone, skin and trimmings, gave us almost 11 pounds of solid meat. We have had old hams that have lost as much as 50 per cent in the cooking and trimming with the bones left in.

# POULTRY

# CHICKEN DONEGAN

*Lillian Marshall printed this recipe, a family favorite from Mrs. Richard Donegan, the wife of a General Electric executive, in 1969. She served the chicken with a peach broil, and we've included that recipe.*

**2 broilers, quartered**
**¼ cup butter or margarine, melted**
**¼ cup soy sauce**
**¼ cup chopped fresh parsley**
**1 cup orange juice**
**1 cup honey**
**1 tablespoon dry mustard**
**1 medium clove garlic, minced**
   **(optional)**

Place the quartered chicken in a flat baking pan and pour over it the remaining ingredients, which have been combined. Bake at 300 degrees for 30 to 40 minutes, or until just not quite done. Drain and reserve the marinade. Place chicken on grill over low charcoal fire. Brush frequently with reserved marinade, turning from time to time, about 20 minutes or until done and brown. Serves 6 to 8.

## PEACH BROIL

Use a large peach half for each serving. Fill each center with a heaping teaspoon of red currant jelly and a tablespoon of sherry. Sprinkle a little allspice over and place under broiler until bubbly.

# CHICKEN-WITH-A-BLUSH

*Cissy Gregg was judging a cooking contest in 1950 when she met Mrs. Arthur Rogosin, 2547 Dell Road in Louisville, and was introduced to her intriguing chicken dish. This is "easy to do," Cissy said of the recipe, "yet has an enticing appearance and sniff-sniff — to say nothing of the flavor."*

*The distinction between fryers and hens may be lost on younger cooks because chickens offered by supermarkets today are uniformly young and tender. In 1950, however, it still was possible to get a "tough old bird" for stewing or slow cooking. By definition, hens are mature female chickens, and therefore, somewhat less tender, and some hens survived into a ripe old age — and tough old stage — by virtue of being good egg-layers. The recipe says that Cissy's fryers were "quite on the other side of youth from hen side," meaning they were young and tender.*

For fryer-sized chickens: Cut the chicken into serving-sized portions. Roll the pieces in flour which has been seasoned with salt, pepper and paprika. For 1 good-size fryer, melt about ⅓ cup shortening in a skillet that can be covered tightly — a chicken fryer works well. Brown the pieces, turning so a good crust will be formed on all sides. When each piece is satisfactorily browned, pour off any excess fat left, leaving approximately a good tablespoonful. Slice 1 medium-sized onion and add to the chicken. Mix together in a cup 3 full-to-overflowing tablespoons chili sauce, 1 tablespoon lemon juice, 1 teaspoon sugar and ½ cup water.

After this is mixed well, pour it over the chicken. Sprinkle again with paprika. Cover and place in a slow oven, about 325 degrees (350 degrees won't hurt, if you are baking something else). Cook slowly until the chicken is spoon-tender and a lush color. Baste several times during the baking period. Ours took about 30 minutes, but our chickens were quite on the other side of youth from hen side.

The juice cooks down to practically nothing, and if the evaporation isn't enough to do this before your chicken is tender, remove the chicken to a hot platter, put the cooking skillet on a spritely fire until it cooks down, then pour the thickened sauce over the chicken on the platter.

We robbed the onion of its flavor, but held the body back as garbage. You can do as you choose.

## THE WAY WITH A HEN

The way with a hen: Cut a young hen (Mrs. Rogosin likes a 4-pound hen or better) into quarters or portions as desired. Peel and slice a large Bermuda onion and lay in the bottom of a small roaster or a Dutch oven. Season the chicken with salt and pepper, and dust the top with flour — just a light sprinkling. Dust paprika over the top of the pieces. Add 1 cup water, pouring it around the chicken. Then on top add 4 good tablespoons chili sauce. Cover tightly and place in a 350-degree or 325-degree oven.

Baste often with the liquid in the bottom of the roaster. Bake for about 2 hours, until the chicken is very tender. Serve on a hot platter with the juice around it. Again, if gravy is too thin when the chicken is tender, allow it to boil down on top of the stove to thicken. If there is too much fat — and some hens come well endowed with fat — skim it off.

Lemon juice and the whiff of sugar can be added to the hen as to the young chicken.

We thought the results were something like a barbecue but not so potent.

Mrs. Rogosin often handles fresh tongue in this manner, too — cooking the tongue until it is tender, de-skinning it and slicing it into a baking pan. She uses the onions, and chili sauce-water mixture with seasonings to blanket the slices, and bakes it until the seasonings take up with the tongue.

# CHICKEN WITH GOLDEN SAUCE

Cut up chicken as for frying. Put in large, deep skillet or Dutch oven with the oil and brown on all sides — about 20 minutes. Add onions and green pepper. Cook about 5 minutes, stirring the onion and green pepper so they cook evenly. Then add seasonings — garlic powder, black pepper, paprika, bay leaf and 5 teaspoons of the salt. (I give the warning about the bay leaf because while I like the flavor, it can go overboard for me quite easily). Add tomatoes and 1½ cups of the boiling water. Cover and continue cooking over low heat until the rice is ready.

While the chicken is cooking, combine 3 cups of the boiling water, the remaining teaspoon salt and saffron. Add rice, bring to a boiling point, cover and cook over low heat until tender — about 20 minutes. Remove cover, let stand over low heat to dry the rice — about a minute. Add to chicken along with 2 pimentoes. Cook slowly for about 10 minutes.

Pour mixture into serving dish, garnish with remaining pimiento strips and chopped parsley.

— Cissy Gregg, 1955

1 2½ to 3-pound young chicken, cut up
⅓ cup olive oil or salad oil
1 large green pepper, finely chopped
1 large onion, finely chopped
¼ teaspoon garlic powder
½ teaspoon pepper
1 teaspoon paprika
1 bay leaf — or a half one
6 teaspoons salt
1 cup canned tomatoes
4½ cups of boiling water
4 pinches saffron
1 cup uncooked rice
3 pimentoes cut in strips
2 tablespoons chopped parsley

# CHICKEN STUFFED WITH CELERY AND APPLES

*Howard Davis created this recipe for Lillian Marshall's Kentuckiana Cooks series in 1967. He was on a special diet, having had surgery, and developed a number of recipes to satisfy his diet needs while feeding all the guests he entertained at home.*

**Roasting hen, 4 to 5 pounds**
**2 cups cubed, unpared apples**
**2 cups celery, cut in 1-inch pieces**

Soak the hen in cold salted water several hours or overnight in the refrigerator. When ready to roast, place the hen on a sheet of heavy aluminum foil. Stuff the cavity with apples and celery.

Overlap the ends of foil over the breast and fold up the ends to hold juices. Don't make an airtight seal.

Place the wrapped bird in a shallow pan and bake at 450 degrees for approximately 1¾ hours. Open the foil the last 10 minutes to brown the hen. This is the quick method Davis uses. For his diet, instead of making gravy in the usual way, he serves the chicken sliced, with mushroom sauce.

## MUSHROOM SAUCE

**1 can cream of mushroom soup**
**¾ soup can light cream**
**1 small can mushroom pieces**
**½ teaspoon salt**
**¼ cup chopped nuts**
**Pinch poultry seasoning, basil or thyme (optional)**

Stir the cream into the soup gradually. Add the salt and mushrooms, liquid and all. Any of the optional ingredients will heighten flavor. Serve very hot over sliced chicken.

# VIRGINIA BRUNSWICK STEW

**2 onions, sliced**
**2 tablespoons bacon fat**
**1 frying chicken (2 to 2½ pounds)**
**Salt and pepper to taste**
**3 tomatoes, peeled and quartered**
**½ cup sherry wine**
**2 teaspoons Worchestershire sauce**
**1 pound fresh lima beans**
**½ cup okra**
**3 ears corn**
**2 tablespoons butter**
**½ cup bread crumbs**

Brown onions in bacon fat and add the chicken, which has been cut in small pieces and seasoned. When the chicken is tender, pour off the fat and put chicken and onions in Dutch oven. Add water to cover, tomatoes, sherry wine and Worchestershire sauce. Cook, covered, over low heat for ½ hour, add the lima beans, okra and corn cut off the cob. Simmer one hour, adding water as necessary, but taking care not to get the mixture too soupy. Add butter and bread crumbs and cook ½ hour longer.
— Cissy Gregg, 1941

# POULET MARENGO

Skin and split chicken breasts. Salt and pepper each piece. Heat ¼ cup butter in large skillet until it begins to foam. Add the chicken breasts and brown them. They'll be golden instead of brown. Spoon two tablespoons sherry over the chicken. Remove from skillet and place in shallow baking dish.

Cover and bake at 300 degrees for 25 or 30 minutes or until tender. To skillet, add ½ pound mushrooms and sauté till tender, adding more butter if needed. Now blend in flour, add chicken stock and simmer, stirring constantly, until thickened. Season with tomato paste, bay leaf, chives, salt and pepper. Simmer slowly for 15 minutes. Meanwhile, cook the lobster tails according to directions on package. Remove meat from shell and cut into bite-size pieces. Add lobster to sauce along with tomatoes. Simmer until tomatoes and lobster are heated through.

Serve chicken breasts on large platter topped with sauce, arranging tomatoes and lobster meat attractively to serve as a garnish. Serves six to eight.
— Lillian Marshall, 1974

**4 chicken breasts, split in half**
**¼ cup butter**
**2 tablespoons sherry**
**½ pound fresh mushrooms, sliced if large**
**2 tablespoons flour**
**1½ cups chicken stock**
**1 tablespoon tomato paste**
**1 bay leaf, crushed**
**2 tablespoons fresh or frozen chives (or a teaspoon dried)**
**½ teaspoon salt**
**¼ teaspoon pepper**
**2 9-ounce packages frozen lobster tails**
**3 ripe tomatoes, cored and quartered**

# LUCKLESS FISHERMAN'S GRILLED MARINATED CHICKEN

*Printed in 1980, this was a popular recipe of Deni Hamilton's.*

Dry the chicken. Mix the juice, garlic powder, onion, wine and tarragon. Place the chicken pieces in a shallow roasting dish or a sturdy plastic bag, and pour marinade over it. Turn pieces every half hour for two hours. To grill, place chicken on grill four inches above glowing charcoal coals, and paint with oil. Turn quickly, and allow to cook until crispy brown, about 20 to 30 minutes. Paint oil on up-side of chicken and turn. Allow to brown on that side until chicken is done through, another 20 minutes or so. You may need to lower grill to get chicken closer to coals for crisping skin. Serves four.

**1 frying chicken, cut in serving pieces**
**½ cup tomato or orange juice**
**¼ teaspoon garlic powder**
**1 sliced medium onion**
**½ cup dry white wine**
**½ teaspoon tarragon, optional**
**Cooking oil**

# CHICKEN 'N' DUMPLINGS

*Read this 1946 recipe for everything you ever wanted to know about "sad" dumplings or read it just for fun. But do read it. It's Cissy Gregg at her best.*

For years it has been a preconceived idea that the real bringer of that "look" in men's eyes was love. Alas, 'tis not true! To prove it to yourself, start up a conversation on love, and if more comes of that than a wan sigh, you have progressed well. But start off with the subject of chicken 'n' dumplin's, and right off you'll be faced with men of strong convictions, ready to go forth to battle for the "kind mother used to make."

All mothers did not make them alike, we have found out. And our dumpling Galahads are willing and eager to go forth in search of a recipe which will produce a facsimile thereof.

Dumplings are not the only item in food we all have definite emotional feelings about. Stories flow freely of happenings where the daughter of a Southern home never could darken its door again because she had gone off and married a man who had to have sugar in his cornbread. Today many of us who have succumbed to this whiff of sweetness in our corn muffins add it behind closed kitchen doors and are driven by conscience to feel as if each pinch was a smudge on our upbringing. We draw another regional line when we think of New Englanders not as people living in the New England states, but those people who, of their own free will, prefer yellow cornmeal to white, coarse water-ground meal.

But with dumplings, the matter changes somewhat. Those who call fat bits of fluff-duff with stewed chicken by the name of dumplings are one kind of people, while those who make sad-flat dumplings to go with their chicken are another kind. The boundaries to hold one kind or the other have nothing to do with geography at all. It's a family affair, and we'll hold on to our type, come what may.

In presenting to you chicken 'n' dumplings, I do not do so with any attempt to change opinion. It is done with the idea that it's time for me to take a stand on dumplings. The matter was brought to my attention by a letter from a fellow Kentuckian who through trying to do his bit in the war effort, was forced to leave his native haunts and associate with people uncivilized enough to hold the opinion that a flat, rolled-out dumpling was nothing but a noodle, after all. Horrors! What war does bring on people!

It makes small difference the course other cooks take. Those who like "pillows" as dumplings on top of their chicken can have them; but around here, when "Ah-h, my dumpling" is said with endearing tones, you can bet your last dollar the speaker-outer has in mind a thin strip of dumpling that nestles down in the gravy in loving companionship with the pieces of chicken.

Cooks vary in their opinion as to how to make flat dumplings. And all three by these ways leave me without a preference. That you'll have to decide for yourself, and, after all, there's very little to it.

Dumpling one: Make the same kind of pastry you would for pie crust. Use more flour than usual on the board when rolling them out. Roll the dough very, very thin. Cut in strips and drop them into the broth.

Dumpling two: Make a richer-than-average biscuit dough. Go to the half-way place between biscuits and pastry and at that point you'll find the perfect proportion for a dumpling. Cook the same as dumpling No. 1.

Dumpling three: Place in a bowl the amount of flour you would want to make up. Two cups of flour, we'll say. Add salt to taste — we used a good teaspoonful. The chicken has been cooked until it is at the place in doneness that, if it had to take one more simmer, it would suffer a complete breakaway from the bones. At this point, tenderly lift it from the stew pot to a serving bowl and keep hot. If the chicken was fat, with a large serving spoon stir up the broth, pushing back the fat a little, then dip up a spoonful of the hot liquid and add it to the measured flour in the bowl. Add enough of the chicken broth to make a rather stiff dough. Roll out thin on a well-floured board, cut in strips, I'd say an inch wide, and drop them into the boiling stew. Cover the pot and cook about 10 to 15 minutes. They must be done, though the thickness the dough is rolled will hold the accurate time needed.

When dumplings go in the gravy, usually no other thickening is needed, since the dumplings carry flour with them to insure their cooking as individual strips. But if thickening should be needed, it's O.K. by us. Pour gravy and dumplings over the chicken and watch all make pigs of themselves.

# CHICKEN AND NOODLES

Melt the butter or margarine in a saucepan and add the green pepper. Then add the sliced mushrooms, either fresh or from a can, and sauté until lightly browned. Shove them to the back of the saucepan and blend in the flour. Work out every small lump. Gradually add cream, stirring all the time, and cook about 10 minutes. Add chicken and salt and pepper and pimentoes. Put the cooked noodles in the bottom of a greased casserole. Then add the beaten egg yolks to the chicken mixture and stir and cook for a minute longer. Top the noodles with the chicken mixture and sprinkle the cheese over all. Set in a hot oven, 425 degrees, for 10 minutes to melt the cheese and bring it all to a bubbling-hot temperature. Serves 12.

This is one of those dishes that really can't be hurt. It can be assembled beforehand and kept in readiness, having a longer heating-up period at the last. It can be cut in half for six, or the seasonings can be changed to suit your whim.

— Cissy Gregg, 1948

½ cup butter or margarine
4 tablespoons minced green pepper
½ pound or 1 cup of sliced mushrooms — but more mushrooms never hurt any kind of dish
⅓ cup chopped pimentoes
3 tablespoons flour
4 cups cooked noodles
4 cups light cream
4 cups chopped chicken (we used one 5-plus-pound hen)
2 teaspoons salt
¼ teaspoon pepper
4 beaten egg yolks
Grated cheese for topping

# BROILED LIME CHICKEN

Mix all ingredients except chicken. Put chicken in mixture, turning to coat all sides and allow to stand half an hour. Arrange chicken on broiler rack, skin side down. Place in lowest part of broiler and cook, turning every 10 minutes and brushing with marinade, about 40 minutes, or until chicken is tender and browned. Serves four.

— Deni Hamilton, 1979

½ cup lime juice
½ cup oil
1 teaspoon garlic salt
2 teaspoons crushed tarragon
¼ teaspoon fresh ground pepper
1 tablespoon grated onion
1 broiling chicken, cut in pieces

# CHICKEN KENTUCKY

*This 1950 recipe wanders a bit, as Cissy Gregg recognized even as she was writing it, but it's essentially a simple baked chicken dish. The chicken is cut down the back and splayed open, butterfly fashion, for baking. The pastry or biscuit-dough strips are optional. Cissy used them for the photograph which accompanied this recipe, criss-crossing them in an attractive pattern. They looked like they were cut with pinking shears — hence, the reference to "pinken'."*

When the fryers get too large to fry, say, 3 pounds or a little better, they're just right for Chicken Kentucky. I say split them down the back, but if you wish, the chicken can be cut into halves or quarters. Rub over with salt. Sprinkle the top skin of the chick-a-dees with flour and place in a roaster. Add pepper and paprika — it makes nice color. Dot with as much butter as you can afford. (Some cooks advise ¼ pound per chick-grown-up, but here I think one must use one's head. If the chick is fat — very fat — don't use so much; for the leaner type, shoot the full volley.) Sometimes bacon strips are placed over the breast. Yes, I like that, unless the chicken is fat in itself.

Perhaps you have lost the directions on this chicken, but we have floured it and you have decided that if it is lean add the bacon strips, and, of course, you have added butter. Now on the side, I will say, we always cooked this kind of chicken in a round roaster. Among my simple kitchen implements I have one of this type to make this kind of chicken comfortable. However, I know it can be cooked in any kind of covered roaster. We did, just to make you happy with what you have.

To go on with directions, lay the chicken in the roaster and add approximately 2 cups of water, boiling hot. Cover tight and cook at 275 degrees for 3 hours. At the end of the time, the chick can be browned under the broiler for a crisp exterior or treated in the way we did it — breast stripped with golden strips of pastry. It can even be biscuit dough, if you like.

For the strip finish, we have ready either the leavings of the biscuits for dinner or of the pie that might be — and roll the dough thin. Cut in strips with a knife or use a pastry wheel that gives a "pinken'" finish. Have them not more than a half inch wide — you're stripping a chick instead of a pie — so don't make it seem hard. Apply these just when the chicken is approximately tender, and then we baste ever so often, as soon as the dough is set, with the fat that is in the bottom of the pan, raising the temperature of the oven to 400 degrees at the very last to brown the strips.

To serve, lift the chicken off onto a hot platter, give it decor if you like. We used the left-over pastry made into tartlets and filled them with jelly. And, oh, the gravy! What's left in the pan may be thickened or not according to the fatness of the chicken. If the fat is too much, take some off, and bind it together with a roux — that mixture of flour and water. This is seldom needed for my taste, but I mention it as a possibility you might meet with. And taste the gravy for seasonings.

What should your goal turn out to be? This I know, the chicken should really be giving — it should almost but not quite fall apart. The slow cooking does something to the meat and the gravy that I enjoy — and hope you do, too.

# CHICKEN CROQUETTES A LA JENNIE BENEDICT

*Jennie Benedict was a popular and successful Louisville restaurateur of the early 20th century. Cissy Gregg printed this recipe in 1961.*

Cook 1 chicken with seasonings such as a little parsley, celery, a piece of carrot — or just as you season a stewing chicken for any use. Grind the meat with 1 can mushrooms. Soak ½ pound of stale bread in the cooked-down broth and add to meat and mushrooms. Add ¼ of a cup of butter and 4 eggs. Mix well all together and cook until well cooked. Season with salt and pepper, celery salt, chopped parsley, a little finely chopped onion and a very little grated nutmeg. Pour out on a platter. When thoroughly cold, shape, roll in crumbs and fry in "boiling fat."

# HELEN DAVIS' NORTH WOODS CHICKEN AND BEANS

*Lillian Marshall wrote in 1968 that this was "one of the most popular chicken recipes ever to appear in these pages." It first was printed almost 15 years earlier, she wrote. Unfortunately, its origins are lost.*

Assemble this dish before bedtime some night and forget it (almost) until dinnertime the next evening.

Soak beans overnight. Drain and place a third of the beans in bottom of a large 4-quart casserole. Sprinkle with salt and pepper, place onions and the salt pork on bean layer. Add another third of the beans, salt and pepper again, then lay the chicken pieces on. Add remaining beans and more salt and pepper, mustard and garlic salt, if used. Add hot water to cover. Cover closely, place in oven at 200 degrees and bake 18 hours.

The only attention the casserole requires during this long, slow cooking is the addition of water occasionally. Two hours before serving, pull up the chicken pieces and remove the bones, then gently stir chicken back into the beans so that each serving will contain an honest share of everything. One hour before serving, remove the cover; the finished product should be nice and moist without being soupy.

**2 pounds dry navy beans**
**A 5-pound fat hen cut in serving pieces or equivalent weight of chicken pieces**
**2 medium onions with 2 or 3 cloves stuck in them**
**¼ pound salt pork cut in ½-inch cubes (more if chicken is not fat)**
**Salt and pepper to taste**
**½ teaspoon dry mustard**
**½ teaspoon garlic salt (optional)**
**Hot water**

# CHICKEN CHOW MEIN

*Everyone knows about the Hot Brown, but at one time, the Brown Hotel's chicken chow mein was more widely consumed among Louisvillians and at least as popular. "I personally know it is one of the most sought-after recipes in Louisville," Cissy Gregg wrote in 1947, after obtaining the "the actual, without-one-deviation recipe" from William W. Gruber, maître d'hôtel. Cissy's observations about the postwar availability of the ingredients are interesting, and today's cook ought to be able to find and substitute two cups of fresh bean sprouts for the canned.*

**2 hens (3 pounds each, dressed) boiled; reserve stock**
**1 pint of fresh mushrooms, sliced**
**3 onions, sliced**
**3 celery stalks, sliced**
**1 No. 2 can bean sprouts**
**1 cup bamboo shoots, sliced**
**1 cup water chestnuts, sliced**
**10 cups chicken stock**
**1½ cups cornstarch**
**1½ cups soy sauce**

After the chickens are cooked, cool, bone and cut the meat julienne style. Reserve one cup of shredded white meat on the side.

Fry mushrooms, onions and celery in oil for a few minutes. Add stock and soy sauce and cook for a while, but leaving vegetables still crisp. Add bamboo shoots, water chestnuts, bean sprouts and chicken, bring to a boil and thicken with the cornstarch mixed with some stock. Season with salt and pepper.

Serve on fried Chinese noodles, allowing 1 No. 2 can for two persons. Top with a garnish made of the reserved julienne of chicken, 2 shredded leeks, a handful of toasted cashew nuts and 1 cupful of shredded pancake. Mix the ingredients of the garnish up well and sprinkle on the chow mein, dished over the fried noodles.

The pancake mentioned above is made by mixing together 2 whole eggs, 2 tablespoons milk, 2 tablespoons flour. Mix well and pour into large enough greased medium-hot skillet to make a very thin pancake. Turn to brown on both sides. Take from skillet and shred into thin strips. The cashew nuts are chopped, but not too fine.

Before the war, water chestnuts and bamboo sprouts could be had from many food specialty stores. But today they have disappeared. And so as a substitution we, as does the Brown, used a canned mixture which contained water chestnuts, bamboo sprouts, bean sprouts and some celery. There are quite a few packers of such a mix on the markets today, but I would suggest that you read the label on your can and see just what is on the inside before you buy. Add in accordance with the amounts — because in all you'll want the equivalent of 2 cups of bean sprouts, 1 cup of bamboo sprouts and 1 cup water chestnuts.

In case you would like to know what you are missing in not having the bamboo sprouts and the chestnuts — we'll try to relay by word the food texture and flavor.

The bamboo sprouts are the tender young shoots of the bamboo. They have a delightful crispness about them. The times I have tasted of their goodness, they had been mixed up with other ingredients, which has left me with the hope there would be at least one more encounter before the experience was placed in past tense.

Before the war, gourmets could find fresh water chestnuts packed in moss which were shipped from the Orient to Chinese firms in New York and San Francisco.

But even before the beginning of the war shut off these shipments, there was not enough of these to meet the growing demands. Eventually, another source was sought and found in the rich, thick black soil and warm climate of Florida. And these that were produced there were so much like the Oriental chestnuts that even the chestnuts couldn't tell themselves apart.

At first nimble fingers peeled the black, slippery shell, leaving the white nut for the consumer. And each one of these was packed in an individual jar. At present the supply is not enough to can them in this way. Instead they are mixed with the other vegetables used in famous Chinese dishes so that many can have at least a little. Some day though, we hope, both the bamboo sprouts and water chestnuts will be marketed again.

Mr. Gruber cautions the maker of chow mein to be careful about the addition of salt. The soy sauce has quite a salty flavor.

From us as makers of chicken chow mein to you as prospective makers, there's really nothing to it at all. But we'll put our small oar in to remind you of a few details you may not think about the first time.

If possible, chill the chicken broth and lift off the fat. Anyway skim it off the best way you can. We used the chicken fat instead of oil to sauté the mushrooms and celery. It took between ⅓ to ½ cup of the fat.

Then the next time we make it, we'll thicken the sauce first and add the julienne chicken last. That will keep the chicken from disintegrating into shreds during the stirring and cooking.

Leeks we could not find, so we substituted scallions, shredded into thin wisps. (It took more time than making the chow mein.)

The noodles can be bought so easy, there's no need to talk about frying them yourself — but it can be done.

# THE C-J HOT BROWN SANDWICH

*"How do you make a REAL Hot Brown?"*

*Cissy Gregg was tired of hearing the question and not having an answer. She wrote that she had "snooped around kitchens" everywhere without coming up with a recipe that she found satisfactory. So she set about re-creating the Brown Hotel classic from scratch. This is her recipe, printed in 1948. Notice that she uses chicken, not turkey.*

*A lot of Hot Brown recipes have passed under the broiler since then. We're inclined to think that Cissy's version was right on the mark, however. She had the advantage of being able to taste the real thing and to adjust her own recipe accordingly.*

The first step toward a completed sandwich is a cooked hen. We simmered ours down in water seasoned with a few peppercorns, salt and bay leaf. When tender, allow to cool in the broth. Then after it has cooled, slice the breast into thin slices. We used only the white meat, but I can't see why that wouldn't be a matter left up to you. If I were to use the dark meat, too, I would distribute both evenly.

The crux of this sandwich is the sauce, which, oddly enough, is a combination of two sauces.

## SAUCE ONE, OR BECHAMEL

⅓ cup butter or margarine
½ a medium-sized onion, minced
1 to 3 cups flour
3 cups hot milk
1 teaspoon salt
A dash of red pepper
A couple sprigs of parsley (if you have it, but parsley isn't a must)
A dash of nutmeg

Melt the butter or margarine in a saucepan. Add onion and cook slowly until a light brown. This must have taken me about 15 to 20 minutes. Add flour and blend until the flour makes a smooth paste, but of course, the onion minces are still in it. Add milk and other seasonings and cook 25 to 30 minutes, stirring constantly and briskly at first until the sauce is thick and smooth. When it is thick and smooth, then continue to cook, stirring occasionally until the time is up. Strain.

## SAUCE TWO, OR MORNAY

2 cups of Sauce One
2 egg yolks
½ cup grated parmesan cheese
1 tablespoon butter or margarine
4 tablespoons whipped cream

Heat the Sauce One and combine with egg yolks. Stir constantly and remove from the fire before it starts to boil — in fact, I used a double boiler at this stage. When hot and thick, add cheese and the butter or margarine. The sauce must not boil or it will curdle. Then for every ½ cup sauce that is to be used for the sandwich, fold in 1 tablespoon of whipped cream. For this it would be 4 tablespoons whipped cream. The cream gives a lift to the browning-off under the broiler.

*Hens with prunes in port-rhubarb sauce.*
*Photograph by Durell Hall Jr.*

## GARNISH

Fry out as many strips of bacon as the sandwiches you are fixing. Also we did a mushroom cap for each sandwich, but that is strictly our own idea.

To assemble, cut the crusts off 2 slices of bread for each sandwich and toast. Put 1 slice of toast on the oven-going shallow dish. Lay the slices of chicken on top of the toast. Enshroud with a goodly portion of the sauce. Place in a very hot oven or under the broiler until the sauce has taken on the glow of a suntan. Cut the extra slice of toast diagonally, and put the tips at each end. Top with bacon strip and mushroom.

A little more grated cheese mixed with bread crumbs can be sprinkled over the top of the sauce, if you like. These are delicious and a full meal.

We did have difficulites in finding the shallow pottery bakers that would be so nice for serving these at home, but there are some just the right size in glass that could be used, or what's wrong in making the sandwich fit the shape of what you have?

**8 slices bread, toasted, with crusts removed**
**4 strips bacon, fried**
**4 mushroom caps, optional**

# LOUISVILLE HOT BROWN

*This is an adaptation of Cissy Gregg's two-sauce recipe — a simpler and quicker recipe. Its authorship is unclear, and it has been printed a number of times over the years.*

Sauté onion in butter until transparent, add flour and combine. Add milk, salt and pepper and whisk until smooth. Cook on medium heat until sauce thickens, stirring occasionally. Add cheeses and continue heating until they blend. Remove from heat. Put one slice of toast in each of four oven-proof individual serving dishes. Top each piece of toast with slices of chicken or turkey. Cut remaining toast slices diagonally and place on sides of sandwiches. Ladle cheese sauce over sandwiches. Place sandwiches under broiler until sauce begins to bubble. Garnish with crumbled bacon and sautéed mushroom slices and serve immediately.

**4 tablespoons butter**
**1 small onion, chopped**
**3 tablespoons flour**
**2 cups milk**
**½ teaspoon salt**
**¼ teaspoon white pepper**
**¼ cup shredded cheddar**
**¼ cup grated Parmesan**
**8 slices trimmed toast**
**Slices cooked chicken or turkey breast**
**Crisp-fried bacon, crumbled**
**Mushroom slices, sautéed**

# LEMON BAKED CHICKEN

*MSG is a flavor enhancer, but it would do no great harm to the recipe to leave it out. In this 1960 recipe, Cissy Gregg suggested serving the chicken with spiced peaches.*

**A broiler-fryer chicken, quartered
   or cut in serving pieces**
**1 tablespoon flour**
**1 teaspoon monosodium glutamate
   (MSG)**
**½ teaspoon salt**
**⅛ teaspoon pepper**
**½ teaspoon paprika**
**1 tablespoon butter or margarine**
**3 tablespoons lemon juice**

Place chicken a shallow baking dish. Combine flour, monosodium glutamate, salt, pepper and paprika and sprinkle that over the chicken pieces. Dot with butter or margarine. Bake uncovered in a moderate oven (375 degrees) for 30 minutes.

Sprinkle with the lemon juice and bake for 20 minutes longer. This recipe serves four to six.

# GOLDEN CHICKEN BAKE

*Cissy Gregg was writing about the poultry breeders' "chicken of tomorrow" for this 1956 recipe. To-day's broiler-fryers usually weigh 3 to 4 pounds, but the larger roasters show up in the supermarket freezer sections.*

**1 pretty-bird, about 5 pounds, half
   way between their 4-6 average**
**½ cup — a stick — melted butter or
   margarine**
**Flour for dusting**
**Salt and pepper**
**Milk, for dipping**

Cut the bird into portions — our portions were large — you can make yours smaller according to the likes of those you are serving. Dust portions with flour, salt and pepper. Dip in milk and dust with seasoned flour again. Our directions said place in baking pan, 11x7x2, and pour the melted butter or margarine over the pieces. We tried that the first time, and liked a larger baking pan where the pieces had more chance to brown on all sides with greater ease, and there was more chance to gather together the drippings. As a matter of fact, use a baking pan where the individual pieces would have a chance to brown individually on all sides — not too large, or too little.

Bake in a hot oven, 400 degrees, for about an hour. (If smaller chicken is used, bake for 45 minutes.) Baste chicken with drippings about every 20 minutes — or at first we basted with margarine or butter melted. Turn as the pieces brown so all are browned and crusty on all sides.

Such chicken should, of course, be served with hot biscuits and gravy. We left the recipe we had been given for our pretty-chicken and went on our own for the gravy. It started with the cutting up. There were pieces of back which we didn't think would add to the chicken platter — we took these bones, the giblets and stewed them slowly until tender, which doesn't take long. What we didn't have in broth we added to with a chicken-bouillon cube. When we had a rich-tasting broth, it was thickened with a little cornstarch moistened to a paste with cold water.

Add to the broth, boil up and season as you wish. That's the best old-fashioned chicken gravy I know of. By the time the oven chicken was golden, we just wallowed it in its juices and saved what was left over for something else. The fair-haired gravy which we made with a topping of chopped parsley couldn't be beat, in our opinion.

# ORANGE FRIED CHICKEN

Shake the chicken, two or three pieces at a time, in a bag containing the flour, salt, paprika, dry mustard and pepper. Coat evenly. Save any leftover flour for the gravy. Cook chicken slowly in moderately hot fat in a skillet, turning as necessary to brown lightly and evenly. Allow 15 to 20 minutes for this cooking. Reduce heat, add a tablespoon orange juice, cover tightly, and cook slowly 20 to 25 minutes, or until the thickest pieces are fork-tender. During this cooking turn chicken once or twice to brown and cook evenly. Uncover last 8 to 10 minutes to recrisp skin. Makes four servings.

For gravy: Pour all drippings from skillet except 2 tablespoons. Add enough water to remaining orange juice to make 1½ cups. Set aside. Add the reserved flour mixture (approximately 2 tablespoons), ¼ teaspoon salt and ⅛ teaspoon pepper to the drippings. Blend thoroughly and cook over low heat until mixture bubbles. Add orange juice mixture and grated rind all at once and cook, stirring constantly, until mixture is uniformly thickened. Cover and simmer 2 to 3 minutes longer. Reseason to taste. This should give you 1½ cups of gravy.

— Cissy Gregg, 1956

**1 broiler-fryer, 2 to 2½ pounds, cut up**
**½ cup flour**
**2 teaspoons paprika**
**2 teaspoons salt**
**½ teaspoon dry mustard**
**¼ teaspoon ground pepper**
**Fat for browning and cooking, about ½ cup**
**Juice of an orange**
**2 teaspoons grated orange rind**

# MRS. SAYLES' CHICKEN WITH DUMPLINGS

*"We went on a search of the dumpling supreme," Cissy Gregg wrote in 1949, "and we think we have it from Mrs. Amanda M. Sayles, 1641 Hale. In a roundabout way, I had learned that Mrs. Sayles wields a very wicked 'dumpling hand,' and when she asked me for some candy recipes, we went into tradin'."*

**1 5-pound chicken**
**4 celery leaves**
**2 onion slices**
**2 bay leaves**
**1½ teaspoons salt**
**7 cups water**

Cut the chicken into servable pieces. Bring water and seasonings to boiling and drop in the chicken pieces. Bring to a boil and then turn down the heat so the water just simmers. Cover the pot and cook at simmering for 2 or 3 hours or until the chicken is so tender it would go to pieces at a harsh word.

## GRAVY

Skim the fat from the top of the broth, and remove the bay leaves. Pour off the broth to measure at least roughly. To each 3 cups full of stock, do this:

Combine ⅓ cup chicken fat and ½ cup flour. Mix to blend until smooth. Add 2 cups milk and blend well together. Add gradually to the 3 cups stock and chicken, stirring until the broth is smooth and has thickened. Season with 1 teaspoon more of salt and ¼ teaspoon paprika. Taste and reseason according to the need.

## DUMPLINGS

**2 cups flour**
**¼ teaspoon celery salt**
**4 teaspoons baking powder**
**3 tablespoons fat**
**⅓ teaspoon salt**
**¼ teaspoon sugar**
**¼ teaspoon paprika**
**¾ cup milk**

Sift flour and measure. Sift with celery salt, salt, baking powder, sugar and paprika. Cut in the fat until it is the size of cornmeal. Add milk and mix until the flour is dampened.

Bring the chicken and gravy to hot-hot. First dip a tablespoon into the gravy and then into the dumpling batter. Don't make them too large, and dip spoon in gravy each time before making another dumpling. Try to place them where the chicken protrudes from the gravy. They should not be dropped at random in the gravy. When the dumplings are all in the pot, cover and steam chicken, dumplings and gravy for 20 minutes without raising the lid of the pot.

Remove to a hot platter, and enjoy what you have made!

# SIXTH AVENUE GETHSEMANI CHICKEN

*Louisville's Sixth Avenue restaurant supplied this recipe to the Cook's Corner column in 1983 in response to a request from a reader. The cheese specified in the recipe is from Kentucky, produced by the Abbey of Gethsemani south of Bardstown, Ky.*

Remove connective tissue or fat from the ham. In a food processor, chop the ham. Add cheese, pulsing a few times. Do not overblend, but leave slightly chunky. Divide mixture into 12 even portions, rolling them into smooth, round balls.

Cut breast in half lengthwise. Place pieces between wax paper and pound to ¼-inch thick. Place one portion of ham-and-cheese mixture on each piece of chicken. Roll. Secure with a toothpick, if meat will not cling by itself.

Dredge roll in flour. Sauté in vegetable oil over medium heat just until evenly browned, about 2 minutes. Place chicken rolls in a baking dish. Bake at 350 degrees for 20 minutes.

Meanwhile, make the wine sauce by bringing brown sauce to a simmer. Remove from heat. Add wine. Fold in butter. When melted, serve about ⅓ cup sauce over each serving. Serves six.

**9 ounces cooked country ham**
**9 ounces Gethsemani cheese, cut in chunks**
**6 10-ounce boneless, skinned chicken breasts**
**1 cup flour seasoned with salt and pepper**
**½ cup vegetable oil**
**3 cups brown sauce (see recipe)**
**6 ounces Madeira wine**
**6 tablespoons butter**

# BROWN SAUCE

Preheat oven to 400 degrees. Place bones in a roasting pan. Roast, turning every 30 minutes, for 2½ hours. During final 10 minutes of roasting, distribute next eight ingredients over bones. Transfer contents of roasting pan to a large pot.

Add water to the roasting pan. Place on stove and deglaze by bringing water to a boil to loosen most of the bits of food that cling to the bottom of the pan. Add pan liquid to the bones. Add wine, plus additional water to cover bones. Boil and skim scum. Simmer, cover off, 12 hours.

Strain through double thickness of cheesecloth. Refrigerate. Skim fat. Store in covered containers. May be frozen. Makes about two quarts.

**5 pounds veal bones, rinsed**
**1 pound chicken bones, rinsed**
**2 cups each coarsely chopped onions, carrots, celery**
**1 tablespoon peppercorns, crushed**
**2 bay leaves**
**2 cloves garlic**
**1 teaspoon thyme**
**2 teaspoons rosemary**
**1 cup fresh packed parsley**
**2 ripe tomatoes, in chunks**
**1 quart water**
**2 cups dry red wine**

# KENTUCKY HOME-FRIED CHICKEN

**3 pounds mixed fryer parts**
**Solid vegetable shortening**

## FIRST COATING

½ **cup flour**
½ **teaspoon each of salt, black**
   **pepper, dried parsley, basil,**
   **oregano, onion powder and garlic**
   **powder**

## SECOND COATING

**1 cup flour**
½ **cup instant dry milk**
**1 tablespoon baking powder**
**1 tablespoon sugar**
**1 tablespoon salt**
¼ **teaspoon each of sage, celery**
   **seed, thyme**
**1 teaspoon paprika**
**1 teaspoon black pepper**

## DIP FOR COATING

**1 egg**
**1 tablespoon club soda**

Wash chicken and pat dry. Combine ingredients for first coating, dredge chicken and let sit 45 minutes. Combine ingredients for second coating. Combine egg and club soda. Dip chicken in egg mixture, then in second coating mixture. Repeat second coating procedure. Deep-fry or skillet-fry in very hot, vegetable shortening, skin-side down first. Turn after 15 or 20 minutes. Reduce heat slightly. Do not let fat burn. Fry 15 to 20 minutes more. Drain well on paper towels. Serves six to eight.

— Elaine Corn, 1982

# THELMA'S COUNTRY CAPTAIN

*It was 1945, and, for reasons she didn't explain, Cissy Gregg was in Fort Sill, Okla., where she "took a good long sniff of the local air in the hope of getting on the scent of some good recipes to bring back to you." This recipe, she said, was "way out front, riding easily."*

*The recipe came from Mrs. Grant Mangum. She and her husband had lived in Louisville before World War II, Cissy explained, "when Colonel Mangum was instructor in artillery for the Officers' Reserve Corps in Kentucky." Cissy said that the recipe originated in Mrs. Mangum's hometown of Columbus, Ga., but that the basis for the name was a mystery.*

Cut up a 3-pound chicken as you would for frying. Heat 2 tablespoons melted butter or margarine in a saucepan or skillet; add the chicken and brown for 10 minutes. (These time limits on browning always confuse me since my chicken usually seems stubborn about changing its color.) Turn occasionally so all sides will be lightly browned. Add 1 finely sliced onion and 1 finely sliced green pepper. Peel one large clove of garlic, cut into halves and stick a toothpick in each half, and add. (The toothpicks are the retrieving help when you have had enough of the garlic.) Brown all of these extras in one side of the skillet — I brown the chicken and shove it to the side, then take on the other members of the force. When the chicken onion, green pepper and garlic have their tinged color, distribute throughout the chicken and add one-half pint of water or chicken broth or chicken bouillon — that's one cup, you know if you'd rather measure it that way. Season all of this with a healthy teaspoon of salt, ½ teaspoon pepper and 1½ teaspoons curry powder. Stir lightly to get the seasonings mixed in properly. Cover the skillet and place in a 350-degree oven for 45 minutes.

In the meantime, have ¼ pound of almonds blanched and roasted to a golden color. If the almonds are to be slivered, be sure to do so before the roasting. We slivered some of them and left others whole. Of course, there'll be a mighty bit of fishing for the whole ones if people serve themsleves, but a few in the shape nature made them is the cook's way of bragging about their presence. Add the almonds to the chicken, along with 3 tablespoons picked-over dried currants. Lightly mix these through the chicken and cook on top of the stove for 5 minutes so the flavor of the newcomers will make themselves known throughout the whole dish.

Dish up on a hot platter and arrange cooked-dry rice in the close vicinity. The original recipe said to place 6 slices of crisp, broiled bacon on top. The supply, however, will help you make the decision about the bacon. We had 3 slices and broke them up into small pieces, then distributed the pieces here and there over the top of the chicken. Maybe the missing 3 slices would make it better, but we couldn't exactly imagine how it could be better than it was.

Serve with Indian chutney.

# CHICKEN LIVERS AND WILD RICE

*This is a recipe from the late Victor Jory, veteran actor and father of Jon Jory, producing director of Actors Theatre of Louisville. In 1971, the elder Jory gave this recipe to Carol Sutton, women's editor, for a feature story she was writing about him. Ms. Sutton was senior editor of The Courier-Journal when she died this year, and one of the last projects she launched was this cookbook.*

*The recipe is not clear on how many mushrooms to use for this dish. Surely no more than an 8-ounce box was intended, maybe less.*

Bring chicken broth and water to a boil; add wild rice, thyme, celery, parsley, bay leaf and other seasonings, and simmer for 50 minutes. If toward the end of the cooking time the rice should become too dry, add a little more chicken broth or water.

Sauté onions and mushrooms in about ½ cup butter until onions begin to wilt. Add chicken livers and sauté, stirring frequently, over a hot fire for about 5 minutes.

Use the rest of the butter to grease generously a casserole. Remove bay leaf from rice. Pour rice and chicken liver mixture into casserole and stir. Add a dash of brandy and sprinkle the cheese over the top. Bake in a 350-degree oven for 15 minutes. Remove, add another dash of brandy and serve.

**½ medium-sized onion, chopped**
**A can of mushrooms, full cap, or a**
  **box of fresh mushrooms**
**¾ cup butter**
**1½ pounds chicken livers**
**½ teaspoon seasoned salt and other**
  **seasonings to taste**
**Bay leaf**
**6 sprigs of parsley, chopped**
**2 ribs celery, chopped**
**Pinch of thyme**
**Parmesan or grated cheddar cheese**
**3½ cups chicken broth**
**A cup wild rice**
**Brandy**

# CORNISH HENS WITH CHERRY SAUCE

6 Cornish hens, halved
Salt
1 stick butter
2 tablespoons gravy browning
    liquid
8 ounces cherry preserves

Sprinkle hen halves with salt on both sides. Melt butter in saucepan and add browning liquid and cherry preserves. When mixture is completely melted, dip each hen-half in it and place, cut-side down, on a rack in a flat roasting pan. Bake in a 350-degree oven for 25 minutes. Pour remaining cherry sauce over hens and bake another 20 minutes or until browned. Serves 12.

— Lillian Marshall, 1975

# CORNISH HENS STUFFED WITH GRAPES IN CHAMPAGNE SAUCE

2 Cornish hens, about 2 pounds
    each
1 lemon
Salt and pepper
Paprika
1 cup whole, seedless grapes
2 tablespoons melted butter
1½ cups brut champagne

Wash the hens and pat dry. Halve lemon and rub cut surfaces over hens. Sprinkle with salt, pepper and paprika. Place hens in a roasting pan. Stuff each cavity with the grapes. Secure with toothpicks.

Roast at 500 degrees for 10 minutes. Reduce oven temperature to 400 degrees. Brush hens with melted butter and pour over with champagne. Roast 30 minutes more, basting frequently with pan juices. The hens' juices should run clear, skin golden brown. Do not overroast. Serve with medallions of duchesse potatoes. Pour pan juices over.

## MEDALLIONS OF DUCHESSE POTATOES

1 large potato
2 tablespoons butter
Salt and white pepper, to taste
⅓ cup heavy cream
1 egg yolk

Peel, cube and boil the potato. While the potato is hot, use a rotary beater to mash and mix with the butter, salt and pepper. Gradually beat in the cream. Vigorously beat in the egg yolk. Squeeze mixture into six medallions through a pastry bag with a large star tip, or shape by hand into balls fluted with the tines of a fork, and place on a baking sheet lined with buttered wax paper. (At this point, potatoes may be refrigerated until just before serving.)

Bake medallions at 400 degrees until lightly browned, about 15 minutes. To serve, lift off sheet and place three beside each hen.

— Elaine Corn, 1983

*Roast goose with bread and cranberry stuffing. Photograph by Durell Hall Jr.*

# CORNISH HENS WITH PRUNES IN PORT-RHUBARB SAUCE

In a small bowl, soak the prunes in the port; set aside while you prepare the rest of the dish.

Cut off and discard the toxic green leaves of the rhubarb. Rinse and coarsely chop the rhubarb. Place in a medium saucepan with the onion, sugar and butter and bring to a boil, uncovered. Simmer 30 minutes, strain and set aside. Mixture will be light pink and slightly thickened.

Rinse the hens and reserve gizzards for another use.

On a plate, combine the flour, thyme, salt and pepper. Lightly dredge hens in flour mixture, shaking off excess.

Melt the 3 tablespoons butter in a heavy, wide skillet. Lay in the hens, breasts down, and brown well. Turn and brown other sides.

Remove hens from skillet. Add the wine and garlic and cook down until the wine is syrupy and about 2 tablespoons remain.

Drain prunes, reserving prunes and adding port to skillet. Cook down by half. Return hens to skillet, breasts up. Pour in chicken stock. Cover, reduce heat and simmer birds 40 minutes, or until done.

Remove hens to a warm serving platter. Strain pan juices into the reserved rhubarb sauce and simmer 5 minutes.

Arrange prunes around hens with red and green seedless grapes. Sprinkle with the grated zest of lemon. Serve with rhubarb sauce. Serves 4.

— Elaine Corn, 1985

1 cup tawny port
16 to 20 pitted prunes
1¼ pounds whole, fresh rhubarb
1 large onion, sliced
3 tablespoons sugar
½ stick butter
4 Cornish game hens
¼ cup all-purpose flour
Pinch thyme
Salt and freshly ground pepper, to taste
3 tablespoons butter
1½ cups dry red wine
2 cloves garlic, bruised
½ cup chicken stock
Red and green seedless grapes, for garnish
Zest of ¼ lemon, for garnish

# CORNISH HENS WITH HERB BUTTER

8 Cornish hens
1 lemon
½ cup butter, softened
1½ teaspoons thyme
1 tablespoon salt

Wash and dry hens thoroughly. Salt the birds, inside and out. Cut lemon into 8 slices. Using 1 slice of lemon per hen, rub each bird inside and out. Then tuck the slice into the cavity. Mix thyme with butter. Put a lump of herb-butter in each hen and dot rest of the butter on top. Tie legs together with string and place in open roasting pan. Bake at 325 degrees for 45 minutes to 1 hour, depending on the size of hens, basting with pan juices 2 or 3 times during baking. It is well to have one 12-ounce hen for each diner. A 16-ounce bird may be split into 2 modest servings.

— Lillian Marshall, 1967

# DOVE IN WINE SAUCE

*The recipe does not say so, but this should suffice for four to six doves.*

1 cup sherry
3 bay leaves
Pinch of marjoram
Dash of onion salt
2 tablespoons Worcestershire sauce
2 to 3 cups water

Salt and pepper each bird to taste. Sear in small amount of bacon fat in frying pan.

Mix ingredients, pour into frying pan,, and cover. Reduce heat to simmer. Cook until meat is tender — about an hour.

— Cissy Gregg, 1956

# MRS. FRED ENSMINGER'S WILD DUCK

*Mrs. Fred Ensminger gave the wild duck and sauce recipes to Lillian Marshall for a 1972 story. She developed the recipes cooking the bounty that resulted from duck hunting at her husband's lodge on Saginaw Bay, Michigan.*

Salt ducks thoroughly inside and out. In each duck put a few celery leaves, ¼ unpeeled apple and ½ small onion. Or stuff with your favorite bread stuffing and put celery leaves, apple and onion on top of duck.

Put ducks in a pan, breast side up, and pour over them unsweetened grapefruit juice until about 1-inch deep in pan. Season with pepper.

Cover and bake at 325 degrees for about 3 hours, basting a couple of times. Remove cover and let brown about ½ hour.

Discard celery, apple and onion before serving. Serve with sauce.

## SAUCE FOR WILD GAME OR RICE

Melt butter in pan. Add mustard and jelly and blend thoroughly. Then, add sherry, stirring constantly until sauce is very hot. Do not boil. Ladle over rice or game.

**4 ounces butter**
**4 tablespoons prepared mustard**
**4 tablespoons currant or wild grape jelly**
**1 cup dry sherry**

# CHRIS' WILD DUCK

*Dr. E. G. (Chris) Christian of Louisville gave this recipe to Lillian Marshall in 1968. A hunter who was accustomed to cooking a variety of game, he had a hunting lodge overlooking Nolin Lake.*

Soak the dressed duck overnight in water in which you have dissolved some salt and a teaspoon of soda. Dry duck well. In the cavity of each duck, place ¼ orange, ¼ onion and ¼ apple. Cover duck with soft butter and sprinkle with salt and pepper.

Place in baking pan and pour over it 2 cups of orange juice or grapefruit juice. Roast, uncovered, in 425-degee oven, about 10 minutes per pound. Wild duck is best served pink, juicy rare.

Remove duck from liquid and discard the apple, orange and onion, Stuff with wild-rice stuffing. Place bacon stips, 2 per duck, over breasts of the birds and return to hot oven for about 10 minutes, or until bacon is done and skin is crisp.

# BROME LAKE DUCKLING

*This recipe was given to Lillian Marshall in 1968 by Norah Cherry, food editor of The Winnepeg Free Press, for an issue of the Magazine honoring Canada on the 100th anniversary of its confederation.*

Wash apples. Pare and core. Cut into thick lengthwise slices. Combine salt, pepper, spices, mustard and sugar. Coat apple slices with sugar-spice mixture. Wash and dry dressed ducks. Fill cavities with apple slices. Skewer cavities closed; lace with string.

Preheat oven to 350 degrees. Place prepared ducks in roaster. Arrange four slices bacon on each duck breast. Combine cider, onion and ginger. Pour over ducks. Roast uncovered 2½ to 3 hours, basting frequently with pan juices. Remove from pan to heated platter. Take out apples and remove bacon. Leave on platter 10 to 15 minutes before carving. Serves 8 to 10.

**4 apples**
**1 teaspoon salt**
**¼ teaspoon pepper**
**½ teaspoon cinnamon**
**½ teaspoon mace**
**¼ teaspoon allspice**
**½ teaspoon dry mustard**
**2 tablespoons brown sugar**
**2 ducklings (4 to 5 pounds each)**
**8 strips lean side bacon**
**1½ cups apple cider**
**½ cup finely minced onion**
**¼ teaspoon ginger**

# JINNY'S WILD DUCK WITH PINEAPPLE

*Louisville native Jinny Schmeer Rose was living in North Carolina when she gave several game recipes to Lillian Marshall in 1968. She specialized in game cookery.*

**1 wild duck**
**6 peppercorns**
**1 tablespoon wine vinegar**
**1 tablespoon minced onion**
**Salt**
**2 bay leaves**
**Water to barely cover**
**3 tablespoons browned flour**
**⅓ cup crushed pineapple**

Cut duck down the back and wash out all blood clots. Soak in salt water at least 2 hours, preferably overnight. Place in pot and add seasonings and water. Stew until tender. Strain out and discard seasonings. To broth, add the flour mixed with the pineapple. Return duck to pot and simmer a few minutes, until duck is well coated. Serve duck and gravy over rice.

# CHINESE ROAST DUCK

**4 to 5 pound duck**
**Salt**
**2 tablespoons minced onion**
**2 tablespoons finely chopped celery**
**1½ teaspoons granulated sugar**
**¼ teaspoon ground cinnamon**
**⅛ teaspoon anise seed**
**⅓ cup soy sauce**
**2 cups water**
**2 tablespoons honey**
**2 tablespoons cider vinegar**
**1½ tablespoons soy sauce**
**3½ teaspoons salt**
**1 teaspoon cornstarch**
**2 teaspoons water**

Wash duck; remove and discard excess fat from body and neck cavities. Rub the inside lightly with salt. Combine the next 6 ingredients with 1 cup of water. Bring to boiling point. Tie duck's neck tightly with string so the sauce will not seep out while cooking. Pour hot sauce into duck cavity. Sew the opening tightly to prevent the sauce from bubbling out. Rub the outside of duck with a little of the sauce that will be left. Place duck on a rack, breast-side up, in a roasting pan. Cook in a preheated 325-degree oven 20 minutes.

Then heat remaining cup of water with the next 4 ingredients and brush over skin of the bird. Continue cooking 1½ hours or until duck is done, basting at 20-minute intervals with the sauce. Remove from oven and drain sauce into a saucepan. Thicken with cornstarch mixed with 2 teaspoons water. Cook until slightly thickened. Serve separately as gravy. Serves 4.

— Deni Hamilton, 1980

# ROAST DUCK L'ORANGE

*This is one of the recipes supplied to Elaine Corn by Vincent Ashby, chef of the governor's mansion, and Gov. Martha Layne Collins' family for the 1984 holiday-entertaining issue of the Magazine.*

Heat oven to 450 degrees. Pat ducks completely dry inside and out. Rub cavities with salt and pepper. Sprinkle skin lightly with salt. Truss ducks and prick skin around thighs, backs and lower part of breast with a sharp knife. Place breast side up in a large shallow roasting pan. Roast for 20 minutes, until skin browns slightly. Draw and discard fat from the pan with a bulb baster. Turn ducks on one side. Reduce heat to 350 degrees and roast 30 minutes. Turn birds to other side and roast 30 minutes, occasionally removing fat from pan. If pierced with a sharp knife, juices from thigh should be clear yellow. If slightly pink roast 15 minutes more. Lift ducks from pan and let juice run from cavity back into pan. Put ducks on a heated platter and cover with foil.

Remove and discard all the fat from the juices that remain. Pour brown sauce into pan. Bring to a simmer over moderate heat, scraping up any browned particles that may stick to the bottom of the pan. Remove pan from heat.

In a 2-quart heavy kettle, stir the sugar and vinegar together and bring to a boil over high heat. Cook until mixture thickens to a golden syrup. Pour in the warm brown sauce. Reduce heat to low and simmer, stirring constantly, 3 to 4 minutes. Stir in the reserved orange juice, lemon juice and currant jelly. Simmer 3 to 4 minutes. Strain sauce through a fine sieve into another saucepan. Swirl in the butter and liqueur. Season to taste with salt and pepper.

**2 5-pound ducks**
**Salt and ground black pepper**
**Brown sauce (recipe follows)**
**⅓ cup sugar**
**⅓ cup white wine vinegar**
**⅓ cup fresh lemon juice**
**¾ to 1 cup fresh squeezed orange juice**
**½ cup currant jelly**
**3 tablespoons butter**
**3 tablespoons Grand Marnier**

# BROWN SAUCE

In a large, heavy kettle, sauté the celery, onions and carrots in the drippings over medium heat until onions are transparent. Stir in the flour and cook until the mixture becomes medium brown. Add tomatoes, purée, parsley and stock. Simmer 2 hours, uncovered, until reduced by half. Skim now and then. Strain and return to pot without heating and stir to prevent skim from forming. Sauce should be the consistency of cream. Serves 6.

**½ cup beef drippings**
**2 tablespoons each celery, onions and carrots**
**½ cup flour**
**2 cups peeled and drained tomatoes, about 3 if fresh**
**1 cup tomato purée**
**½ cup coarsely chopped parsley**
**8 cups rich beef stock**

# ROAST GOOSE WITH BREAD-AND-CRANBERRY STUFFING

For an 8- to 10-pound fresh goose, smear inside and out with butter. Prick an orange and stuff inside goose cavity. Without stitching or tying, place goose on a roasting rack, then place all in a roasting pan. Roast at 400 degrees for 1 hour. Reduce heat to 325 degrees and continue roasting for 1 to 1¼ hours more. Baste frequently. When done, juices should flow beige, not pink.

Note: Here is a goose roasting chart for smaller and larger birds. The first roasting time is for 400 degrees. The second is for continued roasting at 325 degrees:

6 to 8 pounds: 45 minutes, then 1 to 1½ hours
10 to 12 pounds: 1 hour, then 2 to 2½ hours
12 to 14 pounds: 1 hour, then 2½ to 2¾ hours

## BREAD-AND-CRANBERRY STUFFING

**12 to 14 slices home-style white bread (do not use thin-sliced bread)**
**2 cups fresh cranberries, picked over and coarsely chopped**
**¼ teaspoon thyme**
**Salt and freshly ground pepper**
**2 onions, chopped**
**1 stick butter**
**2 cloves garlic, minced**
**1 cup chopped green onion tops**
**1 cup chicken broth**

Tear bread into ½-inch pieces. Lay on a large baking sheet to dry out. Toast until golden. Place in a large bowl with the cranberries, thyme, salt and pepper. Set aside. Cook the onions in butter in a covered skillet for 15 minutes over medium heat until tender. Add garlic and green onion tops. Cover and cook 5 minutes. Add to bread-cranberry mixture in bowl. Combine well, adding chicken stock as needed to moisten mixture.

If using to stuff bird, cool first. Stuff loosely in uncooked goose and roast according to above chart. Stuffing should reach an internal temperature of 165 degrees.

Or, transfer stuffing to rectangular baking dish, dot with butter, spoon over with a little more broth, cover with foil and bake at 325 degrees for 1½ hours, then uncover and bake 20 to 30 minutes more, until top is lightly browned. Makes about 8 cups.

— Elaine Corn, 1982

# BRUNCH QUAILS

*For this 1959 recipe, Cissy Gregg used trenchers to mean slices of bread or toast points on which to serve the quail.*

Sprinkle quails inside and out with salt and pepper and flour. Melt butter in a skillet. Add quails and brown on all sides. Add water and mushrooms. Cover and cook over low heat 10 minutes. Add parsley and cover. Cook 10 minutes longer, or until tender.

I must have known some tough quail in my day because personally, 20 minutes doesn't make them spoon tender, the way I like them. As a rule, I split the quail down the back and brown them under a weight with lots of butter. Add more as needed. Then when they are brown to a turn add hot water a little at a time so they are never in a swimming formation, but keep covered all the time. If you have a pan that is large enough without a cover, use a cooking foil wrap dome. They should be tender. Keep the fat flowing on them for basting and a little moisture — not too much, but enough to make them very good. The drippings from the cooking make excellent gravy. The flour in which the quail were rolled thickens it somewhat. If you have to use more, use more or a little cornstarch mixed with water.          — Cissy Gregg, 1959

**4 quails**
**Salt, pepper, flour**
**¼ cup butter and more**
**½ cup water**
**6 small mushrooms, sliced and whole**
**2 tablespoons chopped parsley**
**Slices of old ham, slightly heated, fried slices of grits or the trenchers**

# QUAIL WITH GREEN GRAPES

Sprinkle quail inside and out with salt and pepper; then flour them. Melt butter in skillet. Add water, cover and cook over low heat, 15 minutes, or until tender. Add grapes and cook 3 minutes longer. Stir in nuts and lemon juice. Serve quail on buttered-toast slices with sauce in the pan.

We learned a clever little trick to use instead of the toast slices. We made trenchers from French-bread slices or rolls.

Select bread slices or rolls slightly larger than a quail. Scoop out center from each to make a cup to hold the bird, then butter and toast lightly. Very delicious, and helps to be a complete miser with the smallest drip of the pan sauce.
          — Cissy Gregg, 1959

**4 quail**
**Salt, pepper, flour**
**¼ cup butter**
**½ cup water**
**½ cup seedless grapes, when in season, or green grapes, seeded**
**2 tablespoons chopped hazelnuts**
**1 tablespoon lemon juice**
**4 buttered-toast slices**

# OYSTER STUFFING

1 stick margarine
1 large onion, chopped
1 cup finely chopped celery stalks
  and leaves
4 cups seasoned stuffing mix
4 cups crumbled cornbread
1 pint oysters, drained and cut up
Salt and pepper
1 teaspoon poultry seasoning
About two cups rich turkey or
  chicken broth

Melt margarine and sauté onion and celery until just soft. Mix stuffing mix and cornbread well. Add onion, celery, any butter left in pan and cut-up oysters. Mix with salt and pepper and poultry seasoning. Pour in broth, a little at a time, until dressing sticks together pretty well when squeezed. You may not need all the broth.

— Lillian Marshall, 1975

# TURKEY STUFFING ALMONDINE

¾ cup whole almonds
½ cup finely chopped onion
1 cup thinly sliced celery
¾ cup butter or margarine
3 quarts soft, stale bread crumbs
¾ teaspoon salt
½ teaspoon powdered sage
½ teaspoon celery seed
¼ teaspoon black pepper
⅓ to ½ cup giblet stock, or rosé or
  sauterne wine

Coarsely chop almonds and toast in shallow pan in 400-degree oven about 6 minutes. Cook onion and celery slowly in butter 5 to 10 minutes. Pour over bread crumbs, tossing to blend. Add salt, sage, celery seed, pepper and almonds. Blend in liquid, amount depending on moisture in bread. Stuffing should be only slightly moist. Makes stuffing for 12- to 14-pound turkey.

— Lillian Marshall, 1972

# BREAD-AND-SAUSAGE STUFFING

1 pound bulk sausage
1 cup butter or margarine
1⅓ cups chopped onions
1⅓ cups chopped celery
4 cups soft bread crumbs
1 tablespoon salt
½ teaspoon pepper
1 tablespoon poultry seasoning
2 tablespoons chopped parsley
1 cup chicken stock or milk

Cook sausage and combine with remaining ingredients. This makes a moist stuffing.

But before you do this we would like to give you our findings on sausage fat. We tried using part of the fat from the sausage to substitute for part of the butter or margarine but it was to rich that way — heavy rich, that is.

You might try making the stuffing in this way: First, fry out the sausage, remove the meat, and add to the bread. Pour off part of the fat left in the skillet, and sauté the onion and celery in it. Lift these out with a slotted spoon and add to the crumbs, adding the other ingredients as given.

For a dry stuffing, toast the bread crumbs in a moderate oven, and add only enough stock or milk to blend thoroughly.

The amount above makes enough stuffing for a 12-pound turkey. Or use it for a 10-pound turkey and have some left over for balls or for five or six stuffing molds. Stuffing in greased individual molds should be baked 30 minutes at 350-degrees.

— Cissy Gregg, 1954

# SAUSAGE-CORN BREAD DRESSING

Fry sausage, stirring to crumble, until done but not brown. Remove to paper towel to drain. Pour off most of fat, leaving only about one tablespoon in skillet. Sauté celery and onion until tender. Reserve with sausage.

Stir cornmeal, flour, baking powder and salt together. Beat eggs into milk, then beat mixture into dry ingredients. Bake in preheated, greased 9-inch skillet for about 25 minutes at 425 degrees. Cool and crumble. Add seasonings, celery, onion and sausage, and stir in enough hot broth to make desired consistency. Grease a 9- by 12-inch baking pan, and with a spoon or ice-cream scoop, make mounds of dressing close together. Bake about 45 minutes to an hour at 325 or 350 degrees, or until lightly browned. Temperature is not critical; you can compromise the heat with whatever else you are baking at the same time.          — Lillian Marshall, 1977

1 pound sausage (hot or mild, as desired)
3 ribs celery, chopped
2 medium onions, chopped
2 cups cornmeal
2 cups flour
4 teaspoons baking powder
2 teaspoons salt
2 eggs
2 tablespoons poultry seasoning
2½ cups milk
1 tablespoon (or more) sage
Hot turkey or chicken broth for consistency

# LEMON-BARBECUED TURKEY WINGS

Combine the cup oil with garlic, salt, lemon juice, onion, pepper and thyme and refrigerate overnight. Cut off the bony tip from each turkey wing and save for making broth another time. Dredge wings in flour. Heat butter and the 2 tablespoons oil together and brown turkey wings slowly in it on all sides. Transfer wings to a Dutch oven. Pour the refrigerated oil mixture over them. Cover tightly and simmer or bake in a preheated 325-degree oven for about 1½ hours or until tender. Serves 8. Recipe can be halved to serve 4.          — Deni Hamilton, 1980

1 cup oil plus 2 tablespoons
2 cloves garlic, minced
1 teaspoon salt
2 cups lemon juice
1 large chopped onion
1 teaspoon pepper
2 teaspoons thyme
8 turkey wings
Flour
2 tablespoons butter or margarine

# SAUTÉED TURKEY BREAST SLICES WITH MADEIRA GLAZE

6 to 8 fresh turkey breast slices
1 egg, lightly beaten
Flour, for dredging
Salt and fresh ground pepper
⅛ teaspoon dried sage
2 tablespoons butter
¼ cup Madeira wine
1 cup chicken stock

Dip each slice of turkey in egg, then coat lightly with flour combined with salt, pepper and sage. Lay on a plate until ready to use.

In a wide skillet, melt the butter over medium-high heat. Carefully lay in the slices. Without reducing heat, cook 1½ to 2 minutes per side, then remove to paper towels. Add Madeira to skillet and let it boil until a syrupy tablespoon remains. Add stock and boil until mixture is reduced by one-half. Place slices in sauce, flip to coat and place on serving plates poured over with the glaze. Serves 4.
— Elaine Corn, 1984

# TURKEY TETRAZZINI

1 medium onion, chopped
¼ cup butter or margarine
¼ cup all-purpose flour
1½ cups turkey or chicken broth
1 cup heavy cream
1 teaspoon salt
⅛ teaspoon pepper
½ cup dry vermouth
¾ cup grated parmesan cheese
1 4-ounce can sliced mushrooms, drained
3 cups cooked, diced turkey
12 ounces spaghetti, cooked according to package directions

Sauté onion in butter until almost tender. Blend in flour, and gradually stir in broth and cream. Stir over medium heat until sauce comes to a boil. Add salt, pepper, vermouth and ¼ cup of the cheese. In a large bowl, combine mushrooms, turkey and cooked spaghetti. Put in a 2½-quart casserole. Pour sauce over top, and sprinkle with remaining ½ cup of cheese. Bake in a preheated 375-degree oven 20 minutes or until bubbly. Serves six.

May be frozen before or after baking. Return to room temperature before putting in oven.
— Deni Hamilton, 1980

# ABOUT TURKEY

*Every year, as Thanksgiving Day approaches, The Courier-Journal kitchen and the Cook's Corner column receive numerous queries about stuffing and roasting turkey. In 1974, Lillian Marshall prepared these guidelines. In one form or another, they are reprinted every year.*

In estimating the size turkey to buy, it is wise to purchase a pound (ready-to-cook weight) per person. If you buy turkey breast, calculate eight to 10 ounces (ready-to-cook weight) per person.

Frozen turkey is best thawed in its original wrapper in the refrigerator, and it will take from two days for a 12-pounder to three days or more for a bird weighing more than 20 pounds. Next best way to thaw, and faster, is in cold water. Leave turkey in its original wrapper and cover with cold water. Change water often during thawing. Cook or refrigerate as soon as it is thawed. A 12-pound turkey will thaw in this manner in approximately six hours; 20-pounds or more will take up to 10 hours.

Some turkeys are self-basting — meaning that butter, fat or stock has been injected into the meat — the wrapper will tell you. If it is, there will be no need for you to baste it as it roasts.

To prevent growth of bacteria, never stuff bird until it is ready to go into the oven. Never partially roast any fowl and finish cooking it the next day. Always remove all stuffing before refrigerating or freezing leftover fowl, and store stuffing separately.

# ROAST TURKEY

Wash and dry thawed turkey, including cavities. Rub inside and outside with a cut lemon (you can use most of the juice for something else) then open up the rind and "scrub" the turkey with it. Next, coat bird well with oil or butter. Mix the seasonings together and massage them into the meat, putting some into cavities as well. Stuff neck and body cavities with stuffing. Close and truss. Place on rack in open roasting pan and roast, uncovered, at 325 degrees until meat thermometer inserted into thickest part of thigh, not touching bone, registers 180 degrees. Or roast according to this timetable:

**12-pound turkey**
½ **lemon**
½ **stick (¼ cup) butter or**
    **margarine, melted, or use oil**
1 **tablespoon salt**
½ **teaspoon pepper**
½ **teaspoon rosemary, crushed well**
¼ **teaspoon thyme**
½ **teaspoon paprika**

| WEIGHT OF TURKEY | APPROXIMATE TIME AT 325 DEGREES |
|---|---|
| 8-12 pounds | 4½ to 4¾ hours |
| 12-16 pounds | 4¾ to 5¾ hours |
| 16-20 pounds | 5¾ to 6 hours |

# TURKEY HASH

*"Nothing could be better than turkey hash," Cissy Gregg once wrote. "It has always been my conten-
tion that all the turkey should be made into hash." The sauce should be "thick and well seasoned," she
wrote. Cissy served this 1952 recipe with cornmeal batter cakes.*

Since the sauce — or gravy — is of utmost importance, we'll start at that point. To
accomplish this, call on every particle that remains of the turkey, except the meat. Don't let
anything go to waste.

In the begining, take all the meat off the carcass. Remove the skin. Cut the meat into as large
pieces as you can and have enough to go through the hash. Place in a bowl and put in the
refrigerator, so it will stay juicy and at its best.

Break up the carcass, toss in the skin, add any gravy that might have been left over, place all
together in a heavy saucepan and cover with cold water. Bring gently to a boil, turn down the
heat and allow the bones to simmer for as long as you can — 2 or 3 hours. Or if you use a heavy
saucepan with a tight-fitting cover, a simmering burner or a thrift cooker, add a little extra
water, if you'll feel better about it, and allow the bones to simmer through the night while your
little head is comfortably resting on your pillow. You just want to be sure you get everything
the bones and trimmings have to offer.

If, when you have simmered the bones, the broth seems a little "pale" in flavor, give thanks
that you are living in modern times which provide chicken bouillon cubes or canned chicken
broth and monosodium glutamate to heighten the flavor.

If time allows, let the broth chill and remove the fat.

Strain the broth. If you care to, add a potato or two peeled and diced. Simmer-boil until
tender. Add salt and pepper to taste. While the potatoes are cooking, sauté a chopped, medium-
sized onion and a rib or two of thinly sliced celery in butter, margarine or turkey fat. Sauté
slowly so the onion and celery cooks but does not brown. Add to the broth.

There are two ways to thicken the hash. One is to make a roux of a tablespoon of butter,
margarine or turkey fat and a tablespoon of flour. Cook it together and allow it to brown or not,
as you like, before adding gradually to hot broth to make a smooth sauce. Then add the meat.
The other way is to add the chopped meat to the clear broth and heat together in a double
boiler, thickening at the last moment by adding a tablespoon of flour, creamed with a
tablespoon of butter, and allowing it to cook for a minute or two until it becomes thickened.

Again some like to thicken the gravy with a little cornstarch blended to a smooth paste with
cold water. This makes a clearer gravy as a background for the meat than the flour-butter
blend.

Just be sure your seasoning is good. Add the cut-up turkey meat only long enough before
serving to be heated through and through.

By the time we had made the broth for the hash, had a look at the cut-up turkey meat, and
tasted the perfection of the seasonings, it suddenly occurred to us that the second exhibition of
our turkey was good enough to make a company meal, and much too good to keep to ourselves.

# SEAFOOD

# POTTED LOBSTER

2 large onions, finely chopped
3 cloves garlic, finely minced
6 lobster tails in shell, thawed if frozen (see note)
½ cup cooking oil
½ stick butter
½ cup brandy
3 tablespoons tomato paste
1 fish bouillon cube dissolved in 2 cups hot water
1 cup dry white wine
Salt and ground black pepper, to taste
1 to 2 teaspoons cayenne pepper
3 egg yolks
¼ cup fresh chopped parsley

Place onions and garlic in a pot with water to cover and simmer, covered, for 30 minutes. Meanwhile, slice lobster according to natural divisions in tails. Heat the oil and butter in a wide, heavy skillet over medium-high heat. Add lobster, shells down, and sauté without disturbing until shells turn red, about 15 minutes. Transfer lobster with a slotted spoon to heated Dutch oven or heavy kettle. Pour in brandy and immediately light with match. Remove from heat and let flame extinguish itself. Keep warm.

Drain onions and garlic. Add to skillet where lobster was sautéed. Add paste, fish stock and wine, stirring until heated through. Add salt, black and cayenne pepper. Sauce should be spicy. Combine a little sauce with egg yolks, then add yolks to skillet, stirring over low heat until slightly thickened. Pour sauce into pot with lobster. Sprinkle with parsley. Serve hot or warm. Serves 10.

Note: Dish may be made with 3 pounds of peeled medium shrimp. Reduce skillet cooking time to 8 minutes, turning shrimp once.

— Elaine Corn, 1984

# SCROD BAKED EN PAPILLOTE (OR IN ALUMINUM FOIL)

2 pounds scrod (or flounder, sole or haddock)
2 tablespoons olive oil or light vegetable oil, such as corn, safflower or sunflower
1 cup thinly sliced onions
2 cloves garlic, minced
2 cups thinly sliced muchrooms
Bay leaf
2 teaspoons thyme or summer savory
2 teaspoons oregano
Salt and pepper, to taste
Additional oil
Fresh chopped parsley

Heat oven to 500 degrees. Cut fish into four equal portions (if pieces are large) and set aside. Cut parchment paper or aluminum foil into large figure 8's, 18 inches long and 12 inches wide.

Heat the oil in a skillet. Add the onions, garlic and mushrooms. Add bay leaf, thyme (or summer savory) and oregano, salt and pepper, and cook until onions are slightly wilted. Brush paper or foil with oil. Place fish portions in center of one rounded half of the figure-8 paper. Spoon filling equally over fish. Sprinkle with parsley. Fold other half of the "8" over, and crimp edges to seal.

Place packages on a baking sheet, and bake 10 minutes, no longer. Bring packages to table and serve individually. Serve with lemon wedges. Makes four servings.

— Elaine Corn, 1985

# GRAVAD LAX
# (SALT- AND SUGAR-CURED SALMON FILLETS)

Remove bone slivers from fillets with tweezers. Place a fillet skin-side down in a glass baking dish. Stir together salt, sugar and pepper. Spoon half the mixture over fillet, rubbing into flesh. Sprinkle dill over cure.

Rub second fillet in same manner and carefully place over first fillet, flesh sides together. Cover dish loosely with foil. Put a brick on fish, or a board weighted down with heavy canned goods.

Refrigerate 3 to 4 days, turning fish now and then. Use a bulb baster to distribute leached juices back between fillets.

To serve, scrape cure off fillets. Place on board and slice diagonally and thinly, following grain of salmon and guiding knife between skin and flesh to release fish from skin. Slip wide knife under fillets and transfer slices to serving platter. Garnish with parsley, large capers and white horseradish.

Serves 12 to 14.

— Elaine Corn, 1984

**2 matching, unskinned salmon fillets, about 2 pounds, from center of fish**
**¾ cup salt, preferably coarse**
**½ cup granulated sugar**
**1 tablespoon peppercorns, coarsely crushed**
**2 tablespoons fresh or dried dill weed**

# OYSTER STEW WITH CREAM

The oyster stew known throughout the land is the one served at the Oyster Bar in Grand Central Terminal, New York. The recipe has been kept within the restaurant for years, but the Oyster Institute got it from them so we could give it to you.

This is a serving recipe, as they would make it to order. You can increase it as you wish.

Place in a deep pan a dash of Worcestershire sauce, paprika, celery salt and a pat of butter. Add 7 fresh oysters and half a cup oyster liquor. Cook until oysters' edges curl. Add 1 cup cream and bring to a boil. Pour in bowl and top with paprika and 1 pat of butter.

Serve hot with oyster crackers.

— Cissy Gregg, 1954

# LEO'S OYSTER FISH STUFFING

*Cissy Gregg used this stuffing for a lake-trout recipe in 1957. She recommended baking it at 400 degrees, allowing about 10 minutes per pound.*

¼ to ½ cup butter or margarine
2 cups bread crumbs or cubes
1 to 2 tablespoons lemon juice
1 tablespoon finely chopped parsley
½ teaspoon sage (if you like it)
½ teaspoon salt
⅛ teaspoon pepper, or to taste
1 pint oysters

We have stuffed fish with a crab stuffing, we looked over a cucumber stuffing, a bacon stuffing and a bacon and mushroom stuffing. Having toyed with these ideas, we took the one we gleaned from Leo Weil of Leo's Hideaway and decided he should know. This makes enough for a 3- to 4-pound fish.

The amount of butter used depends on the type of fish — the leaner the fish, the more the butter or margarine.

Heat butter, add onion and bread crumbs or cubes. Stir over low heat until bread is slightly browned. Add other ingredients and the oysters (we added some of the oysters to the stuffing, and then saved some for the sauce). Stuff the fish, but never fill the cavity more than ⅔ full. Close the cavity with skewers, or sew closed with white thread. Into the oven it goes!

The accompanying sauce was simply a cream sauce, well seasoned, with oysters and sauteed mushrooms added for the special occasions.

# LOUISVILLE ROLLED OYSTERS

*This recipe was printed in the Cook's Corner column in response to requests for information about rolled oysters, the Louisville invention that is associated with Mazzoni Oysters.*

½ cup flour
1 teaspoon baking powder
¼ teaspoon salt
1 well-beaten egg
¼ cup milk or more if needed
18 medium-sized oysters, drained
1 cup or more white corn meal or
    cracker meal, enough in which to
    roll batter-coated oysters
Lard or vegetable shortening for
    frying oysters

Sift the flour, baking powder and salt together. Beat the egg and milk and add to flour mixture. It should be stiff, but if too stiff to coat the oysters, add a little more milk. Beat smooth. Put all the oysters in this and coat them well.

Take three batter-coated oysters at a time and form them in the hand into a croquette. Then quickly roll the croquette in the meal, covering completely. The trick is to prevent the individual oysters from escaping the roll and separating when fried. I find it best to coat them a second time, putting the rolled croquettes back once more into the batter, then giving them another dusting of corn meal or cracker meal.

The six rolled oysters are now ready for frying. They do not suffer one whit if made up in the

*Photograph by Robert Steinau.*

morning and fried in the evening. When ready to fry, treat the oysters as you would doughnuts. Have a pan of deep lard on the stove. Heat to 375 degrees, put the oysters in a basket and lower them into the fat. Do not cook too quickly, as they should be cooked through. I lower the heat as soon as they hit the fat. They should cook on both sides at once if enough fat is in the pan. If not, cook on one side, turn with pancake turner and cook on the other.

This will take about three to four minutes all together. Drain on absorbent paper. Cook only three of these oysters at a time and leave space around them so that they can brown evenly. Serve hot. Six servings.

# LIME TROUT

Trout is often overcooked and mishandled with too much batter and too many almonds. All you need for trout is a little flour, butter or oil, lemon or lime and fresh parsley.

Pat fish dry. Open trout and stuff with a garlic sliver, lime wedge and parsley. Holding edges together, run trout through flour or crumbs seasoned with salt and pepper, shaking off excess.

Heat the oil in a large skillet. When hot, add the butter, taking care the butter doesn't burn. Add fish. Cook on medium-high heat about four to five minutes a side, until well-browned. Turn carefully using two spatulas to prevent fish from breaking.

Transfer fish to a warmed serving platter. Sprinkle fish with parsley and tuck lime wedges between fish. Put remaining butter and lime juice into skillet. Whisk into pan juices until smooth and thickened, just until butter melts. Pour over fish. Serve immediately. Makes four servings.

— Elaine Corn, 1985

**4 Kentucky trout, preferably heads on, gutted and cleaned**
**1 clove garlic, quartered lengthwise into slivers**
**4 thin wedges lime**
**4 large tufts of parsley**
**Flour, for dredging (or use fine crumbs made from biscuits, cornbread or whole-wheat bread)**
**Salt and black pepper, to taste**
**2 tablespoons olive oil**
**2 or 3 tablespoons butter**
**2 tablespoons fresh chopped parsley**
**Additional quartered limes**
**2 tablespoons butter**
**3 tablespoons lime juice (from about 2 limes)**

# CECILIA'S CEBICHE

*Cecilia Ardery, a native of Ecuador, gave this recipe to Carol Sutton, senior editor of The Courier-Journal, for a Magazine food feature in 1981.*

**1 pound fresh shrimp**
**1½ cups fresh orange juice**
**6 tablespoons tomato catsup**
**1 medium-size red onion (cut in half)**
**1 raw carrot (cut in half)**
**2 lemons**
**Hot-pepper sauce**

Chop one-half onion into small pieces. Put the pieces in a bowl with salt and the juice of two lemons.

Peel and devein the shrimp. Put 3 cups of water in a pan. Drop in the other one-half onion, the carrot halves and the celery stalks. Heat. When this has come to a boil and the celery begins to soften, add salt and the cleaned shrimp. Boil for 3 minutes, remove from heat and drain. Wash shrimp in cold water.

Mix the orange juice and catsup in a bowl. Add hot-pepper sauce and salt to taste. Add the chopped onion soaked in lemon juice. Chill shrimp and sauce for about an hour in the refrigerator.

Serve in individual bowls or champagne glasses. The shrimp can either be dropped into the sauce before serving or served around the top of the container. Decorate with parsley and a lemon wedge. Serve with a bowl of popcorn. Serves 6.

# CEVICHE

**½ pound swordfish**
**½ pound orange roughie or flounder fillets**
**½ pound bay scallops**
**½ cup fresh lime juice**
**1 tomato, seeded and cut in chunks**
**1 tablespoon finely minced fresh jalapeño**
**2 tablespoons minced bell pepper**
**¼ cup fresh chopped coriander (cilantro) leaves, or 2 tablespoons dried**
**¼ cup olive oil**
**Salt and pepper, to taste**
**1 avocado, peeled and cut in ½-inch chunks**

Rinse swordfish and orange roughie, and cut into ½-inch cubes. Place in a large bowl with scallops and remaining ingredients. Chill overnight, turning mixture occasionally. Serve ice cold with additional lime wedges. Serves 6.

— Elaine Corn, 1984

# MONKFISH IN WINE AND CREAM SAUCE

Monkfish has rich, lobster-like flesh. The French call it lotte, which sounds better than monkfish. Its head is bigger than its body, and sometimes it is called bellyfish. Monkfish is rich-tasting and may need a fraction of extra cooking beyond the eight-to-10-minutes-an-inch formula. You won't need salt in this recipe, as the fish stock is salty on its own.

Soak the shallots in a few tablespoons of the wine.

Turn the monkfish on its pinkish side and slice into "steaks" about 1 to 1¼ inches thick.

In a wide skillet, heat the butter and oil until hot but not smoking. Add the shallots (and the wine they soaked in) and sauté until softened, a minute or two.

Add mushrooms, the parsley (saving some for garnish), saffron and a spoonful or two of fish stock to loosen mixture in pan.

Place fish on top of shallots and mushrooms. Add remaining wine and stock. Bring to a simmer. Cover, reduce heat and simmer seven to 10 minutes (no longer), turning fish over halfway through cooking.

Remove fish to a warmed serving dish and keep fish warm. Strain vegetables. Place vegetables over fish and return cooking liquid to skillet.

Reduce liquid until thickened, about three to four minutes of boiling. Stir in the cream and reduce again until thick, about three minutes. Season with white pepper to taste. Whisk in remaining butter to finish sauce. Pour over fish. Sprinkle with parsley from on high. Serve immediately. Makes four to six servings.

— Elaine Corn, 1985

2 shallots, finely chopped
1 cup dry white wine
1 to 1½ pounds monkfish, grouper
   or bass
1 stick butter
2 tablespoons oil
½ pound mushrooms, thinly sliced
2 tablespoons fresh chopped
   parsley
Pinch saffron
1 cup fish stock (may use fish
   bouillon)
¾ cup heavy cream or half-and-half
White pepper, to taste
2 tablespoons additional butter

# SHRIMP SCAMPI

*Language purists have fits over the name of this dish. Strictly speaking, it translates as "shrimp shrimp," but the dish has become so widespread and popular under this name that countless restaurant-goers know it only as shrimp with a butter and garlic sauce. Deni Hamilton ran this recipe in 1980.*

1 pound raw, shelled shrimp
1 stick (¼ pound) butter
4 large cloves garlic, minced
White pepper
1 lemon, thinly sliced
½ cup dry white wine
Fresh, minced parsley

Melt the butter, add the garlic, a pinch of pepper and the lemon slices. Sauté very gently until butter and garlic browns ever so slightly. Add the shrimp. Stir and cook over low heat until curled and pink, about five minutes. Serve immediately, sprinkled with parsley. Serves 2 to 4. (This also makes an excellent hot hors d'oeuvre.)

# GRILLED MARINATED SALMON

*This was among the recipes supplied by Louisville hostess Tommie O'Callaghan for a 1983 Magazine food feature by Elaine Corn.*

Whole salmon, fresh or frozen,
   belly slit and gutted
½ pound butter
1 large clove garlic
Juice of 2 limes
Garnishes: Sliced lime, parlsey,
   freshly ground pepper
Dill sauce (see recipe)

Melt butter and mix in garlic and lime juice. Pour over and brush inside of salmon. Marinate in mixture 2 hours or more. Place salmon on grill preheated to medium to low heat. Cook salmon about 20 minutes on each side, brushing on marinade after turning. At serving, garnish with sliced lime, parsley and freshly ground pepper. Serve with dill sauce.

## DILL SAUCE

Combine about 1 cup good mayonnaise, homemade, if you can, with lots of fresh dill. Let it sit, chilled, at least 24 hours so flavors can meld.

# OYSTER FRITTERS

1 pint oysters
2 cups sifted flour
1 tablespoon baking powder
2 eggs, beaten
1½ teaspoons salt
1 cup milk
1 tablespoon melted fat

Drain oysters and chop. Sift dry ingredients together. Combine beaten eggs, milk and fat. Pour into dry ingredients and stir until smooth. Add oysters. Drop batter by teaspoonfuls into fat, heated to 350 degrees, and fry about 3 minutes or until golden brown. Turn gently to brown on both sides. Drain on absorbent peper. Serves about six.

— Cissy Gregg, 1954

# PAN-FRIED OYSTERS

Drain oysters. Combine eggs, milk and seasonings. Combine crumbs and flour. Roll oysters in crumb mixture, dip in egg and coat again with crumbs. Fry in hot fat at moderate heat (about 350 degrees) until brown on one side. Turn carefully and brown the other side. Cooking time, approximately 5 minutes. Drain on absorbent pepper, serve with lemon wedges. Serves 6.

— Lillian Marshall, 1969

**2 cans (12 ounce each) fresh shucked oysters**
**2 eggs, beaten**
**2 tablespoons milk**
**1 teaspoon salt**
**Dash pepper**
**1½ cups dry bread crumbs**
**1½ cups flour**
**Lemon wedges**

# CHESAPEAKE OYSTER LOAF

Cut off the top crust of a loaf of French bread and scoop out the inside. Butter ⅓ of the scooped-out portion, and toast it in the oven.

Fry oysters in butter. Add the cream, celery, salt, pepper, Tabasco sauce and the toasted bread.

Fill hollowed loaf with the mixture. Cover with the top crust and bake 20 minutes at 350 degrees, basting frequently with oyster liquor. Slice and serve very hot.

— Cissy Gregg, 1943

**1 loaf French bread**
**Butter**
**2 dozen oysters, drained with liquor reserved**
**½ cup cream**
**1 tablespoon chopped celery**
**2 dashes Tabasco sauce**
**Salt and pepper**

# TROUT MEUNIÈRE

*Clarified butter is the clear part of melted butter. To clarify butter, melt it and pour off the clear part, leaving behind the white, cloudy portion.*

**½ cup milk**
**¼ cup flour**
**Salt and freshly ground pepper**
**2 medium trout, about 9 ounces each**
**1 tablespoon clarified butter**
**2 tablespoons oil**
**2 more tablespoons butter**
**2 tablespoons fresh, chopped parsley**
**Juice of 1 lemon**

Place the milk in a shallow bowl. In another shallow bowl, combine the flour with the salt and pepper. Dip trout in milk, then dip in flour and shake off excess. In a heavy skillet heat the oil and clarified butter over medium heat. Add the trout and sauté 3 to 5 minutes per side, or until it begins to turn light gold. Remove fish to a platter lightly stroked with butter and keep warm. Add the next 2 tablespoons butter to the skillet and brown. While butter browns sprinkle fish with parsley. Add lemon juice to the butter, let sizzle a second or two and scrape up any browned bits from the bottom of the skillet. Pour lemon-butter over fish and serve immediately. Serves 2.

— Elaine Corn, 1982

# SCALLOPED OYSTERS

1 12-ounce can fresh oysters,
 drained
2 cups soft bread crumbs
½ teaspoon salt
⅛ teaspoon pepper
¼ cup melted butter or margarine
1 teaspoon Worcestershire sauce
1 cup milk
½ cup chopped onions
½ cup chopped bell pepper

While oysters drain, combine crumbs, salt, pepper and butter. Place ⅓ of the crumb mixture in a buttered casserole dish. Cover with a layer of oyster, then onion and green pepper. Repeat layers. Sprinkle remaining crumbs over top. Add Worcestershire sauce to milk, and pour over all. Bake in a preheated 350-degree oven for 30 minutes, or until brown. Serves 6.

— Deni Hamilton, 1979

# ANGELS ON HORSEBACK

1 pint select-size oysters
12 slices bacon
½ teaspoon salt
⅛ teaspoon pepper
⅛ teaspoon paprika
2 tablespoons fresh minced parsley

Drain oysters and lay each across half a slice of bacon. Sprinkle with seasonings. Roll bacon around oyster and fasten with a wooden toothpick. Place oysters on a rack in shallow baking pan and bake in preheated 450-degree oven for 10 minutes, or until bacon is crisp. Serves 6.

— Deni Hamilton, 1980

# BROILED SWORDFISH

To serve four to six people, buy 2 pounds of swordfish steak. Cut into serving pieces. Sprinkle the pieces with salt, pepper and paprika. Preheat the broiler about 10 minutes. Place the fish on the preheated broiler pan 2 inches below the flame. Dot with butter or margarine, and dot generously. Broil 3 to 4 minutes on one side, and turn.

Dot with butter or margarine again and broil 4 minutes — or until light brown. Slip onto a hot platter and serve with lemon butter sauce or black olive sauce.

## BLACK OLIVE SAUCE

Have your sauce butter melted and well seasoned with lemon juice, salt and pepper. Add chopped ripe olives to it. Put on the stove until it's hot and serve over the swordfish.

The amount of ripe olives depends on how much you like them and on your conscience. I love them, so ours was rather "olive-ee."

— Cissy Gregg, 1954

# SNAILS WITH GARLIC BUTTER

Cream butter and add to it the finely chopped shallots, crushed garlic, chopped parsley, salt and pepper. I use Tabasco sauce when I'm dressing them up for myself.

The shells are packed along with the canned snails, so put a little butter in each of the 24 shells. Put a snail in each shell and cover with the remaining butter. Pour wine into a flat baking dish. Arrange the shells in the dish and sprinkle them with fine bread crumbs. Bake the shells in a very hot oven or put the dish under the broiler until the crumbs are golden brown. Serve immediately.

For home use, I serve the snails in the baking dish, with the juices, and as implements have oyster forks for the digging out. In the end there should be chunks of hot French bread to pick up the juices. If you aren't sure of your seasonings, have a little lemon handy. I don't think you'll need it, but it might be a gift to please, and we do want all to like snails.

— Cissy Gregg, 1960

**24 snails**
**⅓ pound butter**
**1 teaspoon finely chopped shallots**
**2 cloves garlic, crushed**
**½ tablespoon finely chopped parsley**
**1 teaspoon salt**
**Pepper, to taste**
**Tabasco sauce (optional)**
**2 tablespoons dry white wine**
**Fine bread crumbs**

# JOE'S FRIED FISH

*Not everyone has enough bacon grease around to satisfy the requirements of this recipe. Cooking oil can be added or substituted to fry the fish, but then, of course, it won't be the version named for Deni Hamilton's father.*

Dry the fish, and roll in the pancake mix, adding a little cornmeal to the mix if desired. Salt and pepper to taste. Cover the fish, and allow to dry in the refrigerator about half an hour (this keeps the coating on the fish as it fries). Heat the bacon grease so that it's at least ½-inch deep in the skillet. Place the fish in the hot grease over medium-high heat, and fry until browned. Carefully turn fish over to brown on other side. Drain on paper towels before serving. Fish takes very little time to cook, so watch out for overcooking. Disregard that old fish-cooking adage to "cook until flakes easily." Following that advice, the fish will be cooked too long, losing its moist texture and some of its flavor.

**Fish (with bone in, about 1 pound per person)**
**Pancake mix (dry)**
**Cornmeal (optional)**
**Salt and pepper to taste**
**Bacon grease**

# MISSISSIPPI RIVER CHANNEL CATFISH

*Lillian Marshall wrote about this and other recipes from a menu planned for a special towboat excursion given in 1968 for a group of government, communications, civic and industrial leaders.*

Skin the fish. Remove all dorsal and stabilizing fins with knife and pliers. Remove innards and clean thoroughly. Chill well. Dip in seasoned flour, then dip in egg wash made by beating egg with 1 tablespoon water. Dip in seasoned cornmeal and fry in deep fat heated to 375 degrees for about 10 minutes, time depending on the size of fish. Seasoned flour or meal means adding salt, pepper and paprika to taste.

# PAN-FRIED TROUT

Rinse and dry trout. Use corn meal, salt and pepper to coat trout. Pan should contain enough peanut or vegetable oil to half cover the trout. The oil should not be smoking, but hot. If the oil is the correct temperature, the trout's tail will sizzle when placed in the hot oil. Place trout in pan so as not to touch other trout. When golden brown, turn with spatula and cook on other side. Serve with sauce on a hot dish, or serve with sauce in accompaniment. Don't overcook.

Serving trout is so easy. You can fillet them for your guests or let them do it for themselves. One more point we would like for you to remember: Trout has no fish-odor to it for handling or cooking, and leaves only the remembrance of how good it was and the great desire for more.

Lemon wedges should always go along with trout or any fish for that matter.

Lillian Marshall, 1962

# HELEN'S OYSTER STEW

*In 1948 Cissy Gregg preceded this recipe with a note that "people who deal with food develop a one-track mind. They can never get off the subject and can never resist probing acquaintances or friends in the search of something new. I met a kindred spirit in New York who has really contributed much to my cooking. The recipes to date have been superlative."*

Combine 3 tablespoons butter and 1 tablespoon oil in a heavy saucepan. Heat slowly and add 2 tablespoons chopped garlic. Cook 3 minutes and add one small onion very finely chopped. Cook 2 minutes and stir in 2½ cups rich milk. (Use top milk or just milk to which a goodly amount of cream has been added — I used the latter method). Add salt and a bit of cayenne. Stir to a boil. Add a pinch of mustard, a pinch of chili pepper, ½ teaspoon dry thyme (this makes it), and ¼ cup oyster juice drained from the oysters. Cook 3 minutes — only! Add one dozen large oysters and 3 tablespoons whipped cream, or you can add real heavy cream, unwhipped. After the oysters are in, do not cook more than 2 minutes. Serve in heated bowls.

The instructions that came with the recipe said it would serve "three or four," and perhaps it would as a first course, but when I have oyster stew, I like a meal of it, and so for four, I doubled the recipe and came out with an empty saucepan and four people who said it was "out of this world," and that they were as full as ticks. It was a meal with only broiled grapefruit added.

# COLD SPICY SHRIMP

In a mixing bowl, combine the shrimp, tomato, olives and green onion. Stir in salt and pepper. In another bowl, stir together sour cream and chili sauce, then combine with the shrimp mixture. Spoon a few tablespoons of filling down the center of each crepe. Serves 2.

— Elaine Corn, 1983

1 cup chopped, fresh boiled shrimp
1 tiny tomato, diced
¼ cup chopped black olives
1 green onion and tops, finely sliced
Salt and freshly ground pepper, to taste
¼ cup sour cream
¼ cup chili sauce
4 basic crepes

## A GOOD BASIC CRÊPE

Beat the eggs and egg yolk. Add the flour and salt alternately with the milk, and keep beating until smooth. Beat in the melted butter. Refrigerate batter 2 hours.

Brush a crêpe pan or round-sided skillet 7 or 8 inches in diameter with oil or melted butter. Pour off excess. Heat pan until hot enough to bounce a water droplet. Using a ¼-cup ladle or measure, dip into crêpe batter and pour batter into skillet.

Quickly tilt the pan to move the batter evenly around the pan as thinly as possible. Cook 1 minute. Shake pan to loosen crepe. Flip, or turn over with a spatula. The first side that cooked is the "good" side. Cook second side 30 seconds more. Stack crepes between pieces of waxed paper until ready to use. Or wrap the stack in foil, freeze, then thaw at room temperature. Makes about 18 crêpes.

— Elaine Corn, 1982

4 eggs plus 1 egg yolk
1½ cups flour
Dash of salt
1½ cups milk
¼ stick butter, melted

# DAVE MAURER'S TROUT IN BEER

*In 1969, Lillian Marshall went to fisherman David Maurer for a food feature on Kentucky fishing. Maurer also was a University of Louisville English professor.*

For each pan-ready fish, tear a sheet of heavy foil large enough to wrap and seal completely. Place a slice of bacon on foil, lay fish on bacon, season with salt and pepper to taste and sprinkle with a little onion salt. Or chop a small green onion onto the fish. Lay another strip of bacon over the fish, then bring up long sides of foil and fold down twice. Fold and seal ends. Lay packet on coals. Depending on the size of the fish and the heat of your coals, turn the fish over after 7 to 10 minutes, or when about half-done. Continue cooking for another 5 minutes. Open the seam carefully and pour in about ¼ cup beer, pinch foil loosely together and let steam for 2 or 3 minutes.

# CASSEROLES

# CASSOULET

2 pounds Great Northern beans
½ pound salt pork
½ pound pork rind
1 pound cut-up lamb, leg or
    shoulder
1 pound pork loin, whole piece
1 4- to 5-pound duck
Salt and ground black pepper to
    taste
1 onion, sliced
2 onions, chopped
3 cloves garlic, minced
2 tomatoes, peeled, seeded and
    coarsely chopped
3 tablespoons tomato paste
2 carrots, halved
2 ribs celery, halved
2 teaspoons fresh thyme, or 1
    teaspoon dried
1 bay leaf
½ teaspoon ground black pepper
4 cups chicken or beef stock
1 pound garlic sausage (or kielbasa)
¾ cup fresh bread crumbs
¼ cup fresh chopped parsley
Fresh thyme, or dried, for garnish

Sort and wash beans well. Place beans, whole pieces of salt pork and rind in a large casserole with water to cover. On low heat, bring beans very slowly to a boil. Boil about 1½ hours covered.

Meanwhile, place lamb, pork and duck in separate roasting pans. Sprinkle with salt, pepper and sliced onion. Begin in oven preheated to 450 degrees and immediately reduce heat to 375. Roast lamb 25 minutes, the pork 1 hour and the duck 1½ hours. Baste the pork and duck with their own juices throughout roasting. Remove meats and cool. Cut the pork in half lengthwise, then crosswise into slices. Cut the duck, through skin and bones, into 1½-inch squares, using a sharp knife or cleaver. Set pieces of meat aside.

When beans boil, add chopped onions, garlic, tomatoes, paste, carrots, celery, thyme, bay leaf, pepper and stock. Add additional water if needed to cover contents of casserole. Cover and return to a boil. Reduce heat and simmer covered 1 hour.

Prick sausage in several places on each link and add to cassoulet. Simmer uncovered 45 minutes, adding water if necessary.

To assemble cassoulet, select a large, presentable, ovenproof casserole (or rinse out the one used to cook the beans). Remove salt pork, rind and sausage from the beans. Dice salt pork. Cut rind into strips. Slip casing off garlic sausage and slice. Spread an inch-thick layer of beans in casserole. Layer a sampling of all meats. Repeat layers until all beans and meats are used, ending with beans. Tuck carrots and celery into beans. Top with bread crumbs. Bake at 350 degrees for 45 minutes. Remove, sprinkle with parsley and thyme and serve. Serves 12.

— Elaine Corn, 1984

# BOHEMIAN CASSEROLE

Slice sausage diagonally into one-inch pieces. Fry in butter in a 10-inch skillet, tightly covered, over medium heat until browned. Remove and drain. Sauté mushrooms and onion about 5 minutes (until onion is tender) in the pan drippings. Stir in rice, water, caraway, salt and sausage. Cover and cook over low heat half an hour. Stir in cabbage, re-cover and continue cooking over low heat until rice is tender, about 20 minutes more. Serves 6.
— Deni Hamilton, 1978

1½ pounds (about 2 links) smoked sausage
2 tablespoons butter or margarine
2 4-ounce cans or ½ pound mushrooms, sliced and drained
1 medium onion, sliced
1 cup brown rice
2⅔ cups water (use juice from canned mushrooms as a part, if desired)
1 teaspoon caraway seeds, crushed
1½ teaspoons salt
2 cups shredded cabbage

# JOE'S MACARONI AND CHEESE

*Deni Hamilton wrote about this recipe in 1978. It is her father's.*

Mix macaroni, cheddar, onion and salt and pepper in a greased casserole. Pour milk over the mixture. It shouldn't quite come to the top of the macaroni. Sprinkle with grated parmesan. Bake in a preheated 350-degree oven for about 30 minutes. Stir the mixture, and continue to bake another 30 minutes. Stir once more; add a bit more milk, if desired, and finish baking for another half hour. Serves 8 or more.

1 pound macaroni, cooked
1 pound mild cheddar, cut in ½-inch squares
1 medium onion, chopped fine
About 1 cup milk
Salt and pepper to taste
½ cup grated parmesan cheese

# EGG CASSEROLE

Cook onion in butter until tender. Blend in flour. Add milk and cook, stirring constantly, until mixture thickens. Add cheese; stir until melted. Place layer of egg slices in 10-by-6-by-1½-inch baking dish. Cover with half the cheese sauce, then half the chips and half the bacon. Repeat layers. Bake in a 350-degree preheated oven for about 30 minutes. Makes eight servings.
— Lillian Marshall, 1977

½ cup chopped onion
2 tablespoons butter or margarine
2 tablespoons flour
1¼ cups milk
1 cup sharp shredded cheese
6 hard-cooked eggs, sliced
1½ cups coarsely crushed potato chips
6 slices bacon, fried crisp and crumbled

# COLLINS FAMILY BROCCOLI CASSEROLE

*This recipe was among those given Elaine Corn by the governor's mansion for the holiday-entertaining issue of the Magazine in 1984. It is from Dr. Bill Collins' mother, Margaret Collins of Versailles (Gov. Martha Layne Collins' mother-in-law).*

**2 bunches fresh broccoli, cut into florets**
**½ stick butter**
**¼ cup all-purpose flour**
**2 cups milk, scalded**
**1 can undiluted cream of mushroom soup**
**2 tablespoons grated onion**
**½ cup grated American cheese**
**1 cup Ritz cracker crumbs**
**½ stick additional butter**

Heat oven to 350 degrees. Steam the broccoli until crunchy and drain. In a saucepan, melt the butter over medium-high heat. Add flour; cook and stir 2 minutes. Add milk and cook until thickened, stirring frequently. Add soup and cook 5 minutes. Place a layer of sauce in a 2-quart casserole. Layer the broccoli over the sauce. Add a final layer of sauce. Sprinkle with onions, cheese and cracker crumbs. Dot with butter and bake for 1 hour. Serves 8 to 10.

# CAPTAIN'S QUARTERS YELLOW-SQUASH CASSEROLE

*Elaine Corn wrote about this recipe in 1984. It is from the restaurant on Upper River Road in Jefferson County.*

**6 to 8 yellow squash, cut up**
**Salt and pepper, to taste**
**2 tablespoons butter**
**1 chicken bouillon cube**
**1 tablespoon grated onion**
**1 egg, beaten**
**1 cup sour cream mixed with ½ cup grated cheddar**
**½ cup crumbled bacon**

Cook squash in boiling water until nearly tender, about 10 minutes. Mash and mix with salt, pepper, butter, bouillon, onion, egg and sour-cream/cheddar mixture. Pour into a casserole. Top with bacon. Bake at 350-degrees for 30 minutes. Serves six.

# KALE AND CHEESE CASSEROLE

**2 pounds kale**
**2 teaspoons chopped onion**
**2½ tablespoons butter or margarine**
**4½ tablespoons flour**
**1¾ cups milk**
**Salt and pepper**
**Buttered soft bread crumbs**
**1 cup grated American cheese**

Remove any wilted leaves and tough stems from the kale. We strip the green leaves off, and when the stems break or seem tender, they go into the pot, too. Wash the kale thoroughly. Cook kale and onion in a small quantity of boiling salted water in a covered pan until tender. Drain. Boil down the liquid to ¾ cup. Melt the butter or margarine in the top of a double boiler. Add flour and mix well. Add the milk gradually and cook, stirring constantly, until thickened. Add the kale liquid, and season with salt and pepper. Add kale. Pour the mixture into a buttered baking dish. Cover with the crumbs mixed with cheese. Bake in a moderate oven, 350 degrees, for about 25 minutes, or until the cheese is melted and the mixture is heated through. I think this would make about 6 to 8 servings, depending on what else you are having and appetites to which you are catering.

— Cissy Gregg, 1960

# ITALIAN POLENTA CASSEROLE

Brown onions and meat together without oil. Add seasonings and tomato paste and stir until blended. Chop tomatoes and add to sauce along with water. Simmer for 10 minutes, or until sauce thickens a bit. Put mixture in bottom of a shallow, greased 1½- to 2-quart casserole. Spoon polenta over, quickly, and spread to cover sauce. Top with a bit of shredded cheese, if desired. Bake in 350-degree oven until warmed through, about 30 minutes. Serves six.

— Deni Hamilton, 1978

**1 medium onion, chopped**
**1 pound hamburger**
**½ teaspoon garlic powder**
**2 teaspoons salt**
**1 tablespoon oregano**
**1 teaspoon basil**
**1 can (2 cups) tomatoes**
**3 ounces (½ small can) tomato paste**
**½ to ¾ cup water**
**Polenta (see recipe)**

## POLENTA

Bring water to boil, reduce heat and slowly sift in cornmeal. Cook over low heat, stirring constantly, until very thick, about 15 minutes.

**3½ cups water (use part chicken broth for better flavor)**
**1 cup cornmeal**
**Salt to taste**

# SOUTHWESTERN CASSEROLE

Steam zucchini about five minutes, and drain well. Sauté meat, seasonings and onions until meat is no longer pink. Drain off grease. Stir in rice, chilies and zucchini. Blend eggs and cottage cheese. Stir into meat mixture. Divide between two shallow two-quart casseroles that have been coated with vegetable spray. Top each with half the cheddar. Bake in a preheated 350-degree oven 30 minutes. These casseroles can be frozen and stored before baking. Each makes six servings at 250 calories per serving.

— Deni Hamilton, 1980

**2 pounds zucchini, sliced**
**1 pound lean ground beef**
**1 teaspoon salt**
**¼ teaspoon each of pepper and garlic powder**
**1 cup finely chopped onions**
**3 cups cooked rice**
**1 4-ounce can chopped green chilies**
**2 eggs, beaten**
**1½ cups cottage cheese**
**2 cups grated cheddar cheese**

# CHICKEN EN CASSEROLE

*Early recipes did not list ingredients and amounts in a separate table. These were incorporated within the recipe instructions, instead. Most people apparently prefer today's recipe styles, although Cissy Gregg made this 1942 recipe, one of her earliest, easy to follow. (A "moderate" oven is about 350 degrees.)*

Separate chicken into pieces at the joints, and wipe with a damp cloth. Sauté in butter until a delicate brown. Put pieces in casserole; add about 1 pint hot broth made from veal or chicken. A boullion cube will do, or just hot water. Cover and cook in moderate oven for 1¼ hours. Melt 2 or 3 tablespoons butter in frying pan and sauté 6 or 8 mushrooms, 12 or more slices of carrots, 2 potatoes, cubed, and 1 sliced onion. Cook until pleasantly browned and add to the casserole. Add 4 tablespoons sherry, more broth if needed, and salt to taste. Cover tightly and return to oven for 30 mintues, or until chicken and vegetables are falling-apart tender.

# ASPARAGUS CASSEROLE

**1½ cups cooked asparagus cuts and tips (we used the canned)**
**8 ounces spaghetti, broken in small pieces**
**2 tablespoons butter**
**2 tablespoons flour**
**1 cup milk**
**3 drops Tabasco sauce or more**
**½ teaspoon salt (we used a little more)**
**½ cup grated cheese**
**¼ cup buttered bread crumbs**

Any mention of asparagus makes us think of a casserole we picked up in New Jersey. It's tremendously good and so easy and economical at the same time.

Cook spaghetti in boiling salted water until just tender. Drain asparagus and reserve the liquid.

Melt butter or margarine in a saucepan, and stir in flour. Add asparagus liquid and milk, stirring constantly until the mixture thickens. Remove from heat. Add seasoning and cheese and stir until smooth.

Put a layer of cooked spaghetti in a greased 1½ quart baking dish. Add a layer of asparagus, then a layer of sauce. Repeat layers until all of the ingredients are used. Cover top with buttered crumbs. Bake 20 minutes in a 350-degree oven. Makes about six servings.     — Cissy Gregg, 1962

# GRITS CASSEROLE

**1 cup grits**
**1 teaspoon salt**
**4 cups water**
**1 stick butter**
**¼ pound pasteurized processed cheese spread**
**¼ pound sharp cheddar**
**3 eggs, slightly beaten**
**⅓ cup milk**

Cook grits in salted water until done. Then add butter, cheeses, eggs and milk. Stir until melted and smooth. Place in 1½-quart casserole, and bake at 350 degrees for 1 hour. Can be made ahead, frozen and reheated. Serves six to eight.

— Cook's Corner column, 1981

# ASPARAGUS CHEESE STRATA

Remove crusts from bread slices and cut bread into cubes. Arrange half the bread in the bottom of a buttered 10-by-6-by-2-inch baking dish.

Cover bread with the cooked asparagus, cut in pieces, and sprinkle with shredded cheese. Cover with remaining bread.

Beat eggs slightly and add milk, minced onion, seasonings and butter. Pour over the mixture in dish. Let stand 20 minutes.

Bake in a moderate oven, 325 degrees, for 45 to 50 minutes, or until puffed and lightly browned. Serve at once. This recipe makes about six servings.
— Cissy Gregg, 1957

2½ cups milk
A pound of fresh asparagus (fresh-frozen or canned)
1½ cups shredded cheese
4 eggs
8 slices bread on the stale side
2 tablespoons minced onion
1½ teaspoons salt
⅛ teaspoon pepper
2 tablespoons butter, melted

# ALMOST ITALIAN CASSEROLE

Brown meat in large sauce pan, stirring frequently and breaking up pieces. Add onion and green pepper, and cook a minute or so until soft. Drain off fat. Stir in tomato paste, sauce, salt, oregano and red pepper. Cover and cook over low heat about 45 minutes.

Meanwhile, gradually add macaroni to boiling water so it continues to boil. Cook uncovered, stirring occasionally, until just tender. Drain well. Layer half the macaroni in the bottom of a buttered 2½-quart casserole. Spoon half the meat sauce over it, then half the cottage cheese; next sprinkle on half the cheddar. Repeat using remaining ingredients.

Bake in a 375-degree oven about 15 minutes, then cover with foil and bake another 15 minutes. Serves six to eight. If you wish, put one layer of macaroni, meat, cottage and cheddar cheeses in each of two 1½-quart casseroles and freeze one, well sealed. Defrost in bottom of refrigerator before baking as usual, and serve to three or four.
— Deni Hamilton, 1977

1½ pounds ground chuck
2 medium onions, chopped
1 medium green pepper, diced
6-ounce can tomato paste
1 cup grated mild cheddar cheese
2 8-ounce cans tomato sauce
1½ teaspoons salt
¾ teaspoon oregano
¼ teaspoon crushed red pepper
Boiling water
2 cups (8 ounces) elbow macaroni
1 cup creamed cottage cheese

# DELUXE CHEESE GRITS SOUFFLÉ

1 cup grits
4 cups boiling, salted water
3 tablespoons butter
3 tablespoons flour
1 cup warm milk
1 cup warm cream
1 cup grated cheddar
½ cup grated parmesan
6 egg yolks
6 egg whites
Pinch cream of tartar

This recipe makes a large mixture. Butter two 1½-quart soufflé dishes, or 1 large soufflé (3-quart) dish, and outfit each with a 2-inch buttered collar. (Folded aluminum foil and transparent tape work well.) Then dust the bottom and walls with parmesan. Or, you may butter and dust a 3-quart rectangular baking dish. Heat the oven to 400 degrees.

Slowly pour the grits into the boiling, salted water. Return to a boil and cook over medium-high heat until the grits are so thick they sputter. In a large saucepan, melt the butter, stir in the flour and whisk the mixture around for 2 minutes until smooth and pasty. Gradually add the milk and cream that have been warmed together, whisking until a smooth white sauce. Loosely blend in the cheddar and parmesan, leaving streaks.

Remove from heat. Beat the egg yolks a minute or so, until light yellow, and add to the grits sauce. Beat the egg whites at high speed, adding the cream of tartar as the whites start to come up, and continue beating until the whites form medium-soft peaks. (Over-beating causes soufflés to fall.) Fold whites into the grits-yolk sauce gently with wide, sweeping strokes and without overblending. Little tufts of white should show. Pour mixture into prepared dishes. Run a knife in a circle through the top of the batter so center will rise into a "top hat" during baking. Place in oven, reduce heat to 375 degrees and bake for 30 minutes if using a straight-walled soufflé dish, or about 20 mintues if using a flat dish. Serve immediately.     — Elaine Corn, 1983

# TURKEY SOPA

1 pint sour cream
3 10-ounce cans tomatoes and green chilies
1 onion, finely chopped
4 cups diced, cooked turkey
8 to 10 corn tortillas, softened in hot oil and cut in half, or 2 cups crumbled, stale tortilla chips
1 cup monterey jack, grated

Lightly grease a 3-quart casserole. Mix sour cream, tomatoes and chilies, onion and turkey. Line casserole with half the tortillas, overlapping slightly. Cover with half the turkey mixture. Add another layer of tortillas, then a layer of turkey and top with grated cheese. Bake at 325 degrees for one hour. May be prepared ahead and frozen. Defrost the uncooked casserole at room temperature for two hours and proceed with baking time. Serves eight.

— Elaine Corn, 1982

# Zucchini Parmesan

Slice zucchini and steam over simmering water for about five minutes, so it's bright green and still crisp. Drain well.

Heat oil and saute onion and garlic in it for five minutes. Add all other ingredients except cheeses and reserved squash; mix well. Add a tomato paste can of water. Simmer one hour over low heat, uncovered, until thick. (You might need to add a little water, but do it sparingly.)

Grease a 2½-quart shallow casserole (like a lasagna pan) and cover the bottom with some of the sauce. Put zucchini over it. (It need not be in neat rows.) Cover with a layer of sliced mozzerella. (Use all you have.) Then douse the top with your remaining sauce. Sprinkle with the grated parmesan cheese. Bake at 350 degrees for half an hour or until bubbly. This seems to be even better if you make it a day ahead, bring to room temperature, then bake. And it freezes well, either before or after cooking. Serves 8.

— Deni Hamilton, 1977

**10 small zucchini**
**2 tablespoons olive oil**
**1 large onion, chopped**
**1 clove garlic, minced**
**2 6-ounce cans tomato paste**
**1 19-ounce can tomato puree**
**½ teaspoon each of oregano and basil**
**¼ teaspoon each of thyme, rosemary and marjoram**
**1 bay leaf, broken in half**
**1 teaspoon salt**
**1 tomato paste can full of dry red wine**
**8 ounces mozzerella cheese, sliced**
**½ cup grated parmesan cheese**

# PASTA & PIZZA

# CAVATELLI AND SHRIMP SALAD

*Louisville restaurateur Don Grisanti created this recipe for a 1980 holiday-entertaining issue of the Sunday Magazine. He was featured in an article by Deni Hamilton.*

1 pound very small shrimp, peeled, deveined and cooked

2 cups mayonnaise

3 tablespoons fresh basil, finely chopped

Juice of 1 lemon (about 3 tablespoons)

2 tablespoons finely chopped red onions

½ cup freshly grated parmesan cheese

3 cups cooked cavatelli

Blend mayonnaise, basil, lemon juice, red onion, parmesan, salt and pepper to taste. Add cooked cavatelli and shrimp. Serve chilled. Serves 4 as an appetizer.

# SIXTH AVENUE CAVATELLI AND SHRIMP SALAD

*Sixth Avenue restaurant gave this recipe to Elaine Corn in 1984. Although Sixth Avenue is a Grisanti restaurant, this recipe obviously differs considerably from Don Grisanti's.*

½ pound cavatelli (small shells)

Olive oil

1 pound small-to-medium fresh shrimp

¼ cup fresh or frozen peas

1 tomato

2 green onions

1 head Bibb lettuce

Dressing (see recipe)

Cook cavatelli in boiling, salted water until *al dente,* still firm to the bite. Drain, rinse with cold water, toss with a few tablespoons olive oil and chill. Peel shrimp and devein. Cook shrimp and peas in boiling water about three minutes from time added to water. Drain, rinse and chill shrimp and peas. Peel tomato by dropping in boiling water 30 to 60 seconds. Halve, remove seeds and dice. Peel green onions, remove root and slice into small rings. Toss cavatelli with all prepared ingredients and dressing. Cover, chill and serve on bed of Bibb lettuce. Makes four servings.

## DRESSING

¼ cup buttermilk

1 cup mayonnaise

4 tablespoons pimento, minced and drained

1½ teaspoons fresh chopped basil

4 tablespoons fresh grated parmesan

Salt and pepper, to taste

2 tablespoons fresh minced parsley

1 small yellow onion, minced

Combine ingredients in a food processor. For a bulkier dressing without machine, mix liquids with remaining ingredients chopped into a fine dice. Let sit overnight in refrigerator so flavors can blend.

# MAMMA GRISANTI'S FETTUCINI ALFREDO

*Mamma Grisanti's gave this recipe to the Cook's Corner column in 1984 in response to a request from a reader.*

Place cream and cheese in a saucepan. Over medium heat (keep it medium so cheese doesn't scorch), cook until cheese is melted and cream is vigorously boiling. Add cooked pasta, salt and pepper. Heat to desired serving temperature. Serve immediately. Makes one serving.

¾ cup heavy cream
¼ cup freshly grated parmesan
Pinch of salt and pepper
¼ pound pasta, cooked

# PASTA IN GARLIC BUTTER FOR ONE

Place the noodles in salted, boiling water. As noodles cook, in about 8 minutes, peel and mince garlic. Heat the butter and olive oil in a small skillet. Add garlic. Toss until golden. Add ½ cup of the water in which the noodles have been cooking, and pepper. Boil. Drain noodles. Transfer to serving bowl. Pour over with butter sauce. Toss gently. Top with minced parsley. Serve immediately. Serves one.

— Elaine Corn, 1982

¼ pound noodles
Boiling, salted water
2 cloves garlic
3 tablespoons butter
1 tablespoon olive oil (optional)
Freshly ground black pepper
Parsley, minced, for garnish

# PASTA WITH CHICKEN AND ITALIAN SAUSAGE WITH FENNEL

Bring a large pot of water to a boil.

In a skillet, melt the butter. Add chicken pieces and sauté over medium heat, turning once, until light brown. Remove and reserve. Add sausage to skillet and sauté, carefully turning once, about 8 minutes in all, until pink cooks out. Remove from skillet and reserve with chicken. Add cream to skillet. Bring to a boil, whisking and scraping up any bits of food on bottom of skillet. Boil 2 minutes. Carefully add peppers, sausage and chicken, stirring gently to combine and coat. Remove from heat.

In the meantime, cook pasta in the large pot of boiling water. Toss, very gently, with chicken-sausage sauce. Serve hot. Serves 6 to 8.

— Elaine Corn, 1983

8 ounces fresh or good commercial pasta
½ stick butter
1 whole chicken breast, skinned and cut into 1-inch cubes
6 links sweet Italian sausage with fennel, sliced ½-inch thick
1 cup cream
2 red bell peppers, roasted, peeled and sliced

# JACK FRY'S SHRIMP AND ARTICHOKE PASTA SALAD

*If you don't have freshly made fettucini for this recipe, the cooking time for the pasta will be longer. Cook al dente. The recipe for this popular pasta salad, featured in a 1984 story by Elaine Corn, comes from Jack Fry's restaurant in Louisville.*

¾ pounds each fresh green and
   white fettucini
½ cup vinaigrette (see recipe)
1 pound medium-to-large shrimp,
   peeled
1 tablespoon red pepper flakes
¼ cup white wine
1 teaspoon thyme
2 jars marinated artichoke harts,
   drained
1 red onion, finely chopped
6 tablespoons fresh chopped
   parsley
Salt and white pepper, to taste

Boil fresh pasta in 1 quart boiling water with ¼ cup olive oil for one to 1½ minutes. Drain, rinse and cool under cold water. Cook the shrimp in boiling water to cover, with red pepper flakes, white wine and thyme for two minutes, starting timing when shrimp are added to water. Drain and rinse under cold water. Toss shrimp with pasta, remaining ingredients and vinaigrette. Cover well and chill. Makes six servings.

## VINAIGRETTE

½ cup cider vinegar
¼ teaspoon salt
1 teaspoon white pepper
1 teaspoon dry mustard
1½ cups salad oil
1 egg

Whisk all ingredients in a mixing bowl by hand with a wire whip.

# STRAW AND HAY

2 cups spinach noodles
2 cups thin fettucine
½ stick butter
¾ cup heavy cream
¾ cup freshly grated parmesan
   cheese
½ of 10- or 12-ounce box frozen
   peas, or 1 pint fresh peas, cooked
8 thin slices prosciutto, cut julienne
   style
Salt and pepper

Cook the pasta *al dente.* Rinse in cold water and place in a pan. Add butter and toss with pasta over medium heat. Add cream and toss. Add cheese, peas, ham and toss, adding salt and pepper to taste. Serve hot. Makes four appetizer servings.

— Elaine Corn, 1983

# ZITI AND THE GARDEN

Place ziti in a large bowl. Blanch string beans two minutes in boiling water. Rinse beans in cold water and drain. Add to ziti with remaining ingredients except blue cheese. Toss salad, turning over with hands until all pieces are coated with oil. Top with blue cheese. Chill or serve immediately. Serves four to six.

— Elaine Corn, 1982

**4 cups cooked and chilled ziti, or other tube pasta**
**¼ pound small, tender string beans**
**4 small zucchini, sliced in coins**
**2 small tomatoes, or 1 large, seeded and cut in strips**
**2 cloves garlic, minced**
**¼ cup apple cider vinegar**
**½ cup olive oil**
**Pinch oregano**
**1 teaspoon fresh, chopped parsley**
**Salt and freshly ground black pepper, to taste**
**Crumbled blue cheese**

# PASTA CON SPINACH

*In this 1972 recipe, Lillian Marshall creates the perfect meal. It has a grain product, dairy products, greens, meat and, of course, wine.*

Put wine in refrigerator to chill. Half-fill a large kettle with water and add a tablespoon cooking oil. Bring to a boil and add spaghetti. Stir occasionally and cook to a chewy consistency; do not overcook. Wash and clean the spinach. Drain lightly, put in heavy covered pot and cook over high heat. Stir with spoon once. When cooked limp (takes only a short time), set aside pot with cover on. Slice the mushrooms, shred the ham and sauté them together in half the butter just until warm, not brown. Press liquid out of spinach and add to the skillet with mushrooms and ham. In serving pot, melt rest of butter. Add pasta and ham combination. Toss well. Sprinkle on the cheese. Bring to table, open wine and eat.

**A bottle dry white wine**
**1 pound fresh spinach**
**¾ pound spaghetti**
**7 or 8 fresh mushrooms (about ½ pound)**
**¼ cup cooked ham**
**1 stick butter**
**¼ cup grated romano or parmesan cheese**

# FETTUCINI PRIMAVERA

*Don Grisanti created this recipe for a 1980 Sunday Magazine article by Deni Hamilton. Grisanti, along with brother Michael, was one of the forces behind the national recognition accorded Casa Grisanti today.*

1 pound fettucini
16 ounces heavy cream
8 cherry tomatoes
½ head cauliflower, cut into florets
½ head broccoli, cut into florets
1 zucchini sliced, (coin size)
1 cup diced mushrooms
4 baby carrots, cut in julienne slices
1 cup grated parmesan cheese
2 ounces pine (pignola) nuts,
   toasted

Cook the fettucini in boiling, salted water until *al dente.* In a large sauce pan, combine heavy cream, cherry tomato, cauliflower, broccoli, zucchini, mushrooms and carrots. Simmer long enough to reduce liquid by one-third. Add fettucine to liquids and vegetables. Add parmesan cheese, pine nuts, salt and pepper to taste. Serve when sauce starts to coat spoon or slightly thickens.

# PASTA WITH PEAS AND PARSLEY SAUCE

¼ cup minced green onions
¼ cup olive oil or butter or
   margarine
1 teaspoon thyme
1 teaspoon basil
Salt and pepper
2 pounds fresh peas

## SAUCE:

3 cloves garlic (or to taste)
A large handful of parsley
⅓ cup pine nuts (pignolas)
⅓ cup grated parmesan or romano
   cheese
Olive oil
Salt and pepper
10 ounces fine egg noodles
¼ cup butter or margarine
For garnish, grated parmesan
   cheese

Sauté the onions in oil or butter. Add the herbs, seasonings and peas. Gently simmer until tender, covered tightly, in 2 or 3 tablespoons water.

For the sauce, crush the garlic (we have a garlic press, if you don't have one, crush it with salt in a small container), add parsley, nuts and cheese. Add olive oil, a little at a time, to make a thick sauce. If you have an electric blender, it works fine, but we gave ours the hand treatment, and even if it wasn't quite the puréed form, it seemed to blend in well with the fine noodles. Add salt and pepper. Boil the noodles 10 minutes in plenty of salted water. Drain. Mix with ¼ cup butter or margarine. Mix the hot peas with the hot pasta, and stir in the sauce. Serve immediately with a light sprinkling of parmesan cheese, or pass the bowl and let all help themselves.

— Cissy Gregg, 1960

# "THE WORKS" DEEP-DISH PIZZA IN WHOLE-WHEAT CRUST

Brush 12- to 13-inch deep-dish pizza pan (removable bottom) with oil. Sprinkle with corn meal. Roll out whole-wheat pizza dough to 2 inches larger than the pan. Place in pan, letting excess hang over rim. Set aside at room temperature to rise slightly. In a medium saucepan, heat the 2 tablespoons olive oil. Add garlic and stir a minute, then tomatoes, sugar, herbs, salt and pepper. Simmer and cook down 20 minutes, stirring now and then. Set sauce aside. Fry the sausage, crumbling as you go. When pink disappears, strain and set aside. Slice zucchini lengthwise into ¼-inch-thick slices. Brown in batches on both sides in a tablespoon of olive oil per batch. Drain on paper towels. Heat the oven to 450 degrees. Brush bottom and sides of dough with oil. Fill with tomato sauce. Arrange mozzarella slices over sauce. Place zucchini over cheese like spokes. Place artichoke hearts and mushrooms between zucchini. Scatter sausage over all. Cut off overhang. Bake 25 minutes. Sprinkle with monterey jack and parmesan and return to oven 5 minutes. Cool in pan 5 minutes before slicing.

— Elaine Corn, 1984

1 recipe whole-wheat pizza dough (see recipe)
2 tablespoons olive oil
2 cloves garlic, minced
3 tomatoes, peeled, cored, seeded and coarsely chopped
Pinch sugar
Dashes of oregano and basil
Salt and pepper, to taste
1 pound bulk sweet Italian sausage
2 medium zucchini
Olive oil
¾ pound mozzarella cheese, sliced
1 can water-packed artichoke hearts, halved
¼ pound fresh mushrooms, sliced
½ pound monterey jack cheese, shredded
½ cup freshly grated parmesan

## WHOLE-WHEAT PIZZA DOUGH

In a medium bowl, dissolve yeast and sugar in warm water. Let stand 5 minutes, until bubbly. In a large mixing bowl, combine the whole-wheat flour, ½ cup of the all-purpose flour and salt. Make a well. Pour in yeast mixture and olive oil and stir briskly with a fork until blended well and dough pulls away from the sides of the bowl. Dough will be sticky. Turn out onto a floured board. Knead 10 to 15 minutes, working in remaining all-purpose flour until smooth and dough regains its shape if pushed or pulled. Drop in a lightly oiled bowl, turning once to coat all sides. Cover and let rise in a warm, draft-free place 1½ hours, or until doubled in bulk. Punch down. Separate into desired portions. Dough may be frozen at this point. Thaw before proceeding. Shape dough as desired or roll out into pizza pans. Makes 1 deep-dish, 3 medium or 6 individual pizzas.

— Elaine Corn, 1984

1 tablespoon yeast (1 package)
1 tablespoon sugar
1½ cups warm water
2 cups whole-wheat flour
1 to 1¼ cups all-purpose flour
1 teaspoon salt
3 tablespoons olive oil

# SHRIMP PIZZAS PROVENCAL

*Makes 2 individual pizzas.*

**1 3-ounce block cream cheese, softened**
**1 tablespoon fresh chopped basil leaves, or 1 ½ teaspoons dried**
**2 tablespoons olive oil**
**2 cloves garlic, minced**
**2 tomatoes, seeded and chopped**
**¾ pound shrimp, peeled and deveined**
**Pinch fresh chopped basil, or dried**
**2 parts all-purpose pizza dough (recipe follows)**
**Oil, for brushing**
**Corn meal**

Heat a pizza stone for 1 hour in an oven set at 500 degrees.

Mash the cream cheese and basil until smooth. Set aside.

Heat the 2 tablespoons oil in a medium skillet over high heat. Add garlic, stirring quickly for 20 seconds. Add tomatoes, shake the pan and cook briefly, 30 seconds at most. Add shrimp, shaking pan again until all shrimp lie flat. With heat still high, cook shrimp about 45 seconds per side. Remove from heat, sprinkle with pinch of basil and set aside.

Roll out 2 portions of dough 8 to 10 inches in diameter. Sprinkle a pizza peel (or other light, wood board) with corn meal and place a round of dough over meal. Brush dough with olive oil. Open oven door and flick dough onto heated stone. Bake 5 to 6 minutes and remove to a rack. Dough will puff irregularly. Repeat for second round. Quickly spread each with cream-cheese-and-basil mixture. Return both to oven 3 minutes more. Remove and top cream cheese mixture with shrimp and serve immediately.

## ALL-PURPOSE PIZZA DOUGH

**1 tablespoon yeast (1 package)**
**1 tablespoon sugar**
**1½ cups warm water**
**3 to 3½ cups all-purpose flour**
**1 teaspoon salt**
**3 tablespoons olive oil**

In a medium bowl, dissolve yeast and sugar in warm water 5 to 10 minutes, until bubbly.

In a large bowl, combine 3 cups of the flour with salt. Make a well. Pour in yeast mixture and oil, stirring briskly with a fork until well-blended and dough pulls away from sides of bowl. Turn out onto a floured surface and knead 10 to 15 minutes, working in the remaining ½-cup flour. Drop into a lightly oiled bowl, turning dough once to coat all sides. Cover and let rise in a draft-free warm place 1½ hours, until doubled in bulk. Punch down and refrigerate about 30 minutes, or until ready to use. Separate into desired portions. Dough may be frozen at this point. Thaw before using. Makes 2 deepdish, 3 medium or 6 individual pizzas.

— Elaine Corn, 1984

## TO BAKE WITHOUT PIZZA STONE

Brush two 8-inch cake pans (or 1 medium-sized) with olive oil and sprinkle with corn meal. Roll out 2 portions of dough 7½ inches wide and place in pans over meal. Do not build up sides. Brush dough with oil. Bake 15 minutes, until puffy and browned. Remove and spread with cream cheese-basil mixture. Return to oven 3 to 4 minutes more. Remove and place shrimp mixture on top, and serve in pan or out.

# VEGETABLES

# BRISTOL BAR & GRILLE ARTICHOKE FRITTERS AND REMOULADE SAUCE

*The Bristol supplied the recipe for this popular appetizer in response to a request from the Cook's Corner column in 1983.*

2 14-ounce cans artichoke hearts, in
    water
3 eggs
1 cup flour
½ cup Dijon mustard
1 teaspoon vinegar
Salt and pepper to taste

Drain and mash artichoke hearts. Mix in eggs, flour, mustard, vinegar and salt and pepper, blending well. Portion and shape fritter by rolling batter in a large spoon. Carefully drop into 5 to 6 inches of oil heated to 375 degrees. Keep fritters separated to prevent raw spots. Fritters need no turning. Fry until golden brown.

Makes about two dozen, depending on size.

## REMOULADE SAUCE

1 small onion, coarsely chopped
4 ribs celery, coarsely chopped
1 bunch parsley, leaves only, and
    coarsely chopped
¼ cup Dijon mustard
½ cup olive oil
1 teaspoon lemon juice
1 tablespoon dried basil
Dash cayenne
2 tablespoons paprika

In a food processor or blender, purée the chopped onion, celery, parsley, mustard, oil and lemon juice. Texture will be somewhat grainy. Add basil, cayenne and paprika during machine's final pulses. Makes 2 cups.

# ASPARAGUS LUNCHEON ROLLS

16 to 24 large cooked asparagus
    stalks
4 to 6 large slices of boiled or baked
    ham, chicken or turkey
Salt
Pepper
Melted butter
Cheese-olive sauce (see recipe)

Arrange 4 asparagus stalks on each slice ham. Sprinkle with salt and pepper, and brush with butter. Roll over to enclose asparagus.

Arrange in shallow oblong casserole or baking pan. Cover with cheese-olive sauce and bake in a moderate oven, 350 degrees, for 20 to 25 minutes to heat and lightly glaze.

## CHEESE-OLIVE SAUCE

(If the raw onion is used, cook until soft in butter.) Measure onion into milk. Cut olives into medium-sized pieces. Melt butter, and blend in flour and salt. Add milk mixture slowly. Cook and stir until thickened and smooth, about 10 minutes. Stir in cheese and olives.

— Cissy Gregg, 1957

**2 teaspoons instant minced onion or 2 tablespoons finely chopped raw onion**
**2 cups rich milk**
**½ cup ripe olives**
**¼ cup butter or margarine**
**⅓ cup sifted flour**
**1 teaspoon salt**
**1 cup grated American cheese**

# FRESH ASPARAGUS WITH LEMON BUTTER

*Cissy Gregg sliced the woody ends from the stalks in this 1954 recipe. Many cooks find it easy to snap them off by hand; they seem to want to break off at just the right point.*

A word about cooking asparagus. It is true that we have asparagus all the year 'round as fresh, frozen. But it still is a herald of spring, and the first fresh asparagus is exciting in flavor as is no other vegetable.

Asparagus must be well washed, since grains of sand can lurk in the petals. Sometimes the petals have to be scraped off before they are freed of sand. To do this, scrape under running water. Also, most asparagus come with a woody base. To find out where the edible portion begins, take trial cuts along the stalk beginning from the lower end. When the knife cuts the stalk easily, you can be sure you have hit the tender part of the stalk. Cut through there.

On cooking, we once gave rules to tie 5 to 6 stalks together in a bundle, then to stand the bundles up in a deep saucepan of rapidly boiling salted water. The boiling water cooks the heavier part of the stalks, and the rising steam tenderizes the buds. But we like another method now. Lay the stalks in a flat pan of boiling salted water. Bring to a boil after adding the asparagus and then turn the heat down so the stalks simmer until tender. Shake the pan once or twice to turn the stalks over.

Since we pay well for the first asparagus, we are for getting its full flavor. Dress with melted butter to which a little lemon juice has been added. Maybe a few toasted bread crumbs may also be included for crunchiness.

# ASPARAGUS SUPREME

⅔ cup ripe olives
1 12-ounce package frozen
   asparagus (or take a shortcut
   and use the canned)
2 tablespoons butter or margarine
2 tablespoons flour
¼ teaspoon dry mustard
¾ teaspoon salt
Dash of black pepper
1½ cups milk
¼ teaspoon Worcestershire sauce
1 cup grated American cheese
2 hard-boiled eggs
6 slices toast

Cut olives into large pieces. Cook asparagus until barely tender if you are using either the frozen or the fresh. Drain. Melt butter and blend in flour, salt, mustard and pepper.

Add milk and Worcestershire sauce, and cook and stir until mixture thickens. Blend in cheese and stir over low heat until cheese melts. Blend in diced eggs and olives. Arrange toast on serving plate, cover with asparagus and top generously with cheese mixture. Serve at once. This is, we would say, four servings.

— Cissy Gregg, 1958

# BOSTON BAKED BEANS

*In 1962, Cissy Gregg delved into stories written about Boston baked beans. She settled on this recipe.*

1 quart dried pea beans
1 medium-sized onion, peeled
½ pound salt pork
½ cup brown sugar, firmly packed
⅓ cup molasses (I use more because
   I like the beans on the sweet
   side.)
1 tablespoon salt
1 teaspoon dry mustard

Come Friday night, put the beans to soak in a kettle full of cold water. In the morning pour the water off, cover with fresh water and bring slowly to a boil. Simmer until you can blow the skins off. Remember: take a spoonful of beans from the pot. If you should put your face down into the steam, you might get badly burned. Just lift the spoonful of beans out, wave them a little and blow.

When the skins blow off, and it takes an hour or more of simmering, drain the beans and place about one cup of the beans in a bean pot or casserole. Add onion. (You may stick the onion with whole cloves or not, as you please.) Add remaining beans until the pot is almost filled.

Score the salt pork to the rind, and scald it. Force down among the beans until it just shows at the top. Combine remaining ingredients and mix with the beans. Add enough hot water to fill the pot. The pork should protrude a little above the water line so that it can brown nicely.

Bake at 300 degrees for at least 8 hours. Add more water if necessary during baking time. The beans should be kept under a blanket of boiling water until the time comes to allow the top to brown off and the salt pork to become crusty. One author said the pork should be "brown as old mahogany."

They were so good to taste, no one would mind having them two days or until the pot is free of the last bean. Wonderful served with brown bread and piccalilli!

# DEVILED GREEN BEANS

Wash and break up the beans and cook in plain salted water until just tender. Taste to find out, and turn off the heat when you think they should cook "just a little longer" — because they will in the seasonings and no one likes mushy beans. Cream the drippings with the other seasonings. Heat and pour over the beans.

Now, they were the directions and you can take them or listen to what I did. I mixed the seasonings with the drippings and melted them in my sauce-pan, if one could call it that in the wildest of imaginations. Then I dumped in the beans which I confess I had cooked in the cool of "Oh, what a beautiful morning" of a day that could be so horrid in the afternoon. Then with two forks, I gently mixed the beans with the seasonings. If you like flavor add a little more of each named seasoning. The original amounts probably would be all right for four cups, but I, same as you, used what amount of beans I had. Allow the beans to simmer long enough to let each ingredient do all that is in its power to do for the good of the beans.

— Cissy Gregg, 1945

4 tablespoons bacon drippings
1 teaspoon prepared mustard, out of a jar
1 teaspoon Worcestershire sauce
Salt, pepper to taste
4 cups cooked beans

# MILLIE'S GREEN BEANS IN WINE SAUCE

Sauté bacon and onions together. Add everything else except green beans and cook until thick. Pour over hot cooked beans.

— Lillian Marshall, 1974

3 slices bacon, diced
1 medium onion, chopped
3 tablespoons sugar
2 tablespoons cornstarch
3 tablespoons tarragon vinegar
½ cup sherry
4 cups French-cut green beans, cooked lightly and drained

# GREEN BEANS SUPREME

⅓ cup chopped onion
2 tablespoons butter or margarine
2 tablespoons flour
A teaspoon salt
¼ teaspoon pepper
1 cup sour cream
2 pounds green beans, Frenched
  and cooked
1 cup shredded sharp cheddar
  cheese

Sauté the onion in the butter or margarine. Blend in the flour, salt and pepper. Add the sour cream, stirring constantly, and cook until smooth and thickened.

Add cooked beans and pour into a shallow baking dish. Top with the shredded cheese. Bake in a moderate oven (350 degrees) for 15 to 20 minutes. This makes about six servings.

— Cissy Gregg, 1959

# GREEN POLE BEANS WITH HAM

*This Cissy Gregg recipe dates back to 1950. Maybe we get a tender variety of pole beans at the super-market these days because many cooks use only a fraction of Cissy's cooking time on their beans. Hull-outs are shelled beans.*

Cooking green beans in ham liquor is more like a "way" with the two foods than a recipe.

Buy the size of ham hock that will not make too ghastly a hole in your budget. Ours was a good-sized one, but that isn't necessary. Place the ham hock in a kettle of water. The water should almost cover the meat. However, the size of your kettle and the amount of beans you are using make a difference. The idea is to hit on the amount of water that will serve for the ham, then the beans, leaving only about a cup of liquor at the finish. Cover and simmer the ham until tender. I prefer the ham to be minus the bean flavor, and cook the beans only in the liquor. But that is a personal matter. Also consider the time element.

Take the cooked ham out of the kettle. Have ready 4 pounds of green pole beans and 1 pound of hull-outs. Have the pole beans washed, strung and broken into suitable lengths. Drop these into the boiling ham broth along with a pod of red pepper. Cover, and when the broth comes to a boil, turn the fire down so the beans will do no more than quietly simmer along. The water can become a little gay but not boisterous. If beans are boiled rapidly and water added they are never as good. Rapid cooking tears the beans open and causes them to be stringy. Keep the water going at the speed where it will not have to be renewed. The usual time given to cooking green beans hangs around 2 to 3 hours. Salt can be added toward the last, and the amount must depend on the flavor of the ham. Don't oversalt beans or any vegetable since it has a way of robbing the flavor.

There is a staunch divided opinion on when to add the hull-outs. My preference goes with those who add them after the pole beans have been cooking about an hour, since I like the hull-outs to be soft all right, but not mushy. Others start them about the same time.

# BUTTER-BEAN MEMORIES

Being a vegetable hound I love these. Maybe this goes back to my childhood, when there were two "older citizens" in my home town who grew "butter beans." One had to get a name on the list early in the year to have these fat luscious butter beans at least once a week. They would come to our home with every bean looking as much like the other as could be — all fat and tender green. They came in a jar, and we had to return the jar for refilling.

Some people I have found can grow "butter beans" and some can't. I don't know that they are choosy, but they have to like where they are.

The size of the butter beans — or limas, if you prefer — will govern the cooking time. We like to put these, shelled and washed, in boiled salted water — just enough to steam them. Then shake the saucepan every so often, gently of course, to have the butter beans tender but not overcooked. For 2 cups of the cooked limas, use about ½ cup sweet cream, a generous piece of butter, salt and pepper, and you have something delicious. Bring to a boil, shake around some, and serve hot.

— Cissy Gregg, 1960

# MAMAJANE'S BUTTER BEANS

*This recipe was from a 1949 Magazine feature by Cissy Gregg on Mr. and Mrs. James Armstrong of Henderson and on the cooking arrangements in their travel trailer. "Wherever the Andersons are," Cissy wrote, "they like their 'butter beans' cooked the way 'Mamajane' cooked them." The feature did not identify "Mamajane."*

Use fresh limas if you can get them, the large kind. The beans can be put on in cold water, plenty of it, salted, with at least ¼ pound of butter for about a pint of shelled butter beans. Let them cook slowly all afternoon. If you use frozen limas, they should be dropped into boiling salted water with the quarter pound of butter added for 1 package of limas, and cook at least 2 hours. There must be plenty of water in each case so there is plenty of juice left. When the water has cooked down to the level of the beans, add enough real cream to give the sauce-juice a cream color, and then cook slowly again until time to serve. In spite of all that Emily Post says about vegetables on plates and never in saucers, Mamajane's butter beans are served in saucers, with plenty of juice around them, and the last drop is captured with a spoon.

# BOURBON CARROTS

Scrape carrots and cut shape into the shape of large olives. Boil 20 minutes and drain.

In a saucepan, heat butter, sugar and concentrate until bubbly. Stir in bourbon. Place carrots snugly in a baking dish. Pour over sauce. Bake uncovered for 1 hour. Serves 10.

— Elaine Corn, 1984

**3 pounds carrots**
**1 stick butter**
**1 cup brown sugar**
**½ cup orange juice concentrate**
**2 jiggers bourbon**

# HONEY-GLAZED CARROTS

*The menu from the governor's mansion, featured by Elaine Corn in the 1984 holiday entertaining issue of the Magazine, included this recipe from Chef Vincent Ashby.*

2 cups chicken stock
1 teaspoon salt
2 pounds carrots, cut in 2-inch
   lengths
½ cup honey
2 tablespoons butter
2 tablespoons brown sugar
½ teaspoon ginger
½ teaspoon cinnamon

Boil the stock and salt. Add carrots and cook, uncovered, 15 minutes. Discard juice from carrots. Combine next 5 ingredients. Pour over carrots. Simmer 5 minutes and serve. Serves 8.

# CARROTS WITH HERBS

8 to 10 carrots (depending on size)
2 tablespoons butter or margarine
2 outer leaves from a head of lettuce
2 tablespoons boiling water
1 teaspoon sugar
¼ teaspoon salt
A dash of pepper
A sprinkling of chopped parsley
¼ teaspoon dried tarragon
2 tablespoons cream

Scrape and cut the carrots crosswise or lengthwise as you wish. Put them in a saucepan with the lettuce leaves, butter, boiling water and sugar. Cover and sauté by shaking the saucepan over the heat. Uncover and stir occasionally.

When the carrots are just barely tender, uncover and remove the lettuce leaves. Add salt, pepper and tarragon. Shake the saucepan over the fire again to distribute the seasonings. Add parsley and the cream. Heat hot and serve.

— Cissy Gregg, 1954

# MINT GLAZED CARROTS

½ cup margarine
8 medium carrots
½ cup sugar
2 tablespoons water
2 teaspoons dry mint leaves, or use
   fresh (the dry will be more potent
   by measurement than the fresh)

Wash and scrape carrots. Cut in strips. Cook until tender, about 10 minutes, in boiling, salted water. Drain. Combine margarine, sugar, water and mint. Stir over heat until sugar is dissolved. Arrange carrots in pan with sugar syrup. Cook, spooning syrup over carrots until carrots are glazed. Serves 4.

— Cissy Gregg, 1953

# ORANGE CARROT RING

Grate the carrots medium fine. Beat eggs with flour until smooth. Stir in orange juice, salt, Tabasco and melted butter. Add grated carrots and minced onion and mix well. Turn into buttered 5-cup ring mold. Bake in moderate oven, (375 degrees) an hour or until golden brown on top. Let stand 5 minutes, then turn out on serving platter. Fill the center with cooked peas and mushrooms or other cooked vegetables of your choice. We tried using orange slices around for garnish, and had them warm but not hot and not cooked. Serves 6 to 8.

— Cissy Gregg, 1962

1 pound carrots, washed and
  scraped
3 eggs
½ cup flour
1½ cups orange juice
1½ teaspoons salt
Dash of Tabasco
¼ teaspoon melted butter
1 small onion, minced
Orange slices, if you want to
  garnish them

# LEMON GLAZED CARROTS

Cook carrots in boiling salted water until barely tender. Heat sugar in skillet until golden brown; add butter, lemon juice and drained carrots. Heat until well glazed. This amount makes about four servings.

— Cissy Gregg, 1956

1 bunch carrots
2 tablespoons sugar
2 tablespoons butter
2 tablespoons lemon juice

# BRUSSELS SPROUTS WITH SLIVERED ALMONDS

Wash the sprouts well and cook them in the half steaming manner, with not too much salted water. If they're young and tender, the water may be salted in the beginning. If the sprouts are large, don't salt the water until they have cooked about 10 minutes. Boil rapidly and, small or large, they will cook in from 10 to 20 minutes. Keep semi-covered.

Remove from the heat the minute they can be penetrated with a fork, and drain thoroughly. Put in a pan with plenty of melted butter or margarine. Roll the sprouts around in the butter over low heat to be sure the flavoring of the butter or margarine penetrates well. Add salt to taste and plenty of fresh ground black pepepr. Don't overheat. Place in the serving dish, and top with slivered almonds, which give any dish a dash.

Black pepper is considered the natural spice for Brussels sprouts, but the French add a pinch of nutmeg also.

— Cissy Gregg, 1961

# BRUSSELS SPROUTS

In buying the fresh ones, it may be helpful to know that 1½ pounds of Brussels sprouts will make approximately 6 servings. Remove wilted leaves from the sprouts, wash and let stand in cold water for 15 minutes. Then place them in a saucepan, cover with boiling water, add salt and cook uncovered 10 to 20 minutes.

Serve them with butter sauce, which has been seasoned with salt and pepper and a little lemon juice.

To me, Brussels sprouts are a delicacy unrivaled by their cousins — cabbage, cauliflower and broccoli. Seasoned with that slight shadow of fresh lemon, they're bound to taste quite delicious.

Please don't overcook Brussels sprouts. We say the same about all vegetables, I know, but it is more disastrous with Brussels sprouts than with most of the others.

— Cissy Gregg, 1950

# PICKLED RED CABBAGE

1 small head red cabbage, shredded
¼ cup salt
1 pint water
1 cup vinegar
1 cup water
½ cinnamon stick
4 whole cloves
6 peppercorns
3 tablespoons sugar

Put cabbage in bowl. Mix salt and pint of water and pour over cabbage. Let stand four hours or overnight. Drain well. Mix rest of ingredients in saucepan and boil for 10 minutes. Strain. Pour hot liquid over cabbage. Allow to stand in refrigerator at least overnight. It's good then, but will get better if left for a week. Serves eight.

— Lillian Marshall, 1975

# SWEET-SOUR RED CABBAGE

1 large head red cabbage
1 medium onion, coarsely chopped
4 tablespoons bacon fat
¼ cup boiling water
2 tart apples, cored and sliced
½ cup vinegar
⅓ cup brown sugar

Remove outer leaves and hard core from cabbage and chop coarsely. Heat bacon fat in skillet and slowly cook onion until tender. Add the cabbage, season, cover and steam 10 minutes. Add apples and ¼ cup boiling water. Cover and simmer over low heat for an hour or until cabbage is tender. Add vinegar and sugar and continue to cook 15 minutes or longer. Serve hot.

— Lillian Marshall, 1973

*Ratatouille. Photograph by Durell Hall
Jr.*

# FRESH CAULIFLOWER WITH PARSLEY SAUCE

Remove outer leaves from cauliflower, leaving small tender leaves attached. Wash. Place whole head in a saucepan with an inch boiling water and salt.

Bring to boiling point without cover. Cook 5 minutes. Cover and cook 15 minutes or until cauliflower is tender, turning head to cook uniformly. Remove from saucepan and place in a serving dish.

Top with fresh parsley sauce. Should make six servings.

**A medium head cauliflower**
**An inch boiling water**
**1½ teaspoons salt**
**Fresh parsley sauce (see recipe)**

## FRESH PARSLEY SAUCE

Melt butter or margarine. Blend in flour. Remove from heat and stir in hot water and bouillon cubes. Cook until mixture begins to thicken.

Add light cream or evaporated milk. Cook until of medium thickness. Add seasonings and chopped parsley.

— Cissy Gregg, 1960

**1½ tablespoons butter or margarine**
**1½ tablespoons flour**
**A cup of hot chicken broth (or a cup hot water and a chicken bouillon cube)**
**½ cup light cream or undiluted evaporated milk**
**1½ teaspoons salt or salt to taste**
**⅛ teaspoon pepper**
**⅓ cup chopped fresh parsley**

# CAULIFLOWER WITH HORSERADISH SAUCE

Soak a head of cauliflower, head down, in salted water for 30 mintues. Then plunge into boiling water, head up. Cook for 25 to 30 minutes or until tender. Drain. Put on hot platter and pour horseradish sauce over it.

## HORSERADISH SAUCE

Combine one cup sour cream with 1 teaspoon prepared horseradish, 1 teaspoon prepared mustard and salt to taste. Heat thoroughly. A little paprika gives a faint but pleasing blush over the top.

— Cissy Gregg, 1949

# INDIA CAULIFLOWER WITH ONION AND TOMATO

1 head cauliflower, broken into
  small florets
1 onion, grated, including juice
⅓ cup vegetable oil
5 cloves garlic, minced
2 teaspoons ground ginger
3 medium fresh tomatoes, peeled,
  seeded and chopped (see note),
  or 4 small canned tomatoes
½ teaspoon cumin
1 teaspoon ground coriander seed
¼ teaspoon turmeric
⅛ teaspoon cayenne pepper
1 tablespoon fresh lemon juice
2 teaspoons salt
⅛ teaspoon saffron, optional

Soak florets 30 minutes in cold water. Meanwhile, grate onion and set aside with its juice. Heat oil in a heavy, wide skillet over high flame. Add garlic, stir a minute, then add cauliflower, which you have scooped out of water with a slotted spoon or strainer. Fry cauliflower 10 minutes, stirring. Remove cauliflower from skillet with slotted spoon and set aside.

To the skillet add the grated onion and juice, a little water and ginger, stirring 2 minutes on high heat. Add the tomatoes, cumin and coriander and cook over medium heat 5 minutes. Add remaining ingredients, except saffron, return cauliflower to skillet, stir well, reduce heat, cover and let cook 5 minutes. Add a few tablespoons of water, if necessary, to prevent sticking. Sprinkle over with saffron, if using. Cover again and cook 3 minutes more. Serve immediately. May be made ahead and reheated slowly, or eaten cold. Serves 4.

Note: To peel fresh tomatoes, drop into rapidly boiling water for 60 to 90 seconds. Rinse under cold running water. Slip paring knife under skins and peel off.

— Elaine Corn, 1984

# CAULIFLOWER POLONAISE

Cut off the stem of a fresh, tender cauliflower and put head down in cold water for about 30 minutes. Take out and drain and put it head up in a kettle of boiling, salted water. Cook uncovered until barely tender. Be careful not to overcook.

When ready to serve, place on a hot platter and have ready a mixture of finely chopped or grated hard-cooked egg mixed with minced parsley. Then in a small skillet melt 3 tablespoons butter or margarine and brown, but don't burn. To this add 2 tablespoons of dry bread crumbs and swish about in the skillet. Take off the fire and add a good healthy downpour squeeze of lemon juice and season with salt. Sprinkle the egg-parsley mixture on cauliflower head first and then pour over the butter-crumb-lemon topping, and lo, the cauliflower is now Polonaised.

— Cissy Gregg, 1947

# PUFFY CORN FRITTERS

Sift flour, measure and sift with salt and baking powder. Combine milk and egg and beat thoroughly. Add to dry ingredients and mix just enough to moisten. Cut the corn off the cob in full kernels and then scrape the cob with your knife as you would for making corn pudding. Stir the corn into the flour mixture with a light touch. Drop batter by tablespoonfuls into deep hot fat, 365 to 375 degrees by a frying thermometer. Fry for 2 to 3 minutes or until they are a pretty, light brown. Drain on absorbent paper. Using a standard measuring spoon, you should get about a dozen and a half of the puffy fritters.

These may be made from canned corn which has been drained. They are wonderful with syrup, too, for breakfast.

— Cissy Gregg, 1955

1 cup flour
¾ teaspoon salt
1 teaspoon baking powder
½ cup milk
1 egg, beaten
1½ cups corn

# CORN PUDDING

*Cissy Gregg relied solely on fresh corn for this 1948 recipe, but for a 1960 corn-pudding recipe, she wrote that frozen corn could be substituted if you "either chop it fine or put it through the meat grinder." She probably would use a food processor today.*

The success of corn pudding is due, in my opinion, to the way the corn is cut from the cob. The mere tips should be cut from the kernels then the rest of the pulp and milk scraped out, using the dull side of the knife. If you have one of the graters that come three to a set and sorta flat-out, I find them most useful for grating the corn off the cob. It seems to me the grating method isn't as "sputtering" as scraping.

Beat the egg yolks, salt, pepper, melted butter or margarine and milk together. Sprinkle the flour over the corn and blend in. Add the corn mixture to the egg yolk mixture. Beat egg whites and fold them gently into the corn group. Pour into a greased casserole dish and bake at 350 degrees for 45 minutes.

2 eggs, separated
½ teaspoon salt
A good pinch of cayenne pepper
2 tablespoons melted butter or
    margarine
1 cup milk
2 cups fresh corn, cut and scraped
    from the cob
1 tablespoon flour
1 tablespoon sugar

# OLD-FASHIONED FRIED CORN

½ cup diced bacon
3 cups canned whole-kernel corn,
  drained
1 teaspoon sugar
¾ teaspoon salt
⅛ teaspoon pepper
¾ cup milk

Fry bacon until crisp. Drain off all the fat but about 3 tablespoons. Add corn, sugar, salt and pepper to the fat. Cook about 10 minutes, or until the corn is lightly browned, stirring frequently. Add milk and continue stirring. Cook and stir until the milk is absorbed, then cook about 5 minutes longer. Add cooked diced bacon. Remove to a hot platter and serve immediately. Wonderfully good for a light meat meal.

Salt pork can be diced and used instead of the regular bacon. But in so doing, reduce the amount of salt to about ¼ teaspoon, and watch it using only that much.

— Cissy Gregg, 1949

# HATTIE COCHRAN DICK'S STUFFED CUCUMBERS

*This dish, the subject of a Magazine feature by Lillian Marshall, was part of a centenary buffet planned by the Phil Hollenbachs of Pewee Valley in 1970.*

*"As a little girl, Hattie Cochran inspired the well-known Little Colonel books by Annie Fellows Johnston," Hollenbach told Lillian. "As Mrs. Albert Dick, she is noted for her delightful parties. This recipe of hers was included in Marion Flexner's famous cookbook, 'Out of Kentucky Kitchens.' I like it especially with baked fish but felt a centenary buffet would be incomplete without it."*

Cut unpeeled cucumbers in halves, lengthwise. Scoop out centers with a sharp spoon, being careful not to break shells. Grind scooped-out cucumber with green peppers, onion and parsley, using proportions to suit your taste. Season with salt, pepper and nutmeg, and mix well. Stuff this mixture into shells. Sprinkle about 1 tablespoon dried bread crumbs over each half-cucumber and dot with butter.

Place in baking pan, add a little water to bottom of pan and bake at 350 degrees for about 45 minutes, or until well-browned.

# SIMPLE DILLED CUCUMBERS

3 medium cucumbers
Salt, to taste
½ cup vinegar
Juice of 1 lemon or lime
3 tablespoons granulated sugar
3 tablespoons brown sugar
¼ cup chopped fresh dill, or 1½
  tablespoons dill seed

Slice cucumbers into paper-thin coins. Place in a colander, sprinkle with salt, let sit 15 minutes, then rinse in cool water. Toss in a large bowl with remaining ingredients. May be made several hours in advance. Serves six.

— Elaine Corn, 1982

# O.S.I. STUFFED EGGPLANT

*"The Old Stone Inn, Shelbyville Road, is one of the places that serves food to be remembered," Cissy Gregg wrote in 1953. "They are always so free with their recipes; when we get calls about 'I wonder what in the world the O.S.I. does to this or that to make it so good,' we just call, state our case and listen. The results come out fine."*

Parboil the whole, unpared eggplant for about 10 minutes. Cut in half lengthwise. Scoop out pulp, leaving a 1-inch wall. Turn the hull upside down in a pan to keep it from darkening. Turn your attention to the pulp. Melt the butter in a skillet and sauté the onion and the parsley in the butter. Cut the pulp in small pieces and combine with the onion and parsley. Add the undiluted cream of mushroom soup. Season with salt, pepper and Worcestershire. An egg can be added if you like. If the stuffing seems too moist, add a few butter-cracker crumbs. Remember never to add soda cracker crumbs to eggplant, the chief cook says. It makes it ugh. The butter-cracker crumbs give it taste quality.

Fill the shell with the seasoned pulp, rounding it up as much as possible. Don't overlook the pulp that was in the top side of the eggplant. We like to cut ours so the top piece is severed just above the stem, and fill the large half with the pulp from both halves. Makes it look a little fuller.

Sprinkle the top with butter-cracker crumbs — buttered, and then with paprika. Place in a pan with a little water in the bottom and bake at 375 degrees for about 25 minutes, or until the stuffing is good and hot and the seasonings are well blended — cooked in, that is. Serve from the shell.

**1 medium-sized eggplant**
**¼ cup chopped onion**
**2 tablespoons, more or less, of melted butter or margarine**
**Chopped parsley to taste**
**Salt and pepper**
**1 can cream of mushroom soup**
**Worcestershire sauce to taste**
**Butter-cracker crumbs**
**Melted butter**
**Paprika**

# FRIED EGGPLANT STICKS

Peel eggplant. Cut French-fry style. Add salt and pepper to one part flour. Dredge eggplant in seasoned flour. Dip into eggs. Roll in plain flour. Fry in a wide skillet in olive oil over medium-high heat, until eggplant is golden brown. Drain on paper towels.

— Elaine Corn, 1983

**1 medium eggplant**
**2 eggs, beaten**
**1 cup flour, divided**
**Salt and pepper**
**½ cup olive oil**

# FRENCH FRIED EGGPLANT

Peel off that beautiful purple skin of the eggplant and cut the eggplant finger-shaped style or according to the way you like it shaped. Place in cold water to which salt has been added. Place a plate on top of the eggplant and weight it down — we usually use another plate to keep the pieces under water. Keep it so submerged for 20 to 30 minutes. Take out and drain on absorbent paper and pat dry.

First roll in flour, then in egg which has been diluted with about a tablespoon of water or milk per egg. Then roll the pieces in fine dried bread crumbs, fine cracker crumbs or in corn meal. Allow to stand a few minutes for the coating to set. Fry in a deep-fat fryer with the temperature about 375 degrees, or fry in a skillet with fat an inch or so deep where the fat is hot enough to heat the hand when placed over the hot fat. In either case roll the skillet so the pieces will brown on all sides, or shake the basket in the deep fat fryer in a way that will do the same. If you have stubborn pieces that won't roll by these methods, turn them with a spatula.

Drain again on absorbent paper and keep hot. But since eggplants are sent to the market in different sizes, and sometimes they are too much for one meal, even though you like them as much as we do, the fried fingers can be placed in a plastic bag and frozen. Then they can be reheated for a meal at a later date.

— Cissy Gregg, 1959

# TO COOK KALE

First comes the washing of kale. And then, with kale's beautiful plumage washed until it glistens, the time comes to strip it. You'll read where it should be cut from "tough stalks and stems and outside circle of tough leaves." I read that many years ago, but I had to learn what was meant by these words. I prepare kale for the pot by "stripping" each stalk of its leaves, leaving intact only the wee ones. Studies show that the stalk isn't the important part of kale. The leaves hold the flavor, and they can be cooked tender quickly. But the stems are tough and stubborn and need long cooking, which destroys the flavor of the leaves.

— Cissy Gregg, 1949

# FRIED OKRA

Cut the ends from tender okra pods and slice into 1-inch pieces or a little thicker depending on the size of the okra. Drop into one of those wonderful gadgets called a "brown paper sack" in which has been placed an amount of flour, cornmeal, salt and pepper. Shake to coat. Remove from bag and shake off excess flour. Fry in heavy skillet, in which has been melted a shallow layer of bacon drippings — or use shortening *(or cooking oil)*. Fry until brown on all sides, turning frequently. We added more salt and pepper to ours, but that is a matter of taste.

— Cissy Gregg, 1959

# OKRA, SOUTHERN STYLE

To cut the okra, we find it best to snip off the tops and drop the whole pod into ice water until you are ready to send them to the pot of boiling, salted water. Chop the onion medium fine, and chop the green pepper into rather large pieces so you know without inquiring that they are there. Peel the tomatoes by blanching, and then when quartering them, take out some of the juice and seeds so the mixture won't be soupy — unless you like it that way.

When the preparation work has been done, drain the okra and cut into the size pieces you like. Cook in boiling salted water for 10 minutes. Meanwhile, melt the bacon drippings or heat the salad oil in a heavy saucepan and lightly tinge the onion and green pepper with a sunburn — don't overdo it and do the cooking slowly. Mix the seasoning and flour together and add, stirring. Add okra and tomatoes and simmer until the vegetables are tender, stirring as little as possible. Get those on the bottom to be on top by "handling" the saucepan which is just another way to say gently shake the pan. Taste to correct the seasoning.

— Cissy Gregg, 1953

1½ to 2 cups cut okra
1 medium-sized onion, chopped
1 green pepper
4 tablespoons bacon drippings or salad oil
4 medium-sized tomatoes, peeled and quartered
2 teaspoons sugar
1 teaspoon flour
½ teaspoon salt
½ teaspoon pepper

# OKRA, CORN AND TOMATOES

Melt the fat in a skillet and sauté the onions in it. Add the okra and sauté 5 minutes. If the okra is large, slice it; if it is the small kind, nip off the stem end and use whole. Add the tomatoes and the rest of the seasonings. Simmer all together until the okra is tender. Cover the skillet for the simmering period.

The combination of okra, tomatoes and corn either charms people to the point where they'll roll their eyes around in their heads at the very thought of it, or it brings forth a grimace and the remark, "Why spoil good tomatoes and corn by okra?" Try it once and see if you don't like okra, especially hitched up with two such great favorites.

— Cissy Gregg, 1946

2 tablespoons butter, margarine or bacon drippings
½ cup finely chopped onion
1 pound okra
2½ cups canned tomatoes, or use about four good-sized fresh ones
1¼ teaspoons salt
½ teaspoon paprika
¼ teaspoon curry powder
2 teaspoons brown sugar

# SAVORY ONION LOAF

6 cups soft bread crumbs
¾ cup diced celery
1¼ cups chopped onions
2 tablespoons chopped parsley
¾ pound bulk pork sausage
1 egg, slightly beaten
¾ cup milk

Mix crumbs, celery, onion, parsley, sausage, beaten egg and milk together until well-blended. Use your hands to shape into a loaf. Put in greased baking dish. Bake, uncovered, in 350-degree oven one hour, or until brown. Serves six. This also makes a savory onion stuffing for roast turkey, duck, or breast of lamb or veal.

— Lillian Marshall, 1978

# ONIONS STUFFED WITH WILD RICE

12 large onions
1 small box wild rice, cooked for 6
   servings according to package
   directions
12 pats butter
2 cups beef stock

Boil unpeeled onions for 10 minutes. Drain and rinse under cold water. Cut off the root end. Peel outer skins. Remove top third. Hollow out centers using a large spoon.

Heat oven to 350 degrees. Place onions in a baking dish. Put a pat of butter in each. Cover dish and bake onions 30 minutes. Keep onions warm after baking. Prepare the rice, using beef stock instead of water. When rice is done, drain well, then stuff into onions. Serve on a bed of steamed spinach. Makes 12.

— Elaine Corn, 1983

# PLAIN BLACK-EYED PEAS

1 pound black-eyed peas
1½ pounds smoked meat or bacon
   ends
1 bay leaf
Pinch thyme
Several pods of red pepper
1 pod garlic
1 large onion
½ teaspoon mustard
Salt and pepper to taste
Few sprigs parsley
Worcestershire sauce
Tabasco sauce

Parboil meat 30 minutes. Wash and soak peas. Add onions, garlic and seasoning meat. Boil slowly for about 1½ hours. Add salt and pepper. Don't be afraid of seasoning. Peas need a lot of seasonings to pep them up. They do absorb a lot of water, so be sure to keep them well covered.

When we cook them — which isn't once a year, by any means — we treat them in the way of baked beans and don't hold back on Worcestershire and Tabasco sauces.

— Cissy Gregg, 1960

# LILIALYCE AKERS' LEBANESE PEAS

*Dr. Lilialyce Akers is associate professor of sociology and women's studies at the University of Louisville. Lillian Marshall included her recipe in a 1967 feature.*

Lightly brown meat in butter or oil. Add onion and tomato, stir and fry lightly together, just for a minute or two. Add peas, season to taste, cook together just for a few minutes and serve hot.

¼ pound ground round steak
1 tablespoon butter or oil
1 onion, chopped
3 tomatoes, peeled and cubed small
A 10-ounce package frozen peas, heated and drained
Salt and coarsely ground pepper to taste

# MR. PEARSON'S PEA SHORTCAKE

*This recipe in "The Countryman's Cookbook," by Haydn C. Pearson, caught Cissy Gregg's eye. Intrigued, she tried it and liked it. You may "smirk over the very idea," she told her readers, "but they laughed at Edison and the Wright Brothers."*

On the bottom of a deep soup plate spread an opened, homemade biscuit. The biscuit should be steaming hot and have a crisp brown crust. On the fluffy white insides spread plenty of butter. Then pour about a pint of peas and plenty of liquor in which the peas were cooked over the biscuit. That's a dish. In fact, it's a whole meal.

# PEAS TIMBALES

Beat the eggs and add the milk. Add the melted butter to the peas after they have been forced through a strainer. Mix altogether and season to taste. Pour well-buttered custard cups about two-thirds full of the pea mixture and place in a pan of hot water. Cook in a 300-degree oven for about 40 minutes or until the timbales are firm. Let stand a minute or two before turning out on a hot platter. Serve with cream sauce.

— Cissy Gregg, 1943

2 cups pea pulp
2 tablespoons melted butter
½ cup milk
2 eggs
Salt and pepper, to taste
A little sugar
A dash of onion juice and lemon juice

# PEAS AND SOUR CREAM

3 pounds of fresh peas
1 tablespoon melted butter
A pinch of sugar
1 cup sour cream
Sprigs of mint or chives

Shell the peas, cook them in as little boiling salted water as is possible. We like to add a handful of washed pea pods to the batch for extra flavor. It's hard to estimate the actual cooking time since all peas are not alike. For young peas, 10 minutes is considered about the right time. Take out the pea pods, drain the peas and put them back in the pot with the butter. Shake the pot over the heat — not on it — until the peas are coated with the melted butter. Add the pinch of sugar. Add the cup of sour cream and fold in quickly until well distributed. The peas will be hot and the cream cold, so you'll have a nice combination of textures and flavors.

Sprinkle if you like with chopped mint or chives, or tuck some mint in the sides where you can smell the fresh fragrance of the mint.

— Cissy Gregg, 1955

# HOPPING JOHN

2 ham hocks
2 quarts water
1 pound black-eyed peas
1 cup raw brown rice
1 bay leaf, broken in half
2 medium or large onions, chopped
1 small red hot pepper, crushed

Put the hocks and water in a pot and bring to a boil. Add the peas and bring back to a boil. Lower heat and simmer 1½ hours. Stir in rice, bay leaf, onion and pepper, stir, cover and cook without stirring until rice is done, about 45 minutes. Serves six to eight.

— Deni Hamilton, 1979

# MISS LUCY'S GREEN PEPPER PIE

*"Miss Lucy" was Mrs. Lucy W. Fonville of Bowling Green, Ky., grandmother of Cissy Gregg's assistant, Mrs. Joan Biggs. For this 1962 recipe, Cissy wrote that "Miss Lucy just cooks, and has small interest in measurements, but we followed these directions and this is what happened."*

4 medium peppers, washed, split
    and seeded
Crumbled crackers
Butter
Milk
Seasonings to taste
Grated cheese

Put the peppers in boiling water which has been salted — there should be enough water to keep them off the bottom of the vessel and in a floating postion. When they are just tender, cube. Put a layer of the crumbled crackers into a greased casserole. Next, put in a layer of the peppers, another layer of the cracker crumbs and so on until you get to an inch of the top. Add dollops of butter, salt and pepper.

Have the milk warm, and we put in a drop or two of Tabasco to help the peppers on their way. Pour the warmed milk over the peppers and cracker crumbs in the casserole, spread a little grated cheese over the top and bake in a moderate oven, approximately 350 degrees, for about 30 minutes.

Miss Lucy says it will serve 6 generously. It's mighty good and we can't honestly say how many can eat it. We weren't long in the devouring of the casserole we used. The casserole we used was about a quart and a half, and our peppers were large and plump. No one can tell you how to measure "crumbled" cracker crumbs, and we wouldn't want to take all initiative out of your cooking, anyhow.

# Stuffed Banana Peppers

*Mrs. C.S. Williamson of Louisville advised Cissy Gregg on this recipe, printed in 1952. She served the banana peppers with spaghetti and meatballs.*

Plan on about 2 peppers per serving, and believe me, they are hot but a good hotness.

Mix all the ingredients together very well. Wash the peppers — about 12 of them — and cut off the stem end. Pull out the seeds and membrane. Stuff with the meat mixture. You can, Mrs. Williams said, save the tops and put them back on the peppers, securing them in place with toothpicks.

Put the stuffed peppers in a baking dish and pour over them either olive oil or salad oil. Pour over enough so there is about ⅛ inch of it in the bottom of the baking dish. Bake in a 300-degree oven for about 45 minutes.

¼ **pound ground beef**
¼ **pound ground pork**
3 **sprigs of parsley, chopped fine**
3 **tablespoons grated parmesan cheese**
3 **tablespoons cracker meal**
1 **teaspoon salt**
1 **egg**
1 **small can chopped mushrooms (optional)**
**Olive oil (or other cooking oil)**

# STUFFED GREEN PEPPERS

**4 medium-sized green peppers**
**1½ pounds ground beef**
**¼ cup chopped onion**
**1½ cups cooked rice**
**¼ cup chopped green pepper from
   the tops**
**1¼ teaspoons Tabasco**
**1 teaspoon salt**

Remove pepper tops. Slice white membrane from inside of each pepper. Drop peppers into boiling water.

Let simmer — some say 5 minutes, some say 15 minutes. We say use your judgment. If the pepper is a thick-housed one, it takes longer than one that is a thin-housed one.

Combine beef, onion, chopped pepper, Tabasco and salt in a skillet. Sauté until pepper is tender. Toss rice to blend with ingredients.

Stuff each pepper with ¾-cup filling. Stand peppers in a greased baking dish. Bake in a moderate oven (375 degrees) about ½ hour or until the peppers are tender.

Only lately have I learned that these may be served hot or cold.

I always like to add tomatoes to the pan and then baste them a little with the juices in the pan. The peppers we have at this time of the year are rather large. We like to cut ours lengthwise and fill them.

— Cissy Gregg, 1962

# GREEN PEPPER CUSTARD

**8 green peppers, skinned**
**1½ cups cubed American cheese**
**6 eggs, slightly beaten**
**2 cups milk**
**Salt and pepper to taste**

To skin the peppers, place them under a broiler and turn on all sides until skin starts to blister. Put them in a paper bag and let stand 15 minutes. Wash the skin off under running water.

Remove stems and seeds from the skinned peppers. Cut them into thin strips. In a greased casserole place a layer of the green pepper strips and then a layer of cheese. Repeat this until all of the peppers and cheese are used up. Combine eggs and milk. Season to taste. Pour mixture over peppers and cheese. Bake in a slow oven, 300 degrees, for one hour, or until the mixture is firm in the center.

This one makes a good main luncheon or supper dish. Should serve about eight.

— Cissy Gregg, 1951

# COLCANNON

Wilt the kale by steaming. Drain well and toss with butter. Reserve. Peel and slice potatoes, then simmer in salted water until tender, about 20 minutes. Drain well and mash. Pour boiling water over the onions, then drain and add to milk. Heat to simmering, then whip the milk and onions into the potatoes until smooth. It should be a little thinner than for regular mashed potatoes. Fold in the buttered kale and season with salt and pepper. Serves six.

— Deni Hamilton, 1980

½ bunch, or about 7 ounces, kale
3 tablespoons butter
2 pounds potatoes
About 1 cup milk
6 green onions, chopped
Salt and pepper to taste

# HERBED PARSLIED POTATOES

Peel off a strip around the middle of each potato. Boil potatoes until tender. Drain. Add parsley, butter, salt and pepper to pan. Shake pan over heat until butter melts. Serve hot.

— Elaine Corn, 1983

8 to 10 new potatoes
Chopped fresh parsley
½ stick to 1 stick butter
Salt and pepper, to taste

# BOILED SLICED POTATOES WITH MUSTARD SAUCE

Use a whisk to blend the onion, mustard, sugar, oil, vinegar, egg yolks and cream. Fold in parsley. Arrange hot potato slices on a platter, overlapping. Spoon over with mustard sauce. Serves two or three.

— Elaine Corn, 1983

2 teaspoons finely minced onion
2 tablespoons prepared yellow
   mustard
1½ teaspoons sugar
1½ tablespoons oil
1½ tablespoons vinegar
2 yolks of hard-boiled eggs,
   crumbled
1½ tablespoons cream
1 tablespoon fresh, chopped parsley
4 boiled thin-skinned white
   potatoes, skins on and sliced

# HOLIDAY BAKED POTATOES

12 baking potatoes
¾ cup hot milk
¾ cup margarine
2 teaspoons salt
¼ teaspoon white pepper
1½ cups shredded zucchini (2 small)
3 tablespoons grated onion
1 3-ounce jar chopped pimentos, drained

Scrub potatoes, prick each with a fork and bake in 450-degree oven 45 minutes or until done. Cut slice from top of each potato immediately and scoop out centers, being careful not to break skins. Add milk, ½ cup margarine, salt and pepper to the hot scooped-out potatoes, mash and whip until light. Cook zucchini and onion in remaining margarine 2 to 3 minutes. Stir zucchini, onion and pimentos into potato mixture. Spoon mixture into shells; place on baking sheet and bake in preheated 325-degree oven 30 minutes. (Potatoes can be prepared several hours in advance and refrigerated. Increase baking time to 45 minutes.) Makes 12 servings.

— Deni Hamilton, 1980

# BAKED STUFFED POTATOES

Anyone can sometimes get tired of family, husband or friends. But who gets tired of a good, luscious baked potato, stuffed or plain? Have you ever been exposed to a surfeit of exotic foods? Once a year I am, when I go to a food editors meeting, and when headed home, I have only two foods in mind — a baked potato, and vegetable soup, American style.

We're taking on the stuffed potatoes for the moment. Even looking at a picture of them gives me the inspiration to do the same for home tonight.

It takes skill to bake potatoes, as simple as that is. First the potatoes must be of similar size for even baking, not oiled, and baked in a 400- to 500-degree oven to make the potatoes come from the oven with a crisp skin.

Test for doneness with a thin skewer so as not to mar the skin. When tender, roll each potato in mitted hands, or just use a clean tea towel as I do.

If the potatoes are tender, cut off the tops lengthwise. Scoop out potato from shell, whip or rice. Add enough hot milk or cream to make fluffy, some butter or margarine, salt and pepper. Refill shells, piling high. (At home, I insure this piling-high business by baking an extra potato.) Top with butter or cheese as desired. Stick back in a hot oven and brown 10 to 15 minutes.

There are all kinds of additions that can be done, too, such as grated cheese on top of the stuffed potato before it goes back into the oven. Maybe you'd like the idea of adding one or two warmed sardines to a potato, sticking them into the top before the last browning in the oven. The stuffed or plain potato makes a wonderful background for almost all creamed sauces, chipped beef and so forth. Well, nothing ever tastes so good as when it has a baked potato for the background.

— Cissy Gregg, 1960

# HASH BROWNED POTATOES WITH SESAME SEEDS

*We didn't find "teenincee" in Webster's, either, but it was pretty clear what Cissy Gregg meant. This recipe was published in 1956.*

Cook the potatoes until they are just tender — they should be firm so they won't mash up in the second cooking. Cut the potatoes into teenincee little squares. Be very neat about it. Keep cutting until you have the 4 cups. Melt butter or margarine in a heavy skillet and add the sesame seeds and finely chopped onion. Cook until the sesame seeds are lightly browned, stirring for the goal of even toasting of the seeds. Add potatoes, salt and pepper, and cream. Cook, stirring occasionally, until the potatoes are a golden brown.

It is remarkable what the few sesame seeds do to this simple dish.

**4 cups diced boiled potatoes**
**¼ cup butter or margarine**
**⅓ cup sesame seeds**
**2 tablespoons minced onions**
**Salt and pepper**
**¼ cup heavy cream**

# ESCALLOPED POTATOES AND HAM

In a buttered baking dish put about one third of the thinly sliced potatoes, butter, flour and salt. Prepare in layers in the same manner until all of the ingredients are used. Add the milk (which we, being old-fashioned, warmed a little before adding to the potatoes).

Cut the slice of ham around the edges to keep it from curling, place on top of the potatoes. Bake at 400 degrees for 1 to 1¼ hours.

As a P.S., we seasoned the potatoes rather well with salt, then added a little marjoram — a small pinch. Then when it came to the ham, we brushed it ever so lightly in the middle with honey. It made the ham a little more merry in the face.

When we moved the ham, we gently put it aside, then put the potatoes on a hot platter with all the juices from the pan and laid the slice of ham on top.

— Cissy Gregg, 1961

**5 cups potatoes, thinly sliced**
**4 tablespoons butter**
**4 tablespoons flour**
**2 teaspoons salt**
**1½ cups milk**
**1½ pound slice of ham**

# NEW POTATOES IN JACKETS

Scrub potatoes well, and try to have them nearly alike in size. Place them in a heavy saucepan with as small an amount of water as possible to steam them rather than boil them — but don't let them burn. Cover tightly and boil until tender; this usually takes from 20 to 25 minutes, but the size will determine the time it takes to cook them.

Drain any water that is left. Place a napkin in a bowl or basket and roll the potatoes in. Even pull a corner of the napkin up over them so they will stay cuddly warm in their nest. For extra seasoning, it's everyone for himself.

— Cissy Gregg, 1949

# FANCY-NAMED SCALLOPED POTATOES

*Cissy Gregg didn't use it on this 1949 recipe, but she wrote that it "has a very fancy name in case anyone should ask you. And that name is* **pommes de terre au gratin dauphinoise.***" We think she put cheese in quotation marks to mean that you could use a cheese of your choice.*

Peel two pounds of potatoes and slice them thinly as for scalloped potatoes. Put the sliced potatoes in a bowl. Sprinkle with salt and pepper to taste, and a dash of nutmeg. Scald one cup of milk in which is a peeled, sliced, middle-sized onion. Strain the milk and beat it into one egg. Pour the egg-milk mixture over the sliced, seasoned potatoes and toss with two forks to mix well. Pour the potatoes and all into a greased baking dish which was rubbed with a cut clove of garlic before it was buttered. Sprinkle the top with grated gruyere or "cheese" and dot generously with butter.

And now, bake in a moderate oven, 350 degrees, for 40 to 45 minutes.

We found that two pounds of potatoes will fill a one-quart casserole to the very top, baked exactly in 45 minutes. Two pounds should serve about six persons, with all the rest of the meal.

# POTATO-CHEESE GRILL

**6 medium potatoes, sliced**
**3 onions, sliced**
**8 ounces cheddar, cubed**
**6 strips bacon, fried and crumbled**
**Salt and pepper to taste**

Wrap all ingredients in foil. Place package on grill for one hour.

— Elaine Corn, 1981

# POTATOES AND ANCHOVIES

*Cissy Gregg collaborated with Kristin von Pawel to produce an authentic Swedish smorgasbord in 1954, and this was one of the dishes. Kristin was the wife of Lt. Col. Ernest Von Pawel, who was stationed at Fort Knox, Ky.*

"Janssons Frestelse" was another hot dish we made, and the name means Jansson's Temptation. It is a dish of anchovies and potatoes, but Kristin was disappointed in the anchovies that we were able to provide. They were the ones put up in oil. Instead of cutting the potatoes up after they are peeled as we do for our scalloped potatoes, Kristin cut them crosswise first and then into narrow strips. The potatoes and anchovies are alternated in layers with potatoes on the top. Pepper was included among the seasonings along with finely chopped onions, but watch the salt. The anchovies will add their salt. Add enough cream so you can almost see it beneath the potatoes, and bake in a 375-degree oven until the potatoes are tender and nicely browned on top. Add more cream as it is needed. It took our Temptation about an hour and a quarter of baking until Kristin said they were done.

And so our day cooking in Sweden so endeth. We hope we have all the Swedish words spelled correctly. If not, do forgive, and thank you, Kristin von Pawel!

# POTATO PANCAKES

Mix potatoes with egg, flour and salt. Place salt pork in a large skillet and fry, stirring, until lightly browned. Add onion and continue cooking until onion is transparent. Remove the cooked pork and onion from the skillet and add them to the potato mixture. Heat fat remaining in skillet very hot and drop in potato mixture by tablespoonfuls, flattening each cake to desired thickness. Brown cakes on each side, drain on absorbent paper and serve hot. Makes 16 large cakes or 24 smaller ones, to serve 8.
— Lillian Marshall, 1972

**2 pounds potatoes, peeled and grated raw**
**1 egg, slightly beaten**
**2 tablespoons flour**
**1½ teaspoons salt, or to taste**
**2 ounces salt pork, finely diced**
**1 small onion, minced**

# SMASHED RADISHES

Wash and trim radishes. Lay each on its side, then crush by pounding it decisively once or twice with a heavy cleaver or bottom of a glass. They should split open but not break in two. Sprinkle with salt and let stand 10 minutes. Drain. Combine soy sauce, vinegar, sugar and remaining salt. Add to radishes and toss gently. Chill. Sprinkle with the oil just before serving. Use on relish dish with sliced cucumbers, green pepper and green onions. Or place a few on a lettuce leaf for a small individual salad. 6 servings.
— Lillian Marshall, 1969

**About 2 dozen radishes**
**¼ teaspoon salt**
**1 tablespoon soy sauce**
**2 tablespoons vinegar**
**1 teaspoon sugar**
**½ teaspoon salt**
**1 teaspoon salad oil**

# RATATOUILLE

½ pound zucchini, sliced crosswise
½-inch thick
1 medium eggplant (about ½
pound) pared and cut like large
French fries
½ cup olive oil
½ pound onions, sliced
1 cup sliced green pepper
2 cloves garlic, minced
1 pound ripe tomatoes or 1 cup
pear-shaped tomatoes, drained
Salt and pepper
3 tablespoons minced parsley
2 teaspoons basil

Place the sliced zucchini and eggplant in a large mixing bowl and sprinkle with a teaspoon salt. Let stand 30 minutes. Drain on paper towels. Heat a little olive oil in large skillet and sauté the zucchini and eggplant, one layer at a time, removing to another container as they cook. Add oil as needed and put in green pepper and onions.

Peel the tomatoes, cut crosswise and gently squeeze seeds out. Cut them coarsely and add to the peppers and onions in the skillet. Cook slowly, shaking pan from time to time, or stir gently, for 15 minutes.

Return eggplant and zucchini to pan. Add parsley, basil, salt and pepper and simmer, covered, for 5 minutes. Uncover, stir gently and cook several minutes or until most of the liquid has evaporated and vegetables are tender. Set aside, uncovered, until serving time. Reheat to serve, or serve at room temperature.

If you prefer, place the cooked vegetables in a casserole in layers and bake at 350, basting with natural juices, for about ½ hour. Serves 6.
— Lillian Marshall, 1969

# QUICK AND DIRTY RATATOUILLE

*Lillian Marshall printed this recipe in 1977, attributing "this sassy version" to Betty Lou Amster, editor of Louisville magazine.*

¼ cup oil
2 zucchini
2 yellow squash
1 medium eggplant, peeled
2 medium onions
2 tomatoes
¼ teaspoon tarragon
½ teaspoon basil
¼ teaspoon chervil
¼ teaspoon thyme

Heat oil in sauce pan. Cut vegetables into bite-size pieces. Put in skillet and toss in hot oil gently so all are covered. Add herbs and salt to taste. Put in covered 2½- to 3-quart baking dish in preheated 350 degree oven for one hour.

# SHAKER SPINACH WITH ROSEMARY

Pluck spinach leaves from thick stems. Wash in cold water several times to rinse off sand. Chop coarsely. Pile in a large saucepan with remaining ingredients, cover and cook, only in water that clings to the leaves, until spinach is bright green, about 5 minutes. Do not overcook. Serves 8 to 10.

— Elaine Corn, 1981

**4 pounds spinach**
**1 teaspoon fresh rosemary, or ½ teaspoon dried**
**½ cup chopped parsley**
**4 green onions, chopped**
**4 tablespoons butter**
**Salt and freshly ground pepper**

# MRS. OWENS' COMPANY SQUASH

*Down in Calhoun, Ky., Cissy Gregg wrote in 1951, "Mrs. J.S. Owens lets me 'pick her brains' sometimes. She seems to have an endless imagination when it comes to handling vegetables. I followed her directions for squash last night and came out very well. We must send you forth to be a little on your own, but I don't think you can go wrong."*

Cook squash with a small onion in a saucepan until barely tender. In a casserole place alternate layers of cooked or canned tomatoes, sliced cooked squash and cracker meal, topping off with cracker crumbs, I used, but meal will do, no doubt. Add cream, salt, pepper and butter or margarine.

Place in a moderate oven, 375 degrees, and bake until browned on top and well blended.

I had fresh tomatoes, so cooked them slightly and used them with the squash. Don't make it too "sloppy" with cream; you can always add a little more if necessary.

# SPAGHETTI SQUASH WITH RED CLAM SAUCE

Halve squashes, scoop out seeds, lay cut sides down in a baking dish and bake at 350 degrees for one hour. Drain clams, reserving juice. In a medium saucepan, combine juice and tomatoes. Simmer until reduced to 4 cups, breaking up tomatoes as they soften and stirring to prevent sticking. In another saucepan, heat the oil. Add the garlic and sauté one minute. Add tomatoes, oregano, basil, parsley, salt, pepper and clams. Heat through. With a fork, remove "spaghetti" from baked squash to a platter, discarding skin. Top squash with clam sauce and serve immediately. Makes four to six servings.

— Elaine Corn, 1983

**3 7-ounce cans chopped clams**
**2 28-ounce cans Italian plum tomatoes, or about 6 cups**
**2 tablespoons olive oil**
**3 to 4 cloves garlic, finely minced**
**2 teaspoons oregano**
**1 teaspoon dried basil**
**3 tablespoons chopped fresh parsley**
**Salt and freshly ground pepper, to taste**
**2 medium spaghetti squashes**

# BEAUMONT INN CUSHAW CASSEROLE

*The Mrs. Pauline Dedman mentioned in this recipe was co-owner of the Beaumont Inn in Harrodsburg, Ky. Cissy Gregg wrote this in 1953.*

The whole cushaw can be used but the choice part of this squash is the neck. Cut the squash in two, and scrape out the bowl, removing the seeds and stringy substances. Cut off the rind. (We found it easier to cut the cushaw into pieces and then cut off the rind.) Next cut the flesh into 1-inch square pieces.

Boil in hot clear water until the pieces are tender but not completely done.

All cooks of large quantities have their own way of measuring food, and this time it is by the casserole full.

Take a casserole 8 inches square and 1½ to 2 inches deep.

To each casserole of cushaw, add 1 cup white granulated sugar and ½ cup light brown sugar. Moisten the sugar with a little of the water in which the cushaw pieces were cooked. Bake in a 375-degree oven until the cushaw is clear. This takes about 35 minutes. Then remove from the oven, sprinkle the top with a little more brown sugar and dot the top well with small chunks of butter. Put back into the oven, and bake until the sugar and butter are melted and the top takes on a glazed tone. It is delicious, and we aren't surprised that it is remembered.

There are two ways of spelling cushaw that I have seen. It can be spelled the way we have, or "Kershaw." Mrs. Pauline Dedman, who sent the recipe to us, says that she prefers the "K" version since that was the way her mother told her it was spelled. And she is under the impression that this longnecked, delicately flavored squash was developed by a man named Kershaw and that's how it came by that name.

In making it several times we did learn about that sentence, "Moisten with a little water in which the cushaw was cooked." The first time we added a little too much and thought it soupier than it should be. The next time we improved on the situation. Then the last time, which was picture time, we mixed the pieces of cushaw and added the sugars. Then with clean hands we gently mixed them together. This process moistened the sugar and then we added only about a tablespoonful extra water to make sure the pieces wouldn't stick to the bottom of the casserole.

# APPLE-STUFFED SQUASH

3 acorn squash
1½ teaspoons salt
⅛ teaspoon pepper
2 tablespoons butter or margarine
3 small red winesap apples
2 tablespoons sugar
12 link sausages

Wash squash and split in half, lengthwise. Sprinkle with salt and pepper and dot with butter or margarine. Peel and core apples. Cut in halves and place a half in the hollow of each piece of squash. Sprinkle with sugar and place in a baking pan. Add a small amount of water to the pan, cover and bake in a hot oven, 400 degrees, for 45 minutes to an hour. Brown sausages in frying pan and place two on each squash half over the apple. Put back in the oven for about 15 minutes. It is one threesome that may make a crowd, but such a good one.

— Cissy Gregg, 1951

# BAKED ACORN SQUASH

Wash the squash and cut in half, allowing a half for a serving. They can be cut lengthwise or crosswise but they make a very pretty serving crosswise. This way they sit on the plate better and Nature has so fashioned them, they have a prettily scalloped edge. Scrape out seeds and fibers.

Place them cut side down in a shallow pan, and add a little water to the pan — not more than ½-inch deep. Bake about 30 minutes upside down in a 375-degree oven. Turn the hollow side up. Put in each a good hunk of butter or margarine, a sprinkling of brown sugar — or white, doesn't matter — a little nutmeg or cinnamon. Continue cooking for another 15 minutes, or until tender, basting the juice in the hollow over the sides once or twice during the latter part of the baking.

Squash is an easy vegetable to cook. It can be baked at a higher or lower temperature if such should help your oven management.

— Cissy Gregg, 1954

# STUFFED WINTER SQUASH

*This recipe was given to Elaine Corn by Fred Wiche, WHAS-TV's "Weekend Gardener," and his wife, Jenny. They were the subject of a Magazine feature by Elaine in 1983.*

Halve squash through the poles and scrape out seeds. Lay in a shallow baking dish, cavity side up. Sauté pork in a heavy skillet, mashing and breaking up as it cooks. Just as pink color disappears, drain off excess fat. Add onion, salt and pepper, and enough tomato juice to bind pork without making mixture runny. Add bread crumbs and more tomato juice, if necessary. Stuff squash, mounding meat. Sprinkle with grated cheese. Pour 1 inch water into baking dish. Bake at 375 degrees for 25 minutes. When served, the whole squash can be eaten. The skin tastes good, too. Serves 2.

**1 medium to large winter squash, such as butternut, acorn, banana**
**1 pound bulk pork sausage**
**1 medium onion, grated**
**Salt and freshly grated black pepper, to taste**
**1 6-ounce can tomato juice**
**1 cup fresh bread crumbs**
**Grated cheddar or swiss**

# MONA'S FRIED SUMMER SQUASH

*Cissy Gregg was served this dish in the lodge dining room at Pennyrile State Resort Park while on a Kentucky press tour in 1955. Mona Sisk was supervisor of the kitchen at the lodge. The original recipe gives no amount for the butter, so we suggest using 2 tablespoons.*

**2 pounds summer yellow squash**
**1 medium-size onion**
**Sugar, salt and pepper to taste**

Parboil or steam squash and onion together. (When squash is tender, there's no need for peeling it. Take off the stem and flower ends, wash, cook up. The onion should be finely chopped.)

When tender, drain well. Place in a heavy skillet or saucepan, and cook to dry out extra moisture. Season with salt and pepper, and a mite of sugar. Add butter and cook, stirring until dry. This should serve about 6.

# MASHED SWEET POTATOES

For these we used orange juice for a whipper-upper. You can use milk, pineapple juice or other liquids.

Boil, drain and mash sweet potatoes, allowing 1 good-sized sweet potato per serving. Moisten with hot orange juice and beat until light. Add butter and salt to taste — and sweet potatoes just lap up butter. Add a dash of sherry wine if you like. Pile into a hot bowl, and sprinkle chopped toasted pecans over the top.

To toast pecans, chop and toast in a skillet with a little butter or margarine.

— Cissy Gregg, 1951

# SWEET POTATOES WITH WESTERN TOUCH

These sweet potatoes can be served from the casserole in which they're baked, or tenderly lifted to a serving bowl.

Boil 4 to 5 large sweet potatoes in their jackets for 20 to 30 minutes or until tender. This will be enough for about 5 people, but you can judge the number for yourself since Nature refuses to cooperate and turn out sweet potatoes in uniform sizes and shapes.

Cool, peel and cut crosswise in 1-inch slices. Cover the bottom of a greased baking dish with a layer of sweet potatoes, sprinkle lightly with salt and brown sugar, and dot with butter. Cover with a layer of very thinly cut whole orange slices, peel and all — except the seeds, of course. Continue with alternate layers of sweet potatoes, seasonings and oranges until all the potatoes are used. Pour ½ cup honey over the top layer, which should be oranges, and dot with butter. Sprinkle on a topping of toasted, slivered almonds. Cover the casserole and bake in a moderate oven (about 350 degrees) for 45 minutes or thereabouts.

— Cissy Gregg, 1951

# SPICY WHIPPED YAMS

*Elaine Corn developed this recipe in 1981 for a low-fat, low-cholesterol Thanksgiving menu.*

Wash yams; place on baking sheet. Bake at 350 degrees for one hour. Cool; remove pulp; discard skins. Mash pulp. Add remaining ingredients except egg whites. When thoroughly combined, gently fold in the egg whites. Transfer mixture to non-stick, ovenproof dish. Bake at 400 degrees for 15 minutes. Yam mixture will rise slightly. Serves 6.

Contains about 5 grams fat and a trace of cholesterol per serving.

**6 yams**
**2 tablespoons unsalted margarine**
**1 teaspoon ground ginger**
**1 teaspoon ground mace**
**1 teaspoon cinnamon**
**2 tablespoons orange juice**
　　**concentrate**
**1 tablespoon honey**
**3 egg whites, stiffly beaten**

# SWEET POTATO-CRANBERRY CASSEROLE

Place sweet potatoes in saucepan, add water to cover, and boil 30 to 40 minutes until tender. Drain, cool slightly, peel and cut into ¼-inch slices. Arrange half the sliced sweet potatoes in a greased 1½-quart casserole and sprinkle with ¼ cup brown sugar. Dot with butter, and sprinkle half the cranberries over the top. Cover with remaining sweet potatoes, sprinkle with remaining brown sugar, add remaining cranberries and pour orange juice over all. Cover and bake in a 350-degree oven for 45 minutes. Uncover, sprinkle the following walnut topping over the casserole and bake 10 minutes longer. Makes about eight side-dish servings.

— Lillian Marshall, 1976

**4 large sweet potatoes**
**Water**
**½ cup brown sugar, packed**
**2 tablespoons butter or margarine**
**1 cup fresh cranberries**
**½ cup fresh orange juice**
**Walnut topping (see recipe)**

## WALNUT TOPPING

Mix all ingredients in a small bowl.

**½ cup chopped walnuts**
**2 tablespoons melted butter or**
　　**margarine**
**1 tablespoon brown sugar**
**½ teaspoon cinnamon**

# FRENCH-FRIED SWEET POTATOES

Wash and peel the sweet potatoes to the amount you think will be used. Cut in thin strips, lengthwise — let's not say too thin, but thin enough. Drop them in a bowl of cold water and hold until frying time like maids in waiting.

Roll the slivers in paper towels or a dish cloth to dry them off.

When the time comes that everything is about ready, drop the sweet-potato pieces into medium-hot fat, and cook them until done, stirring at intervals so they will be well browned on all sides and crisp as a fried potato should be. We don't salt these at first — there's no reason why they couldn't be, but we think that the natural sweetness of the sweet potato should be allowed to shine through, and after all, anyone can use the salt shaker if taste so desires.

— Cissy Gregg, 1962

# STUFFED SWEET POTATOES

6 sweet potatoes
½ teaspoon salt
2 tablespoons butter or margarine
Thin cream to moisten

Bake potatoes. Scoop out centers. Be careful about scooping out the soft insides. Leave a little more for the shell because the skin of the sweet potato is much thinner than that of white potatoes. Mash the scooped out potato and mix with the other ingredients. Stuff the mixture into the shells. Brush tops with a little melted butter or margarine, and reheat in a 425-degree oven until the potatoes are hot all the way through, and the peaks are tinged with brown.

To vary this recipe add a little chopped, cooked, leftover ham, some chopped peanuts, or a little peanut butter.

The liquid may be crushed pineapple with a little juice from the can, or orange juice with a bit of grated peel. Or put a marshmallow on top and bake until the marshmallow melts and browns.

— Cissy Gregg, 1954

# GLORIA'S WAY WITH TOMATOES

They say fingers came before knives and forks, and this is an example. I'm just about as close to Spain as I ever will be, but that doesn't keep us from enjoying what we hear about what they serve in Spain.

Maybe some of this summer's travelers will like to look in on this restaurant and see if we have been informed correctly.

Anyway, our scouts tell us that near Jerez, where sherry comes from, there is a restaurant run by a senorita by the name of Gloria. No doubt she's beautiful, but she is rated highly as a cook, too.

For something to serve with a glass of chilled sherry she dreamed up what we were told has been named, "Tomatoes Gloria."

Gloria chops up an onion, mixes it with a finely diced clove of garlic, places a spoonful of this mixture on a slice of raw tomato, and tops it with a spoonful of mayonnaise and a grating of fresh pepper.

After the formation has been constructed, you eat the slices of tomato with your fingers, at the same time sipping chilled sherry.

No one has informed us if the Restaurant Gloria served bibs along with these tomato slices. It could be that we are just messy, but when we tried doing this, our blouses had to go to the laundry tub the next day.

Perhaps a thin slice of toast under the slice of tomato might help.

It would be a wonderful idea to use the small cocktail tomatoes in similar fashion when they come in season with the summer.                    — Cissy Gregg, 1957

# BAKED TOMATOES WITH BASIL

*This was one of the dishes on the menu from Chef Vincent Ashby and the governor's mansion in 1984. Elaine Corn wrote about recipes from Ashby and the family of Gov. Martha Layne Collins for the holiday-entertaining issue of the Magazine.*

Place tomato halves on a broiling pan. Sprinkle with cheese. Combine basil, salt and pepper, and sprinkle over cheese. Dot with butter. Broil 8 minutes. Garnish with parsley.

**3 large tomatoes, halved**
**½ cup grated combination**
  **parmesan and cheddar cheese**
**1 tablespoon fresh, chopped basil,**
  **or 1½ teaspoons dried**
**½ teaspoon salt**
**¼ teaspoon pepper**
**2 tablespoons melted butter**
**Fresh chopped parsley, for garnish**

# MARINATED TOMATO SLICES

Place tomatoes in a shallow dish, overlapping if necessary. Stir together the olive oil, dill, green onions, lemon juice, garlic and parsley. Add salt and pepper, adjusting to taste. Pour over tomatoes. Cover tightly and refrigerate overnight. Can be made three days in advance. Serves 6.
                    — Elaine Corn, 1983

**12 large, thick tomato slices**
**6 tablespoons olive oil**
**1 tablespoon fresh, minced dill**
**2 green onions, minced, white and**
  **green parts**
**1 tablespoon lemon juice**
**½ teaspoon finely minced garlic**
**2 tablespoons fresh, minced parsley**
**1 teaspoon salt**
**Freshly ground pepper, to taste**

# TOMATOES ROCKEFELLER

2 large tomatoes, halved
2 tablespoons chopped onion
1 tablespoon chopped parsley
½ cup cooked, chopped spinach,
  well drained
1 tablespoon cooking oil or whipped
  margarine
2 tablespoons fine dry bread
  crumbs

Place tomato halves, cut side up, in baking dish. Mix together the onion, parsley, spinach and oil or margarine and spread evenly over the tomato halves. Top with crumbs. Bake at 375 degrees for 15 minutes, or until crumbs are lightly browned. 4 servings.

— Lillian Marshall, 1968

# COUNTRY FRIED TOMATOES

## GREEN

Slice the green tomatoes on the bias if they aren't large (this gives a larger slice). Dip in cornmeal, then in egg — diluted with milk, if you like — and back into the meal.

Fry in shallow fat. Season on both sides and serve hot.

The method for frying the red tomatoes differs somewhat.

## RED

4 medium-large firm tomatoes
Flour
⅓ cup melted butter or margarine
2 tablespoons sifted flour
1½ cups light cream
1 tablespoon instant minced onion
  (or a dash of grated fresh)
1 teaspoon salt

Cut tomatoes in ½-inch thick slices. Dip in flour. Sauté on both sides in a large skillet in the melted butter or margarine. Brown lightly.

Gently remove the tomatoes. Stir flour and cream into the pan drippings. Add onion and salt. Bring to a boil and simmer a few minutes, stirring. Add tomatoes and heat gently. Makes five to six servings.

I like the tomatoes served on toast with a little cheese or cooked bacon on top.

— Cissy Gregg, 1960

# STUFFED TOMATOES

Select large, firm, uniformly shaped tomatoes. Scoop out the centers. Sprinkle the inside with salt and dot with butter. Fill with this stuffing:

One pound hamburger browned in four tablespoons meat drippings; mixed with one cup dry bread crumbs, ½ cup chopped green pepper, ½ cup chopped celery, ⅔ cup water and salt to taste.

Put stuffed tomatoes in a 350 degree oven for 15 to 30 minutes, or until tender.

— Cissy Gregg, 1945

# OLD STONE INN BROILED HALF-RIPE TOMATOES

The greener the better, to their way of thinking. But when they can't find pure green tomatoes, they will settle on the near-ripe ones. Have them small and of uniform size. Wash and cut in half or thirds, according to the size of the tomatoes. Sprinkle the cut side with salt and pepper, and a small inkling of sugar if you wish. Cover the top of the tomatoes with crumbled butter crackers, and put a healthy dab of butter on top of the crackers. Place the thusly treated tomato halves on a baking sheet and slide into a hot oven, 375 to 400 degrees, and let brown — or until the tomato halves or slices are hot all the way through and the topping is hot and crusty, and serve forth with fish, fried chicken or as you wish. We have found them very good with bacon for breakfast.

— Cissy Gregg, 1962

# CLAUDIA SANDERS DINNER HOUSE BREADED TOMATOES

*The Shelbyville, Ky., restaurant named for Mrs. Harland Sanders supplied this recipe to the Cook's Corner column in 1984.*

Combine tomatoes, vegetable oil, onion, salt, pepper and charcoal seasoning. Cook over medium heat until mixture boils. While tomatoes are cooking, melt butter and add flour, mixing thoroughly. Add this to the tomato mixture. Cook until mixture thickens. Stir to keep from sticking. Add the sugar and simmer for 2 to 3 minutes. Mix in the toasted bread pieces just before serving.

**4 cups canned tomatoes (if whole, squeeze or mash them)**
**½ cup vegetable oil**
**1 teaspoon salt**
**¼ teaspoon black pepper**
**½ cup granulated sugar**
**½ cup chopped onion**
**½ teaspoon charcoal seasoning**
**2 tablespoons butter**
**2 tablespoons all-purpose flour**
**3 slices white bread toasted brown and cut into small squares**

# VEGETABLE MELANGE

Everyone does it differently, but we use butter, margarine or olive oil in a saucepan or skillet. We take the okra on first. If it's tender and fresh, moments mean a lot! Turn the okra over in the fat for a few minutes. Add the tomatoes, peeled, and cut in wedges. Don't cook too long — just turn over. Then add the corn kernels and cook a few minutes longer. We stir ours up a little until the corn is tender and season with more butter, salt and pepper — and that's it.

Other seasonings may be added like herbs, seasoning salts or what you have, but we would say start with the vital part — the okra, the tomatoes, the corn and then go on from that point.

To me it is one of the wonderful dishes that summer brings you.

— Cissy Gregg, 1960

# TURNIP GREENS

*Today most cooks try to preserve the nutrients in greens by cooking them a short time in a small amount of water. Few cooks could serve up the stories that accompanied some of Cissy Gregg's favorite dishes, however. This one was printed in 1945.*

When I was a child there was a turnip taboo on our household. It seems that when my father was a boy, a devastating drought hit Kentucky. It has become known as the Drought of the '80s. This was before the day of commercial canneries, and each farm home was dependent on the vegetables grown in the garden and canned at home. The days of scorching, rainless heat played havoc with the summer's supply of food and made winter's table turn a ghastly pallor. Trees lost their leaves in July that year, and nothing was left of the late summer garden. In desperation, the garden was finally plowed and the whole area was planted in turnips. Then the rain god relented, and along came gentle fall rains — just right to produce fine turnips and turnip greens. From that time on, my father's family ate turnips and turnip greens. My father swears that he put all his turnip-eating days in a string together. When he completed them, he had no desire to renew acquaintance.

Out from under the family roof, I ran into turnip greens and pot likker so squarely I could not help giving them respectful consideration. Besides that, I had wondered what the subject of one of Father's best-liked stories tasted like. And then I couldn't believe even a winter of eating them would turn me completly against them.

First pick out tender, perky turnip greens. Wash them well. The little leaves go in the pot as they come; the larger ones I strip from the stem, the same way I handle kale. Into a cooking pot, put 1 quart of water — cold water — for about each 2 pounds of turnip greens. For this same amount, use about ¼ to ½ pound of salt pork. Of course, if you can be choosy about selecting any piece of meat from the pig when it continues to play hard to get, pick out a piece of salt pork with a streak of lean in it. Cut the salt pork into slices about ¼ of an inch thick, and drop them into the pot of cold water. Bring to a boil and simmer the meat by itself for approximately 30 minutes. Then add the well-washed greens. Cover the pot and heat to boiling again, and let the turnip tops wither down. Turn the mess over in the pot at least once so the withering will be complete.

When this has been accomplished, press the leaves down under the surface of the water, and continue cooking uncovered for another 30 to 45 minutes — or until the greens are tender. Should more water be needed to keep the leaves covered, add boiling water. The actual time turnip greens take to cook depends on the age and tenderness of the tops.

Most turnips as greens have small turnips attached. These, I prefer to cook separately and season with the pot likker; but they can be cut up and cooked along with the leaves.

The salt pork does the work of seasoning; but at that, taste and see if a little more salt wouldn't make the mess just right.

# SAUCES

# FRESH MEXICAN HOT SAUCE

*Most cooks are on speaking terms with jalapeño peppers these days but are not as familiar with serranos. They're small — not nearly as plump as jalapeños — and their skins are not as dark.*

**1 bunch fresh coriander, or cilantro**
**4 large tomatoes, seeded***
**1 huge onion**
**4 garlic cloves**
**Juice of 2 limes**
**3 to 4 fresh jalapeño peppers, seeded**
**2 or 3 fresh serrano peppers, seeded**
**Salt and pepper, to taste**

Chop all ingredients and stir gently. Refrigerate about an hour before serving, to meld flavors. Serve with fresh tortilla chips, inside tacos or burritos, on eggs and steak.

*If fresh tomatoes in winter remind you of flannel pajamas, use canned Italian plum tomatoes and proceed as directed.

— Elaine Corn, 1982

# REBECCA SAUCE FOR DIPPING WITH STRAWBERRIES

**½ cup brown sugar, melted**
**½ cup bourbon**
**2 cups sour cream**
**Powdered sugar**

In a small saucepan, melt the brown sugar with the bourbon. Cool. Add sour cream. Thicken with powdered sugar until a dipping consistency. Makes 2½ cups.

— Elaine Corn, 1984

# MAYA'S MARINARA SAUCE

*This recipe was among those in a 1955 Cissy Gregg column on Maya Denise, a native of Milan, Italy, who had become a model in New York. Ms. Denise was visiting Louisville.*

Start with olive oil in a skillet. When it is hot, add peeled garlic (not too much — Italian cooking isn't garlicky). Then add the oregano. (Maya uses as much as will almost fill the palm of the hand.) Stir together and keep cooking slowly, stirring occasionally. Next open up a flat can of anchovies. Add contents, oil, too. The anchovies will break up sufficiently during the cooking and stirring. Keep frying and stirring. Add 3 teaspoons of capers, drained. Fry everything until it's all "nice". Add black pepper (very little). Add a large can of peeled tomatoes. ("Canned tomatoes are so wonderful here," Maya said.) Let everything cook half an hour, stirring occasionally.

In the meantime, cook a pound of spaghetti, but don't cook it too much. ("It should be *al dente,* you know." She looked around for the English word to come to her out of the air, and quickly said "Not too soft, you know.")

Serve the spaghetti with the sauce and plenty of parmesan cheese.

"This sauce is just as good on rice," Maya says.

# GULF HILLS REMOULADE SAUCE

*Cissy Gregg called this "one of the best sauces I have ever tasted or made" and attributed it to Gladys Hill of Ocean Springs, Miss. In 1952, Cissy used a food grinder for the recipe. A food processor or blender would save a lot of trouble today.*

The word "remoulade" in French means ground, and so we did. We put the capers, anchovies, the clove or pod of garlic and the half a bunch of parsley (which was interpreted as "a good fistful") and green onions — all good tops, too, along with the onion and anchovies through the food grinder. It works quite easily if you'll alternate the different textures to push the slow moving ones on their way.

Then we mixed this mixture with the mayonnaise, gently blending them.

You probably wouldn't want to make the full gallon. We based ours on the amount of capers that come in a small bottle — 2¼ ounces — which made us about two-thirds the amount. It wasn't too much, since kitchen visitors hung around eating it on crackers. The little bit we saved, we put in the refrigerator to see as to its keeping qualities. For the time we had it, it seemed to have the same keeping qualities as mayonnaise.

**3 ounces capers**
**1 cup anchovies**
**1 pod of garlic cloves**
**1 pint of Creole mustard**
**Enough mayonnaise to make a gallon**
**½ bunch parsley**
**½ bunch green onions**
**1 small onion**

# GEORGE BAILEY'S MARVELOUS BARBECUE SAUCE

*George Bailey was a photographer for The Courier-Journal and The Louisville Times when he contributed this recipe to Cissy Gregg in 1955.*

Mix all the ingredients and simmer about 20 minutes. Fish out the lemon slice. Cool slightly. Store. Makes about 1 pint.

For a hotter sauce, use about 1 teaspoon Tabasco sauce, says George. Sometimes he adds a little horseradish, or again, chili powder.

George cooks on an electric spit. He brushes the meat while it is cold and continues brushing every 5 to 10 minutes throughout the roasting time. You don't mind standing round and watching it because it is such effortless fun.

He doesn't use a thermometer but finds that an hour and 15 minutes is about right for a rolled rib roast weighing between 2 and 3 pounds. The Baileys like their beef medium done.

**¼ cup vinegar**
**½ cup water**
**2 tablespoons granulated sugar**
**1 tablespoon prepared mustard or salad mustard**
**1 teaspoon pepper**
**1½ teaspoons salt**
**¼ teaspoon cayenne pepper or Tabasco to taste**
**1 thick slice of lemon**
**1 slice onion, chopped fine**
**¼ cup butter**
**½ cup catchup**
**2 tablespoons Worcestershire sauce**
**1½ teaspoons liquid smoke**

# MINT SAUCE FOR LAMB

4 tablespoons minced fresh mint
2 tablespoon sugar (sometimes I
   use white and sometimes light
   brown)
½ cup vinegar

Pour the vinegar over the sugar, and warm and stir until the sugar is dissolved. Add the mint and let stand in a warm place for an hour or more before serving time.

I like to double or even triple this recipe while I'm at it because the sauce will keep. In fact, when the mint bed is really putting out, I make this recipe up and keep it for use later.

— Cissy Gregg, 1953

# MUSTARD SAUCE

*When Cissy Gregg offered this recipe in 1947, none of her readers would have jumped to the conclusion that it would be good on something that races at Louisville Downs. Today, however, you have to have a little "country" in you to know that "trotters" are pigs' feet.*

1 tablespoon flour
4 tablespoons butter or margarine
½ cup stock, consommé, or stock
   made with water and beef extract
½ cup prepared mustard
¼ cup granulated sugar
2 beaten egg yolks
½ cup lemon juice
Salt and pepper, to taste
A dash of cayenne pepper

Melt butter or margarine in the top of a double boiler, add and blend in the flour. When smooth, add the stock, mustard, sugar and seasonings. Cook, stirring every step of the way, until the sauce has thickened slightly. Then add the beaten egg yolks and cook a minute or two longer. But once the egg yolks are in, don't let the sauce boil or even get too hot.

I am a cautious soul, so I cook a sauce of this kind over hot water. And just before the yolks are put in, I turn off the fire and let the rest of the cooking take place with the heat of the water alone. Remove from heat and add lemon juice. Blend well and serve at once.

This mustard sauce was particularly recommended to me for fish or ham loaf, as well as for the "trotters."

# JEZEBEL SAUCE

1 18-ounce jar pineapple preserves
1 18-ounce jar apple jelly
1 5-ounce jar horseradish
1 1-ounce can dry mustard
1 teaspoon white pepper

Thoroughly blend all ingredients. Let stand at least four hours. Keeps indefinitely in refrigerator. Excellent with pork, beef, lamb, egg rolls, chicken, cream cheese and crackers. Makes about 5 cups.

— Cook's Corner column, 1985

# BASIC TOMATO SAUCE

Heat oil. Add onion and garlic. Sauté 10 minutes. Add tomatoes with juice, tomato paste, water, sugar, salt and pepper. Bring to a boil. Reduce heat so sauce simmers. Cook uncovered for 1 hour. Add herbs. Adjust seasoning. Cook longer if thicker sauce is preferred. Makes 4 cups.

— Elaine Corn, 1982

2 tablespoons olive oil
1 big chopped onion
2 minced cloves garlic
1 2-pound, 3-ounce can Italian plum tomatoes with juice
1 6-ounce can tomato paste
1 cup water
Pinch sugar
2 teaspoons salt
Dash ground pepper
½ teaspoon basil
½ teaspoon oregano

# COCOA FUDGE SAUCE FLEXNER

*This recipe was passed on to Deni Hamilton in 1979 by the celebrated Kentucky cookbook author Marion Flexner.*

Stir together the cocoa, sugar, milk, butter and salt in the top of a double boiler. Add the lump chocolate. Cook over simmering water about 15 minutes, stirring constantly, until smooth. Remove from heat and add vanilla. This keeps for weeks in the refrigerator in a 4-ounce glass jar. Reheat by putting the jar over simmering water, and spoon onto ice cream straight from the jar. Especially good over French vanilla or peppermint ice cream.

½ cup unsweetened Dutch cocoa
½ cup sugar
½ cup whole milk or half-and-half
2 tablespoons melted butter
Few grains salt
1 square (1 ounce) unsweetened baking chocolate
1 teaspoon vanilla

# VANILLA SAUCE

Mix sugar and cornstarch together. Add boiling water gradually, stirring constantly. Boil 5 minutes. Remove from heat and add other ingredients. Good with plum pudding.

— Cissy Gregg, 1951

½ cup sugar
1 tablespoon cornstarch
1 cup boiling water
2 tablespoons butter
1 teaspoon vanilla
Dash nutmeg
Pinch salt

# SOUR CREAM TOPPING FOR BAKED POTATOES

*Not many cooks need detailed instructions on how to mix a few seasonings with sour cream for a baked-potato topping, but this is more than a recipe. It's pure Cissy Gregg, and it reflects both her food philosophy and her zest for life.*

Put the sour cream in the top of a double boiler, if you want it warmed, and of course, we use commercially soured cream. If you have chives, fresh in season or frozen, add them to the cream after it has been a little warmed, but don't let it get too hot or the cream breaks down. If you don't have chives this time of the year, there is plenty of "wild onion" sprouting up through the winter snows which in the first place is a cousin of the chive, and if you don't have the onions in your yard, you can use dried chives; or again, I have an onion in my flower box in the kitchen window. I had it in a basket and it seemed to want to sprout, so I stuck it down in the flower box, gave all the usual feeding, and it's going up the window like fire.

These little tender things are harbingers of spring and the hope it holds for everyone. We are rather heretic about seasonings — we add a dash or two of Tabasco sauce to the sour cream for the topping of a baked potato, and we like to add a little salt to the cream. For some tastes it might not be needed, but we like it. Also, as a rule I don't heat the sour cream; I just let it stand at room temperature. Mix in the seasonings and have it ready to meet the heat of the baked potato. There's long been the saying "as hot as a hot potato" and it should be a welcome to the slightly cooling off from the sour cream sauce. We prefer to serve the sour cream separately from the potato, just in case there are novitiates who don't know how good the mixture can be.

# MINT SAUCE FOR ICE CREAM

½ **cup crushed pineapple and juice**
1 **cup sugar**
½ **cup white corn syrup**
**Dash of salt**
1 **cup water**
1 **drop oil of peppermint**
**A drop or so of green food coloring**

Cook all together except vegetable coloring and oil of peppermint, stirring until sugar is dissolved and mixture is slightly thickened. Then mix in green vegetable coloring and oil of peppermint.

To go with the sauce, try making balls of vanilla or chocolate ice cream and rolling them in chopped nuts. Put the balls away in the freezer compartment of the refrigerator or food freezer until serving time.

Then put some of the syrup in the bottom of a compote, settle the ball of ice cream in its midst and serve. It's just mightly good! — Cissy Gregg, 1959

# FRIED PIE SAUCE

1 **cup brown sugar**
1 **tablespoon flour or cornstarch**
1 **cup water**
1 **tablespoon butter or margarine**
½ **teaspoon vanilla**

Mix sugar and flour or cornstarch together until well blended. Add water. Cook, stirring until mixture is of sauce thickness. Add butter or margarine and flavoring. Pass along with pies.

You know, most of those who know about fried

green apple pies don't wait for a plate or sauce — it's from the frying pan to the mouth, and they'll take the sizzling mouth burns along with the sweet morsel. But we suggest that they are good eaten from a plate and with sauce. At least try them like this sometime even if you have to make them two days in succession to get over your point.

— Cissy Gregg, 1948

# SABAYON SAUCE

*Restaurant-goers who are discovering that sabayon is making its way onto dessert menus might be surprised to learn that Cissy Gregg was offering her readers the how-to on this sauce back in 1948. She recommended serving it over a chilled pear, fresh or canned, but it's also good over strawberries and other fruits. The traditional sabayon, or zabaglione, is made with Marsala wine, and most recipes do not use egg whites.*

*One note about this recipe: Be patient about the egg-yolk mixture getting thick. It will. But we also recommend stirring the yolk mixture as it cooks and thickens.*

Mix sugar, egg yolks, salt, sherry and lemon juice together. Cook in the upper part of a double boiler over hot but not boiling water until thick. Add slowly to the 2 egg whites of the whole eggs, beaten stiff.

**½ cup sugar**
**2 egg whites**
**4 egg yolks**
**⅛ teaspoon salt**
**½ cup sherry wine**
**Juice of ½ lemon**

# PEANUT-BUTTER SAUCE

Combine sugar, water, corn syrup and salt in a heavy pan. Bring to a boil and cook over low heat to 220 degrees, or until a small amount of syrup dropped into cold water forms a very soft ball. Remove from heat. Cool without stirring until the syrup has reached room temperature. Add peanut butter and blend until smooth. This sauce can be kept in a covered jar in the refrigerator. It is wonderful for cake, puddings or ice cream.

— Cissy Gregg, 1949

**1 cup sugar**
**½ cup water**
**⅔ cup light corn syrup**
**½ teaspoon salt**
**¼ cup peanut butter**

# PEACH SUNDAE

This is a recipe we came by this week and think interesting. During the "Gay '90s" the city fathers of Evanston, Ill., forbade the serving of ice-cream sodas on the Sabbath.

But some artful dodger prompty created the soda-less "sundae," more luscious than its predecessor.

We are told that to duplicate this dish that became so popular is to take 2 cups crushed, soft, ripe peaches (6 to 8 medium), add ½ cup sugar and ½ cup orange juice in a saucepan.

Bring to a rapid boil. Reduce heat and simmer, uncovered, about 15 minutes or until sauce has thickened. Add ¾ teaspoon vanilla extract and 2 teaspoons lemon juice. Spoon it warm over vanilla ice cream. Or it's good over plain cake or baked custard. It's just plain good!

— Cissy Gregg, 1960

# MYRA'S FAMOUS SAUCE

*This is the recipe for the sauce that accompanies hamburgers served at Myra's Ristorante in Louisville.*

2 cups mayonnaise
⅓ cup ketchup
2 tablespoons chili powder, or more to taste
2 tablespoons ground cumin, or more to taste

Combine all ingredients well. Keep chilled.

— Elaine Corn, 1984

# KENTUCKY SAUCE

*Cissy Gregg proposed ice cream with Kentucky sauce as part of a Christmas menu for 1947. It must have capped off a substantial meal.*

1 cup brown sugar
1 cup white sugar
1 cup water
1 whole orange (the seedless kind is better)
1 whole lemon
1 cup whisky
1 cup pecans
1 cup strawberry preserves

The ice cream you already know how to make or you can buy it, and now we will make the sauce. We have been known to go all out for this or that before, but we did it again on this sauce. It'll finish off the crowd and bring on an inactive afternoon. But by this time a nap is all that can help the situation.

Cook the 2 sugars with the water until the syrup almost spins a thread. Add the cup of strawberry preserves and the pecans, broken up. Last, add orange and lemon rinds, with the rest of the fruit, all chopped very fine. Let stand in the refrigerator to ripen. It just seems to get better all the time. Warm before serving.

# HORSERADISH SAUCE

Mix altogether, taste and reseason, until it's so good it could be eaten on shoe leather. Serve with hot or cold beef.

— Cissy Gregg, 1947

4 tablespoons grated horseradish (ours came from the bottle)
6 tablespoons thick cream
2 tablespoons vinegar
1 teaspoon salt
¼ teaspoon pepper (we used red)
1½ teaspoons prepared mustard, the yellow kind

# THIN AND HOT BARBECUE SAUCE

*Although this is an all-purpose barbecue sauce, Cissy Gregg proposed using the 1954 recipe as follows: One cup of the sauce to 1 pound of frankfurters heated in a pan or chafing dish for about 8 minutes will be about right. Turn the frankfurters over as they heat. Serve on toasted buns.*

Mix all together and simmer 1 hour to blend the seasonings. Take out the garlic and add cayenne pepper to suit your hot-tasting taste buds. This is a sauce you can make in advance and keep stored in the refrigerator. It makes approximately one quart.

½ pound butter or margarine
1 pint vinegar
½ cup water
1 teaspoon dry mustard
2 tablespoons chopped onion
1½ teaspoons sugar
½ cup Worcestershire sauce
½ cup tomato catchup
½ cup chili sauce
Juice of ½ lemon
1 clove garlic stuck on a toothpick

# KENTUCKY SAUCE FOR LEG OF LAMB

*She called it Kentucky sauce, but Cissy Gregg acknowledged in printing this recipe in 1956 that she had come by it in Texas.*

Blend all ingredients together over a low heat. DO NOT BOIL.

4 ounces (1 stick) butter
½ cup apple-mint jelly
½ cup catsup
1 teaspoon sugar
1 teaspoon allspice

# CHEESE SAUCE

1 tablespoon butter or margarine
1 tablespoon flour
1 cup milk
⅛ teaspoon ground black pepper
½ tablespoon salt
¾ cup grated sharp American
   cheese
1 teaspoon fresh lemon juice

Melt butter or margarine. Blend in flour. Stir in milk gradually, along with the salt and pepper. Keep stirring until you have a smooth sauce. Cook until slightly thick. Add cheese and lemon juice. Take off the heat and stir until the cheese is blended with the cream sauce. Serve over asparagas or other vegetables. It is quite a delicious combination.

— Cissy Gregg, 1960

# REMOULADE SAUCE CREOLE

*This version of remoulade was created in 1961 by assistant food editor Gaby Slader. It can be used as an alternative to tartar sauce on seafoods.*

3 hard-boiled egg yolks
½ clove garlic, minced
½ teaspoon prepared mustard
3 tablespoons olive oil
1 tablespoon tarragon vinegar
1 raw egg yolk
1 tablespoon lemon juice
Salt and cayenne to taste

Place the hard-cooked egg yolks in a bowl and mash until smooth. Add the garlic, mustard, salt and cayenne to taste and mix thoroughly. Add the olive oil very slowly, stirring constantly, until it is well blended. Add the vinegar and raw egg yolk and mix thoroughly. Add the lemon juice and again mix well. This makes about 1 cup of sauce.

# WINE BUTTER SAUCE FOR VEGETABLES

3 egg yolks
⅓ cup water
3 tablespoons sauterne or rhine
   wine
1 tablespoon lemon juice
Salt and pepper, to taste
½ cup butter or margarine

Beat the egg yolks until light. Add water, wine, lemon juice, salt and pepper to taste to the beaten egg yolks. Cook slowly in a double boiler until thick, stirring frequently, which for me means practically all the time. Add the butter or margarine, small lump by small lump, beating thoroughly after each addition until all the butter or margarine has been added.

It stays wonderfully smooth and is no trouble at all. I held some over until the next day in the refrigerator, and it was just as good.

When you can say a sauce of this kind is a "fine actor," it is worthy of your friendship.

— Cissy Gregg, 1948

# BUTTER SAUCE FOR ARTICHOKES

Combine all ingredients and heat until bubbly. Serve with hot artichokes as a dip. Makes ½ cup.
— Cissy Gregg, 1961

¼ cup butter or margarine
1 tablespoon or more of lemon or lime juice
½ teaspoon salt
Dash of cayenne
2 tablespoons prepared mustard

# BUTTER SAUCE

Clarify ½ pound of butter by melting it and removing the whitish foam. Repeat the process several times. Save the foam for seasoning vegetables. Season the clear yellow liquid that is left with a little salt, freshly ground pepper and a pinch of nutmeg. Add the grated rind of 2 lemons and heaping tablespoon of chopped chives.

# HOT LEMON SAUCE

Mix sugar and flour thoroughly; add salt. Add water all at once, stirring rapidly. Cook over low heat 5 minutes. Add butter, lemon juice and rind, and cook a minute. Serve hot over fruit cake "leavin's" or any puddings. We thought it pleasantly tart.
— Cissy Gregg, 1960

½ cup sugar
2 tablespoons flour
1 cup boiling water
2 tablespoons unsalted butter
1 teaspoon lemon rind
Grated nutmeg or a pinch of salt (we used both)

# CREAMY MUSTARD SAUCE

Heat the cream. Mix sugar and dry mustard which has been dissolved in a little of the cream. Add to hot cream. Mix the beaten egg yolks with the salt, and stir into the cream mixture. Cook stirring for about 2 minutes — we used the double boiler. Add the vinegar, rather slowly we would say, and cook long enough for the sauce to come back to a smooth consistency. This can be served hot or cold, and it has a wonderful flavor that isn't too "bitey," too sweet, too sour, but we thought just plain good.
— Cissy Gregg, 1960

1 pint of heavy cream
½ cup sugar
4 tablespoons dry mustard
5 egg yolks, well beaten
½ teaspoon salt
1 cup vinegar

# MUSHROOM CREAM SAUCE

2 tablespoons butter
1 heaping (we made it "2")
   tablespoons flour
½ teaspoons salt
A dash of red pepper
1 cup cream
1 cup milk

Melt butter, blend in flour and stir to make it smooth. Gradually add milk and cream and cook until the sauce has thickened. Season to taste. Sauté as many mushrooms as you want to use and add to the sauce. We like to sauté even the canned ones. Maybe it is imagination, but the sautéeing seems to bring out the flavor of the canned ones, and using the fresh ones you sauté to cook them before adding. What's a few more calories, anyway?

— Cissy Gregg, 1951

# MAITRE D'HOTEL BUTTER

This is what most of us amateur cooks call parsley butter. Work ½ cup butter with a wooden spoon until light and fluffy. Then work in 2 teaspoons of lemon juice and 2 teaspoons chopped parsley. Season with salt and pepper.

— Cissy Gregg, 1952

# SAUCE SUPREME

*Sometimes a Cissy Gregg recipe is two or three cooking lessons rolled into one. This 1945 recipe is published the "old" way, with amounts and ingredients incorporated among the instructions, but it also teaches something about stocks, seasonings and sauce-making in general.*

Blend 4 tablespoons of flour with 4 tablespoons of chicken fat, butter or margarine, as you would for a cream sauce — you know, melt the fat first and work in the flour. Do this in the top of the double boiler and let it bubble over a low flame for a minute or so. Now add 2 cups of rich chicken broth well flavored with bay leaves and onion. To get this rich broth, I skim off the fat and boil down the broth until it is about half its former self in volume. And while this boiling is going on, add the bay leaf or two and the onion. But I watch the bay leaf closely — too much of it is definitely too much for me. Stir all the time while the sauce thickens. Season with salt and pepper. When it is just about ready to come off the stove, add ¼ cup of cream and the juice of ½ a lemon.

This sauce is an atomic bomb among sauces — well, almost, anyway.

# BEURRE NOIR OR "BLACK BUTTER"

Heat ⅓ cup of butter in a saucepan until browned but not burned. Then add 1 teaspoon lemon juice, ½ teaspoon salt and a dash of pepper. This enchances so many foods we can't list them all, but we'll say it goes from skate's wings to scrambled eggs. — Cissy Gregg, 1950

# COURIER-JOURNAL MAYONNAISE

*In 1978, Deni Hamilton figured out how to use the labor-saving blender to make three classic sauces, mayonnaise, hollandaise and bearnaise.*

Place all ingredients in blender with half the oil. Cover and turn on blender. Immediately remove cover insert and very gradually add remaining oil in a steady, thin stream. Continue to add remaining oil until thick or until mixture refuses to take more oil. Thickens a bit after refrigeration. Makes about 1½ cups.

**2 whole eggs, room temperature**
**¾ teaspoon salt**
**½ teaspoon dry mustard**
**¼ teaspoon cayenne pepper**
**1 tablespoon white wine vinegar**
**1 tablespoon lemon juice**
**1 cup olive oil, room temperature**

# COURIER-JOURNAL HOLLANDAISE

Place egg yolks, pepper, salt and lemon juice in blender. Heat butter until bubbly, then cover blender and remove lid insert. Turn on blender, then pour hot butter in very slowly in a constant, small stream. Blend just until all butter is incorporated and sauce is smooth. Makes about ¾ cup.

**1 stick butter, melted and bubbling**
**hot but not brown**
**2 egg yolks, room temperature**
**A pinch of cayenne pepper**
**A pinch of salt**
**1 tablespoon fresh lemon juice**

# COURIER-JOURNAL BÉARNAISE SAUCE

In a saucepan, mix vinegar, wine, shallots or chives, salt, pepper, tarragon and chervil. Bring to a boil and boil hard to reduce liquid to about ⅓ of its original volume. With fork, fish out most of herbs and discard. Place yolks in blender. Turn on motor and slowly add reduced vinegar mixture. Immediately begin to add the hot butter in a slow, steady stream, until all is incorporated and the sauce is smooth. Makes about 1½ cups.

**⅓ cup tarragon vinegar**
**½ cup dry white wine**
**2 tablespoons minced shallots or 3**
**tablespoons frozen or fresh**
**minced chives**
**½ teaspoon salt**
**½ teaspoon white pepper**
**2 teaspoons dried tarragon**
**½ teaspoon dried chervil**
**3 egg yolks, room temperature**
**2 sticks, unsalted butter, melted**
**and bubbly hot, but not browned**

# MUSTARD CHEESE SAUCE

*Cissy wrote in 1959 that this recipe was a "good pick-me-up" for asparagus, broccoli, cabbage, cauli-flower or even fish. She said it also could be used as a dip for potato chips, crackers or crisp bread sticks.*

**3 tablespoons butter or margarine**
**3 tablespoons flour**
**2 cups milk**
**1 cup shredded sharp cheddar**
**  cheese**
**1½ teaspoons salt**
**1 teaspoon powdered dry mustard**
**Dash of ground white pepper**
**¼ teaspoon hot sauce**
**⅛ teaspoon garlic powder**
**½ cup milk**
**2 eggs, separated**
**Paprika for garnish**

Melt butter or margarine in a saucepan. Blend in flour. Add 2 cups milk and cook and stir until slightly thickened. Add cheese and seasonings. Blend the ½ cup milk with the egg yolks and add.

Cook a minute or 2 but do not boil. Beat egg whites until they stand in soft peaks; stir into mixture. The recipe makes about 4 cups of sauce, or dip as you prefer.

# HENRY BAIN SAUCE

*Henry Bain went to work for the Pendennis Club in 1881, and he was head waiter when he created his famous sauce. Cissy Gregg printed this recipe in 1962, calling it a "modified" version "because we never make it twice the same way. It will be good with either Master Pig or Ribs of Beef." This particular version of the sauce, she wrote, came "from another well-known and popular Louisville waiter, Livingston Whaley."*

**1 12-ounce bottle chili sauce**
**1 14-ounce bottle catchup**
**1 11-ounce bottle A-1 sauce**
**1 10-ounce bottle Worcestershire**
**1 1-pound, 1-ounce bottle chutney**
**Tabasco or hot pepper sauce**
**Chopped watercress, as desired**

Mix together and add the hot sauce according to taste. It takes more than you think. If the chutney comes with large pieces of mangoes or other chutney fruit in it, chop finely. Chopped watercress may be added as you like.

The sauce will keep indefinitely refrigerated, and it has many uses. Any left may be used for French fried potatoes. Thinned with oil and herb vinegar, it snuggles up to Bibb lettuce.

# BREADS, MUFFINS & BISCUITS

# SCIENCE HILL HOT-WATER CORN BREAD

*This is one of the favorite dishes at the Science Hill Inn in Shelbyville, Ky. Chef Donna Gill gave the recipe to Elaine Corn for a feature in the Magazine in 1985.*

**2 cups white cornmeal**
**1 teaspoon salt**
**1 teaspoon sugar**
**1 tablespoon solid shortening**
**¼ cup half-and-half**
**1½ to 2 cups boiling water**
**Shortening, for frying**

Combine cornmeal, salt and sugar in a bowl. Add half-and-half and boiling water and stir to mix well. In a skillet, melt shortening to a depth of ½ inch and heat to 325 degrees. Using a large kitchen spoon, scoop up spoonfuls of the meal mixture and drop into the skillet. Fry, turning to brown on both sides for five minutes. Serve warm with whipped butter.

# BORDERLAND CORN BREAD

**1⅓ cups flour**
**⅔ cup cornmeal**
**4 teaspoons baking powder**
**½ teaspoon salt**
**⅔ cup milk**
**⅓ cup maple syrup (we used maple-like syrup)**
**¼ cup melted butter, margarine or bacon drippings**
**2 beaten eggs**

When we give this type of corn bread recipe, we start dodging. Some will say we have forgotten our heritage as Southerners, that we have crossed the Mason and Dixon Line. But, we say, when you find something good, nab it. We tried this corn bread, liked it. We made it again and still had the same opinion. So we offer it to you to try.

Sift the flour, meal, baking powder and salt together. Add milk, maple syrup, melted butter or what have you, and eggs together. Then combine the wet ingredients with the dry. Mix until smooth but no more. Pour into a well-greased 9-inch square pan or round pan. Bake 25 to 30 minutes in a moderately hot oven, 375 degrees. Cut into squares or wedges, and serve hot with plenty of butter or margarine.
— Cissy Gregg, 1955

# CORN STICKS

**½ teaspoon salt**
**½ teaspoon soda**
**3 teaspoons sugar**
**½ teaspoon baking powder**
**2 tablespoons oil**
**1 egg**
**½ cup flour**
**1 cup buttermilk**
**1 cup plus 2 tablespoons cornmeal**

Beat all ingredients together, beating well. Heat greased irons until hot enough to sizzle. Fill irons to half full. Bake at 450 degrees about 10 minutes or until brown. The secret of good corn bread is beating well and using hot irons.
— Lillian Marshall, 1970

# CORN MUFFINS

Cream shortening and sugar. Beat in the egg and milk. Sift flour with the baking powder and salt, then add to the milk mixture and beat well. Add cornmeal, stirring only enough to mix. Fill greased muffin pans ⅔ full and bake at 425 degrees for about 25 minutes. Makes a dozen.
— Lillian Marshall, 1967

⅓ cup shortening
⅓ cup sugar (cut this to 2 tablespoons if you don't like a fairly sweet corn bread)
1 beaten egg
1½ cups milk
1 cup flour
4 teaspoons baking powder
½ teaspoon salt
1 cup cornmeal

# DALE HOLLOW HUSH PUPPIES

Combine ingredients, beating until thoroughly mixed. Batter should be quite heavy, thicker than for corn bread. Add oil to skillet in which fish were fried, making it about half an inch deep. It should be sizzling hot. Drop batter by teaspoonfuls into hot oil and fry, turning once, until well browned and done.
— Lillian Marshall, 1974

2 cups self-rising cornmeal
1 egg
¼ cup finely chopped onion
1 cup tomato juice, approximately
Oil for frying

# SIMPLE SIMON CORN BREAD

Put all ingredients into a bowl and mix until smooth. Pour into a well-greased, 9-inch-square pan or muffin tins (or preheated and greased corn-stick pans). Bake at 425 degrees for 20 minutes.
— Lillian Marshall, 1970

1 cup yellow corn meal
1 cup sifted flour
¼ cup sugar
4 teaspoons baking powder
½ teaspoon salt
1 egg
1 cup milk
¼ cup margarine, softened

# BATTY CAKES WITH LACY EDGES

1 cup white corn meal (water
   ground if possible)
½ teaspoon soda
½ teaspoon salt
1¼ cups rich buttermilk
1 egg, beaten
Lard or oil

Sift dry ingredients together. Mix buttermilk and egg and slowly add to dry mixture. Beat until smooth. Melt the lard in a heavy skillet (allow about 1 tablespoon per 4 cakes) and drop in batter by tablespoonful. Cook until brown on one side, then turn and brown on the other side. Serve hot and fresh, preferably with melted butter and honey or maple syrup.

— Deni Hamilton, 1979

# SOUTHERN SPOON BREAD

2 cups sweet milk, scalded
½ cup cornmeal
½ teaspoon baking powder
1 teaspoon salt
3 egg yolks
3 egg whites
2 tablespoons melted butter,
   margarine or drippings

Scald the milk in the top of the double boiler and gradually add the corn meal by sprinkling it over the top of the milk and stirring it in. Cook over boiling water until it is the consistency of mush, stirring frequently. Add baking powder, salt, fat (I don't melt the fat before adding, the hot mush will do that) and egg yolks. Beat the yolks in vigorously. Fold in the stiffly beaten egg whites. Pour into a hot, greased baking dish, about one-quart size, and bake at 375 degrees for 20 minutes. Serve at once from the dish in which it was baked.

One way of getting a proud, high crown on the "spoonie" is to bake it in a casserole that will just about hold the batter. Next make a wide band of double-folded waxed paper or use a strip of cooking foil, and tie it around the top of the casserole so it stands up something like 2 inches above the casserole's top edge. Then the mixture will rise high and make a stunning table appearance.

— Cissy Gregg, 1949

# BEREA SPOON BREAD

3 cups milk
1¼ cups cornmeal
3 eggs
2 tablespoons butter
1¾ teaspoons baking powder
1 teaspoon salt

Stir meal into rapidly boiling milk. Cook until very thick, stirring constantly as when making mush. Be careful not to let it scorch, which means to stir with vigor.

Remove from fire and allow to cool. The mixture will be very stiff when cold.

Add well-beaten eggs, salt, baking powder and melted butter. Beat with an electric beater for 15 minutes. If hand beating is used, break the hardened cooked meal into the eggs in small amounts until all is well mixed. Then beat thoroughly for 10 minutes with a wooden spoon.

Pour into well-greased casserole. Bake for 30 minutes at 350 degrees. Serve from casserole by spoonfuls. — Cissy Gregg, 1951

# NANCY REAGAN'S MONKEY BREAD

*The White House provided this recipe in response to a query from the Cook's Corner column. The molds mentioned in the recipe can be almost anything that can stand the heat of baking — for example, a tube-cake pan, souffle pan or even a regular bread pan.*

In bowl, mix yeast with part of milk until dissolved. Add 2 of the eggs and beat. Mix in dry ingredients. Add remaining milk a little at a time, mixing thoroughly. Cut in butter until blended. Knead dough, let rise one to 1½ hours, until double in size. Knead again; let rise 40 minutes.

Roll dough onto floured board, and shape into a log. Cut log into 28 pieces of equal size. Shape each piece of dough into ball, roll in melted butter. Use half of the pieces in each of the buttered, floured molds. Place 7 balls in each mold, leaving space between. Place remaining balls on top, spacing evenly. Let dough rise in mold. Brush tops with remaining egg. Bake in preheated oven at 375 degrees until golden brown, approximately 15 minutes.

1 package dry yeast
1 to 1¼ cups milk
3 eggs
3 tablespoons sugar
1 teaspoon salt
3½ cups flour
6 ounces butter, room temperature
½ pound melted butter

# HOLIDAY BANANA BREAD

Cream shortening and sugar. Add eggs and mix well. Sift together flour and soda and add to mixture. Stir in mashed bananas. Chop together the nuts, cherries and chocolate chips, then add to batter. Bake in greased 9-by-5-inch loaf pan, or in three greased No. 2 cans, in 350-degree oven. The loaf will take about 45 to 50 minutes, the cans about 30 to 35 minutes. Test for doneness with a straw or wire. The bread also will shrink away from the sides when it is done. — Lillian Marshall, 1973

½ cup shortening
1 cup sugar
2 eggs
2 cups flour
1 teaspoon soda
3 medium ripe bananas, mashed
¼ cup chopped nuts
¼ cup maraschino cherries, halved
¼ cup chocolate chips

# PUMPKIN GINGERBREAD WITH CARAMEL SAUCE

1 cup molasses
2 teaspoons baking soda
1 teaspoon cinnamon
1 teaspoon ginger
¼ teaspoon nutmeg
½ cup sugar
½ cup melted butter or margarine
2 cups flour
1 cup pumpkin pulp
¼ cup boiling water
½ cup floured raisins
2 eggs, separated

Mix molasses, soda and spices. Add sugar, margarine, flour, pumpkin and water, and beat well. Add egg yolks and raisins, and mix. Beat whites stiff and fold in. Pour into a greased ring mold. Bake in a preheated 350-degree oven for 40 minutes. Serve warm, if desired, with caramel sauce. Good at room temperature, too.

## CARAMEL SAUCE

2 egg yolks
1 cup half-and-half
1 pound light brown sugar
1 tablespoon butter or margarine
1 teaspoon vanilla
Pinch salt.

Beat egg yolks, half-and-half and sugar together. Put in top of double boiler over simmering water, and cook until the consistency of thick cream. Stir in butter, vanilla and salt after removing from heat. Serve hot or chilled (it'll be thicker when cold).
— Deni Hamilton, 1978

# SUNSHINE PUMPKIN BREAD

4 cups flour
4 teaspoons baking powder
1 teaspoon baking soda
2 teaspoons salt
2 teaspoons cinnamon
1 teaspoon nutmeg
1 teaspoon ground cloves
A 1-pound, 13-ounce can pumpkin
2 cups brown sugar
1 cup milk
4 eggs
½ cup margarine

Let margarine soften at room temperature. Mix dry ingredients in bowl (except sugar). Mix pumpkin, sugar, milk and eggs in another bowl. Add dry ingredients and softened margarine to pumpkin mixture. Spread mixture into 2 greased loaf pans. Bake at 350 degrees for 50 to 60 minutes.
— Lillian Marshall, 1974

# DILL CASSEROLE BREAD

Heat cottage cheese to lukewarm over hot water. Place in large mixing bowl and stir in the softened yeast. Add egg, beating well, then sugar, dill and onion. Stir or sift the salt, soda and flour together and add gradually to wet mixture. Add a little more flour if neeeded to form fairly stiff batter. Cover, set in warm place and allow to double in bulk, about an hour. Stir down and turn into well-greased 8-inch casserole. Let rise about 45 minutes until not quite double. Bake at 350 degrees for 45 to 50 minutes or until nicely browned and done. Brush while hot with melted butter and cool on rack.

— Lillian Marshall, 1973

1 envelope or package of yeast, softened in ¼ cup warm water
1 cup creamed cottage cheese
1 egg
2 tablespoons sugar
2 teaspoons dill seed
2 tablespoons dehydrated onion or 3 tablespoons fresh onion, minced
1 teaspoon salt
¼ teaspoon soda
2¼ cups flour
2 tablespoons butter, melted

# STRAWBERRY BREAD

Mix together undrained strawberries, eggs and oil. Sift together dry ingredients. Reserving about one-half cup, add dry ingredients to strawberry mixture. Stir to blend well. Stir nuts into reserved dry ingredients and add to batter, stirring well. Pour into a well-greased and lightly floured 9-by-5-inch loaf pan and bake at 350 degrees for one hour or until done. If top starts to overbrown before done, put a tent-shaped piece of foil loosely over it.

— Lillian Marshall, 1976

1 10-ounce package sweetened frozen strawberries, thawed
2 eggs, beaten
½ cup plus 2 tablespoons vegetable oil
1½ cups flour
½ teaspoon baking soda
½ teaspoon baking powder
½ teaspoon salt
1½ teaspoons cinnamon
1 cup sugar, optional
½ cup chopped pecans

# PERSIMMON BREAD

Beat together the sugar, eggs and pulp. Sift together the flour, baking powder, salt and soda. Combine the pulp mixture and the dry ingredients with the oil. Stir in nuts and raisins. Turn into a greased loaf pan and bake at 350 degrees for 45 to 50 minutes or until done.

— Lillian Marshall, 1977

1 cup sugar
2 eggs, beaten
1 cup persimmon pulp
2 cups flour
3 teaspoons baking powder
½ teaspoon salt
½ teaspoon baking soda
½ cup oil
¾ cup chopped nuts
1 cup raisins

# CRANBERRY FRUIT-NUT BREAD

2 cups flour
1 cup sugar
1½ teaspoons baking powder
½ teaspoon soda
1 teaspoon salt
¼ cup shortening
¾ cup orange juice
1 heaping tablespoon grated orange
 rind
1 egg, beaten
¾ cup chopped walnuts
2 cups fresh cranberries, coarsely
 chopped

Stir together the flour, sugar, baking powder, soda and salt. Cut in shortening until mixture resembles coarse cornmeal. Mix juice, rind and egg, and beat. Pour into dry ingredients, and mix just to moisten. Stir in nuts and cranberries. Turn into greased 9-by-5-inch loaf pan. Spread in pan so that center is depressed. Bake in a preheated 350-degree oven for about an hour, until browned and tests done. Remove from pan, and cool on rack.

— Deni Hamilton, 1978

# ZUCCHINI BREAD

3 eggs
2 cups sugar
1 cup oil
1 tablespoon vanilla
2 cups grated zucchini
2 cups flour
1 tablespoon cinnamon
2 teaspoons baking soda
1 teaspoon salt
¼ teaspoon baking powder
1 cup chopped nuts

Beat eggs until frothy. Beat in sugar, oil and vanilla. Beat until lemon colored. Stir in zucchini and flour with cinnamon, baking soda, salt and baking powder. Add nuts. Pour into greased and floured 9-by-5-inch pans. Bake in a 350-degree oven for 1 hour or until done. Makes 2 loaves.

— Lillian Marshall, 1977

# MOLASSES BLACK BREAD

2 tablespoons dry yeast
2 cups warm water
½ teaspoon sugar
¼ cup molasses
¼ cup honey
½ stick butter
2 teaspoons salt
3 tablespoons cocoa
3 to 4 cups unbleached white flour
3 cups rye flour
Cornmeal, for dusting pan

Dissolve yeast in warm water. Add sugar and let stand 5 or 10 minutes, until bubbly.

In a large mixing bowl, combine molasses, honey, butter, salt, cocoa and yeast mixture with electric beaters, mixing well. Add 2 cups of white flour and beat 2 minutes. Beat in 1 cup more white flour. Add 3 cups rye flour and beat until dough leaves sides of the bowl. Dough will be extremely sticky.

Use remaining white flour to dust a work surface. Turn dough onto surface. With heavily floured hands, knead dough until smooth and elastic, sprinkling with additional flour as it becomes sticky. When dough is elastic, cease kneading, even if it is slightly tacky. Immediately place dough in a large buttered bowl, turn to coat all sides, cover with a towel and let rise until doubled in bulk, nearly 2 hours. Punch down. Turn onto lightly floured surface, knead a few times, halve, cover with towel and let rest 10 minutes. Shape into rounds or ovals. Place on greased sheet dusted with cornmeal. Let rise again, about an hour, until nice and big. Brush tops with melted butter. Bake at 375 degrees for 35 minutes. Cool on a wire rack. Slice and spread with herb butter. Makes 2 loaves.

Herb butter: Soften 2 sticks unsalted butter. Mince herb of choice (we used lots of fresh dill) and mash into butter, incoporating evenly. To save, spoon butter down a sheet of wax papper and roll into a log. Partially freeze. Remove from freezer, slice, then re-roll and freeze completely. Retrieve as needed.

— Elaine Corn, 1983

# QUICK MOLASSES BREAD

Mix and sift sugar, flour, baking soda, baking powder and salt. Combine evaporated milk, orange juice, orange rind and unsulfured molasses. Add to flour mixture all at once. Stir just enough to blend. Stir in nuts. Turn into a well-greased loaf pan, 9-by-5-by-3 inches. Bake in a moderate oven, 350 degrees, for an hour. Makes a loaf of moist, even-grained bread. It has the happy faculty of coming from the oven with a smooth top--it was said to do that, and it came through for us. The orange flavor with the molasses was unusual to us but very harmonious.

— Cissy Gregg, 1952

½ cup firmly packed brown sugar
3 cups sifted all-purpose flour
1 teaspoon baking soda
1 teaspoon double-acting baking powder (or the equivalent in the type of baking powder you use)
1 teaspoon salt
¾ cup evaporated milk
¾ cup orange juice
2 tablespoons grated orange rind
½ cup unsulfured molasses
1 cup of coarsely chopped nuts.

# OATMEAL MOLASSES BATTER BREAD

2½ cups milk
⅓ cup molasses
3 teaspoons salt
½ cup shortening
1½ cups uncooked rolled oats
½ cup warm water
3 packages active dry yeast
5 cups sifted enriched flour

Scald milk and stir in molasses, salt, shortening and rolled oats. Let cool until lukewarm. Measure warm water into bowl. Sprinkle in yeast. Stir until dissolved. Add lukewarm-milk mixture. Add flour and stir until well blended. Grease two 8-by-5-by-3-inch loaf pans well. Divide batter evenly between the two greased pans. Press down top smoothly with metal spoon dipped in cold water to form an even surface. Cover. Let rise in a warm place free from draft until doubled in bulk, about 40 minutes.

Bake in preheated 350-degree oven 50 minutes or until loaf is browned on top and when turned out of the pan, dry and well-baked on the bottom.

Ours baked in exactly 50 minutes. The loaves were lovely and would not only bolster up a sparse Lenten meal but be wonderful for toast and sandwiches.

Just to let you know that we do work hard for you, when we got this recipe it called for "3 tablespoons salt". We made it according to the directions — with hesitancy — but we put in the salt just the same. Zow-ey! They must have meant 3 teaspoons, because it worked out that way with us. We give thanks that we don't lead you blindly, even though we do make our own mistakes.

— Cissy Gregg, 1952

# BREAKFAST EGG BREAD

*Elaine Corn noted in this 1983 recipe that this bread "is good for French toast even when it's stale." The dough can be frozen and used later.*

6 tablespoon shortening
1½ cups water, scalded
2 packages dry yeast
1 teaspoon sugar
½ cup lukewarm water
2 tablespoons sugar
2 teaspoon salt
4 eggs, reserving 1 yolk for top of bread
About 7 cups unbleached all-purpose flour

Melt shortening in scalded water. Pour into large mixing bowl. Dissolve yeast and 1 teaspoon sugar in ½ cup lukewarm water. When bubbly, add to melted shortening. Add 2 tablespoons sugar and the salt. Beat the eggs and add. With a fork, stir in 4 cups flour, then 3 cups, stirring vigorously until dough forms a ball and cleans the sides of the bowl. Have additional flour ready for dusting work surface. Transfer dough to work surface. Knead 10 minutes. Sprinkle your hands and surface with flour as necessary. Place dough in clean, oiled bowl. Turn dough once. Cover. Let rise 1½ to 2 hours. Stir down. Pound out air bubbles. Shape.

Braid (free form): Cut dough in half. Roll each part into rectangles. Slice each rectangle lengthwise into 3 equal strands. Braid strands into 2 loaves, mounding centers and tapering ends. Be sure tips are joined together. Place on lightly greased cookie sheets. Lay plastic wrap over. Let rise 45 minutes. Brush with reserved egg yolk mixed with 1 table-spoon water. Bake at 375 degrees for 45 minutes to 1 hour. Cool 5 minutes before lifting off cookie sheet. Makes 2.

Small braids (baked in loaf pan): Slice dough into 3 parts and roll out into rectangles. Slice each rectangle into 3 strands. Braid each loaf. Drop into 3 lightly greased 9- by 5-inch bread-loaf pans. Cover with plastic wrap. Let rise 45 minutes. Brush with 1 egg yolk mixed with 1 tablespoon water. Bake at 375 degrees for 1 hour. Makes 3 medium-size loaves.

Variation: For any size braided loaf, flatten strands. Sprinkle raisins and a little sugar down center of strand, then roll strands so raisins stay in middle. Braid as usual, then let rise, brush and bake as above.

Rounds: Slice dough into 3 parts. Roll each part into a rope. Drop, free-form into a coil onto a lightly greased cookie sheet. Keep center high to make a crown. Lay over with plastic wrap. Let rise 45 minutes. Brush with egg yolk mixed with 1 tablespoon water. Bake at 375 degrees for 45 minutes. Makes 3.

Pull-aparts: Roll pieces of dough into ping-pong-sized balls. Place, sides barely touching, in 3 lightly greased or buttered cake pans. (You may have some dough left over. You can bake it in another shape or chill for 3 days for later use.) Cover. Let rise 45 minutes. Brush with egg yolk mixed with 1 tablespoon water. Bake at 375 degrees for 35 to 45 minutes. Cool in pan about 5 minutes to allow bread to shrink from sides. Remove to cool thoroughly. Makes between 4 and 5 dozen pull-aparts.

— Elaine Corn, 1983

# SOURDOUGH STARTER

*When Lillian Marshall wrote about sourdough in 1970, she had a starter that was three years old "and still going strong," as she wrote. Her sourdough recipes were very popular, and our kitchen is still kept busy answering questions about sourdough bread-making.*

**2 cups whole milk**
**2 cups flour**

First, put the milk in a glass jar or crock and leave it, covered with a cloth, in a warm place (80 to 85 degrees) for about 24 hours, or until it sours. Stir in the flour and let stand again, lightly covered, at the same warm temperature, until bubbly and sour. It will take from 2 to 5 days. If a bit of black mold forms on the inside of the container, just wipe it away. What you're looking for is a good, healthy, yeasty, sour smell. If the sour odor is repugnant, it isn't right. It may be necessary to throw the mixture out and start over; for some reason, it doesn't always work the first time.

Some general notes on sourdough: You should maintain about 3 cups of starter, as most recipes call for 1 or 2 cups. Replenish your starter pot after each use. Immediately after measuring out the amount for the recipe, stir back into the pot enough milk and flour to bring the level up to the original amount. Never, never put anything in the starter pot except the same 2 ingredients you started with. Leftover bits of dough will ruin it. After replenishing, leave the pot out of the refrigerator for a few hours until it starts bubbling again. Then store, covered but not sealed, in refrigerator.

The starter should be used and replenished every 2 to 4 weeks. If a little clear liquid forms on top of the starter after standing for a long time, just stir it back in. It is an alcoholic liquid called "hootch," and it belongs there.

In sourdough baking, soda is used to counteract the sourness. Use the amount called for in each recipe to start, then increase it next time if the product seems too sour.

For storing the sourdough starter, a glass or glazed pottery container is best and should not be filled more than half full, as the mixture rises — sometimes double. A well-fitting lid should be used, but it should not be sealed. Nearly all our sources of information on sourdough emphasize that metal containers must not be used, except possibly for mixing. The acid in sourdough, upon standing, will react with the metal, causing etching of the metal and producing a possibly toxic mixture.

About the recipes:

Amounts of flour given are approximate and depend on the consistency of your starter. We maintain our starter at about the consistency of cake batter.

If it is available, unbleached flour makes a more delicious bread.

If you'd like to try it, you can almost duplicate the bread flour used by bakeries (not sold to the housewife, for some reason) by combining cake flour with all-purpose flour in the proportion of 1 part cake flour to 6 parts all-purpose flour.

A good idea for "proofing" (letting the bread rise): Place the roll of dough inside a large plastic bag and close it up. Do the same for loaves set to rise. This will keep the moisture in.

# SOURDOUGH BISCUITS

Stir the starter with the milk in a mixing bowl. Sift or stir the flour with salt, baking powder and soda. Cut shortening into flour mixture with a pastry blender until particles are the size of tiny peas. Combine the two mixtures and stir well. Turn out on floured board or cloth and knead lightly. Work in a little more flour, if necessary, to make a soft workable dough. Roll out and cut with biscuit cutter. Set to rise for about an hour in warm place, 80 to 85 degrees. Bake at 400 degrees for 15 minutes or longer, until done and browned. Makes about 2 dozen.

— Lillian Marshall, 1971

**1 cup starter**
**¾ cup lukewarm milk**
**2 cups flour (approximately)**
**¼ cup shortening**
**¾ teaspoon salt**
**2 teaspoons baking powder**
**¼ teaspoon soda**

# SOURDOUGH RYE

Mix the starter with the water, molasses, salt and oil. Beat in the rye flour and seeds with 2 cups all-purpose flour. Let rise, covered with plastic wrap, until doubled, about 6 hours. Beat in enough remaining flour to make a kneadable dough and knead until dough loses almost all its stickiness. Shape into 2 round loaves and place on a greased baking sheet. Cover with plastic wrap and let rise until doubled in bulk, about 3 hours. Slash top ¼-inch deep with a sharp knife in an "X". Bake in a preheated 400-degree oven about 40 minutes or until loaves sound hollow when thumped on the bottom.

— Deni Hamilton, 1981

**3 cups sourdough starter**
**1 cup warm water**
**⅓ cup molasses**
**1 tablespoon salt**
**¼ cup oil**
**3 cups rye flour**
**4 tablespoons caraway seeds**
**3 to 4 cups all-purpose flour or bread flour**

# SOURDOUGH PANCAKES

1 cup starter
1 cup warm water
1¼ cups flour
1 egg
1 tablespoon cooking oil
½ teaspoon salt
½ teaspoon soda
1 tablespoon sugar

"Set the sponge" the night before you want the world's tastiest pancakes for breakfast. Blend the starter, water and flour. Cover with a cloth and let stand overnight in a warm room.

Next morning, beat in the egg and oil. Blend the salt, soda and sugar together in a cup, then sprinkle over the batter and stir in. Let the batter rest a few minutes before baking on a hot griddle. Makes about 3 cups of batter.

Most sourdough pancake lovers insist the cakes be small, like a big silver dollar, but no matter the size you make them, they have a flavor no other pancake will give you. A batch of pancakes once a week, even if you never use it for anything else, will make your sourdough pot more than worthwhile.

Any of the usual pancake variations will work, too. You may add blueberries, grated apples or crisp bacon bits to the batter. Always serve very hot, with plenty of butter and hot syrup.

— Lillian Marshall, 1967

# SOURDOUGH WHEAT BREAD

1 package dry yeast
1½ cups warm water (110 degrees)
3 cups whole-wheat flour
1 cup sourdough starter
¼ cup dark molasses
3 tablespoons butter, softened
2 teaspoons salt
2½ to 3 cups unbleached flour or
  all-purpose flour
½ teaspoon baking soda

In large mixing bowl, soften yeast in warm water. Blend in whole-wheat flour, sourdough starter, molasses, butter and salt. Combine one cup unbleached white or all-purpose flour and baking soda. Stir into flour-yeast mixture. Add enough remaining flour to make a moderately stiff dough.

Turn out onto floured surface, and knead five to eight minutes or until smooth. Shape into a ball. Place in a greased bowl, turning once. Cover with a cloth. Set in warm place, free from drafts, and let rise 1½ to two hours or until doubled in size. Punch down, and divide in half. Let rest 10 minutes. Shape into two loaves, and place in two greased loaf pans. Cover. Let rise about one hour or until doubled in size. Bake at 375 degrees for 35 to 40 minutes. Remove from pans and cool on rack.

— Lillian Marshall, 1978

# POTATO BREAD

Combine starter with warm water in large mixer bowl. Add oil, salt and mashed potatoes and mix thoroughly. Beat in 2 cups of the flour until well blended, then gradually work in about 2 more cups with a wooden spoon. Use enough flour to make a soft dough, then turn out on heavily floured board or cloth and work in enough flour to make a rather stiff dough. Form into a ball, place in greased bowl and turn over to grease both sides. In a warm place, about 85 degrees, let rise until doubled; this should take 2 hours or more.

Punch down dough, turn out on floured board or cloth and knead for about 10 minutes until smooth and satiny. Divide into two loaves and form each into a smooth ball. Place loaves on greased baking sheet. With sharp knife, make shallow slits across top of loaves. Brush with egg yolk beaten with water. Cover with oiled wax paper and let rise in a warm place until almost doubled. Preheat oven to 400 degrees. Bake for about 25 to 30 minutes or until the loaves are nicely browned and sound hollow when they are thumped.

— Lillian Marshall, 1973

**1 cup starter**
**1 cup warm water**
**1 tablespoon cooking oil**
**2 teaspoons salt**
**1 cup lukewarm mashed potatoes**
**4 cups unbleached flour, plus about 1 cup on the dough board**
**1 egg yolk**

# NO-KNEAD GOLDEN LOAVES

Combine water with yeast, sugar and salt in a bowl. Gradually add flour to form a stiff dough. Mix well until blended. Place in a greased bowl and cover. Put in warm place and let rise until doubled in bulk — about 1½ hours. Toss lightly on a well-floured board about a minute to coat dough with flour. Divide in half. Shape into 2 round loaves. Place in two 6-inch round casseroles which have been greased and sprinkled with corn meal or place on a greased baking sheet. Let rise in a warm place until doubled in bulk — 30 to 60 minutes. Brush with slightly beaten egg white. Preheat oven to 400 degrees, and bake 40 to 45 minutes.

— Cissy Gregg, 1957

**1½ cups lukewarm water**
**1 package of active dry yeast**
**1 tablespoon sugar**
**2 teaspoons salt**
**4 cups sifted all-purpose flour**
**Slightly beaten egg white**

# HOMEMADE BREAD

*Here is Cissy Gregg's step-by-step recipe for basic white bread, as published in 1951. The recipe doesn't say so, but in Step 2, when you've kneaded the dough, it's best to let it rise in a large bowl. Grease the inside of the bowl with margarine or butter, then place the dough ball in it, turning the dough several times to coat all sides.*

*In Step 5, to test for doneness, turn the bread out of its pan, hold it with a hot pad and thump it on the bottom. It should have a hollow sound.*

**1 cup milk**
**2 tablespoons sugar**
**2 teaspoons salt**
**2½ tablespoons shortening**
**1 cup warm water**
**1 package active dry yeast**
**6 cups flour**
**Flour to dust kneading board**

Step 1: Scald 1 cup of milk. That means to heat the milk until a skim comes on top, but don't boil. Add 2 tablespoons sugar, 2 teaspoons salt and 2½ tablespoons shortening. Set aside to cool until lukewarm. Test it by putting a drop on the inside of your wrist as you would test a formula for a baby.

Measure into a large mixing bowl 1 cup warm, not hot, water. Sprinkle in a package of active dry yeast. Stir until dissolved. Stir in luke-warm milk mixture. Add 3 cups of sifted enriched flour, and beat until smooth. Add 3 more cups of sifted flour, and stir until dough forms an irregular ball and comes away for the sides of the bowl. Turn dough out on a lightly floured board. That's the dough, and 'twas easy, wasn't it?

Step 2: Knead the dough by folding it over on itself toward you and pushing it forward with the heels of your hands. Then turn the dough one-quarter way around, and repeat the pull-push rhythm. As you knead, sprinkle flour sparingly on the board, using only enough flour to keep the dough from sticking to your hands. Knead until the dough is smooth and tightly stretched, feels springy and elastic, and doesn't stick to the board. About 8 to 10 minutes will do the job. Cover with a cloth and let rise in a warm place free from drafts until doubled in bulk.

Step 3: When doubled in bulk, punch down. As the dough collapses, pull in edges and fold them over into center and form a ball. Divide the dough in half.

Step 4: With the hands, press each piece of dough into an oblong, 9 by 8 by 1 inches. Fold outer edges over to meet in center. Pinch center seam and end seams together. Place loaves, with the sealed seams down, in a greased pan, 7½ by 3½ by 2¾ inches.

Step 5: Bake in a preheated 400-degree oven, about 40 minutes. Take the bread from the oven when it is browned all over. It should be slightly darker on the top than on the sides. Remove from

pan as soon as it comes from the oven. Cool on rack
or crosswise on bread pans. When cool store in a
well-ventilated breadbox.

That's all there is to it. And my! doesn't it smell
good?

# WHOLE-WHEAT BREAD

*This was one of the recipes that Elaine Corn wrote about in a 1984 feature on the once-a-month back-stage buffets at the Louisville Ballet. It is Peggy Smith Lindell's recipe. Ms. Lindell prepares the dough at night, Elaine wrote, and by morning it is "ready for baking fresh for breakfast."*

In a large bowl, combine 2 cups all-purpose flour
with the yeast and salt. Stir well. Add honey,
margarine and water. Beat with a wire whisk until
all ingredients all well-blended and no lumps of
flour remain. Add whole-wheat flour 1 cup at a
time, beating well after each addition. With a large
spoon, stir in enough of the remaining all-purpose
flour to make a soft dough that does not stick to the
sides of the bowl.

Turn dough onto a floured surface. Knead 5 to 10
minutes, until smooth and elastic. Divide in half.
Flatten with hands or roll lightly into a rectangle
approximately 6 by 12 inches. Roll tightly from the
6-inch end.

Generously greased two 8½-by-4½-inch bread
pans. Place loaves in pans, turning once to grease all
surfaces, ending with seam-side-down. Cover loosely with wax paper. Refrigerate 2 to 24 hours.

Before baking, heat oven to 375 degrees and let
loaves stand at room temperature for 10 minutes.
Puncture surface bubbles with a toothpick. Bake 30
to 40 minutes. Remove from pans immediately,
brush with melted butter or margarine and wrap
securely in foil. Cool completely before slicing. This
bread freezes well and makes delicious toast.

**3½ to 4½ cups all-purpose flour**
**2 packages active dry yeast**
**1 tablespoon salt**
**¼ cup honey**
**3 tablespoons margarine, softened**
**2¼ cups hot tap water**
**2 cups whole wheat flour**

# PERSIMMON MUFFINS

½ cup persimmon pulp, or about 2
  large persimmons
½ teaspoon baking soda
1 egg, beaten
½ cup milk
¼ cup melted butter
½ cup flour
½ cup sugar
2 teaspoons baking powder
½ teaspoon salt
½ teaspoon cinnamon
½ teaspoon nutmeg
¼ teaspoon ground cloves
½ cup chopped raisins

Heat oven to 400 degrees. Wash and dry persimmons. Cut away from stem. Run through food mill, or carefully strip off skin, if necessary, and quarter. Discard pit and put pulp through sieve, blender or food processor, then measure.

Mix soda with pulp. Beat in egg, milk and butter. Sift flour, sugar, baking powder, salt and spices. Add raisins. Stir persimmon mixture into flour mixture just until moistened. Batter will be lumpy. Spoon into muffin tins. Bake 15 to 18 minutes. Makes 1 dozen.

— Elaine Corn, 1983

# MRS. ROBBINS' SALT-RISING BREAD

*Cissy was a subscriber to the Journal of the New York Botanical Garden, and she opened an issue in 1950 to discover that Christine Chapman Robbins had taken over a substantial number of the pages to describe her research into and experience with salt-rising bread.*

*It turned out that the article supported Cissy's own opinions about salt-rising bread, including the conclusion that "salt can be omitted from the dough without affecting the result." In fact, Bernard Clayton Jr. writes in his "The Complete Book of Breads" that the term, salt-rising, comes from "the old kitchen practice of keeping the bowl of starter nested overnight in a bowl of warm salt, which retains heat nicely."*

*Both Clayton and James Beard, in "Beard on Bread," note that salt-rising bread recipes are notoriously unpredictable. "You may try the same recipe without success three or four times and find that it works the fifth time," Beard wrote. And if the starter doesn't bubble up during the night, Clayton says, "have no patience. It is only a sacrifice of cornmeal and milk. Begin again, but put it together in another way. Use a different milk or another kind of cornmeal. There is no easy explanation of why one combination will work and another will not."*

*Warm temperatures are critical for both the starter and the sponge. Clayton lets his starter develop "on a shelf near the hot water heater in the utility room" and suggests, as an alternative, that you set the starter mixture bowl or jar in "a pan of water over a pilot light on the stove." Beard suggested putting the starter mixture in a gas oven with the pilot light on. With an electric stove, try placing the jar or bowl of starter mixture in a pan of water partially on a burner set at 'warm.'"*

*Cissy's recounting of Mrs. Robbins' recipe follows:*

As all of us who have attempted to make salt-rising bread know, the process is considered in three steps: preparation of the starter; preparation of a batter or sponge to which the rising is added; preparation of the dough and loaves.

## PREPARATION OF STARTER

Heat one cup milk until boiling well. Stir into the milk, ½ cup cornmeal. (She has tried various cornmeals and has secured activity with all, but she believes the water-ground cornmeal has given quicker results.) Place the prepared cornmeal, which should be only moderately stiff, in jar. A wide-mouthed fruit jar holding between 3 and 4 cups is adequate. Cover the jar loosely, and place in a pan of water that is hot to the hand. Wrap the whole up very well in a towel, and place where the water can be kept hot for 6 to 10 hours. (In the winter, Mrs. Robbins places the jar on top of her oil burner at 10 o'clock at night.) If it is cool in the morning, the cornmeal can be reheated by adding a small amount of boiling milk, the water bath renewed, and the whole placed in the oven, preheated to 100-115 degrees. About noon or 1 p.m., it shows a "lightening", an elevation of the mass in the jar. Suddenly the mass is full of bubbles, and you hear the escaping gas. It now is ready to add to the sponge.

## PREPARATION OF SPONGE

Take 2 cups of milk, hot as the hand can bear. Place in a warmed mixing bowl. Add 2 to 3 cups of warmed flour (bread or all-purpose). Stir until well mixed. Add the prepared starter, and mix well with a flexible spatula or spoon. Cover the bowl and place in a pan of water about body temperature. Wrap well and place to rise at the same temperature as for the starter. This should rise in an hour to an hour and a half.
Watch and try to catch it just as it begins to drop a bit. Then use in preparing the dough.

## PREPARATION OF DOUGH

In preparing the dough and loaves, Mrs. Robbins uses the top of the warmed oven and keeps all of the materials warm in the oven. The temperature of the dough should not be allowed to drop during the preparation. Usually, she prepares two large loaves or four half-sized loaves at a time. If the sponge is very active, more can be made.
Add 2 tablespoons of sugar, one tablespoon salt, one tablespoon of vegetable shortening. Add sponge and enough flour to make a soft dough. In kneading, stretch and fold dough 10 to 12 times in the hands or on the board. Mold into loaves. Double loaves are best, since salt-rising loaves tend to split on the side. Use small loaves or a square pan for double loaves. Set to rise at 100 to 115 degrees until double in bulk or until it reaches the top of the pan. This usually takes one to two hours. Bake at 385 degrees for 10 minutes, then lower the temperature to 350 degrees.
We must have learned from the same people since I, too, was taught, in preparation of the sponge, "to try to catch it just as it begins to drop a bit." In this step, if you don't watch, the sponge goes too long, and you get that odor some find offensive.
My baking period usually runs approximately an hour, but all depends on the size of your loaves.

# MARY H. HERRINGTON'S COCOA MUFFINS

Sift the flour, sugar, cocoa and baking powder together. Using your fingers, rub the butter into the dry ingredients. Add enough milk to make a stiff batter. Spoon into greased muffin rings — 8 large ones or 14 tiny ones. Bake at 375 degrees 20 minutes for the large ones, 15 for the tiny ones. Note: These aren't cupcakes; they're like old fashioned "sweetbread," flavored with chocolate. Good dredged with powdered sugar. Or you can cut a cone from the top of each, fill with sweetened whipped cream, then replace the cone.          — Lillian Marshall, 1970

**1 cup flour**
**½ cup sugar**
**¼ cup cocoa**
**2 teaspoons baking powder**
**1 or 2 tablespoons butter or**
   **margarine**
**About ⅔ cup milk**

# SWEET-POTATO MUFFINS

*This recipe and others from the family of Gov. Martha Layne Collins and from Vincent Ashby, chef at the governor's mansion, were featured in a story by Elaine Corn for the 1984 holiday-entertaining issue of the Magazine.*

1 stick butter
1¼ cups sugar
2 eggs
1¼ cups canned sweet potatoes, mashed
1½ cups all-purpose flour
2 teaspoons baking powder
¼ teaspoon salt
1 teaspoon cinnamon
¼ teaspoon nutmeg
1 cup milk
¼ cup chopped pecans
½ cup chopped raisins

Heat oven to 400 degrees. Grease 4 dozen 1½-inch muffin tins. Beat the butter and sugar until creamy. Add eggs and mix well. Blend in sweet potatoes. Sift flour, baking powder, salt, cinnamon and nutmeg. Add to creamed mixture alternately with the milk. Do not overmix. Fold in the nuts and raisins. Fill tins two-thirds full. Bake 25 minutes. Makes 4 dozen.

# YEAST BISCUITS

1 package active dry yeast
1 cup warm buttermilk
½ teaspoon soda
2 teaspoons sugar
½ cup shortening
1 teaspoon salt
2½ cups flour

Dissolve yeast in warm buttermilk. Set aside. Sift together flour, soda, sugar and salt. Cut in shortening. Add yeast mixture to flour mixture. Stir until blended. Knead slightly, then roll ½-inch thick. Cut with biscuit cutter, dip in melted butter and place in greased pan. Let rise about 1 hour. Bake at 425 degrees for 12 minutes.

— Lillian Marshall, 1966

# GET-A-JUMP-ON-THE-DAY BISCUITS

*In 1984, Elaine Corn interviewed Dinwiddie Lampton Jr., president of American Life & Accident Insurance Co. of Kentucky, about food for Derby entertaining. This was one of the recipes from his home.*

3 cups all-purpose flour
4 teaspoons baking powder
1 teaspoon salt
6 tablespoons shortening
1 cup milk

Heat oven to 425 degrees. Sift flour into a bowl, then sift again with baking powder and salt. Cut in shortening. Add milk quickly while mixing well. Knead lightly on a lightly floured surface. Pat out until dough is about ½-inch thick. Cut with floured biscuit cutter. Place side by side in a cast iron skillet or on a baking sheet. Bake 12 minutes or until golden brown. Makes about 1 dozen, depending on size.

# CREAM BISCUITS

Preheat oven to 425 degrees. Stir dry ingredients in a bowl. Stir in cream and blend with a fork, then work with your hands to form a soft dough. If necessary, add water droplets until dough reaches a manageable consistency for rolling. Roll or pat ½-inch thick. Cut with biscuit cutter or use the rims of jars of varying diameter. Bake for 20 minutes or until a light gold. Biscuits will not darken. Brush tops with butter. Makes 1½ dozen, depending on size of biscuit cutter.

2 cups sifted flour
1 teaspoon baking soda
1 teaspoon baking powder
1 teaspoon salt
1 cup cream

# WHOLE WHEAT BISCUITS

Preheat oven to 450 degrees. Sift and then measure the whole wheat. Sift together soda, baking powder and salt. Stir into the whole wheat. Cut in the shortening as you would for any other biscuits. Add just enough milk to make a soft dough. Stir gently to dampen the flour. Then stir vigorously until a soft dough is formed. Knead lightly on a floured board. Pat or roll to ¾-inch thickness. Cut biscuits with a floured cutter. If you like a crisp crust, place the biscuits 1½ inches apart. But if you like soft biscuits, put them close together. Dot each biscuit with a period of butter, or if you desire the varnished effect, paint each with slightly beaten egg yolk. Bake for 12 to 15 minutes.
— Cissy Gregg, 1951

2 cups whole wheat flour
1 teaspoon baking soda
2 teaspoons baking powder
½ teaspoon salt
4 tablespoons shortening
About ⅔ cup buttermilk, or enough
    to make a soft dough

# OATMEAL BISCUITS

Sift together the flour, baking powder, salt and rolled oats. Cut in margarine with a pastry blender. Add milk, mix, then knead on lightly floured board. Roll out to ½-inch thickness and cut doughnut or regular-shaped biscuits. Bake on ungreased baking sheet in preheated 450-degree oven about 10 minutes or until lightly browned. Serve hot or cold. Note: These biscuits may be frozen after they're cut out. Bake until brown and crisp.
— Lillian Marshall, 1973

1½ cups sifted flour
3 teaspoons baking powder
1 teaspoon salt
½ cup uncooked rolled oats
⅓ cup margarine
⅔ cup milk

# BUTTERMILK BISCUITS

2 cups flour
4 teaspoons baking powder
½ teaspoon baking soda
½ teaspoon salt
¼ cup shortening (or combination shortening and butter)
1 cup buttermilk or sour milk

Preheat oven to 450 degrees. Combine flour, baking powder, baking soda and salt. Cut in shortening until mixture resembles cornmeal. Quickly add buttermilk, stirring with a fork just until dough holds together. Knead lightly for about 10 seconds on surface dusted sparingly with flour. Roll or pat to ½-inch thick. Cut biscuits. Place close together in ungreased cast iron skillet or baking dish. Bake for 10 minutes. If desired, halfway through baking, dot each biscuit with butter. Makes 1½ dozen, depending on diameter of your biscuit cutter. — Elaine Corn, 1982

# ANGEL DROP BISCUITS

*Barbara Spalding of Bardstown, Ky., was expecting 42 to 48 relatives for her 1983 Christmas dinner, and she gave this recipe to Elaine Corn for the holiday-entertaining issue of the Magazine.*

4 packages granulated yeast
8 tablespoons warm water
10 cups flour
½ cup sugar
2 teaspoons baking soda
2 tablespoons baking powder
2 teaspoons salt
2 cups shortening
4 cups buttermilk
Melted butter

Preheat oven to 375 degrees. Combine yeast and water, beating until shiny, and let stand. Stir together flour, sugar, baking soda, baking powder and salt. Cut in shortening. Add yeast mixture. Slowly stir in buttermilk. Drop by heaping table-spoons onto well-greased, square or rectangular cookie sheets. Brush with melted butter. Bake until browned. Makes 4 dozen.

# SAVORY BISCUITS

*Cissy Gregg gave this recipe in 1949. She wrote that it produced a biscuit that was "almost as intriguing as a red-head in a well-fitting black dress."*

1 cup flour
2 tablespoons lard or 3 of vegetable shortening
½ teaspoon curry
½ teaspoon salt
1½ teaspoons baking powder
¾ cup milk
¼ teaspoon dry mustard
½ cup grated cheese

Preheat oven to 450 degrees. Sift flour and measure. Sift with baking powder and salt into a bowl. Cut in the lard or other shortening until well mixed. Add milk and seasonings, and mix. Roll out on a floured board, and cut with a biscuit cutter. Prick the top of each with a fork, if you like, and bake 12 to 15 minutes.

*Baking powder biscuits. Photograph by
Robert Steinau.*

# BAKING POWDER BISCUITS FOR TWO

*What's a "good tablespoon?" In this 1948 recipe, Cissy wrote that "good means just don't scrape it off the spoon too well if you like a short, rich biscuit."*

Preheat the oven to 425 to 450 degrees. Sift the flour, and sift again with baking powder and salt. Cut in the shortening with two knives, or crumble it in with the finger tips until it is like coarse cornmeal or about like grains of rice. Add about ⅓ cup milk and stir vigorously with a fork, or work with the finger tips until it is rather stiff and comes free of the bowl in a mass.

Turn out on a lighly floured board and knead lightly. Bring the bottom to the top, using the heel of the hand to press with. Between 10 and 16 "kneads" will bring the ingredients into accord and produce a smooth top to the biscuit. I wouldn't think of dirtying the rolling pin for 1 cup of flour, and so I say, pat the dough out until it is about ¼ to ½ inch in thickness. Cut out with a biscuit cutter and put on an ungreased baking sheet or on the upside-down side of a baking pan. Bake for about 15 minutes.

1 cup flour
1 teaspoon double-acting baking powder
½ teaspoon salt
2 good tablespoons shortening
⅓ to ½ cup milk

# BROWN-CRUSTED BISCUITS

Preheat oven to 450 degrees. Sift flour, soda, cream of tartar and salt together three times, and don't be lazy and skip on this number. Add the shortening by cutting it in as for any biscuit. Then add enough whole milk to make a soft dough. If there is a secret of good biscuits, in my estimation it is having the dough soft. It should be as soft as possible, yet firm enough to roll out. Roll out and cut. Bake for approximately 15 minutes. These get a good crust, and yet the inside is light.
— Cissy Gregg, 1949

3 cups flour
1¼ teaspoons soda
2¼ teaspoons cream of tartar
1 teaspoon salt
6 tablespoons shortening
Whole milk to make the dough

# BRAN BUTTERMILK BISCUITS

½ cup breakfast bran cereal
¾ cup buttermilk
1½ cups sifted all-purpose flour
1 teaspoon baking powder
¾ teaspoon salt
½ teaspoon soda
⅓ cup shortening

Preheat oven to 450 degrees. Add bran cereal to buttermilk and let stand while getting the other ingredients together. To the flour add the baking powder, salt and soda. Sift into a bowl. Cut in the shortening until the mixture resembles fine meal. Then add the buttermilk-bran mixture and mix until the dough follows a wooden spoon around the bowl. Turn out onto a lightly floured board and knead lightly for about 20 seconds. Roll out on a lightly floured board to about ½-inch thickness, and cut with a biscuit cutter. Bake on a lightly greased baking sheet for 12 to 15 minutes. If you like a good brown crust on top, try brushing with milk a few minutes before time for them to come from the oven.

— Cissy Gregg, 1952

# NORTH MIDDLETOWN BEATEN BISCUITS

*This recipe, which Cissy Gregg wrote about in 1949, was from Mrs. Stanley Dixon, of North Middletown, in Bourbon County, Ky., and Cissy said that it was one of her favorites. Four years earlier, Cissy wrote that to beat her own biscuits, she used "elbow strength aided with a wooden mallet which serves otherwise as an ice crusher, and a wooden board underneath the dough." If you have a bread break today, it's probably in your antique collection and not in use in your kitchen.*

7 cups flour
1 cup lard
1 teaspoon salt
2 to 4 tablespoons sugar
1 teaspoon baking powder
1⅓ cups cold milk

This full recipe makes between 6 and 7 dozen beaten biscuits. If you are going to make them by hand, make up half the recipe.

Sift the flour and measure. Then sift flour, baking powder, salt and sugar together three times. Cut in the lard, using the finger tips or two knives or a pastry blender, until these ingredients are of a finer consistency than when mixed for ordinary biscuits but not quite as fine as for pastry. Add the cold milk to make a stiff dough.

If using the bread break, get the dough in a ball, flatten it out and start running it through the machine, which looks for all the world like a clothes wringer. The rollers in this case are turned by hand. Fold the dough over and run back between the rollers. Repeat this process again and again until the dough is slick, glossy and "talks back to you." The talking back comes from popping the blisters that the air forms in the dough. Roll ¼-inch thick and cut with a biscuit cutter. We used the 2-inch biscuit cutter we had but would have preferred a slightly smaller one.

If the dough is beaten by hand, beat the dough out until it is about ¼-inch thick. Fold and beat again. Repeat this until the dough is smooth, glossy and has blisters. (We got far more fascinating blisters beating the dough than when we ran it through a machine.) Finally, roll the dough out to the ¼-inch thickness and cut as suggested. Do not add any more flour in either method of handling.

By hand it takes about 30 minutes to beat them — or use the "200 beats for home-folks and 500 for company" rule. It takes about 15 minutes using a machine or 30 minutes at the most.

All beaten biscuits must have their pricked tops. Some say the best style is three rows, some say four. But these pricks are for more than beauty. If you are using a fork, be sure the fork goes clear through the biscuit and hits the pan. If in doubt that this has been accomplished, look at the bottom of the biscuit to be sure.

You see, the dough has been made into thin layers with the rolling or beating and the folding. In baking, the air between these layers will expand, and the fork pricks aid in holding the biscuit layers together. Many good cooks say a good beaten bisucit should "yawn" during the baking, but this mouth-open appearance isn't quite so attractive according to our way of thinking.

To bake beaten biscuits, the North Middletown recipe calls for a 350-degree temperature for 20 to 25 minutes, but our biscuits were a little larger in size, so we baked them a little longer — perhaps 30 minutes. Other recipes call for a 325-degree oven with a baking time of an hour.

# SODA BISCUITS

*"We have received a number of questionnaires in the past asking for a description of what a true Southern biscuit should be like in form, shape and texture," Cissy Gregg wrote in 1953. "Have you ever actually tried to describe what you consider the right biscuit should be like? We had a heck of a time, and everyone we called in to check with had completely his or her own idea. Thin, fat? Crusty, fluffy? Small, large? Just what is your idea of a biscuit?"*

**2 cups sifted flour**
**½ teaspoon soda**
**½ teaspoon salt**
**⅓ cup shortening**
**1 cup buttermilk**

Preheat oven to 450 degrees. Sift flour, soda and salt together. Cut in shortening, or work it in with your fingers. Stir in milk. Now because some flours will absorb more liquid than others and because the same flour will vary with climatic conditions, the liquid measurement must be approximate. In other words, don't just dump all the liquid in and hope for the best. Take it easy. My preference is a soft dough, and more than likely I'll use the full amount of liquid. Knead on a lightly floured board. Use the light touch in kneading. Pat or roll out to ¼-inch thickness and cut with a medium small biscuit cutter.

Place the biscuits on a lightly greased baking sheet. Brush the tops lightly with melted butter or margarine. Bake for about 10 minutes, or until they have a good suntan on their faces. I do not grease the baking sheet for baking-powder biscuits. Don't ask me why I make this distinction. I just learned that way. Soda biscuits do not rise like baking powder biscuits. You'll find these more like two crisp crusts with very little in between. And don't let anyone tell you cold biscuits aren't good! These are good hot or cold.

# BEATEN BISCUITS

*This is Cissy Gregg's 1945 recipe, producing considerably fewer than the North Middletown recipe. Reading both recipes can fill in the blank spaces in one's knowledge about beaten biscuits.*

**2 cups sifted flour**
**½ teaspoon salt**
**Ice water or chilled milk, using as little as possible**
**1 tablespoon of lard**

Add salt to flour and rub in the lard with the hands. Add the iced liquid — either water or milk, or equal parts of each — to make a stiff dough, kneading all the time. I don't have a kneader, but use elbow strength aided with a wooden mallet which serves otherwise as an ice crusher, and a wooden board underneath the dough. Some people put the dough in a clean cloth, but I don't. Beat until the air is lively with snappings and crackings, and there are blisters on the dough. Cut into small biscuits, place on an ungreased baking sheet, pricked according to fashion, and bake in a 350 degree oven for 35 to 40 minutes.

# MRS. WHITNEY'S CHRISTMAS YORKSHIRE PUDDING

*Mrs. Robert P. Whitney Sr,. mother of the Louisville Orchestra director, helped Cissy Gregg with some Christmas dinner recipes in 1957. She wrote that she had "great success" trying this recipe and that she used muffin cups to bake it. "Mrs. Whitney chooses about an 8-inch square pan. As with much cooking, Mrs. Whitney says you simply have to learn about this interesting recipe. Do it 2 or 3 times, and then you'll know your way with the amount of drippings from the roast that you prefer."*

Beat the eggs and milk together, just enough to mix lightly. Add flour and salt. Into your 8-inch baking pan or into individual muffin or individual glass baking dishes, pour a little of the drippings from the roast of beef. Place them in the oven until they are smoking hot, and we do mean smoking hot. Pour in batter. Bake in a 450-degree oven for 30 minutes. Makes 7 to 8 servings, and it's good any time of year.

**1 pint milk**
**1 cup flour, before sifting**
**Salt, about ⅓ teaspoon**
**3 large or 4 small eggs**
**Drippings from the roast beef**

# YORKSHIRE PUDDING

Gradually mix milk into flour, and when smooth, add eggs and salt. Beat well. Pour melted butter or beef drippings ½-inch thick over bottom of two bread pans. Pour half of mixture in each pan. Bake at 400 degrees for 20 minutes, then reduce heat to 350 degrees and bake 10 minutes longer. Cut in squares and serve with roast beef.

The beef roast will need a little rest to rejoin with its juices, and while this rejoining is going on, the Yorkshire pudding can be baking so it can be served very hot and wonderful with the gravy.

— Cissy Gregg, 1960

**1 cup flour**
**1 cup milk**
**2 eggs**
**½ teaspoon salt**

# CAKES, COOKIES & CANDIES

# MRS. WARD'S CREAM PULLED CANDY

*Mrs. C.T. Ward of Lawrenceburg, Ky., was an educator in Anderson County when Lillian Marshall wrote about her and her secondary passion — candy-making — in 1968.*

**3 cups sugar**
**¾ cups water**
**1 tablespoon butter**
**½ cup heavy cream**
**½ teaspoon vanilla**

Combine sugar, water and butter in heavy 4-quart saucepan and stir over medium heat until all sugar is dissolved. Cover pan for 2 or 3 minutes to steam down last remaining sugar crystals. Drizzle the cream into the sugar mixture slowly, so that the boiling never stops. Reduce heat to very slow boil to eliminate danger of scorching.

Continue to boil slowly without stirring until candy forms a very firm ball when tested in cold water. Mrs. Ward also watches for it to "spin a hair" about an inch long. This would be 250 degrees on a candy thermometer.

Pour candy out on buttered marble slab and allow to cool until you can pick it up comfortably. Pull for a minute or so until it firms up somewhat, then form candy into a ring. Now repeatedly stretch the circle of candy and fold it on itself into a small circle again. Keep pulling the circle and folding it, always keeping it round.

This technique is much easier than pulling it out long, once you get the hang of it. It also is more economical of motion, and it pulls the candy more uniformly. When it holds its shape well, drip the vanilla over it. Pull until it looks "dusty," as Mrs. Ward says, and the ridges hold up well.

Pull candy out into a rope about 2 inches wide on buttered marble and cut with scissors into "pillows" about ½-inch wide. Leave on cool marble until it "creams," and wrap each piece in wax paper.

# EASY CHOCOLATE TRUFFLES

*"Truffles are bite-sized chocolate forms shaped by hand after a chocolate filling is allowed to chill," Elaine Corn wrote for a truffles recipe. "Truffles may be dipped in a chocolate coating that firms on additional chilling. Try not to make truffles too large. One bite is enough for swooning."*

*Elaine should know. Charmed by the chocolate and reeling from the richness, swarms have swooned over her truffles. She wrote the first of these recipes in 1984; the second, 1985.*

With electric beater, beat the sugar and butter until a paste. Melt the chocolate in the top of a double-boiler. Let cool, stirring to bring temperature down. Add liqueur to chocolate, then add sugar-butter paste, beating mixture by hand with a wooden spoon until thick, cool and it forms a ball.

Chill 30 minutes to 1 hour. With cocoa-dusted hands, roll chocolate mixture into small balls. Roll in cocoa sprinkled on waxed paper. Place truffles on a baking sheet lined with waxed paper. Refrigerate about 2 hours before serving. May dip in chocolate coating, if desired. Makes about 2 dozen, depending on size of truffles.

**1½ cups powdered sugar**
**1 stick butter, softened**
**½ pound semisweet chocolate pieces**
**2 tablespoons kirsch, brandy or rum**
**Cocoa, for dusting**
**Chocolate coating (see recipe)**

## CHOCOLATE COATING

Paraffin helps control dipping chocolate with fewer drips and provides more control through changes in temperature. A small amount is harmless. Paraffin is usually found near canning supplies.

Melt all ingredients in the top of a double-boiler, stirring until the mixture is smooth. Remove from heat and let cool to slightly cooler than body temperature, about 90 degrees Fahrenheit on a candy thermometer. Keep temperature as close to 90 degrees as possible throughout dipping process. Return chocolate to heat if coating mixture thickens.

**1 pound semisweet chocolate pieces**
**¼ cup vegetable oil**
**1 tablespoon paraffin**

# TRADITIONAL PRALINES

Grease a cookie sheet, or have ready sheet of wax paper on a flat surface. In a medium saucepan, combine the sugars. Add milk. Cook over medium heat until mixture reaches 234 to 236 degrees on a candy thermometer or until a small amount dropped into a cup of water forms a soft ball. Remove from heat. Add vanilla and pecans. Beat with a fork until blended. Immediately drop by tablespoons onto the prepared sheet. Add a few drops of water if candy becomes too stiff to handle. Let set. Makes 1 pound.

— Elaine Corn, 1981

**1 cup firmly packed dark brown sugar**
**1 cup sugar**
**⅔ cup evaporated milk**
**1 teaspoon vanilla**
**1½ cups fresh pecan halves**

# SOUTH KENTUCKY FUDGE

1 cup buttermilk or sour cream
1 teaspoon soda
2 cups sugar
2 tablespoons butter
1 teaspoon vanilla

Combine soda with buttermilk or sour cream in heavy 4-quart saucepan. Let stand 5 minutes. Stir in the sugar, gradually and continue to stir over medium heat until completely dissolved. Insert candy thermometer. Add the butter and cook, stirring occasionally, until thermometer registers 232 degrees, or until soft-ball stage is reached. Remove from heat. (For soft-ball test, drop ½ teaspoon of boiling candy into a cup of cold water. You should be able to pick up the drop of candy on your forefinger.) Without shaking or stirring the candy, let it cool until just warmer than room temperature, 100 degrees or so. Add vanilla. Beat until it loses its gloss and begins to hold some shape. Pour out on buttered plate and cut into squares immediately. — Lillian Marshall, 1966

# DOUBLE CHOCOLATE TRUFFLES

1½ cups cream
6 tablespoons unsalted butter
1 pound bulk semisweet chocolate, or morsels or squares
2 tablespoons Kahlua, or other desired liqueur, optional
Chocolate coating (see recipe on preceding page)

Place cream and butter in the top of a double-boiler or in a bowl placed over simmering water. Let melt slowly, stirring, then increase heat and bring cream just to a boil.

Remove from heat and stir in chocolate. Stir until melted and mixture is smooth. Continue stirring until mixture cools slightly. Add liqueur. Cover with plastic wrap and chill three or four hours, or overnight. Stir occasionally the first couple of hours.

When firm, roll fondant into bite-size balls no larger than 1 inch in diameter. Place balls on a baking sheet lined with wax paper. Chill until very firm.

To coat, drop fondant balls into coating mixture, holding balls between two forks with long tines. Roll around in dipping mixture until completely coated. Lift out and gently scrape excess coating on rim of pan. Place balls on wax paper and chill as soon as possible.

Let set two to three hours, or overnight. Eat within four days.

Makes between three and four dozen truffles, depending on size.

# MODJESKAS

*Modjeskas were developed in Louisville, named for actress Helena Modjeska, who starred at the old Macauley Theatre on Walnut Street in the 1870s. Cissy Gregg ran this recipe in 1955; the caramel recipe is from 1970.*

Allow cooked caramel to stand 10 minutes before starting to dip. Drop marshmallow half into caramel, then, with a fork, turn it over to coat completely and lift out, pulling the fork over edge of pan so surplus runs back into pan.

Deposit each piece on buttered or oiled surface, such as cookie sheets or clean counter top. When set, wrap each piece separately in square of waxed paper.

When the last of the caramel gets too thick, warm it gently over low heat, or use remainder to make "turtles". Place three pecan halves together and drop a dab of caramel in center, then top with a spoonful of melted chocolate. Or mix with nuts, to be cut in little squares.

**A recipe caramel (see recipe) cooked to 238 degrees**
**About ¾ pound marshmallows, cut in half with scissors**

# CARAMEL

Combine sugar, a cup of the cream, butter, syrup and salt in a heavy 3- or 4-quart saucepan. Put remaining cup cream in a small pan and heat it separately. Bring large mixture to boil, stirring constantly. Wipe down sides of pan with wet cloth or cover with lid briefly to dissolve remaining sugar crystals.

When it begins actively to boil, dribble the hot cup of cream into the boiling mixture, stirring, and don't let the boiling stop in the process. Cook over medium heat, stirring as necessary to prevent scorching, until thermometer registers 238-240. Remove from heat and stir in vanilla.

**2 cups sugar**
**2 cups heavy cream (do not substitute evaporated milk)**
**2 tablespoons butter**
**1¼ cups white corn syrup**
**Pinch salt**
**1 teaspoon vanilla**

# MRS. HARPER'S MAYONNAISE CAKE

*"If you happen to be in the great legion of those desirous of a 'sad' chocolate cake, this recipe is for you,"* Cissy Gregg wrote in 1949. *"Mrs. Robert C. Harper, from Fort Knox, sent me this recipe shortly after we had had a chocolate cake made with mayonnaise in the column. But goodness me, the one we had can't hold a candle to this one."*

*Further along in the column, after giving the recipe, Cissy decided she better explain what a "sad" cake is. "That's one that is very moist," she wrote. "We would hate for you to get the wrong impression of what that way of using 'sad' means."*

1¾ cups flour
1 cup mayonnaise
1 cup sugar
1 cup chopped dates
1 cup chopped nuts (walnuts, Mrs. Harper suggested, but we used pecans)
1 cup boiling water
1½ squares of unsweetened chocolate, melted
½ teaspoon salt
1 teaspoon cinnamon
1 teaspoon vanilla
1 teaspoon baking soda

Dissolve soda in boiling water and pour over chopped nuts and dates. Let stand a few minutes. Mix sugar and cinnamon. Blend melted and cooled chocolate into mayonnaise. Add vanilla. Mix in sugar mixture. To this add the soaked dates and nuts and the accompanying water. Fold in flour sifted with the salt.

Bake in a greased and waxed paper-lined loaf or tube pan in a 350-degree oven for a good hour. We used a 9-inch tube pan, and it produced about a 3½-inch tall cake. Just the height to make a nice slice of cake on a plate.

# MADGE PREWITT'S APPLE CAKE

3½ cups cored, peeled and chopped apples
2 cups granulated sugar
3 cups all-purpose flour
2 teaspoons soda
½ teaspoon salt
½ teaspoon ground cinnamon
½ teaspoon ground allspice
½ teaspoon ground nutmeg
½ teaspoon ground cloves
1 cup English walnuts, chopped
1 cup (½ pound) butter, melted
2 eggs
1 stick (¼ pound) margarine, melted
2 tablespoons hot water
1½ cups confectioners' sugar, sifted

Combine sugar with apples and let stand while sifting the flour, leavening and spices together. Stir a little of the dry mixture into the chopped walnuts. Add melted butter to the sugar-apple mixture, then beat in the eggs. Blend in the dry ingredients and, last, the walnuts. Turn batter into a well-greased 9-inch tube pan and bake in a preheated 375-degree oven one hour. Let cool five minutes before removing from pan, then remove to cake plate and cool to warm.

Beat margarine, hot water and confectioners' sugar together and spread on warm cake.

Mrs. Prewitt advises mixing the cake by hand, because an electric mixer would destroy the texture of the apples.

— Cook's Corner column, 1980

# YE OLDE 'LECTION CAKE

*Election cakes are thought to have originated almost 300 years ago in New England — probably Hartford, Conn. — as part of the processions, ceremonies and general festivities that attended Election Day. The custom spread, and when Cissy Gregg ran this recipe in 1956, she wrote that election cakes were "sold all over New England on Election Day." It is a yeast cake, "very much like our fruitcake," Cissy said.*

Sprinkle yeast in lukewarm water, add a teaspoon sugar and let stand until mixture is frothy (5 to 10 minutes). Pour boiling water over brown sugar and stir until sugar is dissolved. Cool to lukewarm. Stir in dissolved yeast. Add 1¼ cups all-purpose flour and beat until smooth.

Cover and let rise in warm place until light and bubbly — about 30 minutes. Sift cake flour and next four ingredients together into large mixing bowl. Add shortening and next 4 ingredients and beat 300 strokes or for 3 minutes on mixer at low speed. Scrape bowl and spoon or beaters once during mixing. Add light yeast mixture and beat well (a minute on low speed of an electric mixer).

Add currants, citron, pineapple and peel, and mix well. Turn into a well-greased 8½-inch tube pan and let rise in warm place until light, about an hour.

Bake in moderately hot oven, 375 degrees, 55 to 60 minutes. Cool in pan on wire rack 15 to 20 minutes, then remove cake from pan to rack to finish cooling. When cold, spoon pineapple frosting over top, letting frosting run over sides.

**2 packages active dry yeast**
**¼ cup lukewarm water**
**1 teaspoon sugar**
**½ cup boiling water**
**½ cup brown sugar, packed**
**1¼ cups sifted all-purpose flour**
**2¾ cups sifted cake flour**
**1 cup granulated sugar**
**1¼ teaspoons salt**
**1 teaspoon nutmeg**
**1 teaspoon mace**
**¾ cup vegetable shortening**
**½ teaspoon grated lemon rind**
**1 teaspoon vanilla**
**½ cup milk**
**3 eggs, unbeaten**
**½ cup currants or seedless raisins**
**½ cup candied citron, diced**
**½ cup candied pineapple, diced**
**¼ cup candied orange peel, diced**

## PINEAPPLE FROSTING

Put a tablespoon each of light cream, canned pineapple juice and butter or margarine in a small bowl and heat over water until butter is melted. Remove from hot water.

Add ¼ teaspoon each of grated orange rind and grated lemon rind and 1½ cups sifted confectioners' sugar, and beat until smooth. Add 2 tablespoons diced candied pineapple and mix.

# THE ORIGINAL KENTUCKY WHISKEY CAKE

*"The original" carries some pretty weighty implications, but no one disputed the claim after we ran this recipe as an entry in the Cook's Corner column in 1981. Unlike a fruitcake, this cake does not have to ripen and will store almost indefinitely, the column said. Actually, Cissy Gregg ran the recipe first in 1962, attributing it to Thomas H. Buchanan of Washington, Ky.*

**1 pound red candied cherries, cut in pieces or halves**
**½ pound golden raisins**
**1 pint Kentucky bourbon whiskey**
**¾ pound (3 sticks) butter**
**1 pound white sugar**
**1 cup brown sugar**
**6 eggs, separated**
**5 cups all-purpose flour**
**2 teaspoons ground nutmeg**
**1 teaspoon baking powder**
**1 pound shelled pecans, pieces or halves**

Soak cherries and raisins in bourbon overnight, covering mixture tightly so bourbon doesn't evaporate. Cream butter and sugars until fluffy. Beat egg yolks and add to butter-sugar mixture. Beat well. Add soaked fruit and remaining whiskey. Reserve small amount of flour to coat pecans. Add remaining flour, nutmeg and baking powder to butter-sugar-egg yolk mixture. Beat egg whites until stiff and fold into batter. Add lightly floured pecans last.

Spoon into a large tube pan, greased, lined with waxed paper and greased again. Bake in a preheated 275-degree oven three to four hours or until cake tests done (toothpick inserted in center removes with no crumbs adhering).

To store: When thoroughly cool, stuff center hole with soft cloth which has been soaked in bourbon. Wrap in heavy waxed paper. Place in tightly covered container. It isn't necessary to soak cake in bourbon because the cake will be moist and flavorful. Keep very cool, in the refrigerator, if necessary.

The recipe will make six gift-size bourbon cakes when baked in a standard round one-pound coffee tin that has been emptied and greased. After the cake is baked, you can decorate the cans with colored foil, cover the open top with plastic wrap and tie with a ribbon. These cakes stay moist and at their peak for at least six months stored in the refrigerator.

# DRIED APPLE STACKCAKE

*This recipe is from Sidney Saylor Farr, author of "More Than Moonshine," a book about the food and cooking of Appalachia. Elaine Corn interviewed her about her book in 1983 and printed this recipe. Ms. Farr lived on Stoney Fork, in southeastern Kentucky, until she was 15, and she said stackcake came about because mountain people couldn't afford big, layered wedding cakes. As a substitute, women coming to a wedding each donated layers of cake, and the layers were separated by a filling of dried apples.*

Preheat oven to 350 degrees. Cream shortening and sugar; add beaten egg, molasses, buttermilk, and mix well. Sift flour, soda, salt and ginger into a bowl. Make hole in center of dry ingredients and put in creamed mix, stirring until well blended. Add vanilla, stir well, and roll out dough as you would for pastry. Cut to fit nine-inch pan or heavy skillet (this amount of dough will make about seven layers). Bake layers for 10 to 12 minutes, or until lightly browned. When cool, stack layers with cooked, spiced, sweetened, old-fashioned dried apples. Spread between the layers and smooth around sides. Sprinkle top with powdered sugar. Prepare cake at least a day before you serve it. Slice very thin.

Dried apples: Peel the apples and cut into thin wedges, or slices. Spread out on a clean, white cloth and place in sun a few days. Be sure to put a fine wire screen over them to keep out flies and bugs. They can be dried near a wood-burning stove, in a sunny window, or in your oven at very low heat. The apple slices will shrivel up and turn brown. When completely dry, store in cloth bags or in the freezer; the latter will ensure that no pests get into the dried apples.

To cook the dried apples: Put one pound apples in a heavy pan and cover with water. Cook until soft enough to mash. You may need to add water several times to keep apples from sticking to pan. While still hot, mash the apples and add 1 cup brown sugar, ½ cup white sugar, 1 teaspoon cinnamon, ¼ teaspoon cloves and ½ teaspoon allspice.

If you do not have dried apples: Pare and quarter several pounds of cooking apples. Put apples and water in heavy pan and cook until just done. Add 1 cup brown sugar, ½ teaspoon cinnamon, ¼ teaspoon allspice, dash of cloves, and cook until mixture is very thick.

½ cup shortening
½ cup sugar
1 egg, well-beaten
⅓ cup molasses
½ cup buttermilk
3½ cups flour
½ teaspoon soda
½ teaspoon salt
1 teaspoon ginger
1 teaspoon vanilla
**Cooked dried apples (see recipe)**

# EILEEN'S SOUR CREAM CAKE

*Eileen Silver was a friend of Deni Hamilton when Deni wrote for House & Home magazine in New York City. Deni says this recipe, a variation on the standard sour-cream pound cake, is one of her favorites. She ran it in 1979.*

**1 cup butter**
**1½ cups plus 4 teaspoons sugar**
**2 eggs**
**1 cup sour cream**
**½ teaspoon vanilla**
**2 cups flour**
**1 teaspoon baking powder**
**¼ teaspoon salt**
**1 cup chopped pecans**
**1 teaspoon cinnamon**

Cream butter, and add 1½ cups sugar gradually, beating until very light and fluffy. Beat in the eggs, one at a time. Beat in sour cream and vanilla. Mix flour with baking powder and salt. Stir into liquid mixture. Mix remaining sugar, nuts and cinnamon in another bowl. Place about ⅓ of the batter in a well-greased and floured 9-inch bundt or tube pan. Sprinkle with ¾ of the nut mixture. Spoon in rest of batter. Sprinkle with remaining nuts. Bake in a preheated 350-degree oven for about an hour or until it tests done. Cool on a rack after removing from pan.

# STRAWBERRY SHORTCAKE

*"Everyone is most opinionated about the way a strawberry shortcake should be made," Cissy Gregg wrote in 1955. "Some say only pastry should be used to partition off the strawberries; others like sponge cake; again, we have the hot, sweet, buttered biscuit fanciers. This one is sorta half way in between — just not true anything. But it is an old favorite with us."*

## RICH SHORTCAKE

**2 cups flour**
**½ teaspoon salt**
**4 teaspoons baking powder**
**2 tablespoons sugar**
**⅓ cup shortening**
**1 egg, well beaten**
**½ cup milk**

Sift flour and measure. Sift again with salt, baking powder and sugar added. Cut in shortening until the mixture is like coarse crumbs. Add combined milk and egg, stirring until the dry ingredients are just moistened. Turn out on a lightly floured board. Divide the dough into two equal parts. Pat half the dough out to fit an 8-inch round cake pan. Brush the surface with about a tablespoon of melted butter, and top with the patted-out second round of dough. Bake in a 450-degree oven for 15 to 18 minutes.

Separate the two layers, and if you aren't afraid of calories, brush again with melted butter.

## STRAWBERRY PART

Use a lot of strawberries — that's what makes it good. Wash and cap, leaving the caps on a few of them for garnishing. Divide the ones left in half. Slightly mash one half of them and sugar according to the sweetness of the berries. Leave the other whole and sugar lightly, or according to the sweetness of the strawberries. Set the mashed ones in a warm place so they will become juicy. Place the whole ones in the refrigerator.

To assemble, put most of the mashed ones between the layers. Sprinkle over a few of the whole ones. Put the top layer of shortcake in place, spread over the top whipped cream which has been just slightly sweetened.

Add the rest of the mashed berries, and then all over the top literally pour the whole sweetened berries. Spot the uncapped berries here and there. Serve with more slightly sweetened whipped cream.

Strawberry shortcake handled in this manner gives your tongue that interesting mixture of warm and chilled temperatures to ponder over, and also it has the juicy flavor of the mashed berries, yet the firmness of the whole berries. Nothing could be better!

# CLASSIC DOUBLE-STACK STRAWBERRY SHORTCAKE

Heat oven to 450 degrees.

In a mixing bowl combine the flour, sugar, baking powder and salt. Cut in the butter until mixture resembles coarse meal. Make a well in mixture. Combine eggs and milk. Pour into well, stirring quickly to form a thick batter. Spread in two round 8-inch cake pans, mounding sides. Bake 15 minutes. Cool in pans 5 minutes. Remove from pans and cool before assembling.

Meanwhile, combine the strawberries and the 2 tablespoons sugar. Whip the cream until medium peaks form. Stir in vanilla.

Layer half the berries on one shortcake placed on a serving platter. Top berries with one-fourth of the whipped cream. Stack with second shortcake, then remaining strawberries and cream. Serve immediately, if possible. Holds shape in refrigerator about 1 hour. Cut in wedges. Serves 8 to 10.

— Elaine Corn, 1984

## SHORTCAKES

**4 cups all-purpose flour**
**¼ cup sugar**
**2 tablespoons baking powder**
**Pinch salt**
**2 sticks butter or margarine**
**2 eggs, beaten lightly**
**1⅓ cups milk**

## TOPPING

**4 cups sliced strawberries, about 2 pints**
**2 tablespoons sugar**
**1 cup cream**
**½ teaspoon vanilla**

# MISSISSIPPI MUD CAKE

2 cups sugar
⅔ cups cocoa
4 sticks (2 cups) margarine
4 eggs
2 teaspoons vanilla
1½ cups flour
1⅓ cups coconut
1½ cups chopped nuts
1 7-ounce jar marshmallow cream
½ cup milk
1 1-pound box confectioners' sugar

Mix sugar, ⅓ cup cocoa and 3 sticks margarine, beating well. Add eggs, one at a time, beating well. Add 1 teaspoon vanilla and flour, mixing well. Stir in coconut and nuts. Pour mixture into a greased and floured 9-by-13-inch baking pan which can double as a serving dish. Bake in a preheated 350-degree oven 40 minutes or until edges shrink away from sides of pan. Remove from oven and spread marshmallow cream over hot cake. Let cool in pan.

Combine remaining 1 stick margarine, milk, confectioners' sugar, remaining 1 teaspoon vanilla and sifted ⅓ cup cocoa in mixer bowl and beat until perfectly smooth. Spread on cool cake. Frosting sets slowly and can be speeded up by placing pan in refrigerator.

Note: This cake doesn't contain baking powder, salt or baking soda. The consistency is like a fudge brownie.

— Cook's Corner column, 1983

# CHEESECAKE NO. 2

*Elaine Corn ran this recipe, along with two other crustless cheesecake recipes, in 1982 and then let a panel of tasters decide their favorite.*

*"This cake was the control in the experiment," she wrote. "This cake also is my personal standby. I have been making this cheesecake for years. I have added chocolate, bananas, almonds, hazelnuts and brandy. I have presented it to boyfriends, and bosses, with better results from the latter than the former. Without this recipe, I could not have made the other two. It was all I knew to go by. Apparently, it is all I'll ever need.*

*"Summed up by one ardent cheesecake expert destined to go up a dress size: 'Wonderful, classic, lush and plush — this is a serious cake.'"*

2 pounds cream cheese at room
   temperature
1½ cups sugar
6 eggs
Vanilla
Fresh lemon juice and a little rind

Preheat oven to 450 degrees. Beat the cream cheese until smooth. With the mixer running, gradually add the sugar. Beat in eggs one at a time, incorporating well after each addition. Stir in vanilla and lemon. Pour batter into springform pan and smooth top with spatula. Bake at 450 degrees for 15 minutes. Reduce heat to 300 degrees and bake for 45 minutes. Cake is done when center is firm and top is medium-brown. Cool until cake pulls from sides of pan. Remove springform. Serve warm or chilled.

# PECAN BOURBON CAKE

Mix pecans and raisins together and dredge with ½ cup of the flour. To the other 1 cup of flour add the baking powder and sift again. Cream butter and gradually add sugar and continue beating until fluffy. To this add raw yolks of the eggs, one at a time, beating after each addition until the mixture is smooth and lemon-colored.

Add the nutmeg to the bourbon and let stand 10 minutes. Add this mixture to the butter-egg mixture alternately with the sifted flour, beating thoroughly to blend batter. An electric beater can be used for this mixing, if you like. Then with a heavy wooden spoon fold in the raisins and nuts. Lastly, beat the egg whites, with the salt added, until stiff, then fold in.

Grease a tube pan that is large enough to hold a 3-pound cake. Line it well with brown paper and grease the paper lightly. Pour the batter into the pan and let stand for 10 mintues to allow the mixture to settle. Decorate the top with candied cherries and nuts. Bake in a 325-degree oven for 1¼ hours. If the top browns too quickly, cover the surface with a piece of heavy brown paper. Allow the cake to stand ½ hour before removing from the pan. Place on cake rack to cool. To store, wrap in cloth soaked in bourbon, then in foil.          — Cissy Gregg, 1967

1 pound shelled pecans, coarsely chopped
½ pound seeded raisins, cut in half
1½ cups sifted flour
1 teaspoon baking powder
½ cup butter
1⅛ cups sugar
3 eggs, separated
2 teaspoons nutmeg
½ cup bourbon
Pinch of salt
Nuts and candied cherries for decorating

# DEPRESSION CAKE

*This recipe, printed in the Cook's Corner column in 1980, uses no eggs or milk.*

Combine sugar, water, shortening, raisins and aromatic bitters. Bring to a boil and cook for one minute. Cool to lukewarm. Stir in remaining ingredients until well blended. Pour into a greased and floured 9-inch square baking pan. Bake in a preheated 350-degree oven 35 minutes or until firm in the center. Cut into squares and serve warm or cold, dusted with confectioners' sugar.

1 cup firmly packed dark-brown sugar
1 cup water
⅓ cup vegetable shortening
1 cup seedless raisins
1 tablespoon aromatic bitters (or 1 teaspoon vanilla flavoring and 1 teaspoon almond flavoring)
2 cups all-purpose flour
½ teaspoon baking powder
½ teaspoon baking soda
½ teaspoon salt
1 cup nuts, chopped

# LADY BALTIMORE CAKE

*According to "American Heritage Cookbook," when Owen Wister chose Charleston, S.C., as the setting for a novel, he modeled a main character on one of the city's former belles, Mrs. Alicia Rhett Mayberry. Mrs. Mayberry had created a cake called "Lady Baltimore," which Wister duly described and made the title of his book. When "Lady Baltimore" was published in 1906, American Heritage says, the cake became one of the most popular confections in the nation.*

*Lord Baltimore followed his lady. In demonstrating the cakes in 1948, Cissy Gregg paid tribute to the nice symmetry about the recipes: Lord Baltimore uses the yolks of the eggs; Lady Baltimore uses the whites. The Lord uses square masculine pans; the Lady uses round feminine pans. Cissy used a seven-minute icing on both cakes, incidentally.*

**2⅔ cups sifted cake flour**
**3 teaspoons baking powder**
**1 teaspoon salt**
**5 egg whites**
**½ cup sugar**
**⅔ cup shortening**
**1 teaspoon vanilla or grated lemon
  rind**
**1¼ cups sugar**
**1 cup milk**

Sift flour once, measure, add baking powder and salt, and sift 3 times.

In a small mixing bowl beat the egg whites until foamy. Add the ½ cup sugar gradually, beating only until the meringue will hold soft peaks.

In a larger mixing bowl, beat shortening and flavoring together until smooth and plastic. Add the 1¼ cups sugar and beat for 2 minutes. Remember the number of hand strokes that count for a minute, and stop at 1 minute and rest. If it's an electric beater you're using, use high speed and stop at the 1-minute period and let it rest while you scrape down the bowl and beater.

Add flour mixture alternately with milk in small amounts. Add first about ¼ of flour, beat 20 seconds or the equivalent thereof; then add ⅓ of the milk and beat 20 more seconds. Keep this up until all of the milk and flour have been added. Add meringue made of egg whites and sugar, and beat 1 more minute.

Turn into two round 9-inch layers, 1½ inches deep, paper lined and greased, of course, and bake in a moderate oven, 375 degrees, about 30 minutes.

## FILLING

To ½ portion of frosting, add ½ cup raisins, chopped; 6 figs, chopped; ½ cup chopped pecans or English walnuts.

Spread between the layers, and frost with the remaining plain frosting.

## SEVEN-MINUTE FROSTING

Combine egg whites, sugar, salt, water and corn syrup in top of double boiler. Beat about a minute or until thoroughly mixed. Then place over boiling water and beat constantly seven minutes or until frosting will stand in stiff peaks. (Stir frosting up from bottom and sides of pan occasionally with

**2 egg whites**
**1½ cups sugar**
**Dash salt**
**⅓ cup water**
**2 teaspoons light corn syrup**
**1 teaspoon vanilla**

rubber scraper, spatula or spoon.)

Remove from boiling water. For a very smooth and satiny frosting, pour at once into a large bowl for final beating. Then add vanilla and beat a minute or until thick enough to spread.

Makes 4½ cups frosting or enough to cover tops and sides of a 10-inch tube cake. (Note: This also should cover two 9-inch layer cakes.)

— Cissy Gregg, 1962

# LORD BALTIMORE CAKE

This is an easy-mix cake, so before you start measuring and mixing, have the shortening at room temperature. Also line your cake pan with waxed paper and grease. Light your oven and set at 350-degrees. Sift the flour once before measuring.

Now we'll start putting the ingredients together. Measure flour, baking powder, salt and sugar and leave in sifter. In a mixing bowl place the shortening. Mix just to soften. Sift in the dry ingredients. Add egg yolks and one-half of the milk, and mix until the flour is dampened. Then beat 2 minutes. If you have an electric mixer, use it at low speed; if you're your own mixer, 300 strokes equal 2 minutes.

Add remaining milk, and beat 1 minute or 150 strokes. Turn batter into an 8x8x2 pan and bake at 350 degrees for about 1 hour.

**2 cups cake flour**
**2 teaspoons double-acting baking powder, or 3 teaspoons single-acting baking powder**
**¾ teaspoon salt**
**1 cup sugar**
**½ cup shortening**
**⅔ cup milk**
**5 egg yolks, unbeaten**

## FILLING

Use any white frosting or the seven-minute frosting we used. To one-half of the frosting, add 1 cup macaroon crumbs, ½ cup chopped pecans, 12 candied cherries and a little angelica. Fill the cake. Frost with the remaining frosting.

We baked two of these layers or two 5-egg-yolk cakes. We did this to impress your eye [for the Magazine photograph]. We suggest, however, that you try splitting the one layer, filling and frosting as two baked layers would be. In this way you get full benefit of the filling without so much cake.

# MELROSE SOFT GINGERBREAD

*This recipe, printed in the Cook's Corner column in 1980, is from Natchez, Miss., and is named for one of the antebellum homes there.*

**3 cups sifted all-purpose flour**
**1 tablespoon ginger**
**1 tablespoon cinnamon**
**1 teaspoon cloves**
**½ teaspoon baking soda**
**1 cup granulated sugar**
**½ teaspoon salt**
**3 eggs, beaten**
**1 cup molasses**
**1 cup sour milk**
**1 cup butter or shortening, melted**

Sift dry ingredients together. Combine the remaining ingredients and add gradually to dry ingredients. Beat one minute or until smooth. Pour into a large waxed-paper-lined pan, 7-by-11-inches. Greasing the paper-lined pan is optional if your're nervous about sticking. Bake in a preheated 350-degree oven 25 to 35 minutes.

Cool in the pan for a few minutes and then turn out on a rack. Remove paper, right the gingerbread and glaze.

## GLAZE

**1 cup confectioners' sugar**
**2 tablespoons hot water**

Mix sugar and water until it is smooth. Brush over the top of the hot gingerbread.

# GASTON LENOTRE'S CONCORD CAKE

## MERINGUE LAYERS

**3½ tablespoons bitter cocoa powder**
**1 cup powdered sugar**
**5 egg whites (¼ cup)**
**⅔ cup sugar**

## MOUSSE

**5½ ounces semi-sweet chocolate**
**6½ tablespoons butter**
**3 egg yolks**
**4 egg whites (⅔ cup)**
**5 teaspoons sugar**

Heat the oven to 300 degrees. Butter and lightly flour a baking sheet or cover with parchment paper. (I used brown bags). Make the meringue ovals. Mix the cocoa and powdered sugar and sift together. Beat the egg whites until firm, about 5 minutes, adding 1½ tablespoons sugar halfway through. As soon as the egg whites are stiff, add the remaining sugar at low speed, then with a wooden spatula quickly fold in the cocoa-sugar mixture.

Draw three ovals 10 inches by 5½ inches on the baking sheet to guide you when making the meringues. Take a pastry bag with a ½-inch nozzle, fill it with chocolate meringue and make 3 ovals by squeezing out the meringue in a spiral (I found it easier to start piping from the outside). Once this is done, use a pastry bag with a ⅛-inch nozzle to squeeze out all the remaining meringue into long strips. (I used the same pastry bag. I also needed two baking sheets.)

Bake for 1 hour and 5 minutes. Check the color of the meringue after 15 minutes. The meringues should not brown. If they do, lower the heat of the oven. The meringue strips will be done first and should be removed, while the large ovals might need 10 minutes extra baking. When they are cooked, the meringues are hard and can easily be detached from the baking sheet.

The ovals and strips can be prepared a day ahead. While the meringue is baking, prepare the chocolate mousse. Melt the chocolate in a double boiler. Remove from the heat and add the butter, stirring it in with a wooden spoon. Allow the mixture to cool completely. It should be the consistency of a very thick cream. Then stir in the egg yolks one by one.

Beat the egg whites until very stiff. Halfway through, add the sugar. Fold the chocolate mixture into the egg whites with a wooden spatula, making sure the two elements are perfectly blended together. Once the meringues have cooled completely, place one of the ovals on a decorative piece of cardboard, or simply place it on a serving platter.

With a flexible-blade spatula, spread a layer of chocolate mousse over the meringue oval. Then place on top of the chocolate mousse a second layer of meringue, then a second layer of chocolate mousse and finally the last layer of meringue. Cover the cake completely with the remaining mousse.

Cut the chocolate meringue strips into ½-inch sticks. Cover the sides and the top of the cake with these strips. (I found it necessary to press very gently). Refrigerate for 1 hour. Lay a broad ribbon or piece of cardboard (I used a 2-inch wide strip of newspaper) across the cake, then sprinkle the cake all over with powdered sugar. Remove the ribbon (this part of the cake will be darker since it was not covered with sugar) and serve. The cake can keep 48 hours in the refrigerator.

— Elaine Corn, 1984

# ELAINE'S BANANA CAKE

*This is Elaine Corn's own recipe, printed in 1982.*

**1 stick butter or ½ cup shortening**
**1 cup sugar**
**2 eggs**
**4 to 5 ripe mashed bananas**
**1½ cups flour**
**1 teaspoon baking soda**
**1 teaspoon salt**
**Optional raisins or nuts, about ½
  cup, if desired**

Cream the butter and sugar, beat in the eggs and bananas, then the dry ingredients in order. Pour batter into a greased tube pan. Bake at 350 degrees for 40 minutes.

## CREAM-CHEESE ICING

Soften 8 ounces cream cheese. Beat with ¼ cup honey and ½ teaspoon vanilla. If too thin, beat in ¼ cup powdered sugar. If too thick, beat in a tablespoon of milk.

# DAFFODIL CAKE

*This recipe, written about by Cissy Gregg in 1947, produces a cake with a yellow sponge bottom and white angel food's top. The color photo of the cake shows that Cissy also used a drop or two of food coloring to get a pale green icing, even though she left that out in her listing of ingredients.*

*It is a fussy recipe — one that Cissy suggested for a dessert bridge, that is, a party where only dessert is served. Notice that it reflects Cissy's unease at using a lot of sugar at a time when occasional food shortages still were not uncommon.*

## BOTTOM LAYER

**1½ cups cake flour**
**1¼ teaspoons baking powder**
**¼ teaspoon salt**
**1 cup plus 2 tablespoons sifted
  sugar**
**9 egg yolks, beaten until thick**
**1 teaspoon lemon extract**
**6 tablespoons cold water**

## TOP LAYER

**1 cup cake flour**
**1¼ cups sifted sugar**
**1 cup egg whites (8 egg whites
  usually make a cup)**
**½ teaspoon salt**
**1 teaspoon cream of tartar**
**1 teaspoon vanilla**

Bottom layer: Sift flour once, measure. Add baking powder and salt, and sift together 3 times. Add sugar gradually to beaten egg yolks, beating with rotary egg beater after each addition until thick and light. Fold in flour, a small amount at a time, and blend. Add flavoring, then add cold water gradually, mixing only enough to blend. Prepare a 9-inch layer cake pan that is 2 inches deep by greasing only the bottom of the pan, and then line the bottom with wax paper. Turn batter into pan and bake one hour at 300-degrees.

When cake is taken from the oven, allow it to cool in pan before removing, but do not invert pan.

Top layer: Sift flour once, measure. Add ½ teaspoon cream of tartar and the salt. Sift these together 4 times. Beat egg whites with a flat wire whisk until they are foamy. Add the remaining ½ teaspoon of cream of tartar and continue beating until eggs are stiff enough to hold in peaks, but not dry. Fold in sugar carefully, 2 tablespoons at a time, until all is used. Fold in flavoring. Next sift small amount of flour over mixture and fold in carefully. Continue until all flour is used. Turn into a 9-inch by 2-inch deep layer cake pan which has been prepared as was the one for other layer. (Grease only the bottom of the pan, line with wax paper. Don't grease the sides of the pan at all.) Bake for one hour at 300 degrees. Allow this layer, as with the other one, to cool in the pan before removing, but don't invert during that time.

To separate these two luscious layers of cake, we chose a pineappple filling.

## PINEAPPLE FILLING

Combine sugar, flour, cornstarch and blend well. Add pineapple syrup. Place in the top of a double boiler and cook for 20 minutes. Stir all the time until it thickens. Add butter, lemon juice and blend. Remove from fire and fold in egg yolk. Allow to cool. Fold in 1 cup of crushed pineapple that has been well drained. Tint pale green if you like, or leave it natural. When the filling is cold, spread between layers of the daffodil cake.

1 cup syrup from a can of pineapple
½ cup sugar
2 tablespoons flour
2 tablespoons cornstarch
1 tablespoon butter or margarine
1 egg yolk
2 tablespoons lemon juice
1 cup crushed pineapple

## DAFFODIL CAKE ICING

Beat egg whites until foamy, add cream of tartar. Continue beating until egg whites are stiff and dry, then add sugar, 2 tablespoons at a time. Continue beating until all sugar has been used.

2 egg whites
¾ teaspoon cream of tartar
1½ cups sifted confectioner's sugar
1 teaspoon vanilla

This proportion of sugar makes a very soft icing. Should you want a stiffer icing add ½ cup more sugar.

When icing a cake always ice the sides first and bring the icing up towards the top of the cake. Finally, the top surface gets covered up, too. For swirls and the rugged individual personality of the top of the cake, a clean forefinger works well.

There isn't one thing to be said for the way sugar was used in this cake. We fairly wrecked a coupon's worth but look at what a beautiful majestic cake it made.

# CLAIRE TIPSY CAKE

*This beautiful cake is one of the most popular recipes ever printed by Lillian Marshall. It ran in 1975.*

1 cup raisins
⅔ cup Irish whisky
Sponge-cake layers (see recipe)
1 cup apricot jam
Sauce (see recipe)
Custard (see recipe)
Sweetened whipped cream
Slivered almonds

Cover raisins with whisky. Let stand overnight. Drain, reserving whisky for sauce. Split sponge cakes horizontally to make your thin layers. Spread three layers with jam, reserving fourth. Place one layer in glass serving bowl. Sprinkle with raisins and cover with second layer. Repeat, ending with jamless cake layer. Press layers firmly down into dish. Pierce down through layers in several places with a wide-blade kitchen knife. Pour some of the sauce over the surface of the cake. Hold layers away from sides of bowl and pour sauce down to moisten bottom layers. Cover cake with warm custard and refrigerate until custard has set and is cool. Cover custard with a thin layer of sweetened whipped cream. Decorate surface with slivered almonds. Refrigerate several hours before serving.

## SPONGE CAKE

4 eggs
1 cup sugar
¼ cup orange juice
1 cup cake flour
1½ teaspoons baking powder
¼ teaspoon salt

Preheat oven to 325 degrees. Grease two nine-inch layer cake pans on the bottom only. Separate eggs. Beat yolks until pale and thick. Add sugar, two tablespoons at a time, beating well after each addition. Beat in orange juice. Sift flour, baking powder and salt together onto waxed paper. Stir into egg yolk mixture. Beat egg whites with a wire whisk until stiff but not dry. Fold carefully into batter. Pour into prepared pans and bake until firm to the touch, 25 to 30 minutes. Makes two nine-inch cake layers.

## SAUCE

1 cup sugar
½ cup water
1 strip lemon peel
½ stick cinnamon
1 clove
½ cup fresh orange juice
Irish whisky from marinating
  raisins

Combine sugar, water, peel, cinnamon stick and clove in saucepan. Bring to boil and stir until sugar has dissolved. Simmer 10 mintes. Remove from heat and discard lemon peel, cinnamon stick and clove. Add orange juice and whisky and stir. Pour over Tipsy Cake as directed.

# CUSTARD

Beat the egg yolks in a mixing bowl until very pale in color. Add sugar and salt; blend well, then add scalded milk. Place in top of double boiler over simmering water and cook, stirring constantly, until the spoon is coated with custard and nothing drips from it when it is lifted from the pan. Remove from heat and add vanilla. Cool slightly before pouring over cake.

**4 egg yolks**
**⅓ cup sugar**
**⅛ teaspoon salt**
**2 cups milk, scalded and cooled**
**¼ teaspoon vanilla**

# LEMON CHESS CAKE

Cream margarine and shortening together. Add sugar gradually and continue beating until smooth. Add egg yolks and beat well. Add soda to buttermilk. Add flour and buttermilk to margarine-sugar-yolk mixture alternately. Add lemon flavoring, coconut and nuts. Fold in stiffly beaten egg whites. Pour into three 8-inch greased and floured cake pans, and bake in 350-degree oven for 25 minutes. When cool, put pineapple filling between layers and ice cake.

**1 stick margarine**
**½ cup shortening**
**2 cups sugar**
**5 egg yolks**
**2 cups flour**
**1 teaspoon soda**
**1 cup buttermilk**
**1 teaspoon lemon flavoring**
**1 cup chopped nuts**
**1 small can flaked coconut**
**5 egg whites, stiffly beaten**
**Pineapple filling (see recipe)**
**Icing (see recipe)**

## PINEAPPLE FILLING

Mix cornstarch and sugar. Add pineapple and orange juice and cook until thick. Spread between layers of cake.

**2½ cups crushed pineapple, drained**
**2 tablespoons cornstarch**
**¼ cup sugar**
**4 tablespoons orange juice**

## ICING

Have cream cheese and margarine at room temperature. Cream them together, then beat in powdered sugar, lemon flavoring and nuts. Spread on cake.

— Lillian Marshall, 1973

**1 8-ounce package cream cheese**
**½ stick margarine**
**1 pound powdered sugar**
**1 teaspoon lemon flavoring**
**1 cup chopped nuts**

# Jennie Benedict's White Fruitcake

*Jennie Benedict was a caterer-turned-restaurateur who was famous in Louisville in the early 20th century. The Cook's Corner column printed this in 1979, noting that it uses no liquid except the eggs, butter and whiskey. This seems to be characteristic of white fruitcake recipes, the column said.*

1 pound butter
1 pound sugar (2 cups)
10 eggs, separated
2 teaspoons nutmeg
1 pound candied cherries
½ pound candied pineapple
1 pound flour (4 cups)
1½ pounds pecans (shelled)
½ cup whiskey
½ teaspoon salt

Cream butter and sugar. Add egg yolks, nutmeg and fruit which has been mixed with flour, pecans, whiskey and salt. Beat egg whites stiff and fold into mixture. Grease and flour tube pan. Line bottom with waxed paper. Pour in batter and bake in a preheated 250-degree oven for 1½ hours or longer. This recipe makes two cakes or three 8½-by-11½-by-2½ loaf pans. Same cooking time for loaves.

Note: There is no baking powder in this recipe.

# Dolly Varden Cake

*This four-layer cake is named for the Charles Dickens character in "Barnaby Rudge," and she is said to have stood for the very opposite of simplicity. Cissy Gregg tried this recipe in 1950, finding the cake to have an "even temperment." She traced the cake's roots to West Virginia.*

⅔ cup butter
3 cups flour
2 cups sugar
1 cup milk
3 eggs
2 teaspoons baking powder
Flavoring, or if left without
    imagination, use 1 teaspoon
    vanilla

Cream butter and sugar until they are fluffy. Add the eggs. Sift the flour, measure and sift with baking powder. Add the flour mixture alternately with the milk to the egg-butter-sugar mixture. Divide in half. Bake one-half of the batter in two 8-inch layer cake pans, and bake 20 to 25 minutes at 375 degrees or a moderate oven.

## TO THE OTHER HALF OF THE BATTER ADD:

1 tablespoon molasses
1 teaspoon cinnamon
1 teaspoon cloves
1 teaspoon nutmeg
2 cups raisins
½ cup chopped nuts or finely
    slivered citron

Bake this batter in two 8-inch cake pans.

Put layers together alternately with icing. Now I have never seen a Dolly Varden Cake with other than white icing atop. But on our newsprint, the camera snarls at a white mass. So we used a brown sugar seven-minute icing without a single compunction of conscience (recipe below).

The little roses on top of the cake are made from candied orange peel. Just thinly peel off the outside of your breakfast oranges as you would an apple. Put the curlicues in cold water and bring to a boil. Change the water and bring to a boil again. Twice should be enough but you don't want bitterness even in a decorations on a cake. When the strips are tender, drain. Then make a syrup of 2 cups sugar to 1 cup water. Cook until the sugar is dissolved. In the meantime, roll or form the peel into roses, leaves or what not. Drop into the syrup and cook until candied as you would grapefruit or orange peel at Christmas time. While I was doing this I wondered why we were so careless with our breakfast orange and grapefruit peels. They are so good candied.

## BROWN SUGAR SEVEN-MINUTE FROSTING

1½ cups light or dark brown sugar, packed
2 large egg whites
¼ cup water
¼ teaspoon cream of tartar
⅛ teaspoon salt
2 teaspoons vanilla
¼ teaspoon ground nutmeg

Mix ingredients in the top of a double boiler. Set over the bottom filled to a depth of about two inches with boiling water. Beat constantly with an electric mixer over rapidly boiling water until frosting stands in soft peaks. Remove from heat and continue beating until frosting stands in very stiff peaks. Frosts a three-layer cake.
— Deni Hamilton, 1980

# CISSY'S JAM CAKE

*This is a 1984 version of Cissy Gregg's recipe for a Kentucky favorite. It doesn't read like Cissy, so obviously it's been boiled down and polished up over the years.*

Mix whole eggs, which have been beaten, with the melted butter, buttermilk, brown sugar and blackberry jam.

Add flour that has been sifted with the soda, cinnamon, allspice and nutmeg. Mix well. Fold in nuts and raisins. Pour into a 9-inch tube pan that has been greased and floured. Bake in a preheated 325-degree oven 1½ to two hours.

Let cool slightly, about five minutes, and turn it out on a cake rack. While still warm, drizzle bourbon on the bottom and lightly pierce with a fork so the bourbon will seep down into the middle of the cake.

6 eggs
1 cup butter, melted
4 tablespoons buttermilk
2 cups brown sugar
1 cup blackberry jam
3 cups flour
1 teaspoon soda
2 teaspoons cinnamon
2 teaspoons allspice
2 teaspoons nutmeg
1 cup English walnuts or pecans, chopped
1 cup raisins
Bourbon

# MRS. CREASON'S JAM CAKE

*Even though Cissy Gregg's own jam cake recipe was extremely popular, Cissy liked this version from Mrs. Herman Creason of Benton, Ky., mother of the late Joe Creason, a Courier-Journal columnist for many years. Cissy printed this recipe in 1952.*

**5 eggs, beaten**
**2 cups sugar**
**3 cups flour**
**1 cup butter or shortening or part of both**
**1 cup buttermilk**
**1 teaspoon soda**
**¼ teaspoon salt**
**½ teaspoon cinnamon**
**1½ teaspoons cloves**
**1½ teaspoons allspice**
**1 cup raisins or chopped dates**
**1 cup chopped nuts**
**1 cup jam — strawberry preferred, but any kind will do**

Cream butter and gradually add the sugar. Cream together until light and fluffy. Add well-beaten eggs. Sift flour before measuring and add to it the spices and the salt. (The salt isn't necessary if you are using all butter.)

Dissolve soda in buttermilk, and add it and the flour mixture alternately to the sugar-butter-egg mixture, beating after each addition.

Lightly dredge the nuts and fruit with a little extra flour, and add. Next add the jam. Stir to get good distribution.

Grease and paper-line two 9-inch cake pans, 2 inches deep. Bake at 325 degrees for 40 minutes, or until done. Ice with a caramel icing of your choice.

## CARAMEL FROSTING

**1½ cups firmly packed light brown sugar**
**Pinch salt**
**1 cup butter**
**¾ cup flour**
**1 cup heavy cream**
**1 teaspoon vanilla**

Mix sugar and flour. Cream butter until light and add to sugar, beating well. Mix in heavy cream and put in top of double boiler over boiling water. Stir constantly, and cook until about the thickness of medium cream sauce. Takes about 15 minutes after it melts. Allow to cool completely after cooking. Sets up after it's on the cake for a couple hours. Enough for a two-layer cake.

— Deni Hamilton, 1978

# MEXICAN WEDDING CAKES

*Linda Brady makes holiday foods that can be stored and given as gifts, and she supplied this recipe for a 1984 feature by Elaine Corn.*

*"These are my favorite Christmas cookie," Mrs. Brady told Elaine. "I wonder why they appear only during the holidays?"*

*A shortbread cookie, these will keep for many weeks if stored in a covered container, according to Elaine. The dough may be frozen in a large ball or small forms frozen on a cookie sheet which, once frozen, may be bagged for baking later. Mrs. Brady's children also like to help with these.*

Cream butter and powdered sugar. Add vanilla and beat until smooth. Add flour. Mixture will seem dry. Add nuts. Knead dough and begin making small, round balls. Place on ungreased cookie sheet and bake at 250 degrees for 40 minutes. Remove from sheet. While still warm, roll in additional powdered sugar. Makes six dozen.

**2 sticks butter or margarine**
**4 generous tablespoons powdered sugar**
**1 teaspoon vanilla**
**2 cups flour**
**¼ cup chopped nuts**
**Additional powdered sugar**

# MISS JENNIE'S RUM CAKE

*This is another recipe from Jennie Benedict, a famous caterer-turned-restaurateur in Louisville during the early part of the 20th century. This was one of her more popular recipes; Cissy Gregg printed it in 1944.*

Cream the butter and add the sugar, a little at a time. Add ⅓ each of the milk, flour and egg whites, in the order named, beating after each addition and beating well and long after the last addition. But mark this — keep out 2 tablespoons flour, into which mix the baking powder and add this when all the beating is over, the pans greased and lined with paper, and the batter is ready to go in the stove. At the very last, add the vanilla and the salt.

The beating should have special attention.

Bake in two 9-inch greased and paper-lined cake pans for 20 to 25 minutes, at 350 degrees. Turn out on racks and allow to cool before adding the filling.

Filling: Take 2½ cups powdered sugar, ⅔ cup soft, creamed butter. Blend and beat until soft and smooth. Sifting the powdered sugar makes the blending lighter work, too. Add 4 ounces rum. Mix well again. Put into the refrigerator until firm enough to spread. The filling should be ½ to ¾ inch thick. After the filling is spread on the cake, put the cake and filling into the refrigerator until set and the top frosting is ready to cover all.

Frosting: Mix 2 cups granulated sugar and enough water to moisten the sugar well. Boil together until the syrup will spin a thread. Pour slowly in a fine stream over 2 beaten egg whites. Beat! While mixture is hot and during much beating, add 12 to 15 marshmallows, a few at a time. Add one or 2 teaspoons of rum. Ice cake. You might want to decorate with cherries and citron.

**1 cup butter**
**2 cups granulated sugar**
**3½ cups cake flour, sifted once before measuring**
**3½ teaspoons baking powder**
**1 cup milk, not too cold**
**8 egg whites, beaten stiff but not dry**
**1 teaspoon vanilla**
**1 pinch salt**

# PUMPKIN COOKIES

*This is not a recipe for cookies made with pumpkin, but rather a recipe for making cookies in pumpkin shapes. Deni Hamilton used it in 1978.*

**1 cup butter or margarine, softened**
**1 cup sugar**
**1 egg**
**3¼ cups flour**
**½ cup wheat germ**
**¼ teaspoon salt**
**1 teaspoon baking soda**
**½ teaspoon nutmeg**
**1 teaspoon cinnamon**
**½ cup buttermilk**

Beat the butter until light and fluffy. Gradually beat in the sugar and egg. Stir together the flour, wheat germ, salt, soda, nutmeg and cinnamon. Add the flour mixture to the butter mixture alternately with the buttermilk. Chill the dough several hours.

Roll out a small portion of the dough to ⅛-inch thickness on a well-floured board. Cut out with a pumpkin cookie cutter. If you don't have a cookie cutter, use a round shape and form the pumpkins stems by hand. Work quickly with the dough and keep the rest chilled.

Bake the cookies at 350 degrees on an ungreased baking sheet for 10 to 12 minutes or until golden. Frost if desired with orange icing, and use raisins for the pumpkin's nose, mouth and eyes.

## ORANGE ICING

**1 cup plus 2 tablespoons**
**    confectioners sugar**
**1 tablespoon milk**
**Orange food coloring**

Mix the milk and sugar together, adding a little more sugar and milk until reaching the desired consistency. Color orange. Frosts a dozen cookies.

# LOUISE KRIEGER'S GINGER COOKIES

*Louise Krieger is a friend of Deni Hamilton's, and this popular recipe was printed in 1974.*

**1¼ cups shortening**
**⅓ cup brown sugar**
**1½ cups molasses**
**1 egg**
**5 cups flour**
**2 teaspoons ground ginger**
**1½ teaspoons cinnamon**
**1½ teaspoons allspice**
**½ cup boiling water**
**½ teaspoon salt**
**4 teaspoons baking soda**

Beat shortening and brown sugar together until light. Add molasses and egg and beat well. Sift spices and two cups of flour together and add to shortening mixture. Add the boiling water and mix. Stir in one more cup of flour and mix well. Let stand one-half hour in refrigerator. Meanwhile, sift remaining two cups of flour, soda and salt together three times. Stir into the cooled dough and return to refrigerator for another hour or more. (You may leave it overnight, covered.) Roll out a grapefruit-sized portion of the dough at a time, keeping the remainder cold. Roll to about ½-inch thick, using as little flour as possible. Cut with a floured, three-inch biscuit cutter and bake on a greased cookie sheet in a 350-degree oven,

*From foreground: Dried apple stackcake (with strawberry glaze), Miss Jennie's rum cake, Mrs. Creason's jam cake (with caramel icing). Photograph by Robert Steinau.*

for 12 to 15 minutes until set but not browned. Frost while still warm with confectioner's sugar icing and cool completely before storing in a loosely covered crock or cookie jar. Makes 40 to 50 giants.

## BUTTER FROSTING

Cream butter or margine and add part of the sugar gradually, blending after every addition. Add remaining sugar, alternately with the milk, until smooth. Blend in vanilla and salt. Spread on cake.
— Cissy Gregg, 1951

**4 tablespoons butter or margarine**
**2 cups sifted powdered sugar**
**3 tablespoons milk (approximately)**
**1 teaspoon vanilla**
**Dash of salt**

# MRS. EDWARD MILLER'S SPRINGERLES

*Mrs. Edward Miller, who lived at 803 S. 45th St., was renowned for springerle-making, Cissy Gregg reported when she first ran this recipe in 1953. The reprint below, with some changes in the copy, is from 1957, and Cissy reported that she had tried "springerles and springerles and springerles" but had always come back to this recipe. It has remained one of the all-time reader favorites.*

Beat the eggs to the time required by your beating method. You want the eggs to be good and yellow and thick. Gradually add the powdered sugar. Continue to beat. Sift flour and baking powder together and fold in. Add anise oil. And we give a caution about the flour, just as Mrs. Miller gave us: the less flour you can get along with, the better for the tender springerle.

Roll the springerle dough out on a lightly floured board to about ⅓-inch thick, but ½-inch thick might not be too thick if you press the springerle with rolling pin or mold down hard. But either the rolling pin or mold should be well floured. Roll firmly so the designs on the rolling pin or board will be imprinted on the dough. Blow off any extra flour on top of the springerles. Cut into the squares marked off by the springerle rolling pin or board, and place on baking sheets to dry out and set the design. This takes from 12 to 14 hours. Bake on lightly greased sheets at 300 degrees for about 20 minutes. They should be faint yellow but not brown.

These springerles are so tender they can be eaten at any time and made by this recipe was the first time I thought they were worth considering since I didn't cut my teeth on them as a younster. If you made them ahead of time, and want to keep them as long as you can hide them--a half an apple does fine to keep them in condition.

**4 eggs beaten 10 minutes with an electric beater, or 30 minutes by hand**
**1 pound confectioner's sugar, sifted**
**4 cups flour**
**½ teaspoon baking powder**
**½ teaspoon anise oil or less, according to taste**

# MY GRANDMOTHER'S BEST SUGAR COOKIES

*Deni Hamilton got this recipe from Louisville attorney Suzanne Warner, whose grandmother is Bertha Schwindeler of Memphis, Tenn.*

**3 cups sifted flour**
**2 teaspoons baking powder**
**½ teaspoon nutmeg**
**1 cup sugar**
**½ cup butter or margarine**
**2 eggs, beaten lightly**
**Grated rind of a lemon**
**Granulated sugar**

Sift together flour, baking powder and nutmeg. Cream butter, add sugar and blend thoroughly. Add eggs and beat well. Add flour mixture and lemon rind. Mix well.

Roll dough into thin sheet. Cut with cookie cutter. Dredge with granulated sugar and bake in preheated 400-degree oven about eight minutes, or until just slightly brown.

# MOTHER DULL'S TEA CAKES

*There's some irony behind this recipe. Cissy Gregg used it in 1960, attributing it to an "old cookbook" by Mrs. S.R. Dull. Cissy apparently didn't know that Mrs. Dull was food editor at the Atlanta Journal when she wrote the cookbook. In fact, she may have been one of the very first newspaper food editors in the nation. Today's food editors hold regular conferences and trade up-to-date information from their home bases all over the nation.*

**2 cups sugar**
**1 cup lard and butter, mixed**
**½ cup buttermilk**
**3 eggs**
**½ teaspoon soda**
**2 teaspoons baking powder**
**1 teaspoon vanilla**
**Flour (about 6 cups) sufficient to
  make a soft dough**

Cream butter and lard. Add sugar and blend until light and fluffy. Stir in the beaten eggs. Into 1 cup flour, sift soda and baking powder. Add this to the sugar mixture. Add buttermilk and vanilla. Now add enough more flour to make a soft dough. Turn onto a floured board and knead until smooth. Roll out ¼-inch thick. Cut into any shape. Bake in moderate oven, 350 degrees, until brown and done, about 10 minutes. Do not put close enough to touch, as this would spoil the shape. Makes about 120 cakes. If a hard, brittle cake is liked, knead dry sugar into the dough.

This is without doubt the best tea cake or cookie recipe I have ever used.

# LEMON BARS

*This is a recipe from Mary Lou Merritt, hostess, psychiatric nurse and wife of James Merritt, the former dean of the University of Louisville law school. Elaine Corn wrote about Mrs. Merritt's recipes and party-giving ideas for the 1982 holiday-entertaining issue of the Magazine.*

Measure flour, powdered sugar and margarine on the bottom of a 13-by-9 baking dish. Mix together until crumbly, then press into pan. Bake at 350 degrees for 20 minutes, until lightly browned. Meanwhile, in a bowl, mix the remaining ingredients together. Pour over baked crust. Bake again at 350 degrees for 25 to 30 minutes. Recipe doubles easily. Makes 30 bars.

**2 cups flour**
**½ cup powdered sugar**
**1 cup margarine**
**4 eggs**
**2 cups sugar**
**⅓ cup frozen lemon juice**
**1 tablespoon grated orange rind**
**¼ cup flour**
**1 teaspoon baking powder**

# DEE'S KUCHEN

*Lillian Marshall first used one of Mrs. Dee Cunningham's recipes in 1967. Her kuchen recipe has been reprinted several times and has proven to be most popular.*

Scald milk, add butter, sugar and salt. Dissolve yeast in the warm water. Add yeast mixture to the milk mixture. Beat in eggs, then beat in flour.

Cover and put in a warm place for one to 1½ hours. Turn out on a floured board and roll to fit a large greased cookie sheet or two 9-inch cake pans. Pinch the edges to form sides.

Put in a warm place again for 45 minutes to one hour. Meanwhile, choose either the butter or cheese topping. Mix the topping ingredients well and pour on crust after the second rising. Bake at 350 degrees for 25 to 30 minutes.

**½ cup milk**
**4 tablespoons butter or margarine**
**¼ cup sugar**
**1 teaspoon salt**
**1 package yeast**
**¼ cup warm water**
**2 eggs**
**3½ cups all-purpose flour**
**Butter or cheese topping (see recipe)**

## CHEESE TOPPING

**8 ounces cream cheese, softened**
**3 eggs**
**½ cup sugar**
**¼ teaspoon cinnamon**
**1 small can crushed pineapple (optional)**

## BUTTER TOPPING

**1 stick butter, softened**
**1 cup sugar**
**3 eggs**
**½ teaspoon vanilla**
**¼ cup chopped pecans (optional)**

# MOTHER'S JELLY COOKIES

*Elaine Corn wrote about this recipe in 1982. It is from her mother, Vivienne Corn.*

2 cups flour
⅔ cup sugar
½ teaspoon baking powder
¾ cup butter, softened
1 unbeaten egg
2 teaspoons vanilla
Dark jelly (or preserves), such as
   raspberry or blackberry

In a bowl, combine the flour, sugar and bakng powder. Blend in butter with a pastry cutter. Add egg and vanilla and form the dough. If soft, chill. Divide dough into 4 parts. Shape each part into a 13-inch rope ¾ inch thick. Place rolls 2 at a time on ungreased cookie sheets. Using the blunt end of a kitchen knife, make a lengthwise depression down the center of each roll. Fill with jelly. Bake at 350 degrees for 15 to 20 minutes. Cookies will spread. Cool no more than 5 minutes before cutting. Cut diagonally. Cool completely. Makes 2 dozen.

# BUTTER-BATTER RHUBARB COFFEE CAKE

2 cups sliced rhubarb
2 tablespoons butter
¼ cup sugar
1 teaspoon cinnamon
2 sticks butter
1 cup sugar
3 eggs
1½ teaspoons baking powder
Pinch salt
2½ cups sifted all-purpose flour
Glaze of 1 cup powdered sugar
   thinned with 2 tablespoons milk
   or water

Heat the rhubarb, butter and ¼ cup sugar in a saucepan until sugar dissolves and rhubarb cooks down slightly, about 8 minutes. Stir in cinnamon and set aside. Meanwhile, beat the butter until light and fluffy. Gradually add sugar. Beat in the eggs one at a time, mixing well after each addition. Combine the baking powder, salt and flour. Add to butter mixture, stopping mixing as soon as flour is absorbed into batter. Pour batter into a buttered baking dish or tube pan. With a spoon or knife handle, make a trough down the center of the batter. Spoon in cooked rhubarb. Bake at 350 degrees for 45 minutes to 1 hour. Cool completely before pouring glaze in a zig-zag across top of cake.
— Elaine Corn, 1984

*Christmas fruitcake. Photograph by H.
Harold Davis.*

# VIVIENNE CORN'S BLUEBERRY COFFEECAKE

*Elaine Corn wrote about this, her mother's recipe, in 1984.*

Heat oven to 350 degrees. Combine topping ingredients with your fingers until crumbly and set aside. Grease a 9-by-9-inch baking dish. Sift together the dry ingredients. Mix the sugar and shortening on high speed in a large electric-mixer bowl. When fluffy, add egg and continue mixing. With mixer on low, add the dry ingredient mixture alternately with the milk, mixing until just blended after each addition. Carefully stir in the blueberries, and do not be alarmed if batter turns blue; the cake bakes white. Pour the batter into the dish. Smooth top with a spatula. Sprinkle with topping mixture. Bake 40 to 45 minutes. Use toothpick test for doneness.

## TOPPING:

**½ cup sugar**
**⅓ cup flour**
**1 teaspoon cinnamon**
**½ stick butter**

## CAKE:

**2 cups sifted flour**
**2 teaspoons double-acting baking powder**
**½ teaspoon salt**
**¾ cup sugar**
**¼ cup shortening**
**1 egg**
**½ cup milk**
**2 cups fresh blueberries**

# PIES, PUDDINGS & FRUIT DESSERTS

# VINEGAR PIE

*Lillian Marshall used this recipe, from Mrs. C.C. Kelsey of Louisville, in a 1971 "Kentuckiana Cooks" column.*

1 stick butter
1 cup sugar
2 eggs
3 teaspoons vinegar
1 teaspoon vanilla
½ cup broken pecans
8-inch pie shell, unbaked

Cream butter and sugar. Add eggs, one at a time, and mix. Add vinegar, vanilla and pecans. Beat well. Pour into unbaked pie crust. Bake 30 or 35 minutes in 350-degree oven.

# ALBANY BLACK BOTTOM PIE

9-inch graham cracker crust
2 cups milk, scalded
4 egg yolks, beaten
½ cup sugar
1½ tablespoons cornstarch
1½ squares bitter chocolate, melted
1 teaspoon vanilla
1 teaspoon gelatin, dissolved in cold
   water
4 tablespoons water
4 egg whites
½ cup sugar
¼ teaspoon cream of tartar
2 tablespoons bourbon whisky
1 cup heavy cream, whipped
1 tablespoon sugar
½ square butter chocolate, shaved

Add hot milk slowly to beaten egg yolks. Mix sugar with cornstarch and stir into milk. Cook in top of double boiler for about 20 minutes, stirring occasionally, until it coats a spoon. Remove from heat.

Take one cup of the hot custard and add melted chocolate to it, then cool and add vanilla. Stir occasionally as it cools. Pour into crust. Chill.

Dissolve gelatin in cold water and add to remaining warm custard. Cool.

Beat egg whites with the cream of tartar until stiff but not dry, then add ½ cup sugar slowly, beating. Add whisky. Fold the meringue into the plain custard mixture and pour over the chocolate layer in the pie shell.

Top with sweetened whipped cream and garnish with shaved bitter chocolate. Makes 8 servings.

— Lillian Marshall, 1969

# BLACKBERRY PIE

Pastry for double-crust 9-inch pie
1 heaping quart fresh blackberries,
   washed and drained
1½ cups sugar
2 tablespoons flour
2 tablespoons cornstarch
¼ teaspoon cinnamon
1 tablespoon butter

Line nine-inch pie pan with pastry.

In a bowl, combine sugar, flour, cornstarch and cinnamon. Add washed and drained berries and toss lightly to mix. Pour into crust and dot with butter.

Moisten edges of bottom crust with water. Cover with top crust, seal well at edges and crimp crusts decoratively. With a knife, cut vents for steam to escape. If desired, brush top with milk to enhance the browning.

Bake at 425 degrees for 10 minutes, then reduce heat to 350 and bake about 45 minutes longer, until well browned and the juices bubbling out of the slits congeal around the openings. This last is an old-time kind of thing; it does look that way when done. If pie should brown too much on top before it is done, just put a loose piece of foil over it.

— Lillian Marshall, 1974

# MRS. EDDS' RHUBARB PIE FILLING

*Cissy Gregg used this recipe in 1949. It was from Mrs. W.C. Edds of Crestwood, Ky. This is for a 9-inch pie shell with pastry to cover.*

Wash and dry the rhubarb. Do not peel unless the skin is very tough. Cut the stalks into about ½-inch pieces. Beat the eggs, and add sugar and flour which have been mixed together. Beat until the three are as one. Mix the egg-sugar mixture with the rhubarb and fill the pie shell. I like a high, rounding pie even if I do have to put a pan under it in the oven. Believe it or not, this is such a good and well-behaved pie that it didn't drip, but I betcha it would have if that pan hadn't been under it.

To get the shiny countenance on this pie, brush the top with an egg or egg yolk diluted with water or milk when the pie is about halfway through its cooking period. If it doesn't get enough make-up with the first painting, brush it again just before it comes from the oven.

Where there is pie, there should be cheese. We chose this time a soft cheese molded into small balls — one for each serving. Then you'd bettter make a few more since there are always delightful "pigs" who want two scoops of ice cream or two hunks of cheese with pie. And it's only right because these characters always look for the largest piece of pie to go with the double trimmings.

**2 pounds fresh, tender rhubarb**
**2 eggs**
**1 to 1¼ cups sugar**
**2 to 4 tablespoons flour (we used 2 tablespoons and thought it about right for rhubarb)**

# MOLASSES PIE

2 8-inch pie shells
2 cups molasses or sorghum syrup
Juice of 2 lemons
2 tablespoons flour mixed with a
    little water
½ teaspoon cinnamon
½ teaspoon nutmeg
3 tablespoons butter, melted
4 eggs, separated
½ cup sugar

Heat oven to 425 degrees. Partially bake pie shells for eight minutes and remove to cool. Reduce oven temperature to 350 degrees.

In a mixing bowl, stir molasses (or sorghum) with lemon juice. Add flour-water paste and mix thoroughly. Add cinnamon, nutmeg and butter.

Beat the egg yolks with the sugar until very light and stir into molasses mixture. Beat the whites until stiff but not dry and fold into pie mixture.

Pour filling into prepared pie shells. Bake 30 minutes, or until set.

Makes two pies.

— Cook's Corner column, 1985

# THE DUANE PEACH COBBLER

*"When a son comes up with 'My mother makes the best in the world,' no grass grows under my feet until I get my hands on the how-to-make," Cissy Gregg wrote in introducing this 1947 recipe. "And this recipe is one of these."*

*Quite uncharacteriscally, Cissy Gregg did not identify Mrs. Duane or her proud son, and she ran the recipe again as Mrs. Duane's peach pie in 1960.*

Make a pastry and line a square or oblong pan that is about 1½ inches deep. The "master maker" of this cobbler uses a 7x12 pan, we used an 8x8 pan. Cover the bottom of the pan with fresh peach halves that have been peeled and laid in with the pit side up. Sprinkle the peaches with sugar, and the amount depends on the sweetness of the peach — 4 tablespoons sugar should be about right. Then drizzle about 2 tablespoons of water over the peaches to help them along in their cooking.

Put this part of the cobbler in about a 400-degree oven and allow to cook until the peaches are soft and the pastry has cooked and is lightly browned.

While the baking is going on, cream together ½ cup butter or margarine and 1 cup sugar. Then beat in 2 whole eggs. If you are feeling in an expansive mood you could use 3 eggs, but 2 will make a good quantity of sauce for this sized cobbler.

When peaches are tender, take pie from oven and pour over the top the sugar-butter-egg mixture. Then put the pie under the broiler until the sauce has set some and the top surface is a pleasant brown.

This cobbler can be made with canned peaches, too. And so doing there are a few changes to make in the cooking. For instance after you have put the peaches on the crust, use the syrup from the can instead of the sugar and water as with the fresh. And the baking temperature can be increased to 425 degrees. Here the canned peaches are already cooked, and only the pastry needs the heat's attention. For the rest of the way the directions are all right for either canned or fresh peach cobbler.

To serve, allow a half a peach for each person and a proportionate share of the wonderful "goo" that surrounds it.

# OLD TALBOTT TAVERN BROWN SUGAR PIE

*This recipe, Cissy Gregg reported in 1959, is "a family heirloom given to us by Mrs. E.M. Stillwell of the Old Talbott Tavern" in Bardstown, Ky.*

We have made this Brown Sugar Pie in both 8 and 9-inch pie plates and in the individual tart-sized ones. It's like one I remember from home, but my mother didn't know exactly the how-to-do. Do try it. It's rich and should be served in small portions — or so we think.

This recipe, Mrs. Stillwell writes us, "has been a guarded, dark secret in my family for years," then gradually it was let out of Pandora's box, and Mrs. Stillwell thinks everyone should have a chance to try it at home whether or not they get to the Old Talbott Tavern on the day it is being served.

In pie making, pastry comes first.

## PLAIN PASTRY

Cut the shortening into the flour and salt until mixture is the consistency of peas. Sprinkle water over the mixture, 1 tablespoon at a time. Stir with a fork until just enough water has been added to form a soft ball. Do not knead. This makes one crust when rolled out.

1 cup sifted flour (measure after sifting)
½ teaspoon salt
4 tablespoons shortening
Ice water (3 to 5 tablespoons)

## FILLING

Cream sugar and margarine to a smooth paste. Add egg yolks one at a time. Add flour, vinegar, salt and vanilla. Continue beating. Beat egg whites until stiff, and gently fold into the mixture. Pour into an unbaked pie shell, and bake until the filling is set but not firm. (We used a 325-degree oven for approximately 25 minutes.) When the pie filling is set, whip up the jelly with a fork and lightly drizzle over the top of the baked pie.

2 cups light brown sugar
1 stick margarine
1 tablespoon flour
3 eggs, separated
1 tablespoon vinegar
1 teaspoon vanilla extract
Pinch salt
½ cup jelly — Damson plum preferred

## MERINGUE

For the meringue, beat the egg whites until they'll hold a peak and gently fold in three tablespoons sugar. Place over pie, and place back in the oven until the meringue is beautifully sun-tanned.

3 egg whites
3 tablespoons sugar

# MRS. CROSIER'S PERFECT PIE CRUST

*This is among the "most-requested" recipes in the Courier-Journal kitchen. It was supplied by Mrs. Ruth Crosier in 1968, and Lillian Marshall wrote that it was "beautifully tender and flaky." It is a large recipe, Lillian said, "but it keeps well." It makes two 9-inch pie shells plus about a dozen tarts.*

**4 cups flour**
**2 teaspoons salt**
**1½ cups lard or shortening**
**2 eggs, beaten**
**6 tablespoons cold water**

Stir the salt into the flour. Cut in shortening until a mealy texture results. Beat the eggs with the water and mix lightly, but thoroughly with the flour mixture. On floured board or cloth, roll ¼ of the dough at a time, very thin.

Using a saucer about 5½ inches across for a pattern, cut circles out with a knife or pastry wheel. Place about 3 tablespoons filling on each circle. With a pastry brush dipped in water, moisten the outer ½ inch of each circle and fold dough in half to enclose filling. Crimp edges together with a fork dipped in flour.

Place on cookie sheets and bake at 375 degrees for 20 mintes, or until lightly browned. Makes 12 tarts, with pastry enough left for two 9-inch pies. (Rerolling does not seem to harm this pastry in anyway.)

# INDIAN PUDDING

*Cissy Gregg brought the recipe for this traditional New England dessert back from a 1954 food editors' meeting in Maine.*

**3 tablespoons yellow cornmeal**
**⅓ cup dark molasses**
**3 cups milk, scalded**
**½ cup sugar**
**1 egg, beaten**
**1 tablespoon butter**
**¼ teaspoon salt**
**½ teaspoon ginger**
**½ teaspoon cinnamon**
**1 cup cold milk**

Stir cornmeal and molasses into scalded milk and cook over low heat until it thickens, stirring constantly. Remove from heat and add sugar, egg, butter, salt and spices. Pour into a buttered baking dish and bake in 300-degree oven for 30 minutes. Add cold milk. Do not stir. Continue baking at 300 degrees for 2 hours.

This pudding's rich and dark and lush. We ate it served warm with vanilla ice cream.

# HELEN'S WINNER'S CIRCLE PIE

*"Derby Pie" is a registered trademark. The people who own the trademark can call what they make Derby Pie; the rest of us can't. Keep that in mind if your church or organization considers publishing its own cookbook, and don't use the term "Derby Pie" for any recipe in your cookbook. Instead, use a name for your pie that has a Kentucky Derby-type ring to it. People will get the idea.*

*Our food editors have used a number of names over the years. The following recipe was reprinted in 1979. We're not sure where it originated or how far back it goes.*

Mix sugar and flour, add eggs and then butter. Add English walnuts and chocolate chips and vanilla. Pour into unbaked pie shell and bake 30 minutes in a preheated 350 degree oven. You may have to bake it longer because ovens vary. Test with a tooth pick. It should be chewy but not runny. Traditionally served warm.

1 cup sugar
½ cup flour
2 eggs, beaten
1 stick butter, melted and cooled
1 cup English walnuts
1 cup chocolate chips
1 teaspoon vanilla
1 9-inch unbaked pie shell

# GERTRUDE'S LEMON CHESS PIE

*The Cook's Corner column printed this recipe in 1980. It is from Gertrude Rainbolt of Louisville.*

Mix dry ingredients together. Beat in the eggs thoroughly and add the butter, milk and other ingredients. Pour into prepared 9-inch pastry shell and bake in preheated 350-degree oven 50 to 60 minutes or until set.

2 cups sugar
4 eggs
⅛ teaspoon salt
2 tablespoons grated lemon rind
1 tablespoon flour
1 tablespoon cornmeal
¼ cup melted butter
¼ cup milk
¼ cup lemon juice

# CISSY'S CUSTARD PIE

*This is Cissy Gregg's recipe. The Cook's Corner column printed it in this form in 1984.*

Line pie plate with pastry. Be sure there are no bubbles under pastry and no holes in it. For best results, make pastry thicker than usual. Place in refrigerator while preparing filling.

Blend eggs, sugar, salt and extracts. Slowly pour milk into egg mixture, stirring constantly. Pour into crust. Bake in a preheated 325-degree oven 30 to 40 minutes or until knife inserted halfway between outside and center of custard comes out clean. Remove promptly to cooling rack. Do not cut pie until just before serving. Sprinkle with nutmeg if desired.

1 9-inch unbaked pie crust
4 eggs (or 2 eggs and 4 yolks) slightly beaten
½ cup sugar
⅛ teaspoon salt
¼ teaspoon vanilla extract
½ teaspoon almond extract
2½ cups milk, scalded
Nutmeg

# CHESS PIE FOR POSTERITY

*"Here we proudly give you Lena's Chess Tarts, Pauline Goddard Dedman's Chess pie or the Beaumont Inn's Chess pie," Cissy Gregg wrote in 1951. "You can choose the tag you wish. We want to have all three on ours since it was truly one of Lena's fine contributions to good cookery, which Mrs. Dedman has cherished for us, and Beaumont Inn has made it known the nation over."*

**1 cup white sugar**
**1 level tablespoon flour**
**¼ teaspoon salt**
**2 egg yolks**
**1 whole egg**
**3 tablespoons water**
**1 teaspoon white vinegar**
**¼ pound or ½ cup melted butter**

Mix flour, sugar and salt together. Beat the 2 egg yolks and the 1 whole egg together, adding water and vinegar and melted butter. Beat together well, then add the sugar-flour mixture.

Pour into an unbaked pie shell and bake at 350 degrees until set. Ours baked out in 35 minutes, and we had a luscious 9-inch pie.

The companionate 2 egg whites to the 2 egg yolks in the filling were used to make the meringue. They use 1 tablespoon of white sugar for each egg white, and beat it in an electric mixer to form a meringue. Spread on top of the pie and brown-off for 12 minutes in a 350-degree oven.

And so, there is another piece of fine, old, Kentucky cooking. And this column is deeply grateful to its many friends who make our recording of Kentucky cooking possible.

# SHAKER LEMON PIE

*The Cook's Corner column ran this recipe in 1979. It's a Shaker recipe, although it's usually known as "Ohio lemon pie." Some recipes suggest letting the lemon slices and sugar stand overnight before proceeding.*

**Pastry for 2 crusts**
**2 lemons**
**2 cups sugar**
**4 eggs**

Slice two lemons as thin as paper, rind and all. Place them in a bowl and put the sugar over them. Mix well and let stand for 2 hours or more. Beat the eggs together and pour over lemons.

Fill unbaked pie shell with mixture and add top crust. Cut small vents in the top crust to let out steam. Place in a preheated 450-degree oven for 15 minutes and then cut heat down to 350-degrees and bake for 30 minutes or until a silver knife inserted into the custard comes out clean.

# KENTUCKY BOURBON APPLE PIE

Make pastry. In large bowl combine flour, sugar and salt. With pastry blender or two knives used scissor-fashion, cut in cream cheese and butter until mixture resembles coarse crumbs. Knead pastry into a ball. Flatten slightly. Cover and refrigerate one hour. Roll out pastry between two sheets of wax paper. Peel off top paper. Invert pastry into a nine-inch deep-dish pie plate. Remove paper. Flute edge. Refrigerate at least one hour.

Preheat oven to 375 degrees. For filling, arrange apples in pastry shell. In a medium bowl combine sugar, flour and eggs. Stir with a wire whisk until smooth. Slowly stir in melted butter, then walnuts and bourbon. Pour over apples. Bake one hour. Cool. Before serving sprinkle top with confectioners' sugar, if desired.

Makes eight servings.

— Cook's Corner column, 1983

## CREAM CHEESE PASTRY:

**1 cup all-purpose flour**
**1 tablespoon sugar**
**¼ teaspoon salt**
**1 3-ounce package cream cheese, cubed**
**½ cup unsalted butter, cubed**

## FILLING:

**6 cups peeled, thinly sliced cooking apples (about 2 pounds)**
**1 cup plus 3 tablespoons sugar**
**6 tablespoons all-purpose flour**
**3 eggs**
**¾ cup butter, melted**
**½ cup chopped walnuts**
**2 tablespoons bourbon**
**Confectioners' sugar, optional**

# IRISH WHISKEY PIE

Dissolve gelatin in cold water, set aside.

Combine chocolate, hot water, salt and sugar. Bring to boil and cook until smooth. Mix egg yolks and milk. Stir into chocolate mixture.

Melt gelatin mixture over hot water until clear. Add to chocolate mixture with whiskey. Pour into mixing bowl and place over crushed ice or in refrigerator, stirring occasionally, until syrupy.

Beat egg whites and fold into chocolate mixture. Fold in whipped cream and almonds. Spoon into crust and chill four hours. Garnish with additional whipped cream and sliced almonds. Serves six to eight.

— Cook's Corner column, 1981

**1½ teaspoons unflavored gelatin**
**½ cup cold water**
**2 squares (2 ounces) unsweetened chocolate**
**½ cup hot water**
**¼ teaspoon salt**
**½ cup granulated sugar**
**2 beaten egg yolks**
**¼ cup milk**
**3 tablespoons Irish whiskey**
**2 egg whites**
**1 cup heavy cream, whipped**
**¼ cup sliced almonds**
**Additional cream and almonds for garnish**
**1 9-inch baked pastry shell (chilled) or graham-cracker crust**

# THE OLD TALBOTT TAVERN ORANGE PIE

*Cissy Gregg used this recipe in 1952, attributing it to Mrs. B.F. Stillwell, "the power behind the kitchen throne" at the Old Talbott Tavern in Bardstown, Ky.*

¾ cup granulated sugar
½ cup flour
¼ teaspoon salt
1¼ cups water
2 egg yolks
½ cup orange juice
1 tablespoon grated orange rind
2 tablespoons lemon juice
Baked pie shell

Combine sugar, flour and salt in the top of a double boiler. Stir in water, keeping mixture free from lumps. Cook and stir over direct flame 5 minutes. Add egg yolks, slightly beaten, and cook 5 minutes longer over rapidly boiling water, stirring constantly.

Remove from heat and add fruit juice and rind. Chill thoroughly. Turn into baked pie shell, cover with the following meringue.

## MERINGUE

2 egg whites
½ cup sugar
2 tablespoons water
Dash of salt
1 orange
¾ cup moist, sweetened coconut

Put whites of eggs, sugar, salt and water in the top of a double boiler. Beat with a rotary beater until thoroughly mixed. Place over rapidly boiling water and beat 1 minute. Remove from fire and continue beating until the mixture will stand in peaks--about 1 minute longer. Pile lightly on filling. Peel a Valencia or navel orange and separate into sections, removing membrane. Arrange on top of the meringue. Sprinkle with the coconut.

# WOODFORD PUDDING

*Cissy Gregg ran a Woodford pudding recipe as early as Jan. 31, 1942. In 1961 she wrote that it is "quite a favorite of ours."*

*"Whether or not this well-known dessert got its name from Woodford County, I don't know," she said, "but anyone would be glad to claim it." The following recipe was one she grew up with in her home town of Cynthiana.*

½ cup butter or margarine
1 cup sugar
1 cup flour
1 cup blackberry jam
1 teaspoon soda
½ cup sour milk
1 teaspoon cinnamon
3 eggs, slightly beaten
Butterscotch sauce (see recipe)

Cream the shortening with the sugar until light. Add the slightly beaten eggs and mix well. Dissolve the soda in the sour milk. Add the flour which has been sifted with the cinnamon to the sugar-egg mixutre along with the soda and sour milk. Blend in the jam. Bake in a greased, shallow baking dish for about 40 minutes in 325-degree oven. Cut in squares and serve with the following butterscotch sauce.

## BUTTERSCOTCH SAUCE

Mix 1½ cups dark brown sugar with 4 tablespoons flour. Add 1 cup of boiling water and a dash of salt. Stir and cook for six to eight minutes. If too thick, add a little more boiling water. Take off the stove and add 4 tablespoons of butter or margarine, 2 tablespoons of cream and ½ teaspoon vanilla. Blend well and keep warm until served.

# CHERRY CUSTARD PIE

Beat the eggs well, adding sugar, nutmeg and cream. Pour your 2 cups of cherries into the shell, pour over the egg mixture and bake by placing the filled pie shell in a 350-degree oven and turning the temperature up to 400 degrees immediately. It takes about 40 minutes to complete in a 9-inch pie and a little longer for the 10-inch.

The custard should be set firm, but still tender.

To cool, place the pie pan on a cake rack or on an unlighted burner on top the stove. The circulation of air cools the pie more quickly and evenly.

— Cissy Gregg, 1947

**2 cups of drained cherries**
**3 eggs**
**½ cup sugar**
**¼ teaspoon nutmeg**
**¾ cup sour cream or ¾ cup of sweet cream with two tablespoons vinegar added**
**Pie shell**

# FUDGE PIE

Melt 2 squares (2 ounces) of bitter chocolate with ½ stick of butter (4 tablespoons); and add 1 cup sugar, 2 beaten eggs, ¼ teaspoon salt; 1 teaspoon vanilla; ½ cup flour and a cup of chopped walnuts.

We melted the chocolate and the butter together in the top of the double boiler, and the mixing was all done in the same utensil. Spread in an 8- or 9-inch pie pan or an 8-inch square cake pan (we did) which has been paper lined and buttered.

Bake at 350 degrees until firm but still moist. — about 25 minutes, if I remember correctly. Cool slightly and invert on a cake rack. Remove the paper. When cool return to the pan. Punch holes all over the top and pour over it a jigger of rum. Top with whipped cream, sprinkle with nuts and let stand at least an hour before served. Cut in squares or wedges to serve. You don't have to use the rum, but by using rum with the chocolate the effect is of a superlative nature.

— Cissy Gregg, 1952

# AMISH RHUBARB CUSTARD PIE

1¾ cups fresh rhubarb
1 unbaked pie shell
¾ cup sugar
1 tablespoon flour
½ teaspoon salt
2 eggs, separated
1 cup milk
2 tablespoons melted butter

Heat oven to 400 degrees. Chop rhubarb into small bits. Lay in the bottom of unbaked pie shell. In a large bowl, combine the sugar, flour, salt, egg yolks, milk and melted butter and pour evenly over rhubarb. Bake 10 minutes at 400 degrees; reduce heat to 350 and bake 30 minutes more. Beat the remaining egg whites until soft peaks form. While continuing to beat, add 2 tablespoons sugar until medium-stiff peaks form. Spread over warm pie. Return to oven until meringue browns.

— Elaine Corn, 1984

# CHOCOLATE CREME MINT PIE

Cream ¾ cup butter or margarine thoroughly. Add one cup sugar, gradually, creaming well. Beat 3 eggs thoroughly. Blend into the creamed mixture. Then blend in 3 squares (3 ounces) unsweetened chocolate, which has been melted and cooled. Beat until the mixture is smooth. Add ½ teaspoon peppermint extract. Pour mixture into a baked, cooled pie shell. Chill several hours. Top with whipped cream before serving.

It cuts well and is as rich as Croesus.

— Cissy Gregg, 1950

# THE REED CHOCOLATE PIE

*This recipe came to Cissy Gregg from Mrs. McKay Reed Sr., who first made it, by way of Mrs. McKay Reed Jr. Cissy published it in 1957.*

1 package chocolate semisweet
    chips
2 tablespoons sugar
2 tablespoons milk
4 egg yolks, slightly beaten
4 egg whites, beaten until stiff

Melt chocolate chips in top of double boiler. Add sugar and milk. Don't have the water in the boiler boiling, but just hot. Stir to make sure the sugar is dissolved. Beat egg yolks slightly, and add to the chocolate mixture. Stir until smooth. Take from the heat and allow to cool. Beat egg whites until stiff and fold into chocolate mixture. Put in baked pie shell and refrigerate 1 to 2 hours.

Serve with whipped cream and a light sprinkling of shaved bitter chocolate. The bittersweet idea is our own.

# DULCIE'S CHOCOLATE FUDGE PIE

*Lillian Marshall introduced this 1967 recipe by saying that Dulcie Clark of Bowling Green, Ky., had served as guest cook in the Magazine on several occasions during 1966.*

Melt the chocolate and butter or margarine over low heat. Add the sugar, then the unbeaten eggs, one at a time, beating well after each addition. Then add flour, nuts and salt. Beat well. Add vanilla and pour into a well-greased and floured 9- or 10-inch cake or pie pan and bake 25 minutes at 350 degrees. Serve with ice cream if desired.

**3 squares chocolate (unsweetened)**
**2 cups sugar**
**4 eggs**
**½ cup flour**
**1 cup pecans**
**1 teaspoon salt**
**1 teaspoon vanilla**
**1 stick butter or margarine**

# AUNT JENNY'S SUGAR-SAVING HONEY PUMPKIN PIE

*By request, this recipe was printed in the Cook's Corner column in 1983, but it dates back to the sugar-starved days of World War II. A 1942 Spry ad showed Aunt Jenny praising the shortening and urging that everyone serve her honey pumpkin pie to the servicemen coming home for Thanksgiving. "Notice it's sweetened with honey, takes none of your precious sugar!" she says in the advertisement.*

Combine pumpkin, honey, cinnamon, vanilla and salt. Add eggs and milk. Pour mixture into unbaked pie shell. Bake in hot oven (425 degrees) 40 to 45 minutes.

**1½ cups canned or cooked pumpkin**
**½ cup honey**
**½ teaspoon cinnamon**
**½ teaspoon vanilla**
**½ teaspoon salt**
**2 eggs, slightly beaten**
**1 cup evaporated milk**
**1 unbaked pie shell**

# RHUBARB FOOL

**1 pound rhubarb**
**1 cup sugar**
**1 cup yogurt or whipping cream**

Remove and discard rhubarb leaves. Trim off base. Slice stalks into 1-inch pieces. Cook in a heavy pot with the sugar until very soft. Force mixture through a sieve or run through a food mill. Taste for sweetness and add additional sugar, if necessary. (If using yogurt, you'll probably want to add about ½ cup extra sugar.) Chill 1 hour. Whip the cream. Gently swirl into rhubarb mixture, leaving streaks. If using yogurt, aerate well with fork, then fold into rhubarb. Transfer to a clear glass bowl or individual goblets. Chill well. Serves 4.

— Elaine Corn, 1984

# BREAD PUDDING WITH WHISKEY SAUCE

**8 cups stale French or Italian bread, cut in small cubes**
**4 eggs**
**1 egg yolk**
**1½ cups sugar**
**Heaping teaspoon cinnamon**
**Heaping teaspoon nutmeg**
**2 teaspoons vanilla**
**1 stick butter, melted**
**4 cups milk**
**¾ cup raisins**

Place bread in a greased loaf pan or baking dish. In a bowl with electric mixer on high, beat the eggs until frothy and bubbly, about 3 minutes. With mixer running, slowly pour in sugar. Add nutmeg, cinnamon, vanilla and butter, beating until well-blended. On medium speed, beat in milk. Stir in raisins. Pour over bread and let soak in about 45 minutes, tamping down on bread now and then so cubes don't float, until most of the liquid is drawn away from the edges of the dish. Place in oven heated to 350 degrees. Immediately reduce heat to 300 degrees and bake for 40 minutes. Then increase heat to 425 degrees for 25 minutes. Bread pudding should be browned but not burned, and slightly puffed. Serve from hot dish with a little whiskey sauce drizzled over each portion. Serves 10.

## WHISKEY SAUCE

**½ teaspoon cornstarch**
**¼ cup water**
**1 cup sugar**
**1 cup cream**
**1 teaspoon cinnamon**
**2 tablespoons butter**
**1 or 2 shots bourbon**

In a small bowl, combine the cornstarch and water and set aside. In a saucepan, place the sugar, cream, cinnamon and butter. Bring to a boil. When the sauce boils, whip it into the cornstarch. Add bourbon. Keep slightly warm until ready to serve. Makes about 3 cups.

— Elaine Corn, 1983

# CHERRY PIE

*Cissy Gregg turned this simple recipe into a pretty fair pie-baking lesson back in 1962. A reader could even pick up a pointer on darning stockings. If you don't know what that means, ask your mother. Maybe your grandmother.*

**3 tablespoons cornstarch**
**½ cup sugar**
**⅛ teaspoon salt**
**½ cup unsweetened cherry juice**
**2 tablespoons butter or margarine**
**2 cups pitted unsweetened cherries**
**Pie crust**

Make a crust to your liking and line one 9-inch pie pan or six 3-inch pie pans.

Mix together cornstarch and sugar. Then mix with the cherry juice and salt. Cook in a saucepan until thick. Add butter or margarine.

Spread the unsweetened cherries over the unbaked pie crust and pour over the thickened cherry juice. Bake in a hot oven, 425 degrees, 30 minutes for pies and 20 to 25 minutes for tarts.

Some like a two-crust pie for cherry, but I have always taken to the lattice type of covering.

*Blackberry pie. Photograph by Billy Davis.*

Should you also prefer the lattice-topper type, make the bottom crust so it will extend ½ inch over the edge of the pie plate. Cut the lattices from strips of pie crust, lay them over the top of the pie much in the same fashion you would do in darning a stocking, one-over-and-one-under fashion. Moisten the strips and seal edges to the pastry in the pan. Turn the overhanging pastry back over the ends of the lattice and build up a fluted edge.

In all the years I have been making pies latticed, I can't say I have learned just how much juice a pie crust will hold. At the same time I get tired of washing out ovens. So now, even if it turns out to be a thin pie, there's always a baking sheet in the bottom of the oven to catch drippings just in case.

# PRESIDENT EISENHOWER'S PIE

*Yes, this recipe is supposed to have been developed for Ike. Cissy Gregg tried it in 1953.*

**1½ quarts fresh strawberries**
**1 cup sugar**
**3 tablespoons cornstarch**
**2 tablespoons lemon juice**
**1 baked pie shell**

Wash and cap the strawberries, reserving half of them — those that are largest and best looking. Mash the rest of the strawberries and add cornstarch and sugar, mixed together. Cook 5 to 6 minutes until clear and thick. Stir in the lemon juice. Cool. Add the whole berries to the cooled mixture, saving a few for garnish.

Pour into a baked pastry shell. Top with whipped cream just before serving and garnish with whole berries.

For those who use the smaller pie pans, the home economists say that two thirds of the recipe is enough for an eight-inch pie pan.

The berries that are folded in can be sliced. One great advantage the recipe has — the filling can be made and stored in the refrigerator for three to four days without hurting it. If you want to use it for a party, both filling and tart shells can be made ahead and filled as they are needed.

# FROZEN LIGHT LIME PIE

Chocolate-pecan crumb crust (see
   recipe)
1 package plain gelatin
¼ cup cold water
5 egg yolks
¾ cup sugar
1 cup fresh-squeezed lime juice,
   about 7 limes
Grated zest of 3 limes
5 egg whites
½ cup sugar
Lofty meringue (see recipe)

## CHOCOLATE-PECAN CRUMB CRUST

10 double graham crackers (1
   package)
1 cup pecan halves
1 round Mexican table chocolate, or
   2 squares semi-sweet baking
   chocolate
2 teaspoons cinnamon
3 tablespoons brown sugar
½ stick butter, melted

Heat oven to 400 degrees, and prepare crust. Crush between sheets of wax paper with a rolling pin, or run through a food processor, the graham crackers, pecans and chocolate until each is in very fine crumbs. Stir with cinnamon and brown sugar. Pour crumbs into bottom of springform pan. Add melted butter directly into pan and, using fingers, quickly mash mixture until crumbs are held together. Press mixture up sides and over bottom of pan. Bake 10 minutes. Cool. Dissolve gelatin in water and set aside. In mixing bowl set over simmering water, beat yolks and sugar. Add lime juice and cook, stirring or whisking until custard coats a metal spoon. Off heat, add zest and gelatin mixture, whisking well to combine. Beat whites until frothy. Continuing to beat, gradually add sugar until whites form medium-stiff peaks. Fold whites into lime custard. Pour into prepared crust. Cover and freeze.

Elaine Corn, 1984

## LOFTY MERINGUE

1 cup egg whites (about 6 whites)
1 cup sugar
¼ teaspoon cream of tartar

Heat oven to 400 degrees. Beat egg whites until foamy. Continuing to beat, on high speed if using an electric mixer, gradually add sugar and, lastly, cream of tartar, until whites are stiff, glossy and sugar has dissolved. Spread over well-frozen pie with dampened metal spatula, building up tips. Place in oven 10 minutes, until tips brown well. Remove and serve. Garnish with fresh mint. Serves 10 to 12.

— Elaine Corn, 1984

# LILLIE TOMLIN'S FROZEN LEMON PIE

*Comedienne Lily Tomlin was born in Detroit, but her parents were natives of Paducah, Ky., and her mother, Lillie, retured there after her husband died. Elaine Corn used this recipe in 1983.*

Beat the egg whites until stiff. Add ½ cup sugar and egg yolks, beating well. Stir in lemon juice; fold in cream. Set aside. Roll enough vanilla wafers into crumbs to measure 1 cup. Line a buttered pie plate or square baking dish with crumbs. Pour in beaten mixture. Sprinkle with additional vanilla-wafer crumbs. Place pie in freezer at least one hour, or overnight. Before serving, leave out a few minutes. Garnish with a few mint leaves.

**3 eggs, separated**
**½ cup sugar**
**5 tablespoons fresh lemon juice**
**1 cup whipping cream, stiffly beaten**
**Vanilla wafers**

# KENTUCKY STACK PIE

*"Stack pie dates back to the time when basket dinners were the most important part of an outing," according to Cissy Gregg. "There were always lots of people to be fed from a basket and, of course, there must be enough to be generous with friends. There would be room for the base of only one pie, so they simply stacked them on top of each other. It's really a chess pie."*
*The following is a combination of stack-pie recipes Cissy printed in 1948 and 1962.*

Line four or five 9-inch pie pans with pastry. The one that is to be the bottom one is made regulation depth. The others are cut short, or can be. Have these ready for the filling. Then beat the yolks of 10 eggs. Beat well until light. Cream in 3 cups sugar, beating again until light. Add 1½ cups melted butter or margarine and 1 cup cream.

Pour 1 cup filling into each pie shell, and if there is any extra, make the bottom pie a little fuller. We baked two at a time, in a 350-degree oven, until the filling was done. It sorta bubbles up during the cooking, but your fingers will tell you when the fillings are firm and ready to come out. Allow the pies to cool in their pans. Run a spatula around them and out they'll come as easy as can be. Stack one on top of the other and ice with caramel frosting.

## CARAMEL FROSTING

Cook together 2 cups brown sugar and 1 cup cream until the mixture reaches the soft ball stage. Beat until creamy. If the frosting gets too hard before you get it all on the pie, add in a little cream. Serve by cutting in slices clear through the four or five stacks.

# SWEET POTATO PIE

Combine yams, eggs, milk, sugar, figs or dates, orange rind and ginger. Pour into baked pie shell and bake in a 350-degree oven for about one hour, or until filling is set. Garnish with whipped cream and almonds if desired.

— Lillian Marshall, 1976

**1 9-inch slightly baked pie shell**
**1 can (24 ounces) yams, drained and mashed (about 1½ cups)**
**3 eggs, beaten**
**1 cup milk**
**½ cup brown sugar**
**½ cup finely chopped figs or dates**
**1 teaspoon grated orange rind**
**1 teaspoon minced, candied ginger**

# FILLING FOR FRIED APPLE PIES

*Cissy Gregg wrote in this 1959 recipe that fried apple pies are "truly an old-time dish made famous at the time when ingenious housewives dried apples, made a crust, did the flop over, fried or baked them. Truly fried apple pies are turnovers. You can make them made up of pie crust or biscuit crust."*

*If you have dried apples — and Cissy notes that they aren't always easy to come by — soak them before you use them, overnight or long enough for them to become tender.*

*Oh. And yes, the word is "clob." Cissy probably figured we ought to know what that means, just as we ought to know what she meant — in another recipe — when she said to cut the bacon into "snibbles."*

*The pastry recipe which follows was Cissy's from 1962.*

**For each medium-sized apple, allow and combine:**
**2½ tablespoons brown sugar**
**2 tablespoons soft butter or margarine**
**Pinch salt**
**A little cinamon or nutmeg**
**A grating of lemon rind**

Slice the apples up as for sauce and cook until soft. (We peeled ours.) Add the seasonings and allow the sauce mixture to cool at least a little.

Roll out the pastry into circles of at least 2½ inches in diameter, or we made ours a little larger. Put a clob of the seasoned apple mixture in the lower half of the center of the circle, fold over and seal the crescent shape turnover with a little water and reseal by forking the 2 edges together. Fry in deep fat; or these may be baked, brushed with a mixture of an egg yolk diluted with 2 tablespoons of cream. Bake in a 450-degree oven for 15 minutes.

Dried apples are so wonderful for this type or any kind of apple pie, but dried apples are hard to come by, for us.

Fried-apple pies are good, hot as they are, or they may be served with a brown sugar sauce, cream, powdered sugar or — best of all — the young will like eating them drained on absorbent paper and eaten hot, almost to burn the tongue, with only a light brushing of sugar.

## PASTRY FOR FRIED APPLE PIES

**1⅓ cup all-purpose flour**
**⅔ cup cake flour**
**2 teaspoons baking powder**
**1 teaspoon salt**
**6 tablespoons fat**
**1 egg plus enough milk to make ⅔ cup**

Fried apple pies start out with a crust. Oftentimes they are made with plain pastry. We picked up this pastry which may aid and abet you in this mission.

Sift flours, baking powder and salt together. Cut in shortening. Beat the egg and add the milk. Mix as for biscuits. Roll out ⅛-inch thick. Cut into rounds the size you want. Fill according to the desire, placing the filling on one side of the circle. Flap the other half of the circle over the filling. Moisten the edges and press down the edges together with a fork. Most times we stick the tops of the crescent pies with a fork just in case. But this time we thought it let the fat in, and since they fry so quickly, we ended up preferring to leave the crust closed. Fry at 325 degrees until brown. Drain on absorbent paper. These can be made and reheated if it is more conventient.

# CHERRY COBBLER

Mix sugar in with flour, add juice and blend well. Add cherries and butter or margarine and cook until sugar is dissolved and the sauce begins to thicken. Pour into baking dish.

2 cups cherries, pitted and drained
1 cup cherry juice
2 tablespoons flour
¾ cups sugar (you may be able to squeeze down on that amount if you are in the throes of sugar shivers)
2 tablespoons butter or margarine

## BATTER TOPPING

Sift flour, measure and sift with baking powder and salt. Cut in butter or margarine until fine. Add milk and egg which have been beaten together. Make into a very stiff batter. Drop in mounds over the cherry sauce. Bake for 35 to 40 minutes in a 375-degree oven. Serve with hard sauce normally, but we have already used up so much of your sugar we daren't mention it, so use cream of top milk.
— Cissy Gregg, 1947

1½ cups flour
2 teaspoons baking powder
½ teaspoon salt
½ cup sugar
¼ cup butter or margarine
½ cup milk

# PEACHES AND CREAM PIE

Combine flour, tapioca salt and sugar, and spread on the bottom and sides of the pastry shell. Mix together sour cream and ¾ cup brown sugar which has been firmly packed in the cup. Peel 8 good-sized peaches and halve them. Dip each peach half in the sugar-and-cream mixture. Arrange the halves in the pastry shell, cut side down. Pour the remainder of the sugar-cream mixture over the top. Sprinkle lightly with nutmeg or cinnamon, if you like the spicy flavor. Bake in a hot oven, 450 degrees for 15 minutes. Reduce the oven to 350 degrees and bake 30 to 45 minutes longer or until the peaches are tender.

It's rich, need I say, but good!
— Cissy Gregg, 1951

1 9-inch unbaked pastry shell
2 tablespoons flour
2 tablespoons quick-cooking tapioca
¼ teaspoon salt
½ cup sugar
1 cup sour cream
¾ cup brown sugar
8 large fresh peaches or 16 halves
Nutmeg or cinnamon

# OPEN-FACE PEACH PIE

10 fresh peaches, more or less to fill
  the pie
¾ cup sugar
¼ cup flour
¼ cup of water or peach juice
2 tablespoons butter or margarine
2 tablespoons lemon juice
Pastry for one 9-inch crust

Line the pie pan with pastry, and flute the edges according to your own whim. Combine sugar, butter, and flour to make crumbs. Sprinkle half of this mixture in the bottom of the unbaked crust. Have the peaches peeled, seeded and halved or cut into quarters, if they are large ones. Place peaches with cut side down on the pie shell. Cover with remaining crumb mixture. Add fruit juices or lemon juice and water. Bake in a 375-degree oven for 40 to 45 minutes. Serve plain or with whipped cream.

— Cissy Gregg, 1950

# PEACH CRISP

2 cups peach slices (one No. 2½
  can), drained
¾ cup firmly packed brown sugar
¼ cup butter or margarine
½ cup flour
1 teaspoon cinnamon
1 tablespoon lemon juice

Arrange peach slices in the bottom of a greased 8x8x2-inch pan or baking dish. Combine brown sugar, butter or margarine, flour, cinnamon and lemon juice. Crumble all up together and sprinkle over peaches. Bake in a moderately hot oven, 375 degrees, for 45 minutes. Serve warm with cream.

— Cissy Gregg, 1948

# PIEPLANT DUMPLINGS

*Pieplant is rhubarb. In 1954, when Cissy Gregg printed this recipe, the term apparently was so widely known that Cissy didn't think she needed to explain that.*

## DUMPLING DOUGH:

3 cups flour
3 teaspoons baking powder
½ teaspoon salt
½ cup shortening
¾ cup milk

Sift and then measure the flour. Sift again with baking powder and salt. Cut in the shortening and add milk gradually. Mix to form a fairly moist dough. Stir, then knead slightly. Divide the dough into 6 pieces. Roll each piece ¼ inch thick.

## PIEPLANT FILLING:

3 cups pieplant cut into 1-inch
  pieces
3 cups boiling water
½ cup butter or margarine
3 cups sugar

Place ½ cup of the cut pieplant in the center of each piece of dough. Pinch the ends up tightly. You'll wish you had four hands while you are doing this. Dampen the edges of the dough to make them stick together. Place the balls as completed in a buttered baking dish — smooth side down. Dissolve the sugar in the water and add the butter. Pour over the dumplings. Bake in a 375-degree oven for 35 to 40 minutes. Serve hot with the sauce in the dish. A little cream could go along too, if you like.

We thought at first this was going to be pretty sweet. But there is no sugar mixture with the pieplant inside the dumplings, and the combination of tartness and sweetness was very pleasing.

# FRESH PUMPKIN PURÉE

**1 2-to-3 pound pumpkin**

Steamed method: Remove seeds and membranes, then cut the pumpkin into chunks and place on a rack above boiling water in a covered pan. Bring back to boil. Turn down heat, and simmer until tender, about 20 minutes. Peel chunks. Mash. Return to a pot, and turn heat to lowest setting. Simmer, uncovered, stirring frequently, until purée is very thick, which could be up to an hour or more, if the pumpkin was a watery one. The thicker it gets, the more you'll have to stir to keep it from sticking.

Baked method: Cut pumpkin in half, and remove seeds and membranes. Place halves on a greased shallow baking sheet, skin side up, and bake in a preheated 325-degree oven about 1¼ hours, or until tender. Scrape pulp from shells, and mash or process in blender or food processor. If not thick enough, simmer pulp, uncovered, stirring frequently, until desired thickness is reached. Makes about 1½ cups purée.

Microwave method: Cut pumpkin in several large pieces. Remove seeds, and discard membrane, Do not peel. Place in a shallow casserole, and cover with waxed paper. Cook on highest setting about 15 minutes, or until just tender. Turn pieces over, and rearrange them at half time in the cooking. Let stand for five minutes. Scoop out pulp, and discard shells. Mash or process in blender or food processor until smooth. If purée is not thick enough, put back in casserole, uncovered, and cook on high, stirring every five minutes until desired thickness is obtained.

All three methods make about 1½ cups purée.

— Deni Hamilton, 1980

# CHOCOLATE TIPPED STRAWBERRIES

Melt chips over hot water. Wash, but do not stem berries. Drain quite dry on paper towels. Dip tips of berries in chocolate, and place on a waxed-paper lined cookie sheet. Refrigerate to set chocolate. May be prepared a day ahead and refrigerated, covered with plastic wrap. About 8 to 10 cocktail party-sized helpings.

— Deni Hamilton, 1978

**1 12-ounce bag semi-sweet chocolate chips**
**1 quart fresh strawberries**

# STRAWBERRIES ROMANOFF

4 cups ripe strawberries
1 cup orange juice
½ cup sugar
⅔ cup orange liqueur
1½ cups heavy cream, whipped and
  flavored with sugar and vanilla if
  desired
Cognac or brandy

Wash, stem and drain strawberries and put them into a glass serving dish. Mix orange juice, sugar and liqueur; then add to strawberries. Refrigerate for a couple of hours. Make a depression in the middle of the berries and spread whipped cream in a ring around the depression. Heat cognac and take it to table with the dessert. Ignite, pour into depression and serve when flame dies. Serves six to eight.

— Lillian Marshall, 1975

# PUMPKIN FRITTERS

2 eggs, separated
½ teaspoon salt
Pinch pepper
2 tablespoons flour
1 cup cooked pumpkin purée
1 inch oil in bottom of skillet

Beat together egg yolks, salt, pepper, flour and pumpkin. Beat egg whites until stiff, and fold gently into mixture. Drop by spoonfuls into hot oil and fry until browned on one side. Turn and fry other side. Drain on paper towels. Excellent for breakfast with syrup or honey.            — Deni Hamilton, 1980

# SWEET MINI BLINI

6 eggs
½ teaspoon salt
1 teaspoon sugar
1¼ cups all-purpose flour
1½ cups milk
1 tablespoon melted butter
4 medium strawberries, sliced in
  coins
Cheese filling (see recipe)
1 egg, beaten

Beat eggs with salt, sugar and flour. Add milk, beating constantly. Chill 2 hours.

Wipe a skillet no wider in diameter than 4 inches with melted butter. Heat pan to medium-high. Pour batter 3 tablespoons at a time into skillet, tilting pan to coat entire surface. Cook 30 seconds on each side. Slide crepe onto a plate. Crepes may be separated by wax paper, wrapped in foil and frozen.

With crepe in front of you, place a strawberry in center of lower half. Top with 1 to 2 tablespoons cheese filling. Fold bottom edge over filling, fold both sides in and roll securely, sealing edge with beaten egg. Place on cookie sheet as you go.

Freeze blini 2 hours. Transfer to foil wrapping or freezer bag. Reheat uncovered on a cookie sheet at 400 degrees for 20 minutes. Serve on small plates with forks. Makes 24 to 30 pancakes.

— Elaine Corn, 1984

## CHEESE FILLING

Vigorously stir all ingredients until mixture is smooth and thick.

¾ pound ricotta cheese
¾ pound cream cheese
3 egg yolks
4 tablespoons sugar
3 tablespoons Grand Marnier

# ELEPHANT EARS

*Every State Fair season, a new crop of kids goes ga-ga over elephant ears, which sell under a number of names, including tiger ears. The Cook's Corner column printed this recipe in 1983 in response to a number of requests.*

Heat the milk, sugar, salt and shortening only until shortening melts. Remove from heat and cool to lukewarm. Add yeast and stir until dissolved. Stir in flour, 2 cups at a time, beating until smooth after each addition. Put dough in greased bowl, turn once and cover with a damp cloth. Let rise until doubled in size, about 30 minutes. Dust hands with flour. Pinch off golf-ball-sized pieces of dough. Stretch each ball into a thin 6-to-8-inch circle. Heat oil to 350 degrees in a heavy skillet. Fry circles, one at a time, until each rises to surface. Turn and fry second side until light brown. Drain on paper towels. Sprinkle with sugar-cinnamon mixture.

1½ cups milk
2 tablespoons sugar
1 teaspoon salt
6 tablespoons shortening
2 packages dry yeast
4 cups flour
Oil, for frying
¼ cup sugar mixed with 1 teaspoon cinnamon

# PEARS POACHED IN GINGERED WINE

Place the pears in a pan with the remaining ingredients. Bring to a boil and simmer 10 minutes, ladling liquid over pears as they poach. Remove pears and reserve. Cook liquid down by half. Strain and return to pan with the pears over low heat for two minutes. Serve hot or warm. Makes two servings.

— Elaine Corn, 1984

4 Anjou or Bosc pears, peeled, cored and halved
2 cups dry red or white wine (a good jug wine is fine)
1 cup water
½ cup sugar
3 tablespoons crystallized preserved ginger pieces, or 2 teaspoons ground ginger
6 whole allspice
6 whole cloves
1 inch cinnamon stick

# GINGERED-HONEY PEAR TART

## TART SHELL:

**1 cup unbleached white flour**
**1 tablespoon sugar**
**⅛ teaspoon salt**
**6 tablespoons butter, frozen in pats**
**2 tablespoons ice water (4
   tablespoons if mixing by hand)**

Food Processor: Place flour, sugar and salt in work bowl. Top with butter. Pulsate until grainy. With machine running, pour in ice water, processing until dough is a ball. Wrap dough in plastic. Place in freezer 30 minutes, or refrigerate until ready to use.

By Hand: In large mixing bowl, toss flour, sugar and salt with fork. Cut in butter until mixture looks like peas. Mixing with fork, add 4 tablespoons ice water, drop by drop, until mixture cleans sides of bowl. Wrap in plastic and refrigerate until ready to use.

Pat dough into bottom of springform pan, building small ridge with your knuckles. Bake at 425 degrees for 25 minutes. Cool. Remove shell from pan and place on serving plate.

## PEAR FILLING:

**3 medium pears**
**2 cups water**
**½ cup honey**
**¼ cup sugar**
**1½ teaspoons ground ginger**
**Juice and shredded rind of 1 lemon**
**1 teaspoon vanilla**
**1 ring canned pineapple**
**½ cup dark jam, such as Damson
   plum**
**Fresh mint**

Peel, score, halve and seed pears. In skillet, combine water, honey, sugar, ginger, juice and rind of lemon, then add pears in snug arrangement. Bring to boil. Poach 25 minutes, turning pears periodically during cooking. Do not overcook pears. Remove from heat. With pears flat side down, gently stir in vanilla, spooning poaching syrup over pears. Remove pears with slotted spoon. Let cool. In very small pan, simmer jam until it liquefies.

To finish tart: Place pineapple ring in center of tart shell. Arrange pears in spoke fashion. Fill center with jam glaze, then brush glaze over and between pears. (You won't need all of it.) Decorate with mint leaves. Chill or serve immediately. Serves 6.

— Elaine Corn, 1982

# CANTALOUPE AND CHERRIES IN WINE

*This recipe was supplied to Carol Sutton by Victor Jory, veteran actor and father of Jon Jory, executive producer of Actors Theatre of Louisville. Ms. Sutton was women's editor when she interviewed him for a 1971 feature; she was senior editor of The Courier-Journal when she died this year with this cookbook among her few unfinished projects.*

At least 48 hours before you plan to serve this dessert, fill the cantaloupe with port wine and refrigerate it. Do this by cutting a round hole, about the size of a quarter, in the cantaloupe and carefully removing the piece. Pour the wine into the hole until melon is nearly full and replace the circle of cantaloupe.

The afternoon before serving, remove the cantaloupe plug and pour the wine into a bowl. Peel the cantaloupe, remove the seeds, and cut cantaloupe into bite-sized pieces. Put them in the wine. Pour the liquid off the cherries and add them to the cantaloupe in the wine. Refrigerate until serving time.

If you like, a topping of whipped cream can be added to the individual servings at the last minute.

**1 cantaloupe**
**1 can black cherries, pitted**
**Port wine**
**Whipped cream (optional)**

# BEVERAGES

# TWO VISIONS OF THE MINT JULEP

*Nelson was Henry Clay's servant, and Clay's version of the mint julep embodies much of the mystique that surrounds this drink.*

The mint leaves, fresh and tender, should be pressed against the goblet with the back of the spoon. Bruise the leaves tenderly, and remove them from the goblet. Half-fill the goblet with cracked ice. Mellow bourbon, aged in oaken barrels, is poured from the brown jigger and allowed to slide slowly through the cracked ice.

In another receptacle, granulated sugar is slowly mixed with chilled limestone water to make a silvery mixture as smooth as some rare Egyptian oil. Then pour on top of the ice. While beads of moisture gather on the burnished exterior of the silver goblet, Nelson would painstakingly garnish the frosted brim with choicest sprigs of mint, and then present, with a courtly bow, the filled goblet to the nearest guest.

*This version of the mint julep is widely attributed to Courier-Journal Editor "Marse" Henry Watterson, although he is said not to have cared for either mint juleps or bourbon.*

Pluck the mint gently from its bed, just as the dew of the evening is about to form upon it. Select the choicer sprigs only, but do not rinse them. Prepare the simple syrup and measure out a half-tumbler of whiskey. Pour the whiskey into a well-frosted silver cup, throw the other ingredients away and drink the whiskey.

# PARTY MINT JULEPS

**2 cups bourbon**
**1 cup minted simple syrup (see note)**
**Crushed ice**
**Mint sprigs, for decoration**

Combine bourbon and minted simple syrup. Chill overnight, or until needed. The mixture should be very cold. Fill julep cups or tumblers with crushed ice. Into each cup pour the chilled minted bourbon. Insert mint sprigs into ice, so leaves graze rim of glass. Sip through a short straw so the nose of the imbiber draws in the bouquet from the mint leaves.

Note: To make simple syrup, boil 1 cup water and 2 cups sugar for five minutes. Cool. Add ½ cup packed mint leaves and let brew overnight or 12 hours, stirring occasionally. Strain syrup through a fine sieve, discarding mint. Makes 1 cup syrup, or enough for five juleps.

— Elaine Corn, 1984

# CLARET PUNCH

*Claret is what the British call Bordeaux wine. It is a dry red French wine, and any dry red would do for this recipe — French, California, Italian or other.*

Combine all ingredients in a large punch bowl. Serve chilled. Makes 1¼ gallons.

— Elaine Corn, 1981

**3 quart bottles claret, chilled**
**¾ cup sugar**
**½ teaspoon ground nutmeg**
**3 7-ounce bottles carbonated water**

# SHACKELFORD'S BEER

*In 1980, a reader asked the Cook's Corner column about "beer corn." This was the response.*

Nevyl Shackelford, public information specialist for the University of Kentucky College of Agriculture, writes two weekly columns for the university, and he dips into folklore — particularly Kentucky folklore — on a regular basis. He is familiar with "beer corn" that was passed around from neighbor to neighbor.

Kentuckians went to the sorghum mills, according to Shackelford, after molasses was made and picked up the "cane crushings" that were left over. These cane crushings were carried home and washed thoroughly several times. Let the crushings dry, then store in a covered jar for the next beer making. Here is Shackelford's mother's recipe:

**Sorghum to taste**
**1 tablespoon beer corn**

Fill a half-gallon jar with water and sweeten with sorghum. Add beer corn and fasten a clean cloth over the top of the jar. Do not close it tightly because it will explode. Let it "work" about a week in a warm place, like a window sill. Remove the beer corn, dry it and store for another making. The beer is now ready to drink. The beer corn (or cane crushings) look green when they go in the beer and become snow white during the beer-making process.

# HOT MULLED WINE

*This festive drink was on the menu that restaurateur Don Grisanti created for a Sunday Magazine article by Deni Hamilton in 1980.*

Slice the fruit garnishes about ¼ inch thick and place 1 clove in the rind of each slice. Use as much fruit and cloves as you like. It's simply a matter of taste, as with the sugar. Warm all ingredients together. Do not boil. The key to good seasoning here and elsewhere is to be able to detect the subtle flavors of each spice but for no one flavor to overpower any of the others. Garnish each cup with some of the fruit or a cinnamon stick.

**4 26-ounce bottles dry red table**
  **wine**
**½ fresh lemon**
**½ fresh lime**
**1 orange**
**4 cinnamon sticks**
**12 cloves**
**½ cup granulated sugar**

# PEACH FUZZIES

1 6-ounce can frozen lemonade
   concentrate
1 6-ounce can cold water
6 ounces vodka
1 10½-ounce box frozen peaches, or
   4 to 5 fresh peaches, peeled,
   pitted and cut into chucks
About ½-cup crushed ice

Put all ingredients into blender and slush until frothy. Makes eight small cocktails.

— Lillian Marshall, 1975

# HOT CRANBERRY PUNCH (NON-ALCOHOLIC)

2 cups cranberry juice
2 cups pineapple juice
1 cup water
½ cup brown sugar
2 teaspoons whole cloves
2 teaspoons whole allspice
2 sticks cinnamon

Mix the juices, sugar and water in a percolator. Put the spices in the basket and perk for 5 minutes. Serves 6. To serve 18 to 20, triple the recipe and use an automatic coffee-urn set at medium strength.

— Lillian Marshall, 1973

# PARTY PUNCH (NON-ALCOHOLIC)

3 quarts unsweetened pineapple
   juice
3 cups orange juice
1½ cups lemon juice
1½ quarts cranberry juice
2½ cups sugar
4 28-ounce bottles ginger ale,
   chilled
2 28-ounce bottles club soda, chilled

Combine juices and sugar. Chill several hours. (An ice ring can be made of a portion of this mixture.) Just before serving, pour the juice over an ice ring in a punch bowl. Carefully pour in ginger ale and soda water. Float orange slices on top if desired. 75 servings.

— Lillian Marshall, 1976

# SPARKLING BURGUNDY PUNCH

A large can unsweetened grapefruit
   juice
2 packages frozen raspberries (do
   not drain)
¼ cup lemon juice
½ cup sugar
3 bottles sparklng burgundy

Mix all ingredients well except for burgundy. Make sure sugar is dissolved. Stir in burgundy and serve with mint or lemon slices. Serves 40.

— Lillian Marshall, 1977

# IRISH COFFEE

Fill a warmed, clear-glass coffee mug two-thirds full of hot coffee. Add 2 teaspoons sugar and stir to dissolve. Add about 2 tablespoons Irish whiskey, or enough to suit your taste, but do not stir. Top with unsweetened whipped cream, through which you're supposed to sip the beverage. Top with a cherry, if desired. Serves one.

— Deni Hamilton, 1979

# HOT MULLED CIDER (NON-ALCOHOLIC)

This should serve about 8, but we made ours to fit our fat teapot and let the candle underneath keep it warm to the last drop.

Place cider in a saucepan, add sugar and spices. Simmer along at a slow rate of speed for 15 minutes. Strain and serve in mugs with a dash of nutmeg.

Just keep tilting the fat pot until that's all there is, there isn't any more, and no more even from the kitchen. If it isn't too sweet, we think it merely whets the appetite.

— Cissy Gregg, 1951

**2 quarts cider**
**½ to 1 cup brown sugar (We chose the lesser sweetening; you do as you choose.)**
**1 one-inch stick cinnamon**
**6 whole cloves**
**1 teaspoon whole allspice**

# HOT CIDER PUNCH (NON-ALCOHOLIC)

*This recipe, from the family of Gov. Martha Layne Collins, appeared in the 1984 holiday section.*

Combine all ingredients in a large kettle. Bring to a simmer, but do not let punch boil. Garnish with orange slices. Serves 35.

**1 gallon apple cider**
**2 cups orange juice**
**2 cups cranberry juice**
**8 orange slices, pulp garnished with whole cloves**
**4 cinnamon sticks**

# HOT BUTTERED RUM

1 cup rum
6 twists lemon peel
10 whole cloves
2 cinnamon sticks
2 tablespoons brown sugar
5 cups boiling apple cider
1 stick butter
1 teaspoon freshly grated nutmeg

Place rum, lemon peel, cloves, cinnamon and brown sugar in a jug or heavy pitcher. Add boiling cider. Float butter on top, stirring. Sprinkle with nutmeg. Pour into individual glasses or mugs with a swizzle cinnamon stick. Serves 6.

— Elaine Corn, 1983

# BREAKFAST IN A GLASS

2 eggs
1 cup milk
1 cup fresh fruit (banana, strawberries, blueberries, plums, pears)
2 tablespoons honey
2 tablespoons wheat germ
1 teaspoon vanilla or almond extract

Combine all ingredients in a blender. Makes two servings.

— Elaine Corn, 1981

# HOSPITALITY TEA PUNCH (NON-ALCOHOLIC)

4 quarts cold water
5 level tablespoons loose tea (or 15 tea bags)
2 cups lemon juice
4 cups orange juice
1½ quarts grape juice
2 cups sugar
1 quart ginger ale

Bring 2 quarts cold water to a rollicking boil in a saucepan. Remove from heat. Immediately add the tea. Brew 4 minutes. Stir and strain into a large vessel containing the juices, sugar and remaining 2 quarts of water. Stir well and pour over a block of ice set in punch bowl. Stir in the ginger ale. (Your favorite liquor may be substituted for the grape juice, if desired). Makes about 50 cups of punch.

— Lillian Marshall, 1970

# ULTIMATE SMOOTHIE

Blend all ingredients on high until completely smooth and thick. Garnish with melon. Serves 1.
— Elaine Corn, 1984

1 banana
¼ cup blueberries
5 or 6 strawberries
Juice of 1 orange, about ½ cup
3 tablespoons honey
½ cup plain yogurt
Melon slice, for garnish

# PEACH JULEP (NON-ALCOHOLIC)

Blend all ingredients, except the soda, until smooth. Pour into serving glass and add soda. Stir lightly. Serve immediately. Serves 1.
— Elaine Corn, 1984

2 peaches, pitted and coarsely chopped
2 tablespoons honey
2 tablespoons lemon or lime juice
1 tablespoon mint leaves
½ cup club soda or seltzer

# BANANA BREAKFAST DRINK

Combine all ingredients in a blender. Makes two servings.
— Elaine Corn, 1981

1 cup plain yogurt
1 banana
½ cup milk
2 tablespoons honey
2 tablespoons orange-juice concentrate

# LEMON-FRUIT SANGRIA

In a pretty pitcher, combine the wine and sugar. (Chill a few hours if ingredients are not cold. You may want to chill everything before mixing.) At serving time add the fruit, club soda and ice cubes to the pitcher. Pour in the cognac and watch it cascade around the fruit. The Sangria is ready to drink as soon as you finish making it. If you are serving more than 4, a double batch is a good idea.
— Elaine Corn, 1981

3½ cups dry white wine, chilled
¼ cup sugar
3 lemons, thinly sliced
1 orange, sliced
Small bunches green grapes
1 10-ounce bottle club soda, chilled
1 tray ice cubes
¼ cup cognac or other brandy

# GLÖGG

1 cup raisins
2 teaspoons whole cardamom
1 cinnamon stick
1½ cups water
6 cups Bordeaux or any dry red
   table wine
¾ cup sherry
¾ cup brandy
¾ cup sugar
¼ cup blanched almonds, unsalted

Rinse raisins and drain. Peel and crush cardamom, and combine in a saucepan with water, cinnamon and ½ cup of the raisins. Simmer 30 minutes. Heat but do not boil wine, sherry, brandy and sugar. Strain raisin mixture and add liquid to heated wine mixture, stirring to combine. Place almonds and remaining raisins in individual glasses or mugs. Pour over with glögg. Serves 8.

— Elaine Corn, 1983

# SCARLETT O'HARA

8 jiggers cranberry juice
5 jiggers bourbon
3 jiggers lemon juice
8 ice cubes, crushed

Shake well — and there it is! Serves 4 to 8. We thought a little sugar might be added, but that is a matter of taste.

— Cissy Gregg, 1956

# THE PENDENNIS CHAMPAGNE PUNCH

12 lemons, juiced
Powdered sugar
1 quart carbonated water
½ pint maraschino liqueur
½ pint curacao
1 pint brandy
2 quarts champagne

To the juice of a dozen lemons, add enough powdered sugar to sweeten to taste and 1 quart carbonated water. Place a large block of ice in the punch bowl and stir these all together. Add the remaining ingredients. Mix together. Some people like to add 2 cups tea, strained, into this mixture for added body.

Decorate with fruits in season. This will give between 4 and 5 quarts of punch and should make something like 40 servings.   — Cissy Gregg, 1949

# TOM AND JERRY

12 eggs
1 pound confectioner's sugar
1 jigger of whisky per serving
Boiling water

Beat the eggs slowly but very well. Add the sugar, and just keep on beating. For each serving, pour 1 jigger of bourbon into a cup. Fill each cup ⅔ full of boiling water. Put a spoonful of the egg mixture on top. Give each cup a dash of nutmeg and serve.

— Cissy Gregg, 1957

# GEORGETOWN EGGNOG

Separate eggs, and beat yolks until light. Add ⅔ of the cup of sugar and beat and beat. They should be thick and lemon colored no matter how your arm aches for relief. Slowly pour the whisky over the yolks and beat all the time. When this much of the task is completed, set aside and turn your attention to the whites.

Beat the whites of the eggs stiff but not dry, and add the remaining ⅓ cup of sugar, beating it in as you would in making meringue. Then slowly pour the whisky-sugar-egg yolk mixture into the whites, folding it in gently. If you'll do this the egg nog will never separate like having the cream come to the top and the liquid settling to the bottom of the bowl.

Next whip the cream, and fold it into the egg white-yolk-sugar-whiskey mixture. Then, even though you have just about beaten yourself into a state of exhaustion, no one can help but stand back and admire your accomplishment. It is all ready now for the punch bowl. Once there, don't forget to add the sprinkling of nutmeg, putting freckles of perfection on the satiny complexion of the egg nog.

In making large quantities of egg nog this way we suggest that you make the first quart of cream mix as given in the recipe. Then for the second quart of cream allotment, reduce the sugar to ⅔ of a cup and the whisky to ⅔ of a pint.

— Cissy Gregg, 1947

**6 eggs, beaten separately**
**1 cup white sugar**
**1 pint of whisky**
**1 quart of heavy whipping cream**

# HAPPY NEW YEAR COFFEE NOG

Combine egg yolks, instant coffee, salt and vanilla. Beat until thick. Add the ¼ cup sugar and beat again until very thick. Slowly add the brandy and the milk. Chill thoroughly. Then beat egg whites until stiff, but not dry, and gradually add the ½ cup sugar. Fold the egg-white mixture into the egg-yolk-coffee mixture. Then fold in the whipped cream. This should be served with small spoons or plastic straws. It will make approximately 12 or 13 servings of 6½ ounces.

— Cissy Gregg, 1954

**2 egg yolks**
**⅓ cup instant coffee, dry**
**Dash of salt**
**1 tablespoon vanilla**
**¼ cup sugar**
**¾ cup brandy**
**2 cups milk**
**2 egg whites**
**½ cup sugar**
**1 cup heavy cream, whipped**

# PLANTATION EGGNOG

*Cissy halved the amounts from a recipe in "Charleston Receipts" and prepared it for a Sunday Magazine photograph in 1952, then served the eggnog to the reporters and editors of the city desk. It should have served 45. "Maybe it would if the 45 were little ladies and gentlemen," Cissy wrote. "It disappeared so fast, we couldn't count the imbibers, but we know the number was far less than 45. The verdict was that it was extra special and the best we had ever made. But don't go too much by that because they say the same thing each year."*

**5 dozen eggs, separated**
**4 cups granulated sugar**
**1½ quarts whipping cream**
**1 pint coffee cream**
**1½ quarts bourbon whisky**
**1 pint rum**
**1 pinch salt**

Beat the egg yolks well. Then gradually add the sugar and beat until the mixture is light, lemon-colored and spongy. Add the whisky in small portions — about a tablespoon at a time. Then add the rum in the same manner. Add the coffee cream. Beat the egg whites, with the salt added, until stiff. Fold into the yolk mixture. Whip the cream and add last. This makes 6 gallons of eggnog, and 'tis said it will make between 90 and a hundred servings.

# SOUTHERN EGGNOG

**3 cups sugar (or less)**
**Yolks of 12 eggs**
**1 quart of bourbon whisky**
**1 quart of double cream**
**Nutmeg as you wish**

If one more glass of eggnog is your meat for New Year's, we suggest a favorite formula as it comes to us from the Pendennis Club. The Pendennis rather stands as an institution which marches on with the years. Whether you have your own favorite eggnog recipes or use this one, we feel that you, as we, will be happy to keep it among other eggnog recipes we like.

Mix the sugar with the egg yolks. Then drip — and we do mean drip — in a quart of whisky, stirring constantly. You'll get along better if you have an electric beater because it is like making mayonnaise — the emulsion must be maintained. This beating can be done by hand, but the hand better be supported by good muscle.

Whip the quart of cream very stiff, and after the mixture of bourbon, eggs and sugar has been completely mingled, stir in the whipped cream. Sprinkle a little nutmeg on the top of the mixture after it has been poured into a punch bowl.

There endeth the Pendennis Club's recipe for eggnog. But they add a P. S. which says to wit: Some people like, also, to add the stiffly beaten whites of 6 eggs to this recipe just before serving. We have no advice on this last to offer, since we know that while there are countless recipes for eggnog, all are much alike, each someone's pet.    — Cissy Gregg, 1953

# NON-ALCOHOLIC VANILLA EGGNOG

Beat egg yolks until thick and lemon colored. Gradually beat in sugar. Stir in milk, heavy cream, vanilla and rum extract. Add salt to egg whites and beat until they stand in soft peaks. Fold into the mixture. Garnish with nutmeg. Serve in punch cups. This makes about 10 servings.
— Cissy Gregg, 1956

**4 eggs, separated**
**⅓ cup sugar**
**3 cups milk**
**1 cup heavy cream**
**2½ teaspoons vanilla**
**1 teaspoon rum extract**
**Dash of salt**
**Ground nutmeg for garnish**

# COLD SHERRY EGGNOG

Beat eggs with the sugar. Mix in the wine and the milk. Serve in tall glasses, garnished with whipped cream and a dash of nutmeg. Serves two.
— Cissy Gregg, 1942

**2 eggs, well beaten**
**4 teaspoons sugar**
**¼ cup California sherry**
**1¾ cups milk (chilled)**
**Whipped cream**
**Nutmeg**

# KATHY'S HOT BUTTERED RUM

*The Kathy who produces this winter drink is Mrs. Harvey Sloane, and she gave the recipe to Lillian Marshall for the 1974 holiday-entertaining issue of the Magazine.*

Heat water to boiling, and dissolve sugar and butter in it. Add rum and heat but do not boil. Makes 16 half-cup servings.

**1 quart water**
**5 tablespoons sugar**
**1 stick (½ cup) butter**
**1 quart light rum**

# PATRICIA WILLETT'S EXCELLENT BOURBON PUNCH

*Cissy Gregg attributed this punch to Patricia Willett of Bardstown, Ky. and said Mrs. Willett had done a lot to popularize the use of bourbon as a flavoring in cooking.*

Mix all ingredients, and sweeten with a simple syrup to your taste. Patricia says they boil 2 cups sugar with a pint water rapidly for 10 minutes and sweeten with it, but if you wish to add more or less to yours, that's what it means when you say "sweeten to taste." Makes one gallon.

**1 pint ice tea (regular strength)**
**1 pint pineapple juice**
**1 quart orange juice**
**1 pint lemon juice**
**1 quart ginger ale**
**1 pint bourbon whisky**

# FISH-HOUSE PUNCH

*Thelma Linton, a lifelong Kentucky cook, supplied this recipe for the 1984 holiday-entertaining issue of the Magazine. Elaine Corn wrote a feature story about Mrs. Linton.*

**2 cups sugar**
**1 quart lemon or lime juice or**
   **combination**
**2 cups water**
**2 fifths dark rum**
**1 fifth cognac**
**2 to 3 ounces peach brandy**

Dissolve sugar in citrus juice and water. Stir in remaining ingredients. Let "brew" 3 to 4 days on porch or mudroom. Serve over shoe-box-size ice block. Serves 50.

# WARM-THE-COCKLES WASSAIL

**1 whole orange, studded with cloves**
**7 or 8 good-sized tart apples**
**6 (12-ounce) bottles ale**
**2 fifths amber rum**
**1⅓ cups sugar**
**¼ teaspoon ground ginger**
**1 long stick cinnamon**

Preheat oven to 350 degrees. Place orange and apples on a cookie sheet or shallow pan and bake, uncovered, about 10 minutes for small apples or 13 minutes for large ones. They should be soft, but not mushy. Put into bottom of empty punch bowl. In large saucepan, combine ale, rum, sugar, ginger and cinnamon. Turn on high heat and warm, stirring, until sugar dissolves. Do not boil. When warm but not steaming hot, remove from heat and pour over hot apples and orange in punch bowl. Serve warm. Makes about 30 punch-cup-sized servings. If this seems too strong to your liking, you may add a pint to a quart of unsweetened apple juice or cider to the mixture when heating.

— Deni Hamilton, 1975

# HAPPY HOLIDAY PUNCH

*Lillian Marshall picked up this recipe, among others, for a feature story on the 25th anniversary party of the Newcomers Club in 1977.*

Combine juices, vodka or gin and liqueur in a punch bowl. Add bitters. Pour carbonated beverage down side of bowl, and stir gently to blend. Add ice mold or ice cubes. Float cherries on top. Makes 22 four-ounce servings.

**3 cups orange juice**
**2 cups unsweetened pineapple juice**
**2 cups vodka or gin**
**1 cup any orange-flavored liqueur (Cointreau, Curacao or Grand Marnier)**
**Few dashes aromatic bitters**
**A 28-ounce bottle lemon-lime flavor soda**
**Maraschino cherries for garnish**

# INDEX